Yasmin Saikia is the Hardt-Nickachos Chair in Peace Studies at the Center for the Study of Religion and Conflict and Professor of History at Arizona State University. Her books include *In the Meadows of Gold: Telling Tales of the Swargadeos at the Crossroads of Assam, Fragmented Memories: Struggling to Become Tai-Ahom in India* and *Women, War and the Making of Bangladesh: Remembering 1971*.

Chad Haines is Assistant Professor of Religious Studies and Global Studies at Arizona State University and faculty affiliate with the Center for the Study of Religion and Conflict. He is the author of *Nation, Territory and Globalization in Pakistan: Traversing the Margins*.

WOMEN AND PEACE IN THE ISLAMIC WORLD

Gender, Agency and Influence

Edited by

YASMIN SAIKIA AND CHAD HAINES

I.B.TAURIS

LONDON • NEW YORK • OXFORD • NEW DELHI • SYDNEY

I.B. TAURIS
Bloomsbury Publishing Plc
50 Bedford Square, London, WC1B 3DP, UK
1385 Broadway, New York, NY 10018, USA
29 Earlsfort Terrace, Dublin 2, Ireland

BLOOMSBURY, I.B. TAURIS and the I.B. Tauris logo
are trademarks of Bloomsbury Publishing Plc

First published in Great Britain 2015
Paperback edition published 2021

ISBN: HB: 978-1-7845-3017-4
PB: 978-0-7556-4403-2
ePDF: 978-1-7867-3984-1
eBook: 978-0-8577-3725-0

Series: Library of Modern Middle East Studies 164

Typeset by OKS Prepress Services, Chennai, India

To find out more about our authors and books visit
www.bloomsbury.com and sign up for our newsletters.

To the nameless strangers of Palestine, Pakistan, Iraq and Syria whose random acts of kindness and hospitality illuminated for us the potential of peace in the everyday.

CONTENTS

PREFACE AND
ACKNOWLEDGEMENTS

Women and Peace in the Islamic World has many points of origin. The initial idea of bringing together these collected papers germinated from the international conference, 'Women, Islam and Peace', funded by the Hardt-Nickachos Peace Studies initiative at the Center for the Study of Religion and Conflict (CSRC) in Arizona State University (ASU). Two faculty seminars we coordinated on 'Islam and Modernity' and 'Pluralism and the Other in Islam' for two years, brought together a dynamic collective of Islamic Studies faculty at ASU, and deepened and expanded our conceptual interests in Islam. These seminars at ASU were funded by ASU's Institute of Humanities Research (IHR) and we are deeply thankful to the IHR for the support.

Out of these research clusters we forged a new and informal group called ISRA (Islamic Studies Research Alliance). The faculty group meets every month and in these gatherings we read, discussed and debated our ideas about the scholarship of Islam and Muslim societies. However, there was a visible dearth of literature on Islam and peace. As well, we found a predictable narrative concerning Muslim women and there was very little variation from the established literature on Islamic feminism and piety. We asked our colleagues to help us to think through our ideas of Muslim women as peacemakers. We were particularly keen to probe how women live Islam and what changes they are able to engender in their communities for peaceful living through accommodation and understanding with different others. This led us to think and read more on the concept of the everyday, because that is where we started seeing Muslim women's work happening and developing something quite unique – a new way of thinking and living peace. For us, the two co-editors of the book, it became our lens of investigation for an entire year. We are particularly thankful to Hasan Davalcu, Chouki el Hamel, Nabil Kamel, Jim Rush and Shahla Talebi for the multiple conversations that sharpened our knowledge and thinking on the subject of ordinary Muslim women as peacemakers.

Beyond these academic discussions and deliberations, the Sonoran desert in Arizona has been a source of inspiration. What appears to be the plain and lifeless desert is actually full of living activities. The desert is the ground of fertile renewal, every minute. It is, however, rarely noticed because the on-the-ground activities in the desert are almost invisible and thus imperceptible. Occasionally, the desert comes to life in a dramatic way and puts forth a grand display of multi-colored blooming cacti. Some of these cacti take five, ten, or even 40 years to bloom, and when they do they make the desert dance in splendor. The desert that nurtures this beauty truly is a place of wonder. The desert taught us the everyday is a site of multiple and wondrous happenings and that the potential is endless. The alchemy of the everyday and ordinary people works in a similar combination. At work together, continuously, their efforts promise hope and beauty. This collection is the outcome of the cross-fertilization of ideas that were generated in the international conference, IHR seminars, discussions of the ISRA group, and the book of nature of the Arizona desert. For the heterogeneous origins of this book, we are deeply grateful and have been enriched because of it.

At an individual level, our heartfelt thanks go to the Linell Cady, Director of the Center for the Study of Religion and Conflict. Linell is the best leader one can think of working with for developing a project that is continuously evolving. Our benefactors Professor Ann Hardt, her late husband, Anthony Nickachos, along with ASU President Michael Crow have provided us with the much needed funds for creating a space to think, read and discuss about peace as an intellectual and humanistic endeavour. Our ongoing work on peace studies at CSRC emerges from their support and encouragement. Carolyn Forbes, Assistant Director at CSRC, has been a great sounding board for our ideas. Carolyn has also helped us in many different ways to see this book to its completion. Matt Correa, Nigah Muhgal and Emily Fritcke at CSRC assisted us with the technical issues as well as research on bibliographies. Laurie Perko, Manager at CSRC, did all the background work to put together the international conference and managed the finances. Jerryll Moreno and Doann Houghton-Alico read and edited the manuscript. We are thankful to this team of people who helped us to produce this book. At I.B.Tauris, our editor Azmina Siddique shepherded the manuscript through the entire process, beginning with the initial proposal to its completion for publication. We are deeply thankful to Cemalnur Sargut for her love and friendship. Each of the individual authors worked to keep the deadline and produce new and original work for this book. We thank them for their trust in our endeavour. The responsibility of the remaining shortcomings of this book is of course our own as editors.

Yasmin Saikia and Chad Haines

INTRODUCTION

SITUATING PEACE, ISLAM AND WOMEN IN THE EVERYDAY

Yasmin Saikia and Chad Haines

Peace is a yearning and an aspiration for people worldwide. Yet, in our contemporary times, peace is the most elusive goal. Generally, scholars and the public think of peace as the cessation of violence and war. This narrative, controlled by State interests, conjured and spun-out by the media, moves people out of the arenas of high-powered discussions on conflict resolution, the sites of peace brokering. Curiously, this approach deems peace as a by product and transforms people into bystanders, if not outright victims, who play the role of passive recipients of peace, delivered by the powerful. In this volume of essays, we suggest a conceptual and methodological shift by reading peace in small acts of human interactions in the *everyday*. The shift from the dramatic and big actors to the complex and subtle issues of the everyday requires careful attention to ordinary people and their activities, as well as, a sufficiently detailed understanding of how people conceptualize peace. This makes peace an active process that combines people and the everyday for meaningful realization in our present time.

Our focus is on a particular group of actors, Muslim women, whose voices and actions reconstruct for us an alternative narrative of peace inhabiting the site of the everyday. We situate women's contributions, framed through the lens of an Islamic ethic, in the multiple dialogues taking place in the everyday. The voices of these women are rarely heard because scholarly attention is mostly focussed on big players and actors.[1] Women's dialogues, happening in less visible arenas outside the dominant areas of the public sphere, are not private matters though. They are engagements about day-to-day concerns that affect society as a whole. When listening to some women's voices that are close to the surface, negotiated on the site of the everyday, we hear emphasis on the daily acts of hospitality, neighbourliness and sociality that are human concerns. These intimate issues allow us to hear the voices of women who are concerned with the moral ethics learnt from religion. It is important for us to qualify here that our emphasis on women's dialogues is not to reproduce binaries – women do peacework in everyday interactions with others, while Muslim men are not actors in these matters. That would be too simplistic. In addition, the focus on the intimate issues informing the dialogues should not lead us to assume that women's voices are a soft murmur or a cacophony of noises in the private domain. We highlight some of the human issues that women speak, alerting us to language that is critical for enabling dialogue. Women's dialogues, one can say, are a new horizon for imagining peace in the everyday.

The significance of the everyday is that it is a place of meaningful actions where Islam guides Muslim women's deliberations and for making the journey a shared and collective effort. Taken together, women, Islam and the everyday create a new horizon for thinking about peace as both a moral process and a personal strategy creating a continuous site for human transformation with deep roots in Muslim consciousness and Islamic thought.

The chapters in this volume cover a wide array of geographical areas from Aceh to Bosnia. They are the diverse voices of individuals and collectives of Muslim women and the multiple experiences encompassing communal living in quiet segregated women's spaces to the chaotic zones of war. In its breadth, this volume shows the persistence of women's daily actions and the integration of religion, which allows us to interpret the everyday differently as the site of hope and to lay the groundwork for peace. In so doing, the testaments here also open up the possibility of studying Islam as a lived tradition that counters dominant stereotypes depicting Islam as inherently violent and hyper-patriarchal. Through case studies, theological discussions and personal dialogues, the contributors consider multiple peace processes occurring in the Muslim world, and Muslim women enlighten us to the influences of religion shaping their sensibilities as agents of peace.

Through these conversations, three issues interweave to shed light on the possibilities of peace: the everyday, Islam and Muslim women.

Everyday

The everyday is a site of action and knowledge production that creates the transformative possibilities of human life and the conceptualization of peace as a lived practice of ordinary people. Given the day-to-day routines of work and family, for the majority of people there is no magic in the everyday; few pay attention to it or discern change. Further, the overt concern, particularly in media, about the violent spectacular in the Muslim world and the focus on a few leaders and perpetrators eclipse the vast spaces inhabited by the majority of ordinary Muslims and their everyday acts of peace through civility and lived ethics. Women's generally unnoticed lives are thickly interwoven in ordinary tasks and are not considered a site of new and positive developments for providing leadership on peace thinking. Yet, it is the recurring actions of ordinary people, produced on a seemingly unchanging surface of the everyday, that create the possibility of new developments. They are the authors of change. When people navigate the everyday and perform ordinary actions, they move beyond the idea of lives as mimetic projects robotically acting out traditions, roles and cultures to rise up to their human capacity effectively demonstrating agency. Shifting from consumers of beliefs to active agents as users and producers who create new meanings in words and performances, ordinary people's negotiations in the everyday demonstrates both process and sensibilities.[2] Through close attention to the everyday in Muslim societies, we can trace a pattern of peace that ordinary Muslims unselfconsciously author and practice.

The negotiations that occur in the everyday lack adequate documentation in the corpus of Muslim world studies, but to understand it, we have to accept that the 'inhabitation of the ordinary' is the unrecorded site of transformation and peace.[3] In the ordinary lived experiences of being Muslim, one may not notice overt actions proclaiming grand religious ideas, theological concepts or unusual acts of heroism or resistance drawing upon religious knowledge. For Muslims basic concepts, such as *halal* (licit) and *haram* (illicit), inform everyday relationships and actions determining the moral compass of a person. What becomes ordinary, acted-out-routines of accepting and doing what is permitted and avoiding or resisting the prohibited reflect meaningful ways individuals draw upon a diversity of reference points as guidance for living in the world. The everyday is the site where people imbibe and reproduce Qur'anic interpretations, moral values and ethical ideas in ordinary actions or where people reject or reinterpret them to fit their immediate needs and interests.

Despite the everyday ordinary nature of lived religion for the vast majority of Muslims, the concerns for ethical living and the site of the everyday is the 'place of relations' with others.[4] In everyday encounters, Muslims speak and act; in meeting others, they perform their identities, gender, age, social class and other aspects of reflecting a sense of ethical living and selfhood in relationship with one another. In their articulations and exchanges, they interact, share, discuss, bargain and argue with others. They also show civility, concern and hospitality. Producing cultures of being Muslim, the everyday is a site of sociality comprised of performances and speech acts. In the rarely glanced everyday Muslim cultures of being in the world, we begin to see something potent and powerful – a site of peace where living with others is negotiated. Ordinary Muslims are involved in transforming their worlds, and quite surprisingly, many in the world at large seem to barely notice. Such incognisance calls for our attention, but the important question is, *what kind of transformation occurs in the process of the everyday and how does it happen?*

As a site for performing selfhood and values, as a series of unfolding social interactions forging meaningful relationships and as a striving for self-improvement, the everyday is a dialogical process. On the one hand, the everyday is a cacophony of voices negotiating, compromising, adapting and contesting meaning. Muslims are in constant negotiation amongst themselves as a diverse population asserting different interpretations of Islam. Be it jihad, veiling for women, how to stand while saying one's prayers, which duties are compulsory, what the role of the State is in matters of religion and so on, a variety of Muslims express their opinions and engage in dialogues, debates, contestations and squabbles over what is right. On the other hand, through ordinary events, gestures and words, people are in constant dialogue with multiple reference points to guide and interpret the realities around them. Islam, modernity, secularism and fundamentalism, even Marxism or Liberalism, or a combination thereof informs Muslims' dialogues with one another and with their worldviews. In these encounters, exchanges, discussions and debates lies the possibility for transformation. The everyday is a struggle for the betterment of self and the deeper understanding of the requirements of their religious beliefs. The fluidity of meaning and possibilities of ideas and actions keep the doors of *ijtihad* (interpretation) open.

Thus, the significance of the everyday is inherent in our understanding of Islam. From an Islamic perspective, the everyday that we focus on here is grounded on the three sites discussed above. The first is the everyday as the performance of the ordinary, where daily events are imbued with significant meanings. The second plane is the everyday as a site of encounters where personal relationships are forged. Finally, the everyday is the articulation of dialogues of multiple, complex and unfolding interactions negotiated between schools of philosophy and theology that occur in the public and private spheres. The recognition of the everyday in these three realms has large consequences. If indeed ordinary Muslims are the agents and actors of true change and the leaders of peaceful thinking in the Muslim world, we have to reconsider the very concept of Islam and who speaks on its behalf. We have to begin to see the overlooked and to acknowledge the troubling consequences of not seeing the everyday and the lives of ordinary Muslims for rethinking a new conceptual frame of Islam and everyday peace. Our effort in this book is to direct our readers to take a steady look at this site and engage its importance.

Islam

Islam, meaning submission to God, proclaimed a universal message of a single human community referred to as *ummah*. The original *ummah*, which first emerged in Medina in the seventh century, was inherently heterogeneous; its values, organizations and members were plural and comprised of Christians, Jews and Muslims. Eventually the *ummah* spread beyond the foundations in Medina to include the pagans of Mecca as well.

The forging of a new kind of community marked the shift from the existing system in seventh-century Arabia, which was based on divided clan and tribal affiliations and loyalties. When the Prophet Muhammad emigrated from Mecca to Medina in 622 CE he created this new *ummah* emphasising horizontal relationships between the groups that came together to form community. For Malik Bennabi the *hijra*, or migration of the Prophet Muhammad and his early followers, marks this shift from the past to a new future, which was a movement that resulted in the establishment of a new society based on mutual agreement of shared rights and responsibilities between immigrant Muslims and local Jewish, Sabean, Christian and pagan communities. Cooperation and reciprocity with others who were different from the immigrant groups of Muslims but were considered equal to them in social matters was the highlight of the *ummah*, and it was formalized in the Constitution of Medina.[5]

This reading of Islam, which emphasizes the communal nature, identified participation of each individual as critical in the continuity of the community, which, in turn, fostered pluralism, countered claims to a privileged exclusionary group and emphasized the rights and duties of individuals. 'An emphasis on kinship at this early stage would, after all, have flown in the face of the Qur'anic espousal of individual merit and personal piety in establishing a person's moral and social standing and would have been rightly perceived as a throwback to the *Jahili* period [the time of ignorance].'[6] Further, the horizontal communal polity built on social relations rejected vertical power structures that Bennabi refers to as 'colonizability'. The early history of Islam, until the death of the Prophet Muhammad, in Bennabi's reading, is the exemplary moment of Islamic history. It was a period of forward movement based on inter-faith understanding with a pluralistic connotation. The righteous behaviour of individuals constituted the principle requirement for membership in the *ummah*. Subsequent to the expansion of Islam to far-flung areas across the globe, the communal principles of the early Muslim community based on mutual dialogues with others were repeatedly ignored. Today, we witness countless attempts to colonize Muslims, be it from Islamists or Western imperialists.

It is a challenge today to situate Islam's inclusive ethos given the contemporary political climate and civilizational discourses that imagine exclusionary traditions. Muslims and non-Muslims, scholarly studies and popular representations, are fraught with assumptions about borders between cultural and religious worlds. Most egregious, of such bounded representations, are those of Samuel Huntington and Niall Ferguson. One can also think of the ideas of Muhammad ibn Abd al-Wahhab, Mohammad Abdu and Abul A'la Maududi among the Islamists who constructed a separatist interpretation of Islam, undoing 1400 years of historical interactions and dialogues. Counter to these ahistorical claims, scholars like Fazlur Rahman and Mohammed Arkoun call upon Muslims to continuously rethink and regenerate Islam in the context of their present conditions.[7] The significance of interpreting Islam in the present that Arkoun and Rahman emphasize becomes evident in the lived practices of many Muslim women, which the chapters in this book highlight. Women's keen awareness of circumstances and conditions allow for rethinking the individual's capacity to renew community drawing upon Islamic values.

The values guiding Muslims can be summed up as *islam* (submission, what one should strive towards), *iman* (faith, what one should have) and *ihsan* (good and beautiful, what one should do). *Ihsan*, William Chittick and Sachiko Murata assert, is the most important reference point for Muslims in ordering relations with self and others, as well as humankind and God, because it means taking one's inner faith and expressing it in one's actions.[8] *Ihsan* calls for a humane awareness that allows for seeing the good and positive in the other. The importance of *ihsan* is invoked in many Qur'anic injunctions enjoining people to do what is good and righteous and forbidding wrong by upholding rights and developing patience (e.g., Qur'an 3:114; 5:9; 5:85–7; 6:82).

The practice of *ihsan* thus calls upon individuals to develop a social and moral ethic that guides them to live in harmony and in community. It is a matter of doing good in the everyday as an active member of the *ummah*.[9] The ideal of doing good is most notably evident in the practice of *zakat* (purifying alms) and *sawm* (fasting) during *Ramadan*, which require one to share one's wealth and appreciate the condition of the other, particularly the hunger of the poor and the needy. The practice of congregational prayers and pilgrimage of *hajj* that brings the *ummah* together and enables a reassurance of a common human journey towards a spiritual goal are also practices that improve *ihsan*. Islamic scholars like Ebrahim Moosa, Abdullahi Ahmed An-Naim and Abdolkarim Soroush emphasize the ethic of human responsibility that forges social relationships with others and in so doing improves and transforms the individual. In their opinion, the proper functioning of society is one of the principle concerns of Islam that requires a constant self-consciousness of living with others.[10]

The focus on everyday ethics of living *ihsan* provides an understanding of Islam beyond fixed theological frames. It allows for re-engaging and contextualizing the methodological issue of 'how' to be Muslim, which is one of the most important issues that the majority of Muslims struggle with. For some, implementation of Shar'ia[11] is the shortcut method for providing the rules as a package deal for how to be Muslim, but it is hotly debated. The question that lingers for Muslims worldwide – many of whom follow different *fiqh* (schools of jurisprudence) – is, who has the power to command one set of rules? The remaining question is what are the reasons for these laws and in relation to whom? Refocussing on *ihsan* as the methodological option recentres agency in ordinary individual Muslims who, through their practical experiences, reform and live the principles of Islam in their everyday lives; and allows us to see Shar'ia as a lived set of personal practices of living in community and not a set of laws dogmatically imposed.

The essays in this collection reinforce the capacity of Muslim women who are engaged in peace work and renew their commitment to community. The dynamic between women's work on the site of the everyday and Islamic values as guidance offers a new location for thinking about peacemaking in our contemporary times.

Women

The place of women accorded in Islam is the liberating starting point for the majority of Muslim women. Many rights empower Muslim women: the right of choice in marriage and to initiate divorce; the right to inherit property; the right to education of both scriptural and practical knowledge; the equal rights and duties of worship; and, the right to pursue civil, political and commercial interests in the public domain.[12] Orientalist commentators paid scant attention to Muslim women's rights. On the contrary, many representations focus on issues of oppression, such as polygamy, veiling and presumably high-fertility rates in Muslim communities; the representations construct a persuasive knowledge that Muslim women are without agency and in need of saving.[13]

Particularly, early Western travellers' accounts and art depict Muslim women as either cunning manipulators or erotic bodies devoid of positive and defined individual personality. This over-generalized representation allows for imagining the Muslim woman as the other of their European or Western female counterparts. With the expansion of colonialism into the Muslim world since the late eighteenth century, another image of Muslim women was conjured: that of a dormant and weak population that was forced into perpetual servitude and abuse by Muslim men – their fathers, husbands and brothers.

The interpretation of Muslim men as 'uncivilised' and oppressive gave fillip to the white man's burden to free Muslim women from the terror of the Muslim male tyrants. This notion worked well for the colonial mission of conquest and rule in the Muslim world. Colonial administrators saw themselves as saviours of Muslim women from their own societies and passed laws regarding polygamy, legal age of consent for marriage and so on. In consequence, the ideas that Islam is the enemy of women, and Muslims are inherently inferior to the Western cultures and people became an established assumption and passed as knowledge. Many Western women's discourses, including Victorian feminist discourses of the nineteenth century and contemporary human rights discourses, transform Muslim women into a 'project' that needs rescuing. There is a vast difference between image and reality in Muslim women's lives though. Some rethinking is essential in this area. We cannot ignore or be apologetic to the subordination of Muslim women today in many Muslim societies and the discrimination practiced against them, but pointing fingers at Islam for this outcome is a misconstruction that fails to engage the voices and understandings of patriarchy of Muslim women themselves.

We see Muslim women in many different positions and circumstances; some of them occupy extremely high positions, such as Prime Ministers and political leaders in Islamic countries like Pakistan, Bangladesh and Indonesia. In sharp contrast, there are places where Muslim women do not have the right to exercise their full citizenship (e.g. Saudi Arabia) and are subordinated at every level of public life. It would be a simple failure of imagination not to take into account that the Muslim communities are diverse and have their own cultures and patriarchal structures informing their practices of the religion and the place of women. As well, the experiences of social, economic and political emasculation of Muslim societies during colonialism can hardly be overlooked in considering and evaluating the lesser position of Muslim women in the contemporary world today.

One cannot make easy generalizations regarding the place of women in contemporary Muslim societies. Engagement with this question has produced a variety of responses in academic circles as well as in popular media and television. The material available expands our understanding of the issue and the different approaches to it. Our primary concern in this book is how Muslim women themselves have been responding to these concerns by privileging their focus on peace and through ongoing dialogues and their roles in reforming Muslim communities. We engage the production of knowledge by women about their communities and the problems that persist, and we move beyond to document and analyse how Muslim women confront these challenges and negotiate their places as active agents of change. The examination of Muslim women's roles in multiple everyday sites allows us to locate specific groups of women and see how they work in their local settings, as well as the larger processes influencing their actions and reactions. The empirical evidence gives us sufficient confidence to interpret Muslim women as agents of peace. Many of the essays in this volume are in conversation with several strands of established scholarship in the field of Muslim women's studies, and some follow their own self-made paths that open the way for new questions and issues for further investigation.

There is a vast body of literature written by Muslim women in their own languages – Arabic, Urdu, Bahasa, Persian, Hindi, Bangla, Swahili, English and other languages. As far as we know, Fatima Mernissi's *Beyond the Veil*, published in 1975, is the first English language scholarly book that provides an insider's perspective into Muslim women's lives.[14] This was followed in 1977 by Basima Bezirgan and Elizabeth Fernea's edited volume titled *Middle Eastern Muslim Women Speak*.[15] These scholars pioneered the participation of Muslim women in the dialogue about Muslim women and brought together a variety of voices of ordinary Muslim women alongside the issues of importance in the contemporary world. They also addressed the lived and historical aspects of Muslim societies beyond the textual doctrines of theology and religion.

The academic literature in the field of Muslim women's studies grew in the 1980s. Broadly speaking, the trends in the early period of Muslim women's writing focussed on the role of religion and the status of women in Muslim societies. Critiquing the pernicious effects of patriarchal institutions in depriving women their rights, Nawal El Saadawi's *The Hidden Face of Eve* (1980), Nayra Atiya's *Khul-Khaal:*

Five Egyptian Women Tell Their Stories (1982) and Soraya Altorki and Camillia El-Solh's edited volume *Arab Women in the Field* (1988) blazed a trail of insights and raised important questions for the study of the diversity of Muslim women's lives.[16]

Muslim women's writings from the late 1980s demonstrate confidence in interrogating the violations of women's rights done in the name of religion and dispel some myths regarding Muslim women as voiceless subjects: Haifaa Jawad's *The Rights of Women in Islam* (1998); Fatima Mernissi's *The Veil and the Male Elite* (1991) and *The Forgotten Queens of Islam* (1993); Ziba Mir-Hosseini's *Islam and Gender* (1999); Nilüfer Göle's *The Forbidden Modern* (1996) and Amina Wadud's *Qur'an and Woman* (1991, 1999).[17] Margot Badran argues that this early group of Islamic feminists did not label themselves as such, but they were part of a new discourse producing knowledge that reshaped how Muslim women saw themselves as equals in their societies.[18]

In the post-9/11 world, Muslim scholars using the conceptual framework of Islamic feminism and empowerment have been speaking back and correcting the misconception of Muslim women as victims of tyranny. Drawing upon the Qur'an and the *Hadith* literature, these feminist scholars criticize the patriarchal readings of Islam, and they do not hesitate to show how men have taken over the guardianship of the religion by assuming power against women but not always successfully. The '*Tawhidic* paradigm' of Amina Wadud equalises the rank of men and women.[19] Leila Ahmed, Asma Barlas, Irene Oh and Zakia Salime, to name a few scholars, have reinforced the reading of women as equal in religion.[20]

The meaning of agency through piety is the subject of a new and promising body of Muslim women's scholarship. Saba Mahmood, Sadaf Ahmed, Elora Shehabuddin and Lamia Shehadeh have produced important works that challenge the 'bafflement' of Muslim women as victims and show women's agency in religion beyond dogmatic approaches.[21] In so doing, these works also confound simplistic essentialising of Muslim women and the binary theories of subordination and resistance – the lenses through which Western scholarship and representational theory generally view Muslim women. These new studies offer realistic and nuanced perspectives on religion and feminism that speak back to the Western liberal–secular model from Muslim women's perspectives that exercise their agency by reclaiming piety. This renewed look at the purposeful use of religion resignifies the place of religious values in the lives of Muslim women for a different and liberatory outcome.

Methodologically too, women's scholarship from its early inception in the 1970s has consistently shown a bold approach. Muslim women scholars show intellectual sophistication and the human ability to interact with their subject of study by engaging in the sites of 'intimate knowledge' production and reading religious texts alongside ethnographic analyses of community based on fieldwork, interviews, participant observations and oral history. They enable us to 'see' Muslim women in their human capacity.

The sample of current scholarship mentioned above addresses a wide range of issues. Each example offers a sophisticated analysis and is intensely involved with the topic of understanding Muslim women. Each confirms that the assumptions regarding Muslim women are open to debate, discussion and rethinking, repeatedly. No single lens can sufficiently enable us to understand the diversity of historical contexts, cultural milieus, political conditions and economic circumstances in family and society that produce different realities for Muslim women. Each scholar's contribution allows us to know better and dispel some form of misconception that improves understanding. We may not know the entire story of Muslim women's lives and roles; but we can begin to see patterns within multiple societies and witness how Muslim women carry out active and challenging tasks in their societies, and they have done a fine job in forging ahead. This knowledge about and by Muslim women is cumulative and growing.

In the popular public domain of book production and consumption, Muslim women are a subject of intense scrutiny. The literature covers a wide range – from novels and memoirs to biographies and spiritual writings. Books written for the wider public audience are more accessible, and at times, they present reductive and simplistic solutions to difficult problems. On the one hand, for example, Asra Nomani's *Standing Alone in Mecca* is a story of an American woman's struggle against sexism and intolerance in her local Muslim community in Charleston, West Virginia, which stands in sharp contrast to the principles of equality and acceptance that Islam as a religion provides to Muslim women.[22] On the other hand, according to Ayaan Hirsi Ali in her 2008 title, *The Caged Virgin*, Islam is the problem because it denies her freedom and rights as a human, and it feeds into the prevailing Islamophobic discourse.[23] Irshad Manji, another popular writer, noted in *The Trouble with Islam Today* that the loss of Islamic ethics in public life is perhaps the reason for the less-than-acceptable treatment of Muslim women.[24] Her solution is that Muslims should open the gates of *ijtihad* for questioning their learned assumptions and presumptions. These are dominant voices of Muslim women in the popular and public domains, and because of this, they are all the more important to engage. Unfortunately, many of these books reproduce the essentialized depictions of Muslim women and Islam critiqued by Edward Said, conflating and homogenizing Muslims across the rich and diverse spectrum of cultures and religious orientations.[25] Their principle concern is asserting the domination of Western values for reforming Islam and Muslims rather than shedding light on the realities of Muslim women and their work for changing self and community from the inside, which is fundamental and far more powerful for spurring real change to happen.

Our book continues in the strain of the academic conversations for enhancing understanding of Muslim women's humanity and agency in the context of the everyday. It is written for the general reader, as well as scholars; we have not tried to segregate the knowledge. We have kept the voice of our respective disciplines, but with the aim to share and generate conversations within and beyond our specific areas of research and field expertise. These are essays drawn from multiple sources of academic knowledge and from personal experiences. Our effort is to convey to Muslim insiders and outsiders the concerns of Muslim women regarding their societies and the determinations they have in building a peaceful world for themselves and others around them. The tasks women do every day are generally unnoticed, again sometimes to the women themselves, because they are not actively seeking labels to be heroes or leaders. They, however, allow us to see how everyday acts have the capacity for improving civility and sociality; these are simple acts improving human relationships and improving people's humanity. Women's actions on the site of the everyday signal the prospect of enhanced and peaceful human communities that we present as essential for knowing Muslim communities.

Book Summary

The authors of this volume draw upon a rich array of personal experiences, research and work in the field. Their commitment to Muslim women's concerns for peace through critical evaluation of the sources of knowledge that women draw from, and careful analysis of this material suggest new ways of appreciating and understanding the diverse roles Muslim women play in the development of peaceful and just communities. The authors recognize that often in the international arena of peace-building, women's work is rarely accorded due respect or recognized as 'small successes'. Despite this, the women persist in their ordinary everyday acts to chart the pathways of peace. This kind of scholarship, illuminating what is generally overlooked and is located in the unglamorous site of the everyday, requires the piecing together of disparate contexts and historical conditions. The careful attention to women's everyday actions and responses produces fine-grained scholarship. Through personal observations and reflective scrutiny, the individual authors of each essay delineate the outlines of peace from Muslim women's perspectives and share with the readers their wealth of intimate knowledge that create confidence that Muslim women can be lively and vitally important contributors to peacemaking. The power of Muslim women's work lies in their everyday actions that lay the foundation for peace.

Peace, as discussed above, cannot be actualized as an imposition brokered by militaries or diplomatic missions; it works best when ordinary people become participants in the process. This is qualified in peace literature as 'positive peace'.[26] As an ongoing activity that depends on the involvement of an expanding circle of participants, the work of peace improves by accommodating a variety of opinions, approaches and strategies. Peace, like violence, is not undivided and monolithic. There is no defined and singular path to peace, but engaged and critical awareness of the lived realities of violence and its destructive outcomes can generate thoughtful ideas, useful strategies and effective policies that can effect change for improving communities. The essays in this book suggest that the capacity for individual involvement in the peace process are promoted in various ways by Muslim women and that the ripple effect of these small acts of peace are an inherent aspect of Islamic belief. Our ability to see and appreciate these acts of peace by individual Muslim women and Islamic women collectives can provide new insights for developing a democratic outlook towards understanding the role of variety in peace work and illuminate the spaces where peace is an everyday activity.

There are four interweaving sections of the book; each delves into various aspects of women's lived experiences struggling for peace in their communities. The first section raises significant conceptual issues and questions pertaining to some of our basic assumptions about Islam and women. The second section highlights Islamic concepts, philosophies and practices that Muslim women activists draw upon. In the third section, the essays describe women's work through formal institutions and established cultural traditions, and the fourth section focusses on the interpersonal relationships women forge in their everyday routines. The conclusion is a response of a Western feminist scholar engaging the work of Muslim women in peacemaking as it is represented in this book. It raises questions of the differences between Western feminists' and Muslim feminists' approaches to peace. In order to situate feminist theory of peace within the lived reality of Muslim women's work for peace, in the epilogue we offer a public conversation between two Muslim women peaceworkers, a Sufi sheikha and a social activist. Their conversation drives home the point that much work remains for bringing into dialogue the diverse and often divided worlds of ideas and work, Western and Muslim feminists, peaceworkers and peace theory.

In the very first chapter of the book, miram cooke asks us to heed
to a basic observation that 'neither violence nor peace has a gender'.
She reflects on how women are just as prone to act violently and
promote war, as they are to be harbingers of peace and justice. Peace is
not just the cessation of war, cooke argues, but it is also about 'human
rights, societal transformation, empowerment and dialogue'.
Recognizing this human aspect of peace opens possibilities for
engaging Muslim women as human beings, like other women
worldwide, with agency, beliefs, fears, joys and struggles for their
families and communities within, and against the structures of
patriarchy and global exploitation. Chad Haines focusses on the
potential of dialogue to improve the capacity for human interaction
towards peace. Haines analyses how dialogue, process and cacophony
are conceptual frames for understanding different cultural worlds as
well as an inherent aspect of being Muslim; further, he argues, they
provide a corrective to imposed Liberal ideas of peace and belonging.
Using the Arab Spring and the symbolic significance of Cairo's Tahrir
Square as his starting point, Haines transforms the basic question
about peace asked in the West – how to bring peace to the Muslim
world – into: what does Islam have to say about peace, about world
peace? Opening the channels for dialogue can engender reward and
reinforcement for peace and change the outlook towards the Muslim
world. Calling attention to an Islamic perspective for democratising
the peace processes in the Muslim world is a previously 'unthought'
possibility.[27] In the next chapter in this first section, Richard Martin
traces contemporary Muslim discourses to the Medieval *Mu'tazalite*
philosophical tradition. The rationalist school, Martin suggests,
offers contemporary Muslim feminists pathways for challenging and
debating male-centric Qur'anic interpretations. In the past decade
Muslim apologists for terrorist violence have documented the
theological ideas of Islam as a religion of peace (*salam* in Arabic is
cognate with 'Islam') creating a debate about the proper way Islam is
to be interpreted.

The chapters in the second section explore women's activism in
reshaping social institutions and creating new ones to assert their
rights and claims to peace and justice. The Islamic concepts in which

women engage are part of the dialogical processes that give shape to diverse Muslim societies and communities; and thus the culturally specific institutions and traditions in which women operate. In Bangladesh, Elora Chowdhury shows how non-governmental organizations (NGOs) encode the elite interests and norms of society that reflect class structure. Counter to elite imaginings of gender issues, 'the indigenous women's movement [. . .] has integrated more nuanced intersectional analysis of gender, ethnicity, militarism, nationalism and class in thinking about violence'. Chowdhury argues and directs our attention to the on-the-ground concerns of Muslim women in Bangladesh and their everyday small acts that generate real changes. Similarly, in Aceh, Indonesia, Muslim women are social actors with a long history of significant leadership roles. Asna Husin follows the lives of three Acehnese women and traces their emergent 'gender consciousness' as rooted in Islamic education, family and the needs and demands of their conflict-ridden society. Local cultures of patriarchy, national issues and gender shape women's roles, which are more than predefined by a religious dogma, as it is often perceived by non-Muslims. Rarely discussed or acknowledged, Souad Ali analyses the shifting terrain of Sudanese women preachers from the disjuncture of colonialism to the assertion of nationalist agendas in Sudan. She relates this history to the work of American-based Muslim academics, such as Nimat Hafez Barazangi and Amina Wadud, and their call for a holistic and feminist Qur'anic exegesis.

The chapters in the third section demonstrate the contributions Muslims can make in peacework by sharing some of the Islamic concepts Muslim women draw upon in their everyday acts for peace. Ayse Kadayifci-Orellana focusses on the work of several remarkable women struggling to bring peace to their communities in Kenya, Somalia and Afghanistan. She emphasizes how, 'basing their arguments in Islamic texts and the Prophet's examples enables Muslim women to respond to conservative interpretations much more effectively than secular arguments urging democratisation and Westernisation'. Arzoo Osanloo focusses on the Islamic concept of forgiveness and relates the encounter between a woman whose son was murdered and the family of the perpetrator for arriving at a different and humanistic outcome. Osanloo shows how forgiveness becomes a humanitarian act performed by an individual, and this move, beyond the legal language of justice of the State and human rights discourse, allows for transcendence. An ordinary human act produces a long lasting and positive outcome at multiple levels. It is an empowering site of transformation and peace. Similarly, Azza Karam reflects on the diverse articulations of feminism amongst Muslim women from non-religious, to religious and to Islamist. Karam cautions that it is important to remain open and keep the multiple public discourses that arise from the Arab Spring present in the public sphere to create a paradigm shift that encompasses feminist consciousness and peaceful transformation. The chapters in this section shed a different light and show that Islam is more than a religion of scholars who interpret and debate, but that it works as guidance for Muslims to participate in developing moral communities in their everyday lives.

In the everyday, women enact their cultural traditions and produce improved social relations based on the interweaving of local and Islamic ideas. The chapters in the final section reflect on the minute and ordinary acts of women who carve new pathways and develop various ethics of peace. Within the institutional confines of Aligarh Muslim University (AMU), Yasmin Saikia engages the interpersonal ethics of friendship, tolerance and dignity performed by female hostel borders. The value system of AMU and Islamic ethics of *adab* (etiquette, refinement, respect and humanness) provide women with the tools to negotiate their initial strangeness with one another and actualize their capacity for *insaniyat* (humanity) by seeing the *insan* (human) in others – an inclusive other of fellow students, professors, wardens and janitors. Shahla Talebi situates women's imaginings of peace and justice within the cultural expressions and performance of forming community through memory and remembrance of the martyred. Drawing upon Shi'a traditional practices of mourning in Iran, she interconnects memory with *shahadat* (witnessing) and *amanat* (divine entrustment) that provides the foundation for a sense of peace that is 'inviting and binding in grief and joy [for] those who work to create rather than destroy communities'. In a similar way,

Zilka Šiljak focusses on the concepts and practices of *merhamet* (compassion) and *komšiluk* (neighbourliness) to suggest ways women are rebuilding war-torn Bosnia, and engaging in interfaith and intercommunity dialogues with erstwhile enemies who are now peace-builders working towards a common goal. She finds that the interpersonal ethics are fragile and easily usurped if their application was to be narrowed to ethno-nationalist agendas, which would divide communities once again, rather than seeing the humanity across imagined borders.

The essays in this book draw our attention to a myriad of issues and the role of social institutions, and traditions as sites of liberation, as well as, oppression that force women to negotiate their place in society. Evidently, women who are conscious of their situation and the urgent need to work within their traditions often manage to provide original interpretations for carrying on the work of justice and peace. This reminds us that Muslim women are human beings with agency and beliefs; Islam is a lived tradition with diverse possibilities for followers to define what it means to be Muslim; and peace is a possibility with the active engagement of individuals and collective participation. Islam, like every religious tradition or philosophical school, is neither inherently peaceful nor violent. We as individuals, negotiating our everyday lives, social institutions and cultural traditions make choices to act peacefully or violently. We find within our belief systems the moral and ethical codes to guide our everyday behaviours that lay the groundwork for creating peaceful communities. There is no right or wrong kind of Islam to inspire us to imagine peace. 'Peace is service to others and self, a human duty', as Cemalnur Sargut, a Sufi sheikha, sums up brilliantly for all of us to pay heed.

Notes

1. Sally Merry, *Human Rights and Gender Violence: Translating International Law into Local Justice* (Chicago: University of Chicago Press, 2006); Lila Abu-Lughod, *Do Muslim Women Need Saving* (Cambridge: Harvard University Press, 2013); Irene Oh, *Islam, Human Rights and Comparative Ethics* (Washington, DC: Georgetown University Press, 2007).

2. Michel de Certeau, *The Practice of Everyday Life*, transl. Steven Rendell (Berkeley: University of California Press, 1984).

3. Veena Das, *Life and Words: Violence and Descent into the Ordinary* (Berkeley: University of California Press, 2007).

4. Maurice Blanchot, *Friendship*, transl. Elizabeth Rottenberg (California: Stanford University Press, 1997).

5. Malik Bennabi, *On the Origins of Human Society*, transl. Mohamed El-Tahir El-Mesawi (London: The Open Press, 1998); also see, Mohammed El-Tahir El-Mesawi, 'Religion, society, and culture in Malek Bennabi's thought', in Ibrahim M. Abu-Rabi' (ed), *The Blackwell Companion to Contemporary Islamic Thought* (London: Blackwell Publishing, 2006), pp. 213–56.

6. Asma Afsaruddin, *The First Muslims: History and Memory* (Oxford: OneWorld, 2008), p. 23.

7. Fazlur Rahman, *Islam and Modernity: Transformation of an Intellectual Tradition* (Chicago: University of Chicago Press, 1982); Mohammad Arkoun, *Rethinking Islam: Common Questions, Uncommon Answers* (Boulder: Westview Press, 1994).

8. William Chittick and Sachiko Murata, *The Vision of Islam* (New York: Paragon Books, 1994).

9. Abdulaziz Sachedina, *The Islamic Roots of Democratic Pluralism* (New York: Oxford University Press, 2001); Michael Cook, *Commanding Right and Forbidding Evil in Islamic Thought* (New York: Cambridge University Press, 2010).

10. Ebrahim Moosa, 'The dilemmas of Islamic rights schemes', *Journal of Law and Religion* 15/1–2 (2000), pp. 189–215; Abdullahi Ahmed An-Na'im, *Islam and Global Justice* (Philadelphia: University of Pennsylvania Press, 2011); Abdolkarim Soroush, *Reason, Freedom, and Democracy in Islam*, transl. and edited Mohammad Sadri and Ahmad Sadri (New York: Oxford University Press, 2002).

11. Shar'ia literally means path to a watering hole and reflects a wide, diverse, and debated corpus of interpretations of proper behaviors for being Muslim. However, it comes to be defined as "law", which reflects a very modern understanding of the state and practices of adjudication.

12. Barbara Stowasser, *Women in the Qur'an, Traditions, and Interpretation* (New York: Oxford University Press, 1994); Leila Ahmed, *Women and Gender in Islam: Historical Roots of a Modern Debate* (New Haven: Yale University Press, 1992); Fatema Mernissi, *Women and Islam: A Historical and Theological Inquiry*, transl. Mary Jo Lakeland (London: Basil Blackwell, 1991).

13. Lila Abu-Lughod, 'Do Muslim women really need saving? Anthropological reflections on cultural relativism and its others', *American Anthropologist* 104/3 (2002), pp. 783–90.

14. Fatema Mernissi, *Beyond the Veil: Male-Female Dynamics in a Modern Muslim Society* (Cambridge: Schenkman Pub. Co., 1975).

15. Elizabeth Fernea and Basima Bezirgan (eds), *Middle Eastern Muslim Women Speak* (Austin: University of Texas Press, 1977).

16. Nawal El Saadawi, *The Hidden Face of Eve: Women in the Arab World*, transl. and edited Sherif Hetata (London: Zed Press, 1980); Nayra Atiya, *Khul-Khaal: Five Egyptian Women Tell Their Stories* (Syracuse: Syracuse University Press, 1982); Soraya Altorki and Camillia El-Solh, (eds), *Arab Women in the Field: Studying Your Own Society* (Syracuse: Syracuse University Press, 1988).

17. Haifaa Jawad, *The Rights of Women in Islam: An Authentic Approach* (London: MacMillan, 1998); Fatema Mernissi, *The Veil and the Male Elite: A Feminist Interpretation of Women's Rights in Islam*, transl. Mary Jo Lakeland (New York: Basic Books, 1991); Fatema Mernissi, *The Forgotten Queens of Islam*, transl. Mary Jo Lakeland (Minneapolis: University of Minnesota Press, 1993); Ziba Mir-Hosseini, *Islam and Gender: The Religious Debate in Contemporary Iran* (Princeton: Princeton University Press, 1999); Nilüfer Göle, *The Forbidden Modern: Civilization and Veiling* (Ann Arbor: University of Michigan Press, 1996); and Amina Wadud, *Qur'an and Woman: Rereading the Sacred Text from a Woman's Perspective* (New York: Oxford University Press, 1999 [1991]).

18. Margot Badran, 'From Islamic feminism to a Muslim holistic feminism', *Institute of Development Studies Bulletin*, 42/1 (2011), pp. 78–87.

19. Amina Wadud, *Inside the Gender Jihad: Reform in Islam* (Oxford: OneWorld, 2006).

20. Leila Ahmed, *Women and Gender in Islam: Historical Roots of a Modern Debate* (New Haven: Yale University Press, 1993); Asma Barlas, *Believing Women in Islam: Unreading Patriarchal Interpretations of the Qur'an* (Austin: University of Texas Press, 2002); Oh, *Islam, Human Rights and Comparative Ethics*; Zakia Salime, *Between Feminism and Islam: Human Rights and Shari'a Law in Morocco* (Minneapolis: University of Minnesota Press, 2011).

21. Saba Mahmood, *The Politics of Piety: The Islamic Revival and the Feminist Subject* (Princeton: Princeton University Press, 2005); Sadaf Ahmed, *Transforming Faith: The Story of Al-Huda and Islamic Revivalism among Urban Pakistani Women* (New York: Syracuse University Press, 2009); Elora Shehabuddin, *Reshaping the Holy: Democracy, Development, and Muslim Women in Bangladesh* (New York: Columbia University Press, 2008); Lamia Shehadeh, *The Idea of Women in Fundamentalist Islam* (Gainesville: University of Florida Press, 2008).

22. Asra Nomani, *Standing Alone in Mecca: An American Woman's Struggle for the Soul of Islam* (New York: HarperCollins, 2005).

23. Ayaan Hirsi Ali, *The Caged Virgin: An Emancipation Proclamation for Women and Islam* (New York: Free Press, 2008).

24. Irshad Manji, *The Trouble With Islam Today* (New York: St. Martin's Press, 2004).

25. Edward Said, *Orientalism* (New York: Vintage Books, 1978).

26. Johan Galtung, *Theories of Peace: A Synthetic Approach to Peace Thinking* (Oslo: International Peace Research Institute, 1967). Also see, Johan Galtung, 'Violence, peace, and peace research', *Journal of Peace Research*, 6/3 (1969), pp. 167–91.

27. Muhammad Arkoun, *Rethinking Islam*.

PART 1

DELIBERATIONS: QUESTIONING THE NORMATIVE

CHAPTER 1

UNGENDERING PEACE TALK

miriam cooke

'Bedell, meanwhile, is dressed in her desert camouflage. She has a Beretta M9 strapped to her thigh and an M4 rifle over her shoulder.'[1] Zoe Bedell, a 2007 Princeton graduate, is in charge of the US Marine Corps' Female Engagement Teams in Afghanistan. Trained for 'combat lifesaving techniques', these female marines are part of the US military's counterinsurgency project to reach out to Afghan women. Theirs is a new assignment – win the hearts and minds of the men through the women. Armed women marines like Bedell are complicating the usual association of women and peacemaking. While women's groups and networks around the world have long worked for peace, other past and present women like the Amazons, Joan of Arc, Golda Meir and, most recently, women suicide bombers have not. Women are not created peace loving *in utero*; they are told they are. Sara Ruddick argues that women are not inherently peaceable.[2] Rather, they practice a form of maternal thinking that adapts women to violence on behalf of peace. Their special conflict resolution skills, she writes, are learned. The mother cares for her child often devotedly.

Are men – automatically associated with war – more engaged in peace-building than women? In its 112-year history, the Nobel Peace Prize has been awarded to 86 men – 4 of them Muslims – but only to 15 women – 2 of them Muslim women – a ratio of 1 woman to 7 men.

Male poets from Homer to Osip Mandelstam have long sung odes against the reckless violence of war and advocated renunciation of arms. The heart-wrenching voices that called for peace in the early twentieth century were those of the young men who had been to the World War I front and fought in the trenches. Rupert Brooke, Wilfred Owen and Siegried Sassoon turned chemical warfare into passionate poetry that conveys the horror of war and need for peace. These men did not use the language of peace to demand peace. They described the devastation of war so that its senseless destruction might provide instruction on how to cultivate its opposite.

Men's principled objections to war, often articulated by those who have seen combat and its devastations, have taught us that warmongering and peace-building are not natural; they are learned behaviours. Men are not born violent; they have to be whipped into violent shape. Private Pyle in Stanley Kubrick's 1987 *Full Metal Jacket* was a large man with the look of someone who could be shaped and trained into the ideal military agent. However, no amount of abuse and punishment could turn him into the opposite of what he was born to be – a man who could not commit violence. To make any changes in the perception of men and women's instincts and behaviour, this gendering must first be marked and then deconstructed. Only then can war and peace options begin to be ungendered and universalized. The acknowledgment of women's potential violence and men's peace-building work provides a corrective to the rosy picture of women waving white flags and men wiping blood off their blades. Depending on the context, Muslim and non-Muslim women, like Muslim and non-Muslim men, nurture and kill.

In what follows, I examine the disjuncture between expectations for how men and women should react to violence, and I question the instinctive gendering of war and peace activism with a focus on Muslim women.

War–Peace Continuum

Peace-building is not only opposition to war; it is concerned with human rights, societal transformation, empowerment and dialogue.

It is 'designed to assist the warring parties in transitioning from a prolonged, violent conflict into a durable peace [...]. War is the product of the mind; it only looks as though it is the product of generals and weapons.'[3] Peace and war coexist; they define each other negatively. Peace and war – like heaven and hell – are the outer limits on a continuum. To be more precise, peace should be thought in the felicitous terms coined by Johan Galtung in 1964: 'positive peace' – the struggle for a constructive resolution of violence – and 'negative peace' – the absence of violence that does not, however, preclude its happening. The poles of the continuum would then be war and positive peace with negative peace bridging the divide.[4]

War is much more than the direct inflicting of physical harm, and peace is much more than stopping that violence. The technologies of war that have been domesticated for 'peaceful' purposes permeate the environment in which we live.[5] Chemotherapy was developed out of chemical warfare, non-invasive pressure monitoring was a by-product of military submarine technology and the Internet grew out of Defense Advanced Research Projects Agency's data gathering for transnational espionage. Long before Eisenhower coined the term 'the military–industrial complex', war and technology were historically intertwined. Paul Virilio writes of the 'pure war' that marks the relationship between a State and its people, and McLuhan and Fiore elaborate on an analysis of what they call the 'war environment' in which we all live. This does not mean that bombs are constantly dropping. It means that even when bombs are not exploding, conflicts continue, and scientists imagine new and better weapons. Our thinking is still geared towards war, and at best we are enjoying negative peace.

The violence of war, Galtung theorizes, is of two kinds (direct and indirect) that function at three levels: physical, cultural and structural.[6] *Direct-physical violence* is the way we generally think of war – bombs and 'rape and pillage'. *Indirect-cultural violence* varies socially and regionally in terms of what are considered to be acceptable levels of injury. It is at work in local forms of patriarchy. In many cultures, physical or epistemic violence against women is not coded violence but considered to be a part of the norms and values of that society. *Structural violence* is the most difficult to pinpoint and to eradicate because it is a systemic modus operandi. Structural violence is the war at home that is inherent in the military, but at home, it is carried out without all the gear and without calling what is being done 'war'. In the heart of civilian society, structural violence shapes the ways misogynist religious authorities twist scriptures to privilege men at women's expense. Sociologist Fatima Mernissi is unequivocal about how this works in Muslim societies. She shows that 'not only have the sacred texts always been manipulated, but manipulation of them is a structural characteristic of the practice of power'.[7] Citizens deprived of their human rights are suffering from structural violence. In other words, they are targets in the war the State has waged on some of its citizens. A case in point is the Islamic Republic of Iran.

Shirin Ebadi, Nobel Prize laureate and judge at the age of 23, has devoted her life to fighting for peace in her native Iran. When she was stripped of her judgeship in 1979 because the Islamic authorities believed women to be incapable of practicing Islamic law, she determined that she would fight for her people's rights in whatever way possible. During the eight years of war with neighbouring Iraq many Iranians fled the country, but she stayed. After Islamic authorities granted her permission to resume her legal practice, Ebadi defended the disenfranchized without thought of the personal cost.[8] Law provided her with the weapon to fight the structural violence of the Islamic Republic of Iran.[9] In 1988, the last year of the Iran–Iraq War in which hundreds of thousands were killed, 4500 dissidents were executed.[10] The government's goal, like all wars' goal, was to 'impose a climate of fear'.[11] During the 1990s Ebadi took on some very difficult cases that 'illustrated the tragic repercussions of the theocracy's legal discrimination against women'.[12]

In her memoir, she tells the story of the family of a girl who was raped and murdered, and her parents were expected 'to finance the executions of their daughter's convicted murderers'.[13] The case involving a young man who killed his stepsister brought Ebadi to the world's attention and gave her a voice with which to fight for peace and, in other words, to end the war the Islamic Republic of Iran was waging on its people, especially its women. She also refers to her work in military terms. 'Is there an alternative battlefield?' she asks when explaining the need to argue her cases from within an Islamic framework.[14] She describes her legal work as, 'doing battle in the revolutionary courts of Tehran', and, 'I have been under attack most of my adult life'.[15] Use of the words 'battlefield' and 'battle' clearly indicate her understanding of the state of war she has lived and contested. Nor did the danger subside after she received the Nobel Peace Prize in 2003 and became the first Muslim woman and only the tenth woman to have been awarded the honour. In fact, the threats accelerated, and to her dismay the Iranian government sent guards to protect (monitor?) her. The war goes on.

Nobel Women's Initiative

Since structural and cultural violence are without clearly identifiable agents, they may be imperceptible and thus hard to fight; it is only at the physical level that we are fully aware of war's violence. Although peace-building needs to address each level, it has been direct-physical violence that has been the reason for peace initiatives. To posit peace as an achievable end and to plumb the depths of war's imbrication in our lives as discourse and practice, these structural and cultural levels must be revealed.

This is what the Nobel Women's Initiative has tried to do. In 2006, Ebadi joined the six living female Nobel laureates to create the Nobel Women's Initiative. They insist on the connections between physical, cultural and structural violence. Their mission statement redefines peace as:

> more than the absence of armed conflict. Peace is the commitment to equality and justice; a democratic world free of physical, economic, cultural, political, religious, sexual and environmental violence and the constant threat of these forms of violence against women – indeed against all of humanity.[16]

In 2007 the Initiative convened its first conference, Women Redefining Peace in the Middle East and Beyond, to:

compare successful strategies in countering violence against women and in promoting women's human rights [...]. We came to understand that our work on women's rights, religious fundamentalisms, nuclear weapons, government reform, corporate and media responsibility, and so on, is linked, whether we acknowledge the linkages or not, and that all of our work is contributing to building cultures of peace.[17]

The Initiative emphasized that women should be involved not only *during* peace negotiations, but also *after* in their implementation. The conferees called for support of the Iraqi people, an end to the Israeli occupation of the Palestinian territories, support for the Million Signatures Campaign (a grassroots petition to abrogate discriminatory laws against women in Iran), support for disarmament campaigns and support for the people of Darfur, Burma and the women peace activists in Serbia and Uganda.

Three years later, the Nobel Women's Initiative held another conference on redefining peace. The 2009 conferees demanded an end to all State violence against women, protection of women and children in conflict situations, and women's greater participation in formal peace negotiations. A representative of UNIFEM (United Nations Development Fund for Women) 'noted that worldwide, only 2.4 per cent of signatories to the major peace agreements signed since 1996 are women, and women have made up less than 6 per cent of the negotiating delegations in peace negotiations'.[18] Women's peace-work, the female Nobel laureates insisted, should translate into participation in international conventions.

Sometimes, as in the tiny oil state of Qatar in the Arabian Gulf, it does. Sheikha Mozah bint Nasser Al Misnad, the Emir's consort, has been advocating the centrality of education and dialogue to peace-building in a tumultuous Middle East. A woman's face is the official look of peace to the world. She was instrumental in the 2005 launching of the post-9/11 Alliance of Civilizations Project (AOC). Addressing the structural and cultural levels of war's violence, she works for the justice without which peace is impossible. In a November 2011 interview, she said 'the mission of the AOC is to build bridges between people of different cultures to foster peaceful coexistence and cooperation via intercultural dialogue [to build] a better understanding specifically between the Muslim world and the West'.[19] Sheikha Mozah is fighting for peace in the war-torn Middle East and for mutual cross-cultural understanding. Her weapons are education and dialogue.

Muslim Women Warriors

Women's participation in their people's wars is not new. Since the beginning, Muslim women were involved in war. In the second chapter of the Qur'an, men and women are told that they must fight, however loathsome they might find it to be:

> Fighting is written for you even though you hate it. But it may well be that you hate what is good for you and that you love what is bad for you. God is the one who knows and not you. (Q 2:216)

Women like Nusayba bint Kaab al-Maziniya should be added to the stories of nurses accompanying Muhammad and his followers to battle. During the 625 CE battle of Uhud between the Muslims and their Meccan opponents, Nusayba defended Muhammad with her sword and bow and arrows, and she saved his life. So popular a figure has Nusayba become that references to her bravery are present on several Islamic websites. One site quotes Muhammad saying to Nusayba's son, 'Your mother! Bind her wound! May Allah bless you, the people of a house! The stand of your mother is better than the stand of so-and-so'. And then he said, 'Whenever I looked to the right or left I saw her fighting in front of me'.[20] The cost of peace for early Muslims was war with their opponents.

Another early Muslim woman warrior is Muhammad's grand-daughter, Zaynab bint Ali. She fought at Karbala in 680 CE, the founding moment of Shi'ite identity and piety. Zaynab stood up to the second ruler of the Umayyad Caliphate, the tyrant Yazid, who was responsible for the persecution of her family and the murder of her brother Husayn. She demanded justice and warned him that she and her descendants would never forget his evil. She was the first to hold a lamentation assembly for Husayn, thereby setting a precedent for the ritual *Zaynabiyat* (Shi'ite women's assemblies for the remembrance of Husayn), which is still performed in Shi'ite communities all over the world, but especially in Iraq. These early Muslim women were not armchair advocates of peace and harmony. They had a message, and they were willing to risk all to deliver it. It was a message of peace delivered in unpeaceful ways.

This is what Shirin Ebadi, and other women like her in the Nobel Women's Initiative, is doing today. In Ebadi's work with Iranians who are deprived of their human rights, she has risked much in her search for the justice that is the *sine qua non* of peace. In 2000 she found her name on a government list of assassination targets.[21] Yet despite her fear, she persisted in her advocacy of equality and life for all. Without justice, equality and freedom there could not be peace.

Networking for Peace

Today many Muslim women's groups are networking for peace. In Afghanistan, women have been mobilizing against misogynist authorities throughout the past 30 years. In the late 1970s the Revolutionary Association of the Women of Afghanistan opposed first the Soviets and then the Taliban. In 1984 nine women from Algeria, Sudan, Morocco, Pakistan, Bangladesh, Iran, Mauritius and Tanzania formed Women Living Under Muslim Laws (WLUML). As an international network of information, solidarity and peace-building, WLUML prioritises the fight against Islamists when they target women. In 1990 they initiated a project on Qur'anic interpretation that brought together 30 women from 10 countries to provide Muslim women everywhere with the appropriate information and language to contest readings of scripture that endorse gender injustice. The 1991–4 Women and Law Project examined the ways in which Muslim Personal Law has discriminated against women, sometimes in contradiction with their countries' Constitutions.

In December 2010 I attended a women and peace conference in Cairo. Like the Nobel Women's Initiative, the goal was to imagine a 'world free from military, patriarchal, imperialist and religious domination (and) the promotion of a space for non-violent and peaceful conflict resolution, at a local and international level'.[22] The conference called for a global–local solidarity among feminist movements as 'an essential precondition for real democracy, just peace and full equality regardless of gender, class, religion or other characteristics'. The organizers insisted on the primacy of secularization and urged the need to counteract the growing influence of religious fundamentalism. Women from 25 Muslim societies gathered in Cairo to discuss solutions to the violence plaguing their societies.

Using Islamic language and frameworks to promote peace and an end to the Islamists' war against women, they demanded attention to women's rights in Islam. They knew that in a context saturated with religion, it was essential to produce new Islamic-informed under-standings of the roles and status of women in Muslim societies. Papers detailed the violence unleashed against women in the name of Islam, but they did not provide signposts through the maze of the physical, structural and cultural violence that underlies the visible manifestations of the war waged against them. The conference had two outcomes: (1) a call for *another* conference to foster global peace, security and stability at both the local and global levels; and (2) a petition to stop the flogging of Sudanese women when caught venturing outdoors after dark. Participants were asked to distribute the petition to concerned Embassies around the world. After the first wave of enthusiasm waned, the dejection was palpable. However, nobody anticipated the groundswell of change that was just ahead. Although, the conference took place a few days before the outbreak of the Arab Spring in Tunisia that moved to Egypt in late January 2011, there was no intimation among the conferees that the kind of popular, pro-peace and democratic uprising that they were demanding was ready to explode.

The Arab Spring

The Arab Spring unleashed a grassroots struggle for justice and against poverty and State-sponsored violence against their peoples. No longer able to ignore the structural violence of the pure war their governments had long waged against them, women and men called for the freedom, rights and justice that give substance to the word peace. Muslim women embraced modern media and allowed the world to watch when in April 2008, a veiled Muslim woman, Usra Abu al-Fatah, organized a protest against the increasing cost of food. Now known as the 'Facebook Queen', she was one of the founders of the 'April 6' youth movement that many claimed was the forerunner of the 2011 Egyptian Revolution. It was another veiled woman, Asma Mahfuz, who on 25 January called on Egyptians and especially on Egyptian men to come to Tahrir Square:

> If we still have honour and we want to live in dignity on this land, we have to go down on January 25 [...]. Whoever says it's not worth it because there will only be a handful of people, I want to tell him you are the reason behind this, and you are a traitor just like the President or any security cop who beats us in the streets. Your presence with us will make a difference, a big difference![23]

And it did. The demand for justice and peace drove Husni Mubarak out of the President's office.

Shortly thereafter, Tawakkul Karman led the uprising to oust Yemen's authoritarian leader, Ali Abdullah Saleh. When she became aware of her leadership role, she decided to uncover her face so that the people might see her and relate to her. For her inspiration and direction, Karman became the second Muslim woman to win the Nobel Peace Prize. In her acceptance speech, she articulated her beliefs about the importance of gender justice in the struggle for peace:

> I have always believed that resistance against repression and violence is possible without relying on similar repression and

violence [. . .]. So, when women are treated unjustly and are deprived of their natural right in this process, all social deficiencies and cultural illnesses will be unfolded, and in the end the whole community, men and women, will suffer. The solution to women's issues can only be achieved in a free and democratic society in which human energy is liberated, the energy of both women and men together [. . .]. The Arab people who are [in revolt] a peaceful and civilised manner have, for so many decades, been oppressed and suppressed by the regimes of authoritarian tyrants.[24]

Men and women must be equally engaged in peace-building. The Arab Spring has shown the world that the battle for dignity and human rights, the core values of peace, has no gender.

This is a critical moment in Arab–Muslim history. Not since the mid-twentieth-century successes of the anti-colonial struggles have so many Arabs risen up against unjust regimes and demonstrated that death is a price worth paying to end decades of oppression and 'peace' without justice. The setbacks, especially for women, are dispiriting, but they are also galvanizing new energies.

Religions and the Gender of Peace

Tawakkul Karman and Asma Mahfuz used Facebook to mobilize the masses and to oppose dictators without arms, but with determination to instigate change. Wearing the veil that symbolizes commitment to Islam, they did not invoke religion. It was implicit in their appearance and influential in the mass response to their call to action. Can religions – that sometimes provide a crucial justification and act as an effective mobilizer for people to kill and die – play a role in peace-building? Many believe that they can. There are numerous Muslim groups networking for peace. Among them is Muslims for Peace.[25] With messages focussed on peace and justice, religions would seem to be ideally placed to oppose violence. Jesus admonished his followers to turn the other cheek. Muhammad named his religion Islam, a word derived from the same root as peace, *salam*, the internationally recognized greeting Muslims exchange with each other. In this volume (Chapter 8), Arzoo Osanloo notes that although the Qur'an permits vengeance, more importantly, it advocates forgiveness: 'But he who shall forego vengeance out of charity will atone for past sins' (Q 5:45). In other words, even in the face of extreme provocations, when revenge is religiously sanctioned, mercy to the enemy is the greatest grace. It is a way for the injured person to hope to become whole again.[26]

Peace has less to do with religion, than with ideas about how men and women are expected to act in war. While men are expected to gird their loins for violence, women are expected to keep the home fires burning. Clichés? Perhaps. But these clichés persist despite the radical changes in warfare. In April 2011, the USA's National Public Radio broadcasted a series of programmes on *Women in Combat* to explore how gendered expectations in the military had changed. Although in the USA we have become more accustomed to reading about women and war, and to seeing images of uniformed women with guns, listeners commented, 'I don't like to see women hurt', 'men are supposed to protect', and so on. Space may no longer be split and gendered when war is declared; yet old behavioural attitudes persist. In the era of 'carpet-bombing' when all are fair game, men are still expected to protect; and women and children to be protected.

Gendered expectations for warlike and peace-loving behaviour have to be questioned. Neither violence nor peace has a gender, but the instinctive feminising of peace-making is problematic because it portrays men who are committed to opposing lethal conflict as weak. Sharon Macdonald asks how peace movements can confront:

> the accusation that they offer a weak, passive and negative alternative to war [...]. The association of women with the private and the domestic, rather than the public political, sphere may also be built into a politically enfeebled picture of peace movements. Their vision is said to be limited or naïve, and their concerns are depicted as those of individual rather than national security.[27]

This marginalization of peace as women's work may be overcome by breaking the essentialized link between women and peace. In order to prevent peace-oriented activities from being feminized and then automatically dismissed, women's behaviour must be understood to be as variable as men's behaviour.

Women's Peace Literature

In my work on Arab women's literary, peace-oriented interventions in what I called the 'War Story', I approached peace through what it is not. I wrote about war not peace when analysing Arab women's war fiction that articulated their desires, struggles and aspirations for peace.[28] I did not want the expected coupling of women and peace to tune people out. They shrug – how nice! Who cares? Above all, I wanted readers to recognize that even when Arab women did not pull a trigger, they were involved in a form of combat and that to pay attention to what they were saying about it was crucial to any project for its ending.

My work on Arab women writers and peace–war straddled two strands of women in the military discourse that Ilene Rose Feinman called 'feminist egalitarian militarism' and 'feminist antimilitarists'.[29] Feminist egalitarian militarists believe that more women in the military do not undermine it, nor do they spoil cohort morale. It is a woman's right to fight, like the men. Yes, combat is a right, but it is also a privilege because only those prepared and allowed to kill and die for king and country can become true citizens. In 1930 Evadne Price, aka Helen Zenna Smith, published her semi-autobiographical *Not so Quiet...* about her experience in the trenches as an ambulance driver. A feminist egalitarian militarist, she argued that women like her were in combat because they were exposed to the same dangers that the men faced. Smith was recoding the actions of women ambulance drivers so that their dangerous work should be called combat, and the stakes in this naming become apparent. Women who perform combat duties, the place par excellence where nationalist commitment can be demonstrated, may be granted full citizenship.

While feminist egalitarian militarists are committed to changing perceptions of women in the military so that their actions can be recognized and they can receive the civic reward they deserve, feminist anti militarists are pacifists. They oppose not only the direct violence of war but also its structural imbrication in daily life. They are clear that the military–industrial complex must be challenged and deconstructed.

Lebanese Hanan al-Shaykh's Zahra is not legible as a combatant, yet she fights in her own way for peace. She does not oppose the war with its own instruments, but with her woman's body. She climbs the stairs to the roof where a sniper, the emblem of war's mindless cruelty, lies in wait. She seduces him, and while she is with him he is distracted from his deadly task. Their affair progresses, she becomes pregnant, and she tries to humanize him. She wants to know his name. She wants him to share in her nervous anticipation of their baby. She wants to change him from a killer into a man of peace. However, Sami's not ready for peace. As she exits the building, he shoots her. Zahra may have failed to end even only one individual agent of violence, but she had tried to understand it and thus to change it. What mattered was her engagement with the structural violence that fuelled the engine of the Lebanese Civil War.[30]

Palestinian women's literature on the people's activities after the Israeli occupation of the West Bank in 1967 reveals that women invented a new way of fighting that stemmed the advance of the occupiers. Already in the early 1970s novelist Sahar Khalifa and poet Fadwa Tuqan described women's tactics and how successful stone-throwing and tire-burning were in disabling the Israeli military on the physical and structural levels. Their actions were called *sumud*, which means steadfastness. With the eyes of the world on the confrontation between unarmed women and children and uniformed soldiers in tanks, the female refugee presented a heroic figure who disabled military training and hardware. They were waging war by other means and forging a painful path to peace. Their *sumud* was a form of combat that maintained a fragile peace. In 1987, however, things changed. Palestinian men adopted women's ways of fighting. Centralized commands and young men wearing helmet-like kaffiyas throwing Molotov cocktails replaced the spontaneous, non-lethal actions of unarmed women and children. By 1991 the Intifada exhausted itself and the Israeli military machinery cranked back into action. Women's non-lethal violence had kept the peace.[31] The next step should have been the reward for nationalist service and contributions to creating a culture of peace. The reward is on hold; the culture of peace they fought for remains a dream. Gender segregation is not the answer to the search for peace. As Tawakkul Karman said in her Nobel acceptance speech, 'I have always believed that human civilisation is the fruit of the effort of both women and men'.[32]

Conclusion

Peace without justice is meaningless. It does not end conflict but ploughs it under with deeper, more resilient seeds of hatred, despair and revenge. Peace-building that strives only for a cessation of the physical violence without insisting on the justice that comes from dealing with structural and cultural violence is truce-building at best. Without justice, peace risks being reduced to some problematic acceptance of tyranny and injustice in the name of stability, security and harmony. The women and men of Tunisia, Egypt, Libya, Bahrain, Syria and Yemen have recognized the need to resist and to be on the front lines of the war for dignity, freedom and real democracy. Seeing the connections between 'iron fist', 'stability' and authoritarianism, they say 'No' to the kind of 'peace' that tyrannical rule brings.

New thinking requires shifting the lens. Women fighting predators intent on destroying their young are not exceptions; they are doing what has to be done to preserve those they cherish. Men working for peace are not exceptions; they are doing what they know is right and necessary to keep the world whole. The fact that some men are inherently peaceful and some women are born fierce does not mean that either group is any more emblematic of their gender, than are their opposites. Children must be taught this variability from the youngest ages so that they will grow up knowing how:

historic links between feminism and pacifism are counterbalanced by the instances when women have embraced revolution with hope and war with enthusiasm. There has not been a consistent women's response to war and revolution any more than there has been a uniform feminist position on women's relation to organised violence.[33]

Once it is understood how multiple are women's engagements with war and peace, men's essentialized links to war and violence can, and should, be questioned. Conflict resolution and peace-building should be as much a part of mainstream curricula, as violence and war are.

This chapter has made a case for recognizing the gendering of war and peace as a first step towards undoing their binary logic. Once these extremes at either end of the continuum of conflict engagement and management have been marked, their assumptions can begin to be questioned and deconstructed. The goal is to universalize the work of peace-builders. Arabian Nusayba bint Kaab, Iranian Shirin Ebadi, Qatari Shaykha Mozah, the Palestinian women of the Occupied Territories, Egyptian Asma Mahfouz and Yemeni Tawakkul Karman, as well as, Lebanese Hanan al-Shaykh's fictional Zahra are only the tip of the iceberg of women's peace-building. However, in each case, men's cooperation was essential to the success of these women's efforts to build peace. Nusayba fought side-by-side with the Prophet Muhammad. Ebadi insists that it was her father who inspired her peacework and that her husband was always supportive. The Palestinian women's peace initiative could only thrive with the backing of their men; when the men took over the women's ways of resisting the Israeli occupation and sidelined the women, they failed. The revolutionary women leaders of the recent Arab Revolutions appealed to the men to join them. Without this support, women's peace-building is doomed to fail, as when the sniper refused to accede to Zahra's peace project that would have turned him into a father and responsible member of the community.

Positive peace-building is everyone's business. Women may be better placed than men to perceive war's three-tiered violence because they are often subject to its structural and cultural dimensions. However, without men they are no better equipped to deal with them.

Notes

1. E. B. Boyd, 'Women to women: In Afghanistan, Zoe Bedell '07 led female Marines in a new role', *Princeton Alumni Weekly* (1 June 2011). Available at http://paw.princeton.edu/issues/2011/06/01/pages/5436/index.xml?page=2& (accessed 2 May 2012).

2. Sara Ruddick, *Maternal Thinking: Towards a Politics of Peace* (Boston: Beacon Press, 1989).

3. Shai Har-El, 'From peace process to actual peace', *World Policy Blog* (3 April 2012). Available at http://www.worldpolicy.org/blog/2012/04/03/peace-process-actual-peace (accessed 18 April 2012). Har-El is the founder and president of Middle East Peace Network.

4. Johan Galtung, 'Editorial', *Journal of Peace Research* 1/1(1964), pp. 1–4.

5. Marshall McLuhan and Quentin Fiore, *War and Peace in the Global Village* (New York: Bantam Books, 1968), pp. 125–6.

6. Johan Galtung discussed these levels of violence during his keynote address at the global conference 'Women and the 21st Century – Feminist Alternatives', in Cairo, Egypt, 16–18 December 2010.

7. Fatema Mernissi, *The Veil and the Male Elite: A Feminist Interpretation of Women's Rights in Islam*, transl. Mary Jo Lakeland (New York: Basic Books, 1991), pp. 8–9.

8. In 2000 she was jailed in the infamous Evin prison. See: Shirin Ebadi, *Iran Awakening: One Woman's Journey to Reclaim Her Life and Country* (New York: Random House, 2006), pp. 156–77.

9. Ibid., pp. 51–2.

10. Ibid., pp. 90–1.

11. Ibid., p. 103.

12. Ibid., p. 111.

13. Ibid., pp. 112–22.

14. Ibid., p. 122.

15. Ibid., p. 204.

16. Nobel Women's Initiative, *About Us*. Available at http://nobelwomensinitiative.org/about-us/ (accessed 13 April 2012).

17. Jody Williams, 'Conclusions', *Conference Report: Women Redefining Peace in the Middle East and Beyond, Nobel Women's Initiative* (2007). Available at http://nobelwomens initiative.org/wp-content/archive/stories/pages_from_nwi_confernence_report_2007-low_res-conclusions_section.pdf (accessed 2 July 2013).

18. Nobel Women's Initiative, '"Real" democracy guarantees equal rights, security & peace' (13 May 2009). Available at http://nobelwomensinitiative.org/2009/05/real-democracy-guarantees-equal-rights-security-peace/ (accessed 13 April 2012).

19. Sheikha Moza Bint Nasser, 'Q & A: Her Highness Sheikha Moza Bint Nasser', *Qultura* (December 2011), p. 1. Available at http://www.qatar4unaoc.org/wp-content/uploads/2011/12/SHEIKHA+MOZAH + INTERVIEW.pdf (accessed 16 April 2012).
20. Hamza Qassim, 'Umm Umara: The prophet's shield at Uhud', *Nida'ul Islam* 22 (Feb/March, 1998).
21. Ebadi, *Iran Awakening*, p. xv.
22. Text from *Women and the 21st Century – Feminist Alternatives* call for papers; this conference was a sequel to the 2009 *Peace and Security – Feminist Alternatives* conference held in Skopje.
23. See http://asmamahfouz.com/ (accessed 12 April 2012).
24. Tawakkul Karman's Nobel Peace Prize acceptance speech (10 December 2011). Available at http://www.nobelprize.org/nobel_prizes/peace/laureates/2011/karman-lecture_en.html (accessed 13 April 2012).
25. See http://www.muslimsforpeace.org (accessed 22 April 2012).
26. Ebadi recounts the case of a mother staying the execution of her daughter's murderer. See Ebadi, *Iran Awakening*, p. 126.
27. Sharon Macdonald, Pat Holden and Shirley Ardener (eds), *Images of Women in Peace and War: Cross-Cultural and Historical Perspectives* (Madison: University of Wisconsin Press, 1988), p. 21.
28. miriam cooke, *War's Other Voices: Women on the Lebanese Civil War* (London: Cambridge University Press, 1987); miriam cooke, *Women and the War Story* (Berkeley: California University Press, 1996).
29. Ilene Rose Feinman, *Citizenship Rites: Feminist Soldiers and Feminist Antimilitarists* (New York: New York University Press, 2000).
30. See Chapter 3, cooke, *War's Other Voices*.
31. See Chapter 4, cooke, *Women and the War Story*.
32. Karman, Nobel Peace Prize acceptance speech.
33. Ruth Roach Pierson, '"Did your mother wear army boots?" Feminist theory and women's relation to war, peace and revolution', in Sharon Macdonald, Pat Holden and Shirley Ardener (eds), *Images of Women in Peace and War*, p. 225.

CHAPTER 2

DIALOGICAL DIN AND EVERYDAY ACTS OF PEACE: AN ISLAMIC PERSPECTIVE

Chad Haines

Over the past two decades we have witnessed some dramatic global shifts, eruptions, destructions and the unleashing of new creative forces. We struggle to comprehend, keep up with and be part of the unfolding sociocultural, political, economic and religious transformations forging new relationships and interconnections. Some of these new associations are virtual, some are grounded, engendering re-evaluations of how we have theoretically, empirically and ontologically come to understand our place in the world. Our modern global connections open up new horizons of identity, such as transnational nationalism and global religious movements, which expand our ontological points of reference and unveil covert connections that interweave histories and cultural formations.

One of the particular challenges is the intensification of exposure to diverse and divergent ways of being in the world, defying our modernist desire for drawing borders between us and them. The presence of diverse cultural practices, assumptions and social formations counter nationalist hubris and religious orthodoxy, and often challenge the limits of our own orientations and assumptions about how the world is; in so doing, they intensify conflicts, social marginalization and the denial of justice to those mapped outside emergent 'we' groups. Simultaneously though, new possibilities of community and belonging open unique possibilities for creating and living in communities of tolerance and peace.

Symbolically, the uprisings that marked the beginning of the Arab Spring in January and February of 2011 were the formation of a creative community that transcended the normative markers that came to define and fix identity in much of the Arab world. Muslims and Christians, lower class and upper class, the deeply religious and the completely secular, urbanite Cairenes and rural *fellaheen* (peasants), men and women, youth and elders came together on the streets across various countries demanding respect and basic rights. In Muslim history there are deep roots for both creative and pluralistic comings together as well as claims to fixed and rigid interpretations of being Muslim, an outward worldly cosmopolitanism and an inner-looking orthopraxy. Theologically, these opposing orientations are mapped along different strands, one of the dominant being the historic debates between Asharites and Mu'tazilites,[1] but other formations and interpretations also exist that encode peace and tolerance in Muslim communities such as Sufi strands of love and belonging, ethics of *ummah* (community), traditions of hospitality and moral expressions of *adab* (manners and comportment).

In this chapter I shift focus away from entrenched theological debates, to reflect on these Muslim histories and practices of everyday living. I posit how modes of change, sociality and being that, while not unique or original to Muslims, but that are defined and enacted within a referential world of Muslimness, come to assert a lived peace. My concern ultimately is not with what is being referenced – how tolerance or peace or rights are viewed by some within an Islamic, Qur'anically sanctioned definition. Rather, my concern is to reflect on Muslim acts of peace, enacted in ways of being in the world that significantly shifts both our dominant concern of Islam tied to its textual/theological roots, but also our mapping of peace solely as a liberal project, inherently tied to the modern world order of the nation state and particularistic Christian values. In this chapter I do not attempt to unveil a progressive or Liberal Islam, but rather to suggest ways in which everyday Muslimness expand and enrich our understanding of peace and ultimately our possibility for living in peace.[2]

What I am challenging is that our studies of Islam are predominately compartmentalized as solely studies of Islam. I ask instead, what is it about our studies of Islam that speaks back to the gatekeepers, both within the academy as well as those of the public sphere? How might Islam emerge not just as an object of study but as an active creative field of theorising, studying and representing the world around us? The question is more than merely trying to provide a corrective to Islamophobic depictions. The issue is, whether there is an Islamic theory that can be applied to social processes beyond Islam.

In the global context, at least from images produced in the United States, Islam has become of central concern; it is now viewed as the new threat to Western Christian Liberalism and the American Nation State. From the collapse of the Soviet Union to that of the World Trade Center, from the racist and gendered violence of the Balkans to the Revolutions sweeping across the Arab world, Islam has entered centre stage. Islam is dissected, picked apart, placed under the microscope and more often than not reconstituted in a perverse, Frankenstein-like image that is objectified, subjectified and essentialized in ways that transcends even Edward Said's damning critique of *Orientalism* over three decades ago.[3]

Through the prism of Muslim cosmopolitanism, of which Tahrir Square is an encapsulating moment,[4] this chapter first outlines several theoretical approaches that open new possibilities of moving beyond the politics of difference; exposing the glaring theoretical lacuna in much that is written about Muslims today. The second part highlights various Muslim concepts and practices that draw our attention to unique ways of envisioning peace as an everyday practice that counters both Western Liberal and Islamic fundamentalist ideologies. The argument is not to assert that Islam is inherently a religion of peace. It is not, just as Christianity is not inherently a religion of forgiveness; of all Christians turning the other cheek. Such ideals guide believers, but ultimately it is the translation of those concepts into living, everyday ethics that fosters peace and forgiveness. This chapter is a reflection on the possibilities of peace in the everyday practices of Muslims.

Muslim Cosmopolitanism: Jihad of Possibilities

Cosmopolitanism offers possibilities for being a part of and seeing connections, a way of being in the world, as well as, an epistemological model for interpreting social processes. While cosmopolitanism can be usurped into nationalist projects, as one might witness in the global nationalism of India[5] or the assertions of a global Turkey, it opens new horizons for countering the inherent atavism associated with the nation state that divides the world into discrete sociocultural worlds. Such divisions underlay popular and scholarly interpretations of our human pasts and presents; most debilitating to our humanity is how geographies of inclusion and exclusion are grounded by the nation state idea.[6] Such imagined spatial divisions are reified in academia through the institutionalization of 'area studies' and the naturalization of the nation state that come to bind histories, anthropological subjects and civilizational regions.[7] Despite the consensus that nations, as territorially bounded communities with common traditions, are not primordial but are imagined and socially constructed, academic studies continue to define ancient pasts of very modern political entities and assume culturally-bounded ethnographic communities.[8] The nation state, nationalist ideologies and national histories are inherently anti-cosmopolitan.

The 25 January uprising in Cairo in 2011, when Tahrir Square was occupied for 18 days, was in its original moments, an aspiration for cosmopolitan possibilities.[9] Symbolically, Tahrir Square transcends the borders of the Egyptian, Arab or Muslim worlds to inspire more grounded visions of human communities and possibilities. Tahrir Square was and is more than a confluence of particular historical processes, social movements and political demands; it was not the by product of any particular ideological mandate for political reform that fermented in Egypt for years. Tahrir Square was inclusive, open to all seeking dignity and basic rights; it was cosmopolitan. The open-ended and dialogical communities that emerged during those 18 days in winter 2011, and the memories, art and passion for social activism that were borne from the uprising forefront basic philosophical concepts inherent in Islamic and Muslim thought and historical processes.[10] These concepts challenge the mapping of discrete cultural worlds and suggest new ways of coming to understand not just Muslims in the world, but humanity itself. This humanity is not one rooted in capitalist consumer culture, but one that is expressive of a cosmopolitan orientation and predicated on an underlying assumption of our common and shared humanity.

Eric Wolf reminded us three decades ago that the 'billiard ball' approach to history and anthropology permeates much of our understanding of human history and sociocultural development.[11] More recently, the billiard ball became an inherent 'clash'.[12] Despite being critiqued by many scholars, the clash thesis informs popular perceptions about Islam and Muslims produced and circulated globally, and I argue that in much academic study of the Other – perhaps with a toned down sense of clash – there remains deep rooted assumptions of distinct histories and geographies that can be understood by their geographical (area studies and/or nationalist) particularisms.[13]

Cosmopolitanism, encapsulated in Tahrir Square but also a lived reality for many Muslims on the streets of diverse cities, challenges our underlying assumptions of bounded particularities and forces us to engage new modes of understanding the public sphere based on *comings-together* not differences, that draw on intercultural inter-connectivity, not division, and that allow for sociocultural fluidity, not fixed particularities. This chapter highlights the conceptual ideas of these comings-together as rooted in Muslim histories and thought. These concepts provide a humane and universal foundation for peace and tolerance free from the hegemony of Liberal modernity that informs our sociopolitical world of exclusionary nation states and that gives shape to segregated and absolutist urban spaces. In so doing, the concept of peace is shifted away from just a theological term and thus repositions the terrain of dialogue away from whether Islam is *salam* (peace) or not. This latter debate is one purely of interpretation that ultimately has no answer, pitting 'good Muslims' forever against 'bad Muslims'.[14]

Academic Pursuits: Jihad of Difference

Along with the global transformations that are reshaping geopolitical realities, academia too has witnessed major intellectual displacements in the past 20 years as we have pushed ourselves to transcend some of the entrapments of the 'post-modern turn' and forged new theoretical perspectives. In doing so, we listened to and engaged new voices that speak up and speak back to the established gatekeepers of the academy. Over 30 years ago Audrey Lorde admonished us that, 'the master's tools will never dismantle the master's house', calling for an open and honest engagement with the differences amongst us – including race, class and sexuality.[15]

Despite the move towards intellectual tolerance and engagement, Islam and the Muslim world often remain beyond such reflective and relative considerations among academics. One does not have to visit the extremes of entrenched Islamophobic Orientalism, such as in the work of Niall Ferguson, to be bludgeoned with Liberal intolerance.[16] An inherent assumption of Ferguson's argument that is widely held is the existence of 'the West' that is then objectified, enlightened and compared to the rest. Even Richard Rorty, the grand debunker of meta-narratives, naturalizes the West and dehistoricizes Islam in the hopes for its Western-like enlightenment.[17] Although he is far from an Islamophobe, Rorty's underlying assumption about the West and the Enlightenment reflects ideological blinders rooted in reified geo-civilizations of difference asserting a hegemonic 'pragmatic Liberalism' dogmatically faithful to a particularistic secular creed.

Despite the naturalization of a divided world of diverse civilizations (depicted either as a 'clash' or celebrated as a multicultural richness), different discursive trends open up new possibilities for critically questioning the construction, maintenance and naturalization of borders. Feminism, border studies and queer theory all interrogate our epistemological, methodological and ultimately our ontological moorings; each opens new critical questions that, I suggest, interweave in creative and productive ways with Muslim studies.[18] First, the questions and processes focused upon by these three theoretical approaches are useful tools for approaching studies of both

Muslims and Islam. Second, in their emergent stages, all of these theoretical approaches were at the margins of academia but are now mainstreamed in a variety of ways, allowing their theories to speak to more than just women, the borders and gays. Muslim studies too can be mainstreamed by moving it beyond just the study of Muslims. Third, Muslim studies draws our attention to similar issues of being in the world that require greater critical attention.

Feminism is a powerful intellectual lens that highlights the structures that bind us and the possibilities for ontological transformation, various strands of which interweave with other distinct scholarly traditions to suggest a unique outlook on social phenomena. By embracing differences, feminist theory in particular made significant inroads and transcended early attempts to compartmentalize the emergent field as solely concerned with women to raise significant questions about state formation, globalization, empire, violence and identity construction. Simultaneously, feminist theory offers creative methodologies and modes of representation that call forth moments of reflection, listening and voicing.

These epistemological and methodological tectonics create new terrains for displacement − crossing and transcending borders − that open new doors of engagement in feminism studies.[19] Of particular, significance is the genealogy of feminism's ontological project, which charts new cartographies of being in the world in recognition of and in celebration with difference. Critical feminism reminds us that there are multiple ways of being in the world and coming to understand, epistemologically and ontologically, our basic humanity through our differences.

We are also seeing and being active participants in engaging flows, connectivity and creative cultural formations through the perspective of borderland studies. Border studies shift our lenses away from the centre to the borders, and back again as we question the production and imposition of particular hegemonies and the construction of peoples and lives on the margins.[20] While borders are social constructs, they do inform people's mental maps of inside and outside, centre and periphery; and they direct the flows and traffic that structures marginal and bypassed spaces.[21] Border studies thus direct our attention to the fringes and sheds light on the connections, flows and perceptions that challenge the naturalization of centrist maps and ideologies.

While feminism forefronts an ontological project and border studies suggests pathways to understanding differences, queer theory draws our attention to embodiments of desire, the performance of subjectivities and more 'troubling' questions on the naturalization and hegemony of what is perceived as normal.[22] Queer theory reminds us that borders are not just geographical constructions, but a societal imagining of those included and excluded that reproduces power and social hierarchies. Who belongs within a social order is not merely definable by membership in the national community; queer theory challenges us to reflect on internal hierarchies based on moral imagining, and the construction of particular normative ideas.

I suggest that Islam, like particular strands of critical feminism, border studies and queer theory pushes us to cross borders, appreciate flows and processes, celebrate the cacophony of differences and acknowledge the transformative possibilities of our everyday lives rather than perceive differences as threats. More than a mere apologetic to counter internal debates and external representations of Islam as singularly violent and intolerant, there is a need to recognize the extent to which these ideas flourish amongst Muslims and are part of the debate about what it means to be Muslim in the world today. Audrey Lorde challenged feminism's entrapment in Western Liberal bourgeois exceptionalism through a feminist perspective; similarly an Islamic lens challenges strands of Islam whose genealogies are rooted in epistemological maps of colonial modernity and Eurocentrism that reproduce violent exclusionary ideologies. Simultaneously, it challenges Western Orientalist essentialist representations and atavistic mappings of civilizational difference.

Back-Alley Cosmopolitanism: Jihad of Community

Just as with any social movement, political party, philosophical school and religious tradition, there are many Muslims attempting to define the religion within their narrow interpretations from a normative position. However, Tahrir Square reminds us that there are also many Muslims who envision their place in the plural global world, who accept difference, who practice tolerance, and who have the agency and will to recognize the humanity in one another. Such Muslim ways-of-being in the world are not limited to the unique disruptions of Tahrir Square; they are everyday realities for many Muslims across the world. There are particular ways in which Muslims interact and organize informally that counter and disrupt absolutist and normative claims on their lives − be those absolutist claims imposed by Islamists, neoliberal globalists, secular fundamentalists, or Liberals.[23]

Absolutism as a structure of control and oppression, as a claim and attempt to control and as a prism for interpreting urban spaces (particularly in studies of West Asia and North Africa) is an everyday reality. Tahrir Square is a testament to the triumph of absolutism, those 18 days in the winter of 2011 being an out-of-the-norm expression of cosmopolitanism. Prior to the 25 January Revolution, Tahrir Square, as all of Cairo and Egypt, was controlled by an oppressive and violent police state; today it has returned to such an absolutist space, despite various attempts to reassert the ideals of the original Revolution.

As a professor at American University in Cairo (AUC) from 2004−8, whose campus was located on Tahrir Square, I spent many days on and passing through the Square. What one witnessed and experienced in Tahrir Square during the days under Mubarak was anything but liberation.[24] Every day the Square was surrounded by riot police, whether there was a demonstration or not. Police lined the main intersections through Tahrir and constantly pulled over cars, taxis and busses to collect bribes. There were the young, unemployed men hanging out in front of Kentucky Fried Chicken watching the young, chic AUC students eating their lunches inside. There were the women, young and old, veiled and unveiled, hurrying by attempting to avoid the unending catcalls and verbal sexual harassment. Tahrir Square was a site of oppression, fulfilling the dictatorial needs of the State that offered absolutely no aspirational line for the mass majority of Egyptians to grasp on to so that they could at least hope for a better tomorrow.

Absolutist spaces in Cairo included militarized and policed spaces, such as Tahrir Square, as well as, the increasing presence of neoliberal absolutist spaces: gated-communities like Al-Rehab City and Palm Hills and malls like CityStars where security guards at the entrances keep out Egyptians wearing the traditional *galabia*.[25] They also include the manner in which public spaces along the Nile River are being transformed into private parks that charge admissions and the neoliberal reconstruction of the Nile riverfront just north of downtown that displaced tens of thousands of poor residents to construct five-star hotels, shopping malls and office complexes.[26]

Cities around the world are grappling with the same processes as Cairo, but each has its unique landscape for controlling residents and passers-by. Islamabad, a modernist city planned and built in the 1960s, is an example of an entire city landscaped as an absolutist space. The layout of streets to control traffic flow, the design of market centres to limit access to upscale areas and the segregated governmental site reflect the dictatorial demands of Field Marshal Ayub Khan, the military ruler at the time of the city's planning.[27]

In the back allies of Dubai, the *ashwaiyyat* (informal areas) of Cairo and in markets like Aabpara in Islamabad, one witnesses the limits of absolutism and the forging, through everyday actions, of dialogical spaces. These are the spaces where feminist ideas of subjectivity and inclusionary politics play themselves out. It is here that borders are crossed and where normative ideas are debated. These spaces exist despite absolutist claims that continue to creep into everyday realities. The 'cosmopolitan worldliness' that Hamid Dabashi calls to be rediscovered by Muslims, was not lost with Western colonialism, as he suggests.[28] It continued to exist in the dialogical spaces of the back allies and informal areas of Muslim cities.

Such cosmopolitanism and dialogical spaces are not unique to Muslims; they are evident in multiple cultural traditions, in every corner of the world. There is nothing particularly unique about Muslim dialogical spaces. However, there are ways in which Muslims negotiate dialogical spaces that reference Islamic concepts and ways of being in the world. Within these alternative spaces we witness that different possibilities for being Muslim do exist. These spaces and practices are not a Muslim anomaly; their spirit is deeply rooted in Islamic ideas, practices and histories. They draw our attention to Islam as a lived tradition. In the everyday, as well as the *longue durée*, Muslim practices and histories reflect possibilities for peace and tolerance.

Regretfully, those lived realities are rarely acknowledged today as we become blinded by ideological constructions of the Other. Rather than viewing Islam as a lived tradition, researchers typically see Islam as an institutionalized object of study with a variety of theories, perspectives, methodologies and representational tools imposed upon it. Islam is incorporated at the margins of academia, just as feminism, queer studies and border studies, were before it. It is an object of study upon which theories are imposed and applied to interpret Muslims, but rarely do theories emerge from within Islam that speak back to the academy.

How do we invert the dominate narrative about bringing peace to the Muslim world – or, more maliciously, is the Muslim world even capable of peace – to, what does Islam have to say about peace, about world peace? How can Islamic ideas and practices be employed to study peace and to implement it around the world – not just amongst Muslims – as avenues of creating peace in our everyday lives? Ultimately, we can ask, is there an epistemology of back alleys that informs our understanding of peace? An example of this inversion is the abnormal focus on Muslim women by the Liberal Establishment in the United States and Europe. By seeing Muslim women as agents in defining and creating their own identities, as well as in fostering peace as a social practice, we can strategically challenge the deeply embedded simplistic notions of the oppressed Muslim woman. One articulation of this was the US invasion and colonization of Afghanistan in October 2001 when leading American women activists and academics heralded the 'civilising mission' of 'Empire' to save Afghan women from Afghan, Muslim men.[29]

I want to qualify that what I am not suggesting here is the 'Islamization of knowledge'. Islamization offers important intellectual insights into the construction of knowledge by Muslims and creates exciting new perspectives on social and scientific subjects. Islamization however, is ultimately limited in that it defines the 'knower' within a narrow corpus of Muslim academics. It is as if only women can employ feminist theories, or only gay scholars can critically engage queer theories, and that those theories only pertained to their subjects. Just as Islamic banking was created to cater to the ethical needs of modern Muslims, Islamic knowledge provides tools for Muslims to interpret the world around them. While esteemed scholars such as Fazlur Rahman and Muhammad Naquib al-Attas developed an extensive corpus of writings delineating Islamic knowledge, their works are confined to Muslim scholars reproducing Islamic studies as an academic silo. I propose two broader questions: first, are there ideas, practices and theories that emerge from Islamic concepts and Muslim history that shed light on social processes of non-Muslims? And, how can Muslim theories enter into dialogue with other social theories to foster more dynamic knowledge about the world we live in and practices for living in it?

Responding to the 'Clash': Jihad of Reinterpretation

In an attempt to reposition Islam and wrestle its messages and meanings away from self-declared public 'experts', such as Daniel Pipes and other ideologically-driven scholars, Islamicists (scholars of Islam) have charted several paths over the past two decades. They offered theological reinterpretations, historical analyses and alternative readings of Islam to reposition and redefine not just the field of study but the tradition itself. These reinterpretations speak back to bigoted Orientalists and Islamic fundamentalists simultaneously, whose messages ultimately 'bear a grotesque resemblance' to one another.[30] Here I focus on jihad – one of the more controversial concepts in Islam today – to reflect upon emergent responses to renewed objectifications of Islam.

One approach to confronting the Frankenstein image of Islam created by both Islamophobes and Islamists is the theological, to return to the authoritative sources of the Qur'an and *Ahadith* (plural; collection of writings on the actions and sayings of the Prophet Muhammad) to assert the 'true' meaning of jihad. Writing for a predominately non-Muslim audience, Khaled Abou El Fadl decries the 'great theft' of Islam and calls upon moderate Muslims to wage a counter jihad against the extremists and absolutists who have hijacked the religion.[31] Jihad for El Fadl becomes a tool of 'enjoining the good' by enacting the Qur'anic 'moral imperatives such as mercy, justice, kindness, or goodness'.[32]

The theological interpretations espoused by El Fadl have long genealogies in Islamic philosophy. They are not new reimaginings of Islam refashioned to meet the normative demands of Liberalism that espouses tolerance and pluralism. They are part of the cacophony of being Muslim. But, they ultimately provide little to counter absolutist and fundamentalist assertions, which also have a long genealogy in Islamic thought.[33] Indeed, one might ask, is there any tolerance in El Fadl's interpretation for the absolutists? Further, who ultimately will decide whose readings of Islamic texts are correct? It is an unresolvable debate. Attempting to assert one's own understanding as the 'true' Islam and another's interpretations as a 'hijacked' version constructs a normative position that will itself require policing and enforcing that then counters any claim to moderation, tolerance and pluralism. Countering Orientalist and absolutist representations by privileging Qur'anic exegesis in fact only provides greater legitimacy to their interpretations as it reproduces a Qur'an-centric Islam, ignoring other established methodologies for studying religion. As well, this approach establishes an Islamic hermeneutical process that Islam is only about Islam, reinforcing the idea of Islam both as a distinct field of study and as a distinct civilizational force.

A second approach to providing alternative visions of Islam is to situate Islamic ideas, like jihad, in historical context. Mahmood Mamdani argues 'historically, the practice of the lesser jihad [of social rebellion] as central to a "just struggle" has been occasional and isolated, marking points of crisis in Islamic history'.[34] Mamdani argues that since the first few centuries of the founding states of Islam there have been only four extensive calls for jihad until the Afghanistan War in the 1980s.[35] In its modern manifestation, jihad must be linked not to Islamic movements but rather to US foreign policy in Afghanistan. It was President Jimmy Carter's National

Security Advisor, Zbigniew Brzezinski, who stood near the Khyber Pass in 1980 and called for the Afghans to wage jihad against the Soviet invaders. Mamdani and others offer an important historical corrective that situates contemporary jihad and terrorism within the confines of American geopolitics and military strategy rather than as emerging *sui generis* from within Muslim societies. Unravelling the real-politics of jihad as terrorism is an important historical study, but it fails to suggest a path to moving beyond what has now become an institutionalized practice around the world. Further, no new conceptual tools are called upon to suggest unique means of envisioning peace.

A third interpretative response is related to the first. It forefronts certain strands of Islamic thought associated with love and spirituality, particularly those associated with *Sufism*. Here we see scholars and activists emphasizing Islam's semantic link to *salam* (peace); the significance of the inner jihad; the struggle for full submission to God; and the fostering of social justice and peace. Omid Safi, in his extensive writings, draws upon Sufi ideals of love to wage a new jihad that encompasses our humanistic possibilities. He asserts the right to dream that, 'God's love encompasses all of God's children, Jewish and Muslim, Christian and others'.[36]

While I fully sympathize with the Sufi approach, and I am drawn to its transformative power, I recognize that the politics for engaging Islamic absolutism, secular fundamentalism and Orientalist Islamophobia require a multi-pronged approach. There is a point where asserting a more liberal, feminist or Sufistic interpretation of the Qur'an falls short of countering the real-politics of institutionalized inhumanity. That is, for all the critiques of jihad by Muslim academics, for all of the emphasis on Qur'anic interpretations that focus on justice, non-violence and peace and for all of the arguing – till you are red in the face – that Islam is a religion of peace Muslims continue to commit horrendous acts of violence in the name of Islam, liberal secularists continue to depict Islam as the problem and many Western observers continue to imagine bearded *jihadis* knocking on their doors with scimitars drawn. Pointing out that in the past, few Muslim rulers called for jihad does not stop self-proclaimed leaders today from using jihad as a rallying cry to arms for Muslims. We have our interpretations, they have theirs; they continue their jihads, we continue to defend 'true' Islam, and around and around we go with no end in sight, and no transformation.

My own approach laid out here focuses on Muslim ways of being in the world and advances the humanistic approach that underlies the work of such scholars as Safi and Dabashi.[37] My concern is to focus on lived practices in the everyday, as well as across the *longue durée* of Muslim history, and to draw our attention to the cosmopolitan worldliness of Muslims. The initial uprisings of the Arab Spring brought that cosmopolitan worldliness out of the quiet streets of the everyday into the public space of global ecumenism and offered humanity new possibilities for imagining peace.

And thus, I return to Audrey Lorde's message, 'the master's tools will never dismantle the master's house'.[38] We as scholars of Islam and Muslims, both as insiders and outsiders, have a double challenge of creating new tools for studying Islam, but they must be tools that also dismantle the multiple oppressions within. Just as when Audrey Lorde first presented her paper as a critique of feminists who failed to create – from her perspective as a black, lesbian poet – an inclusive feminism, there too must emerge a rethinking of Islam that directly engages with and challenges the construction and policing of a normative, absolutist Islam by insiders and outsiders.

This questioning of the normative is where Islam can perhaps play its most important transformative role. To map out what I mean by this, I briefly focus upon three Islamic ideas and practices to trace out the creative, inclusive potentialities of Islam and to suggest how these ideas are interwoven into the everyday fabric of Muslim lives. These ideas, I suggest, are integral for informing an Islamic perspective that challenges the imposition of all forms of normativity, be it liberal secularism or Islamic absolutism. I argue that it is the emancipatory power of community, of the coming together of disparate individuals with diverse and even conflictual interests that represents Islam's contribution to imagining peace.

Personal Becomings: Jihad of Dialogue

Tahrir Square was not an anomaly. The coming together of so many in a shared sense of belonging occurs every day on the streets and alleys of Cairo and around the Muslim world. For many, it is a remembering of the possibility of being Muslim that is often forgotten in the malls, gated-communities and slums that have come to dominate people's lives. That is, the public spaces of the urban centres of the Muslim world, and beyond, create possibilities for communities. This is in contrast to the global spaces of neoliberal capitalism grounded in the mega-malls designed to orient shoppers to particular stores rather than to social interactions as in the old bazaars and souks.

Many stories and remembrances about Tahrir Square and those 18 days in 2011 are in circulation; they are stories and memories of community, of belonging and of sharing. In my conversations with participants in the demonstrations, one kind of story seemed to dominate, particularly among activists from the upper classes of Cairo. One student of AUC (an elite private institution) related how one afternoon she was sitting with a group of her friends and they started to make tea for themselves on a special gas stove one of them had brought. As she was making the tea she noticed a tea-seller pushing his cart by. Rather than making the tea, she turned off her stove and instead bought tea from him. She remembered in the recounting of her story the significance of recognizing her social responsibility, which was that the tea-seller was trying to make a living and that there was a social dynamic that they had to participate in; there were social relationships they had to abide by and that community was in interactions and exchanges.[39]

From those 18 days, many similar stories, as well as the different ways community came together, are retold. Without prompting or organizing, people formed security chains around the demonstrators who policed themselves to make sure no weapons were brought into the Square.[40] More striking are the stories of what happened away from Tahrir Square in the many streets of the city after the police disappeared. There was great fear of looting and vandalism. So organically, individuals from neighbourhoods organized 'neighbour-hood watches' where young men sat guard around the clock. One informant related how familiar faces from the neighbourhood she resided in, people known but not really known, became protectors, informants and friends. Young men from her area helped her household out – a household made up only of women.[41] Interestingly, very little looting occurred in Cairo – a city of over 20 million people – despite the lack of any noticeable police force patrolling the streets for over two weeks. Not surprisingly, one of the few places where looting was reported was an area known as New Cairo, a Dubai-like development on the southern outskirts of Cairo. New Cairo is full of gated-communities where in fact no community existed for the residents to form neighbourhood watches of their own. These stories reflect the power of community as one of the symbolic meanings of Tahrir Square. Community is not comprised of individuated residents, but rather neighbours, neighbours communi-cating with one another and building social relations. At the heart of this idea of community is dialogue, a willingness and ability to reach across the silent barriers of social divides and share, organize and assist one another.

Dialogue is an inherent aspect of being Muslim, of being human ultimately. Anyone who has visited Cairo and experienced the chatter of taxi drivers, or the invitation of shopkeepers in the famed Khan el-Khalili market to sip hibiscus tea and talk as they attempt to woo you into buying souvenirs is all too familiar with the incessant dialogue on the streets. However, the dialogue is also deeply rooted in acts of piety. While often representations of Islam are of a dogmatic nature in which each religious act is carefully scripted, the reality is quite different. As a graduate student in Madison, Wisconsin, some years ago I first started to explore Islam as a set of personal beliefs. Through this exploration, I moved outside my safe little box of seeing Islam as a field of study, or Muslims as the other I lived amidst while serving as a Peace Corps volunteer in Mali, or while conducting research in Pakistan. The intimacy I sought out was reciprocated by inclusion in the personal lives of many, including participating one year in a series of *Iftar* dinners to break the fast during Ramadan. I clearly remember a gathering one evening at a Muslim friend's house for *Iftar* when my normal interlocutor was not present. They were mostly Indians, but there was also a Syrian family and several North African Arabs. As the sun set a discussion broke out on the proper way to break the daily fast. Each had their own set of traditions, but each also claimed a position of authority in referencing a particular *hadith* or scholarly position. Does one pray first, eat just a date and then pray, eat a full meal or just a small meal? While ultimately it was quite a minute concern, it was the process of engagement that intrigued me. There was no heated argument, only a sharing of traditions, authoritative claims and ultimately a coming together as we each ate and then joined in a communal *Maghreb* (evening/sunset) prayer.

Within Islam, at the personal level, there is an inherent dialogical nature of teaching, learning and creating community. Many years ago, the Brazilian social activist and theorist Paolo Freire wrote *Pedagogy of the Oppressed* mapping out a dialogical pedagogy as a means of creating a world free from oppression.[42] He saw modes of learning as potentially liberatory, but also as potential modes of hegemony. He called oppressive pedagogy 'banking' where knowledge is deposited into the mind of a pupil to be extracted at a later point – no analysis, no thinking and no creativity. We are surrounded by this form of learning – be it through MOOCs (massive open online courses) in the USA, the rote memorization of the Qur'an in a *madrassah* (Islamic religious school) in Pakistan, or the cramming of facts by a Japanese or Indian student before their annual examination.

Dialogical exchanges as learning offer a direct challenge to any normative system predicated on fixed modes of behaviour and fixed knowledge, be they 'liberal' or 'Islamic'. Normative/bank-style learning reproduces social hierarchies and oppression and segregates communities by denying interactions and exchanges. Dialogical communities and social interactions are part of the everyday reality of Muslims just as they are of others around the world. Such processes are not unique to Islam, but they are also not foreign either. Tahrir Square made visible this strategic aspect of our humanity, reconnecting us with the possibility of dialogueing with one another, as human beings, not as a label prejudged or as a lesser being to be taken advantage of. Dialogue is an equalizing force that connects us across our social differences – differences that do not have to be divides.

Transforming our Worlds: Jihad of Process

Dialogues lead to connections and build community. They are a way of connecting and learning. Learning is an unfolding process that is institutionalized in Islam through a variety of practices. One can think of *Hajj* (pilgrimage to Mecca) and the radical impact it had on not just a figure such as Malcolm X, but many others who also found it to be an internal conversion. Abdellah Hammoudi's *A Season in Mecca* relates the multiple journeys one takes to Mecca through the various rituals of the *Hajj*. Each ritual is a halting and 'new departure' that sets one off for the next stage and the inner voyage of becoming Muslim.[43] *Hajj* is a once-in-a-lifetime opportunity; but not at the beginning of one's life, for the majority of Muslims it is performed in the later part of their lives when their social responsibilities are taken care of and they can afford the journey without entering into debt. It is something the vast majority of Muslims aspire for, moving them towards a unique spiritual experience. As an aspiration and as an experience, the *Hajj* reflects how being Muslim is not a fixed state, robotically acted out day-in and day-out, but a journey of learning and experiencing new ways of being Muslim. Through *Hajj*, Islam is an unfolding process of becoming in the world.

The spiritual aspect of becoming Muslim is also reflected in the rich and diverse history of Muslim communities coming into being as Islam spread out of the Arabian Peninsula to the far corners of the world. It was first enacted by the Prophet Muhammad who, after several significant battles against the pagans of Mecca, finally conquered the city. Despite the fact that the pagans attempted to assassinate him, harassed and killed many of his followers and endeavoured to destroy Islam in its founding, when Prophet Muhammad entered into Mecca he did not kill its inhabitants or force them to convert to Islam. Through his example and that of his early followers, he allowed the pagans of Mecca to witness the power of Islam, and eventually, over time, they converted. There was a process of transformation that was not enforced in a single event, but that was allowed to unfold.

This unfolding is part of the history of Islam's spread around the world. Here I reflect upon the work of Richard Eaton, a historian of Islamic South Asia. During a personal discussion I had with him, he raised an important question, one he has been studying for several decades. Eaton first began with the basic question of how to explain the fact that when one looks at a demographic map of South Asia today, including the countries of Pakistan, India and Bangladesh, the majority of Muslim populations exist on the frontiers; in what is now Bangladesh and Pakistan. That is to say, conversion to Islam occurred outside and beyond the reach of the Islamic rulers of Medieval India. What drove Islam to the margins, and how do we understand this movement and socio-religious transformation?[44]

In Eaton's study, more important than his answer to the question of why, was how. What became clear is that conversion to Islam did not occur overnight; it was not an instantaneous, born-again revelation. Conversion, Eaton argues, is a process that takes generations, if not hundreds and hundreds of years.[45] This is a fascinating issue to reflect upon when we recognize that every Muslim is in fact a descendent of a convert – be they Arab, Persian, Punjabi, Bengali, Indonesian or American. Built into Islam, as a global religion, is a process of engagement with the question, what does it mean to be a Muslim? Islam as process implies that what might be perceived as normative today is in fact a social construction that constantly needs to be challenged, questioned and pushed.

Conversion, Eaton explains, is in fact the wrong lens through which to study the spread of Islam. Conversion as a religious practice, and thus as an analytical concept, is borne out of Christianity. Its particular orientation as a religion is defined by orthodoxy, unlike Islam and Judaism that are orthopraxic, that is, they place emphasis on practice rather than merely belief. Conversion is a Christian experience: where faith is defined by belief that is revealed. It is not a process but an event.

Islam is an unfolding and transformation of one's place in the everyday as one engages, learns, participates and ultimately becomes Muslim. Any attempt to delimit Islam along particular fixed codes, be it a call to state-institutionalized Shari'a or dogmatic representations of the Muslim Other, counters Islam's processual spirit. As such, when we observe Muslim everyday lives and fully appreciate the aspirations articulated in the Arab Spring that spilled onto the streets in early 2011, we are beckoned to question any claim of a normative position. Normative claims are just that – claims. As claims, they are part of the dialogue, part of the process, not as achievements or fixed facts, but as part of the unfolding, never imposed. For as soon as they are imposed, the spirit is killed.

Heterogeneous Possibilities: Jihad of *Din*

Islam as process reinforces the first issue I raised on the importance of narrative, but narrative not just to impose a particular belief system. I mean narrative as dialogical in which each individual has a voice in defining their personal relationship with God. In so doing, there are a lot of voices to be heard. In *Muslims through Discourse* John Bowen recognized this multiplicity of voices amongst Muslims.[46] He aptly pointed out that the term 'religion' in Arabic, *din*, was appropriate given din's meaning in English – a noisy clamour, a cacophony of voices. Dialogical, processual *din* – this is Islam, and it perhaps sums up what Islam has to offer as a means of fostering a more inclusive world view that acknowledges and engages differences, rather than attempting to erase them by crafting a singular, normative, perspective. For better or worse, this move towards dialogical, processual Islam does not mean that calls for a normative Islam are going to evaporate. Whether they come from violent extremists or progressive Muslims, indeed they are part of the din. It is in accepting them as part of the cacophony that in fact extremist positions are undermined, for they lose their legitimacy when there is no longer a battle over a singular normative framework.

It is here that I wish to turn attention back to Tahrir Square, a site I was fortunate enough to get to know quite personally, much before the Egyptian Revolution.

On 25 January 2011 Egyptians transformed Tahrir and shed the yoke of oppression for one of hope. It was a capturing of the present *a la* Walter Benjamin who, in his critique of teleological history and orientations to the future, saw the present as pregnant with potential and ripe for productive political action. In that present, as Benjamin argued in 1940, 'each individual becomes a unique and indispensable bearer of responsibility for the support and development of their community'.[47] In his attempt to hang onto power, Mubarak resorted to futurist claims of the need for security and protection of the nation. The people didn't buy it. As well, the US government and many American commentators made similar claims, particularly in their expressions of fear towards the Muslim Brotherhood. The Egyptians didn't buy it.

In not buying it, the Egyptian people rejected political codes of security and the West's fear of Islam, rather opting for imagining a new *ummah* predicated on a coming-together in the present. They rejected the tools of the hegemonic forces. Perhaps that present is lost, as old normative forces raise their ugly heads, creating sectarian violence between Muslims and Christians, attempting to impose normative codes and instilling fear once again in the hearts of Egyptians.

In this struggle for being equal members of a processual, dialogical *din* rather than subjects of an imposed normative code, there is a multitude of voices. Those in Tahrir Square made theirs heard. However, there are many others who speak, yet remain absent from the table. Here I think particularly of Mukhtar Mai of Pakistan. Some years ago Mukhtar's younger brother was accused of harassing a woman from another tribe in their village in Pakistan's Punjab. When the tribal elders met to mete out justice, the punishment was that men from the offended tribe would be allowed to gang rape Mukhtar. Unlike many women who have experienced similar fates, Mukhtar refused to remain silent. Not only did she seek out legal redress, she also chose to transform her disempowerment into empowerment for herself and others. A woman with only a third grade education, Mukhtar started a series of schools in her village. Among her students are the children of the men who raped her. Mukhtar rejected the normative codes of peace defined by her tribal society and practiced ethics of everyday community instead.

In closing, I reflect upon miriam cooke's comment (Chapter 1) that perhaps peace is not achievable, but is an aspiration. I am also reminded of a quote from Nikos Kazantzakis' fictional biography of St. Francis. At one point while wandering through the woods and appreciating the natural sounds and sights with his friends, Francis wonders, 'perhaps God doesn't exist, perhaps God is the search for God'.[48] While I don't want to enter into a debate on the existence of God, I would suggest a change in wording, 'Perhaps peace does not exist, perhaps peace is the search for peace.'

Notes

1. See Richard C. Martin, 'Negotiating Islamic feminism: Echoes of Medieval theological disputes in modern Islam' (Chapter 3 of this volume) for the revival of *Mu'tazila* thought in contemporary Islamic feminism. See also Richard C. Martin, Mark Woodward and Dwi S. Atmaja (eds), *Defenders of Reason in Islam: Mu'talizism from Medieval School to Modern Symbol* (Oxford: OneWorld Publications, 1997).

2. Significant contributions to the study of Islam posited as critiques of fundamentalist interpretations are often couched within liberal frameworks, such as: Khalid Abou El-Fadl, 'The place of tolerance in Islam', in Joshua Cohen and Ian Lague (eds), *The Place of Tolerance in Islam* (Boston: Beacon Press, 2002); Khaled Abou El Fadl, *The Great Theft: Wrestling Islam from the Extremists* (New York: Harper, 2005); and, Nader Hashemi, *Islam, Secularism, and Liberal Democracy: Toward a Democratic Theory for Muslim Societies* (New York: Oxford University Press, 2012).

3. Edward W. Said, *Orientalism* (New York: Vintage Books, 2003 [1979]).

4. My focussing on Tahrir Square highlights the uniqueness of the original uprisings that commenced 25 January 2011 and ended with the resignation of Hosni Mubarak on 11 February. Since then a variety of groups have laid claim to Tahrir Square and to the original revolutionary ideas, but each ultimately is polluted by ideological and communal differences, rather than the spirit of coming together. For an extended discussion on the creative possibilities of Tahrir Square, see Hamid Dabashi, *The Arab Spring: The End of Postcolonialism* (London: Zed Books, 2012).

5. Chad Haines, 'Cracks in the façade: Landscapes of hope and desire in Dubai', Ananya Roy and Aihwa Ong (eds) in *Worlding Cities: Asian Experiments and the Art of Being Global* (London: Blackwell, 2011), pp. 160–81.

6. Thongchai Winichakul, *Siam Mapped: A History of the Geo-Body of a Nation* (Honolulu: University of Hawaii Press, 1994).

7. Prasenjit Duara, *Rescuing History from the Nation: Questioning Narratives of Modern China* (Chicago: University of Chicago Press, 1995).

8. Benedict Anderson, *Imagined Communities: Reflections on the Origin and Spread of Nationalism* (London: Verso, 1991); Akhil Gupta and James Ferguson, 'Discipline and practice: "The field" as site, method, and location in anthropology', in Akhil Gupta and James Ferguson (eds), *Anthropological Locations: Boundaries and Grounds of a Field Science* (Berkeley: University of California Press, 1997), pp. 1–46.

9. Also see Hamid Dabashi, *The Arab Spring*.

10. Sadly, much of the originating comings-together of Tahrir Square are lost as people latch on to markers of difference. Ideology, religious belief and interpretations, class interests and geo-political manipulations re-emerged, denying the spirit of Tahrir Square and transforming it into a battleground over differences rather than a new and original *ummah*. Nevertheless, the symbolic significance of Tahrir Square is not lost, and it is that value that I focus on.

11. Eric Wolf, *Europe and the People without History* (Berkeley: University of California Press, 1982).

12. Samuel P. Huntington, 'The clash of civilizations', *Foreign Affairs* 72/3 (Summer 1993), pp. 22–49.

13. One can easily think of the vast majority of history texts that trace ancient histories of very modern political entities and construct those histories as bounded along the territorial lines of contemporary nation states.

14. Mahmood Mamdani, *Good Muslim, Bad Muslim: America, the Cold War, and the Roots of Terror* (Lahore, Vanguard Books, 2005).

15. Audrey Lorde, 'The master's tools will never dismantle the master's house' in her *Sister Outsider: Speeches and Essays* (Berkeley: Crossing Press, 1984), pp. 110–13.

16. Niall Ferguson, *Civilization: The West and the Rest* (London: Penguin, 2011).

17. Danny Postel, 'Last words from Richard Rorty', *The Progressive* 71/8 (August 2007). Available at http://progressive.org/mag_postel0607 (accessed 8 July 2013).

18. Here I suggest a shift from the emphasis of 'Islamic studies' with its inherent concern with theological interpretations and practices of piety, to a focus on 'Muslim studies' highlighting human social practices, in all their diversity, that are not necessarily religious, but come to represent the corpus of possibilities of being Muslim in the world.

19. For new terrains of displacement, see Caren Kaplan, *Questions of Travel: Postmodern Discourses of Displacement* (Durham: Duke University Press, 1996); for crossing see M. Jaequi Alexander, *Pedagogies of Crossing: Meditations on Feminism,*

Sexual Politics, Memory, and the Sacred (Durham: Duke University Press, 2005); and for transcending borders, see Chandra Talpade Mohanty, *Feminism Without Borders: Decolonizing Theory, Practicing Solidarity* (Durham: Duke University Press, 2003).

20. Kathleen Stewart, *A Space on the Side of the Road: Cultural Poetics in an 'Other' America* (Princeton: Princeton University Press, 1996); Chad Haines, *Nation, Territory and Globalization in Pakistan: Traversing the Margins* (London: Routledge, 2012).

21. Chad Haines, *Nation, Territory, and Globalization in Pakistan.*

22. Judith Butler, *Gender Trouble: Feminism and the Subversion of Identity* (London: Routledge, 1990); Michael Warner, *The Trouble with Normal: Sex, Politics, and the Ethics of Queer Life* (Cambridge: Harvard University Press, 1999).

23. For a critique of liberal absolutism and the triumphal claim to an, 'actually existing democracy', see Nancy Fraser, 'Rethinking the public sphere: A contribution to the critique of actually existing democracy', *Social Text* 25/26 (1990), pp. 56–80.

24. 'Tahrir' in Arabic means liberation.

25. Mona Abaza, *Changing Consumer Cultures of Modern Egypt: Cairo's Urban Reshaping* (Leiden: Brill, 2006); Safa Marafi, 'The Neoliberal Dream of Segregation: Rethinking Gated Communities in Greater Cairo (a case study of Al-Rehab City gated community)', MA Thesis (Cairo: American University in Cairo, 2011).

26. Farah Ghannam, *Remaking the Modern: Space, Relocation, and Identity in a Global Cairo* (Berkeley: University of California Press, 2002).

27. These evaluations of the city draw upon my personal research undertaken in Islamabad in 2009, 2011 and 2012.

28. Dabashi, *The Arab Spring.*

29. Lila Abu-Lughod, 'Do Muslim women really need saving? Anthropological reflections on cultural relativism and its others', *American Anthropologist* 104/3 (2002), pp. 783–90.

30. Akeel Bilgrami, 'The importance of democracy', in Joshua Cohen and Ian Lague (eds), *The Place of Tolerance in Islam* (Boston: Beacon Press, 2002), p. 61.

31. El-Fadl, *The Great Theft*; see also El-Fadl, 'The place of tolerance'.

32. El-Fadl, 'The place of tolerance', p. 14.

33. See Chapter 3 in this volume: Martin, 'Negotiating Islamic feminism'.

34. Mamdani, *Good Muslim, Bad Muslim*, p. 51.

35. Ibid.

36. Omid Safi, 'A Muslim spiritual perspective on Israel Palestine (with a dash of Obama)', *Tikkun* (12 June 2009). Available at http://www.tikkun.org/article.php/20090617013141275 (accessed 8 July 2013).

37. Omid Safi, *Memories of the Prophet: Why the Prophet Matters* (New York: HarperOne, 2009); Hamid Dabashi, *Being Muslim in the World* (New York: Palgrave Macmillan, 2013).

38. Lorde, 'The master's tools'.

39. I would like to thank my colleague Nabil Kamel for sharing this story from his own research in Cairo following the original uprisings.

40. As related to me by Ahmed Mohamed Abd el Hamid Farag in an interview conducted on 14 February 2013.

41. Thanks to Eman Shoukry for relating this story in an interview on 12 February 2013.

42. Paolo Freire, *Pedagogy of the Oppressed* (New York: Continuum Press, 2000 [1968]).

43. Abdellah Hammoudi, *A Season in Mecca: Narrative of a Pilgrimage* (Cambridge: Polity Press, 2006), p. 251.

44. Richard Eaton, *The Rise of Islam and the Bengal Frontier, 1204–1760* (Berkeley: University of California Press, 1993); Richard Eaton, *Islamic History as Global History* (Washington: American Historical Association, 1990).

45. Eaton, *Islamic History as Global History.*

46. John R. Bowen, *Muslims through Discourse: Religion and Ritual in Gayo Society* (Princeton: Princeton University Press, 1993).

47. Jenna Reinbold, 'Radical Islam and human rights values: A "religious-minded" critique of secular liberty, equality and brotherhood', *Journal of the American Academy of Religion* 78/2 (2010), p. 458.

48. Nikos Kazantzakis, *Saint Francis*, transl. Peter A. Bien (New York: Simon and Schuster, 1962).

CHAPTER 3

NEGOTIATING ISLAMIC FEMINISM: ECHOES OF MEDIEVAL THEOLOGICAL DISPUTES IN MODERN ISLAM[1]

Richard C. Martin

miriam cooke has challenged the widely held belief that women are by nature more effective peacemakers than men (Chapter 1 of this volume). The axis of cooke's analyses is discursive practices. She focuses on 'the strategies that Muslim women writers have developed to translate conflict-laden confrontations into constructive discourses and outcomes'. The purpose of this chapter is to investigate another genre and discursive practice in which some Muslim feminists have sought to negotiate conflict among Muslims theologically. This chapter draws attention to the contemporary revival of interest among liberal and progressive Muslim intellectuals, including some feminists, in the Medieval rationalist school of theology known as the *Mu'tazila*. Their goal has been to find an alternative *Islamic* justification to support their challenge to male-centred interpretations of the Qur'an and the *Sunna* (the collections of sayings and actions of the Prophet Muhammad). Is dialogue possible between progressive and Islamist feminists? Although many scholars of Islamic feminism are pessimistic in the face of hardline resistance, this chapter concludes with the suggestion that recent theories of 'communicative reasoning' may hold promise for managing conflict among religious disputants.

An assumption often made about women as peacemakers is the anti-Hobbesian assumption that conflict and violence are unnatural disruptions of the social order – that peace is the natural condition, which conflict and violence disrupt. cooke argues that late twentieth-century Muslim women's groups and networks have acknowledged and confronted violence and war mongering in order to engage it and deconstruct its rationales in attempts to prevent conflict from developing into lethal violence.

Islamic feminists have generally challenged traditional male-dominated discourses about women in one of two ways: (1) by challenging either male-dominant interpretations of the Qur'an or the *Shari'a*, that is, through scriptural reinterpretation; or (2) by interrogating the premises of *fiqh* (traditional jurisprudence) and *kalam* (theological reasoning). The claim made in this case is that theological reasoning is another strategy that has emerged to serve the interests of some feminists who seek to base their positions on elements from within traditional Islamic discourses, albeit historically contested ones.

Medieval scholars practiced a form of dialectical theological reasoning and disputation called *'ilm al-kalam* that means literally 'the science of speaking'. *Kalam* evolved as a discipline that grounded theological reasoning in premises or foundational value systems, such as the Qur'an and the *Sunna* of the Prophet Muhammad, and for some, it is also based on the teachings of the Shi'a *Imams* on which disputants might potentially agree as Muslims. However, the impulse to dispute meanings was energized by different or conflicted points of view, known in Arabic as *ikhtilaf*. This chapter contends that the performative structure of theological debate served to frame and manage discursive conflicts, and thus if possible, to prevent the devolution of inter and intrasectarian disputes into social violence. I have referred to this function of medieval theology as the poetics of disputation.[2] This chapter is a continuation and extension of a project begun much earlier. Several contemporary Muslim feminist writers have appealed to the *kalam* school known as the *Mu'tazila*, whose proponents are often labelled as 'rationalist' theologians with a liberal approach to theological ethics.[3] This chapter describes and comments on the recent reference to *Mu'tazili* theology by some Muslim feminists in their disputes with other feminists about the role of women in modern Muslim societies. Is the conscious turn towards theology (*kalam*) significant; and if so, why? What does this have to do with peace-building?

Peacemaking is seen as necessary in order to steer human society away from conflict, violence and war. In addition to asking if women are by nature more effective peacemakers as some feminist theory suggests, is structural conflict implicit in judicial and theological reasoning? The first decade of the twenty-first century has seen the development of two contrasting and competing answers debated in what might be called the Islamic public sphere. Muslim insiders and sympathetic non-Muslim scholars often assert that Islam is, almost by definition, a 'religion of peace' (*islam/salam*) or at least a form of civil society that inherently seeks a just and stable public order. In this view, the causes of social violence are attributed to non-Islamic sources and un-Islamic behaviours. In the same decade, a growing number of pundits, conservative think-tanks, politicians and non-Muslim religious leaders boldly declared that on an intrinsic level, Islam is a religion of violence – especially towards women, non-Muslims, democracy and other modern liberal social concerns. Ziba Mir-Hosseini has referred to the now blatant combat over Islam in the global media and on the internet as 'the pervasive and rhetorical tricks of either glorifying a faith, without acknowledging the horrors and abuses committed in its name, or condemning it by equating it with those abuses'.[4] Neither position in its extreme gets at the complex ways in which contemporary Muslim women can be and often are engaged in resolving social and communal conflict – it is a problem that challenges Islamic studies more generally.

Theology as Religious Practice

Islamic theology has functioned to confront (and ideally to resolve) differences among Muslims who support different interpretations and understandings of Islam. Theological disputation (*munazara, mujadala*) may be described as engaging in rule-bound verbal arguments to try to resolve social and intellectual conflicts. In other words, peace-building among Muslim disputants on issues that 'mattered' required spokespersons for the various positions to engage each other according to behavioural norms that were grounded in Islamic understandings and cultural customs. In the classical period, the institutional term for subscribing to and interpreting Islam according to a particular school of thought was *madhhab*; intellectual, legal and theological identity was established by adhering to a particular *madhhab*, such as the *Hanafi* school of law among the four main Sunni schools, or the *Mu'tazili* school of theology as opposed to the *Ash'arite* or *Maturidi* schools. In law, there has been a long-held view among scholars that the major Sunni schools agreed to disagree on interpretations and applications of reasoning from scripture and tradition to questions regarding proper religious practice, personal family law, social conflicts and crimes that could be clarified by a *mufti* (one who could provide a nonbinding legal opinion) or, in the case of conflict between two parties, adjudicated by a *qadi* (state appointed judge). (Shi'i *madhhabs* operated under similar rules of custom and religion.) Theological schools such as the *Mu'tazila* and the *Ash'ariyya*, on the other hand, were less inclined to agree to disagree and more disposed to seek to take control of the discourse in the public sphere. A Muslim who became uncompromisingly devoted to defending his school was said to be *ta'assub fi madhhabihi* (i.e. fanatic, factional). The possible negative effects of the extremes were usually mitigated, however, by entering into a debate under rules of engagement, which managed the potential for conflict and provided canons of audience criticism and appreciation for those who attended and judged the success of the debates.

Feminist Disputations

Much of the debate among Muslim feminists has centred on the interpretation of the Qur'an and the Shari'a as sources for constructing positions and theories regarding the normative role of women in society. The general feminist move, as noted above, has been to challenge the preponderant male-oriented understanding and social ethos of the submissive role of women. The debate has usually centred on traditional interpretations of the Qur'an and Shari'a as the sites where customary male-oriented *episteme*s (what might be compared to the concept of *'ilm* or 'ways of knowing' in traditional Islam). These have been challenged by Muslim feminists and scholars of Muslim feminist theory. However, as some feminists have pointed out, because of the nature of the absolute authority of the Qur'an and the *Sunna,* to argue directly from these sources tends to restrict the kinds of reasoning that one can deploy *if* one feels bound to traditional ways of reasoning from and interpreting those sources.

Historian of religion Anne Sofie Roald claims that feminists working against the background of the modern Christian tradition of historical–critical analyses of the Bible are empowered by critical methodologies, whereas such analytical methods have generally been regarded as unacceptable in Muslim scholarship.[5] This criticism seems to point to a loose distinction between Christian and Islamic feminisms that suggests a minor limitation for the latter, but not as a condition that has in fact closed the Qur'an to critical reinterpretation by Muslims. Roald's claim must be qualified by the fact that not all Christian feminists are receptive to historical or higher criticism of the Bible. Nonetheless, the status of the Qur'an is as the direct revelation of God to Muslims through the Prophet Muhammad – in contrast to the biblical text that for modern Western Christians especially can be subjected to textual and historical criticism – that has induced most Muslims, including modernists and progressives, to approach the Qur'anic text differently than other literary and religious texts.

9/11 – The Conflict within Islam

In the summer of 2003 a few months after US President George W. Bush naively declared an end to the conflict in Iraq from the deck of an aircraft carrier in the Gulf, Akeel Bilgrami, a secular Muslim philosopher, published an essay titled 'The Clash

within Civilizations'. In it he explains, 'the clash I have in mind [...]
is between the values of [most Muslims] and the values of
[absolutists]'.[6] He elaborates on what is easily discerned as a Western,
liberal understanding of the intra-Islamic conflict today:

> [M]ost Muslims are not absolutists or 'fundamentalists', to use
> the more misleading term [...]. Most Muslims, even when they
> are devout, have no particular vision of their creed. That is to
> say, they have no particular desire to perpetrate atrocious (and
> self-defeating) acts of terrorist violence in Islam's name [and]
> [...] unlike absolutists they do not particularly reject, as a
> *religious* threat coming from 'infidels', the various ideas and
> freedoms entrenched in Western political practice.[7]

His claim is that 'this clash within Muslim populations is between
secularists and absolutists'. Bilgrami's dichotomous representation
of the problem makes an important point; however, it is much too
simplistic, and it overlooks more nuanced Muslim responses to
absolutist Islamist positions. For example, he essentializes a
category of 'absolutist', which his readers will tend to identify with
the more widely used label, 'Islamist'. Islamism, too, has been
essentialized in public discourse to rope-off an imagined body of
Muslims who are all prone to terrorism, violence towards women
and the West and who demand theocratic States based in Shar'ia and
the like. Bilgrami's taxonomy does not recognize Islamists who seek
to conserve traditional Islamic values within modern, global,
political realities.[8]

Nevertheless, Bilgrami points to the serious nature of the
conflicted understandings of Islam among contemporary Muslims.
In fact, Bilgrami has occasionally found himself defending absolutist
criticisms of Islam. He reports responding to a claim that author and
journalist Christopher Hitchens had made at a talk Hitchens gave at
Columbia University a few years prior. In it Hitchens had made, in
Bilgrami's recounting, 'the extraordinary claim that the very
category of "moderate Muslim" was incoherent, that it was doubtful
that you can have religious convictions and not be given to

fundamentalist tendencies and sympathies'.[9] Bilgrami speculated that one cause of Hitchens's equation of religion with antisocial absolutism (fundamentalism) was as he put it, 'a certain powerlessness and even unwillingness on the part of "ordinary" Muslims to confront the absolutists'.[10] Bilgrami worried about the math; if a significant number of Muslims are comfortable with secular world views and living in a secular civil society, then why have the minority – the absolutist Islamists – become, in effect, the tail that wags the dog in many cases? Akeel Bilgrami, the non-believing secularist Muslim, holds what I refer to as a 'hard' distinction between moderate (secular and liberal) Muslim world views on the one hand and absolutist positions on the other. This 'clash *within* Islamic civilisation' has been the concern of a number of Muslim and non-Muslim writers during the past decade. In most cases below, however, I nuance Bilgrami's term 'absolutist' with the phrase 'absolutist Islamists' to allow that many Islamists, and Islamist feminists in particular, are less than absolutist in their preferred moral and religious lifestyle.

A serious concern, then, is how such *intrareligious* conflicts can be negotiated. Are there peacemaking discourses and scenarios possible between moderates and Islamist absolutists? In preparing to write this essay, I wanted to know if such discourses among secular, moderate and Islamist feminists were taking place. I asked the question of a few contributors to this volume who know much more about Islamic feminisms than I do. The initial response I got was not encouraging; colleagues who study Islamic feminisms or write as Islamic feminists do not find much conversation between 'absolute' Islamist feminists and more liberal and secularist Muslim feminists. Indeed, those I communicated with expressed doubt that productive dialogue is possible at the present moment. Yet, there are indications that some conversations across Islamic feminisms are occurring in local cultural–political contexts. For example, Fatima Sidiqi, a Moroccan feminist and author of 'Morocco's Veiled Feminists', reports that in Morocco, 'a unique combination of activism by secular and religious women' is taking place, which has helped Moroccan society make 'real progress' in a period of religious revival. She wrote in 2006 that 'the Women's movement in Morocco – which now bridges secular and religious communities – is setting an example of the power of social thought in a traditional society'.[11] This suggests that political action is deeply associated with purposive discourse or, to cite the work of Jürgen Habermas to which I return below, that communicative reasoning is tantamount to communicative action in a discourse community. Another interesting indication that Islamists and Muslim moderates, and secularists can share social and political values was demonstrated in the uprisings of the Arab Spring movements in Tunisia, Egypt and elsewhere in 2011. However, as of this writing, it remains an open question; the 'revolutions' are still evolving and far from achieving stable political outcomes. The following section examines some recent cases of Muslim feminists excavating early Islamic theological discourse as a way to pry open more possibilities for dialogue between Islamist and more moderate feminist positions.

Islamic Feminisms and Theology

Margot Badran is among those scholars writing on feminism in Islam who has concluded that the chance for productive conversation between Islamist feminists and other Islamic feminists is unlikely.[12] In *Feminism in Islam: Secular and Religious Convergences*, she follows others in distinguishing between Western and Islamic feminisms. And, she characterizes the latter as inherently divided between Muslim *secular* feminisms on the one side and *Islamic* feminisms on the other. Secular feminism in Islam developed over a century ago. It was, in Badran's words:

> Located within the context of a secular territorial nation-state composed of equal citizens, irrespective of religious affiliation and a state protective of religion while not organised officially around religion [...]. Islamic feminism, by contrast, burst [recently] on the global scene as a new discourse or interpretation of Islam grounded in *ijtihad*, or independent investigation of the Qur'an and other religious texts.[13]

Badran's thesis is, as her title implies, that these two forms of Muslim feminism are not 'hermetically sealed', and they are in occasional dialogue and often converge with each other. A third type of feminism in contemporary Islam is, however, *absolutist* Islamic feminism, which 'promote[s} political Islam and its patriarchal version of religion' and chooses not to be in dialogue with the other two groups.[14] (Badran calls members of this group 'Islamist feminists'.) This confirms Bilgrami's concern about the failure of dialogue – a fundamental requirement for peacemaking – between moderate and absolutist Islamist Muslims, specifically among Muslim women.

Some Muslim scholars have sought to engage, or at least resist, the claims of Badran's *Islamist* feminism to be *the* Islamic feminism by exploring medieval theological modes of contesting different understandings of the Qur'an and the *Sunna*. For some, the ninth-century *Mu'tazili* methodology for framing and disputing differences can be read as an approach to theology that is at once rationalist in epistemology, liberal in ethics and open to dialogue with other schools of thought within Islam, as well as with non-Muslim traditions.

In the early 1990s Mark Woodward and I, along with Dwi Atmaja, a former graduate student at Arizona State University, wrote a book on the re-emergence of the medieval rationalist school of theology known as the *Mu'tazila*. In it, we noted that the Moroccan feminist Fatema Mernissi had found in rereading some of the early theological texts and sectarian debates that they resonated with her own project of deconstructing male-dominant interpretations of the Qur'an and the *Sunna*. What seemed important to us in Mernissi's interpretation was that the context in which those debates took place, and the modern context in which Mernissi has been writing, were both highly politicized theological discourses.

Mernissi concluded that the new ingredient that dialectical theology contributed to the growing discourse about an Islamic solution to internal communal conflict was a discursive reasoning process literally called *kalam* (talking) or theological reasoning and argument. She states:

By introducing reason into the political theatre, the Mu'tazila forced Islam to imagine new relationships between the ruler and ruled, giving all the faithful an active part to play alongside the palace. Politics was no longer just a Kharijite dual between two actors, the imam and the rebel leader. A third element came on the scene: [namely] all believers who are capable of reasoning. The two conflicting trends [...] continued, under various names, to be active throughout Muslim history.[15]

In *Islam and Democracy*, Mernissi highlighted the role of *reasoning* in the interpretation of texts, including foundational texts. The 'active part' that the faithful began to play alongside the palace, in Mernissi's paradigmatic construal of early Islamic history, was within the context of competing interpretive communities, whose discourses were formed and deployed in what Edward Said referred to as the 'politics of interpretation'.[16] Theological reasoning for Mernissi, seemed to function in a manner akin to what Said called 'secular criticism', although early theologians such as the *Mu'tazilites*, as we have already noted, were often engaged in critiquing texts and arguments.

Mernissi did not explore the relevance of tenth-century *kalam* for contemporary feminist argumentation. Khaled Abou El Fadl, however, has. And he has done so with a much broader and deeper historical analysis than has Mernissi of the texts that bear witness to the early Islamic disputations. He has gradually concluded that the *Mu'tazili* positions hold the most relevance for moderate Muslims like himself, although his reference to the *Mu'tazila* in the 1990s was guarded and often in footnotes.[17] I believe it was not until sometime post-9/11 that he declared himself to be a follower of the *Mu'tazili madhhab*, which has caused considerable blowback, especially from conservative Sunni Islamists.

Abou El Fadl's discussion of the *Mu'tazila* is important because his historical and ethical analysis of the early sects and schools of thought makes greater sense of the conflicts among different theological and ideological discourse communities today. In a passage that is strikingly consistent with the *Mu'tazili* linguistic theory of the *khalq al-qur'an* (Created Qur'an), he asserts that when God expresses himself in the Qur'an, the *kalam Allah*, he does so perfectly with respect to himself as divine speaker, but insofar as he does so in a human language with its creaturely imperfections, human knowledge of God is imperfect and not absolute.[18] He adds:

> I am not arguing that the [jurists'] search for the Divine Will should be abandoned; I am arguing the text does not embody the full Divine Will and does not embody the full authorial intent either. The text embodies indicators to the Divine Will and to the authorial intent as well.[19]

In addition to following indicators in the text, Muslim feminists must apply their own reasoning powers and moral sensibilities, sometimes even when the resulting judgments seem to contradict the text. Here, Abou El Fadl adopts the classic *Mu'tazili* argument in their debate with the *Ash'ariyya* and with the *Hanbaliyya* (the Sunni law school that followed the conservative populist patronymic founder of the school, Ahmad ibn Hanbal (d. 855)) as posed in the following question: does God will to send down laws to humans because the laws are themselves good (holy), or are the laws good because he sent them down?[20] The *Mu'tazilites*, in concert with Socrates in the Euthyphro, believed the former had to be the case – God reveals divine commands and prohibitions that can be known *a priori* to be good. It follows, then, that moral reasoning is independent of the text but must be applied to the text. What happens when, as Abou El Fadl puts it:

> A person can read a text that seems to go against everything that he or she believes about God [...] and [one] might even exclaim, 'This cannot be from God, the God that I know!' What does one do in such a case? The appropriate response is to exercise what I have called a *conscientious-pause* [...]. I argue that as long as a person has exhausted all the possible avenues toward resolving the conflict, Islamic theology requires that a person abide by the dictates of his or her conscience.[21]

Here Abou El Fadl is referring to the Muslim subject as free, based on *'aql* (divinely granted reasoning powers) to interrogate the text rationally, which is perhaps somewhat akin to Martin Luther's concept of the 'priesthood of all believers' and what Mernissi referred to (above) as the 'element of reasoning believers'. Between the text and the *mu'min* (believing Muslim) is the act or process of reasoning, which in this context is inherently theological. This is true regardless of whether or not such reasoning is expressed in formal scholastic theological terms or the kinds of theological reasoning applied to problems within the Muslim *ummah* today, which have very noticeable echoes from the early sectarian disputes and the rise of schools of *kalam*.

Mu'tazilism, Modernism and Feminism

A couple of decades earlier, the Pakistani scholar Fazlur Rahman had written a modernist Muslim manifesto, *Islam and Modernity: Transformation of an Intellectual Tradition*.[22] It provided an intra-Sunni critique of conservative *Jama'ati* and *Salafi* trends in what came to be labelled 'fundamentalism' in the 1980s and established grounds for a modernist construction of Islam. Although Rahman was critical of what he considered to be the dry intellectualism of the *Mu'tazila*, his later writings evinced certain features of the *Mu'tazili* project. This is nowhere more clearly articulated than in the opening lines of his monograph, *Major Themes of the Qur'an*:

> Muslims and non-Muslims have written extensively on the Qur'an. The innumerable Muslim commentaries on the Holy Book often take the text verse by verse and explain it. Quite apart from the fact that most of these project tendentious points of view, at great length, by the very nature of their procedure they cannot yield insight into the cohesive outlook on the universe and life which the Qur'an undoubtedly possesses.

Rahman mentioned more recent attempts to rearrange passages and verses topically, which had certain utility for modern interpreters, but he concluded that these attempts also 'are of no help to the student seeking to acquaint him/herself with what the Qur'an has to say on God, man, or society'.[23] He argued instead for a 'synthetic exposition' that could expose the underlying and unifying message of revelation on God, humans and morality. Like Abou El Fadl and the Muslim feminists discussed in this paper, Rahman admitted that a literal reading of the text presented problems that resisted a coherent understanding of the text according to modern ethical sensibilities regarding gender justice.[24] His hermeneutical approach was to separate the sociocultural context of the times in which the revelation was received from the underlying universal message of the revelation. Like *Mu'tazili* theologians nearly a millennium earlier, Rahman argued for deeper readings of the text to illumine an underlying rationally and morally coherent message. *Major Themes of the Qur'an* is a theological as much as it is an exegetical or judicial project.

Like Abou El Fadl, Amina Wadud also directly or indirectly expresses *Mu'tazili* insights in staking out a Muslim feminist position in *Inside the Gender Jihad*.[25] As a progressive Muslim feminist intellectual, Wadud wanted to think through such problems as women's justice and the basis of Muslim participation in global human rights from a distinctly Islamic point of view. She stated, 'I concluded early in my search that one way to resolve my questions about gender was to direct myself to *Islamic theology* rather than Muslim social contexts or commentary, present or historical.'[26]

The *Mu'tazili* theologian's independent moral reasoning as interpreter of the Qur'an and the *Sunna* (that is, the teachings must make rational moral sense consistent with the overall message of the Qur'an) comes to bear upon the passage that Islamic feminists have had the most difficult time accepting literally or reinterpreting more positively:

Men are in charge of women by [right of] what Allah has given one over the other and what they spend [for maintenance] from their wealth. So righteous women are devoutly obedient, guarding in [the husband's] absence what Allah would have them guard. But those [wives] from whom you fear arrogance – [first] advise them; [then if they persist], forsake them in bed; and [finally], strike them. But if they obey you [once more], seek no means against them. Indeed, Allah is ever Exalted and Grand. (Q 4:34)

Wadud speaks forthrightly on the moral difficulty this well-known verse causes her as a Muslim woman:

Even though I have tried through different methods there is no getting around this one, even though I have tried for two decades. I simply do not and cannot condone permission for a man to 'scourge' a woman or apply *any kind* of strike to a woman [. . .]. This also has implications in implementing the *hudud* (penal code) ordinances. This verse, and the literal implementation of *hudud*, both imply an ethical standard of human actions that are archaic and barbarian at this time in history. They are unjust in the way that human beings have come to understand justice, and hence unacceptable to universal notions of human dignity. I have had what Khaled Abou El Fadl calls a 'conscientious pause' regarding the application of the *hudud* ordinances and the verse on wife beating.[27]

Like Mernissi and Abou El Fadl, Wadud does not resort to deploying the medieval dialectical methods of *kalam*. She nonetheless argues a position reminiscent of *Mu'tazili* theological ethics, which places upon the believing Muslim the need to make rational, moral sense of revelation and the divine commands and prohibitions.

Kecia Ali, another Muslim feminist trained in religious studies, analyses the task of interpreting the Qur'anic message in support of gender justice using a *Mu'tazili* theological argument without labelling it as such:

Those Muslims who strive for gender equality, considering it an essential component of justice, must address the central issue: what is justice and on what basis does one know it? Is something good because God says so? Or does God say it is good because it is, inherently, so? If what God says – and indeed, what the Prophet, 'a beautiful example' (Q 30:21), does – is automatically good, then what happens when this clashes with one's own view of what is just and good? Arriving at a working resolution of this dilemma requires a consciousness of history and an acceptance of the role of the individual conscience.[28]

This passage resonates with *Mu'tazili* theological ethics as articulated by Khaled Abou El Fadl and is given concrete application by progressive Muslim feminists. Ali explains in an extended footnote that this dichotomy of theological ethics is traceable to the disputes between the *Mu'tazilites* and *Ash'arite*s, although she does not develop the significance of the two positions. She explains further that the problem extends to Christianity and Judaism as well, citing C. S. Lewis's, *The Problem of Pain*, who asked in similar terms 'whether God commands certain things because they are right, or whether certain things are right because God commands them'.[29] Regarding Ali's passage above, Rhouni comments to the effect that arguing from history and personal conscience were very much in conversation and dispute among the tenth-century *Mu'tazila* and *Ash'ariyya*.[30]

Ziba Mir-Hosseini has referenced the *Mu'tazili* school of theology more directly in her writings on feminine justice. She writes as an ethnographer, as well as a Shi'i Muslim feminist activist in the wake of the Iranian revolution, in the context of which she has become a strong advocate for gender justice. Here is how she poses the problem:

Muslim jurists claim, and all Muslims believe, that justice and equality are intrinsic values and cardinal principles in Islam and the sharia. If this is the case, in a state that claims to be guided by the sharia, why are justice and equality not reflected that regulate gender relations and the rights of men and women? Why do Islamic jurisprudential texts [...] treat women as second-class citizens and place them under men's domination?[31]

Mir Hosseini like Mernissi is a social scientist and not an historian of religion, as are Wadud and Ali. Nonetheless, she advises the reader that (like Wadud and Ali) as 'a believing Muslim woman I am a committed participant in debates over the issue of gender equality in law'.[32] She bases her argument, following Abou El Fadl, on the distinction between *Shar'ia* and *fiqh*. The distinction, in her words, is that 'while the sharia [comprising the Qur'an and the *Sunna*} is sacred, universal and eternal, *fiqh* is human and – like any other system of jurisprudence – subject to change'.[33] Islamic religious and legal thinking go astray when jurists and other Muslim intellectuals conflate their juristic interpretations (*fiqh*) with Shari'a, that is, regard their *interpretation* of the Shari'a to *be* Shari'a. Thus, Mir-Hosseini contends, as she says, that 'patriarchal interpretations of the shari'a can and must be challenged at the level of fiqh'.[34]

Mir-Hosseini, however, also identifies the Medieval *Mu'tazili/Ash'ari* theological *disputations* as an *Islamic* context for understanding contemporary conflicts between revolutionary Iranian Islamists and modernists. Again, citing Abou El Fadl, Mir-Hosseini argues that the problem of advancing an Islamic theology of human justice, including gender justice, is to be found in the tenth- and eleventh-century's *kalam* disputations between the *Ash'arite*s and the *Mu'tazilites*:

> The dominant *Ash'ari* school holds that our notion of justice is contingent on religious texts; whatever [the texts} say is just and not open to question. The *Mu'tazili* school, on the other hand, argues that the value of justice exists independent of religious texts; our sense and definition of justice is shaped by sources outside religion, is innate, and has a rational basis. I adhere to the second position, as developed by Abdolkarim Soroush.[35]

Commenting on this passage, Rhouni offers that 'Mir-Hosseini's statement shows that reviving latent Islamic theological debates, especially the ones with respect to the concepts of "revelation" and "justice", is crucial to Islamic feminists advocating gender equality today'.[36] But do progressive Muslim feminists do so in order to prove the Islamic-*ness* of their position in contrast with Islamist and other feminist positions? In the case of Wadud and, to a lesser extent, Mernissi, Rhouni's speculation is that they in fact are trying to link the *Mu'tazili*/*Ash'ari* debate to the context of contemporary intra-Islamic disputes. They are, as Rhouni states:

> building on Mu'tazili thought by posing new questions equipped as they are by new tools, like gender and comparative religious studies. This may support the description of Islamic feminism as neo-Mu'tazilites. It also clearly indicates that Islamic feminism is an active contributor to the redynaminization of Islamic theology, namely through asserting the significance of gender as an important category of thought.[37]

That the progressive neo-*Mu'tazili* feminists are using *Mu'tazili* ideas to pose new questions in the contemporary fields of gender and religious studies is a useful way to see the importance and limits of neo-*Mu'tazili* studies.

Thus, we may conclude that some contemporary feminist appeals have found the rationalism and ethical humanism of the Medieval *Mu'tazilite* theologians amenable to their own understanding of the Shar'ia and for their own ethical responsibility to establish a just society. These 'neo-*Mu'tazilites*' do not attempt to challenge their Islamist opponents with the dialectical methods of disputation that dominated discourse from the ninth to eleventh centuries. Nor do they attempt to revive the scholastic categories of the medieval *mutakallimun* (dialectical theologians). However, they do seem to attach importance to reviving *Mu'tazili* theological ideas in the form of a modern *Islamic* discourse that, even though its ancestors lost the public debate to *Ash'arism* as the main Sunni school of theology, its rationalism and potential for liberalism and progressivism is seen by some as relevant today. By drastically curtailing and changing the political and discursive contexts in which *Mu'tazili* ideas are being reintroduced, the original meanings are also being changed.

Why Theologies Conflict?

It was noted above that among the pre-modern Islamic law schools jurists generally agreed to disagree on how to answer the problems and questions put to them. Such was not the case among the theological schools. Theological opponents were charged with heresy and anathema, often with the force of the sultan or governor to back up the theologians who enjoyed the favour of the court. This is a problem that neo-*Mu'tazili* feminists are aware of and are experiencing. To try to understand the political significance of a theological approach to social and political problems, let us step back for a moment from the neo-*Mu'tazilism* of contemporary Muslim feminists to consider the case of the *Mu'tazili/Ash'ari* conflict in Nishapur in the eleventh century and ask what lessons might be drawn from it.

In 1053 the vizier of Nishapur, Abu Nasr Muhammad bin Mansur al-Kunduri, bearing the weighty title of *'Amid al-Mulk* (Supreme Commander), secured an order from the Saljuq sultan he served, Tughril Beg. The order enjoined all *khatibs* (preachers) during Friday prayers to curse the name of the theologian Abu l-Hasan al-Ash'ari, the doctrines of his school and the Shi'a as well as the populist sect of the Karramiyya. The official theology henceforth was to be that of the *Mu'tazili madhhab* (meaning both school of that name and its body of doctrine). The order was valid for all of *Dar al-Islam* (lands under Islamic rule), or at least the land under the rule of the Saljuq sultan. However, it was only enforced in the province of Khurasan, especially the city of Nishapur, where al-Kunduri lived for a while. Al-Kunduri was *Hanafi* in *fiqh* and *Mu'tazili* in *kalam*. Being *Mu'tazili* and *Hanafi* implied more than simple doctrinal choices for him and for the families of the *ulama* (religious notables) with the same *madhhab* identity − the patrician scholars and their families who, along with and sometimes against other patrician *ulama*, ruled Muslim urban society. The notion of *madhhab* in theology and law implied cultural boundaries that were sites of intellectual debate and occasional social conflict. Indeed, the real target of this public denunciation of *Ash'ari* doctrine, according to Richard Bulliet, was the *Shafi'i ulama* of

Nishapur, who had been engaged in factional fighting with *Hanafi* jurists for several decades.[38]

Nonetheless, the results of this order were devastating for *Ash'arite*s as well. It remained in force in Nishapur for nine years until it was reversed by al-Kunduri's more judicious successor, the famed Saljuq vizier, Nizam al-Mulk. We are told that street-fighting actually broke out between the two camps of *ulama* and that mosques and *madrassas* were destroyed. The public discourse against the *Ash'arites/Shafi'ites* was led by Kunduri's choice as head *khatib* in Nishapur, Abu l-Hasan 'Ali (b. al-Hasan) al-Sandali (d. 484/1091). A *Mu'tazili* in *kalam*, al-Sandali is characterized in the sources as being *ta'assub fi madhhabihi*, that is as mentioned above, a factional fanatic in his adherence to the *Hanafi/Mu'tazili* alliance in law and theology. To recall just one well-known consequence of al-Kunduri's and al-Sanadali's intolerance, the famous *Ash'ari* theologian 'Abd al-Malik al-Juwayni (d. 478/1085) was forced from Nishapur into exile in Mecca and Medina where he taught *Shafi'i* law and earned the title *Imam al-Haramayn* (teacher of the two holy cities), eventually returning to Nishapur after Nizam al-Mulk's institutional restoration of the *Shafi'i madhhab*.

One lesson to be drawn from this example in Bulliet's study is that Islamic cultural forms of discourse and conflict management were not always effective practices of peacemaking or conflict reduction. In the mid-twelfth century, disputes between the *Ash'arite* and *Mu'tazilite* patrician families devolved into communal violence that within a decade destroyed Nishapur, one of the great medieval Islamic cities.[39] Another interesting significance of Nishapur for present purposes is the role of theology in framing and conducting such disputes. Bulliet suggests that the historical narrative of the feud between the *Shafi'ite* and *Hanifite* schools of law in Khurasan in the eleventh and twelfth centuries were not publicly debated in court or in terms of *fiqh* but rather in what could be seen as *attacks* against the respective theological *madhhab* affiliated with the law schools, namely the *Ash'arite*s and *Mu'tazilite*s. 'The persecution of the *Shafi'ites* carried out by 'Amid al-Mulk al-Kunduri and his *Hanafi* allies in the mid-eleventh century was ostensibly based on theology. It was not

Ash'arite law that was proscribed; it was *Ash'ari* Theology.'[40] Disputants in these debates engaged each other not as the jurists they were trained to be in legal argument, but as theologians (*mutakallimun*, 'speakers') strongly associated with the respective affiliated schools of theology.

Although the Muslim feminist scholars discussed above have argued for feminine justice on the battle grounds of scriptural interpretation and Islamic jurisprudence, they have taken the additional step of identifying, directly or indirectly, with the Medieval *Mu'tazili* school of theology. Why make this move? Their opponents among more conservative and Islamist feminists enunciate positions that can be identified with *Ash'ari* and more anti-modernist *Hanbali/Salafi* theological arguments. Nonetheless, *Ash'ari* and *Hanbali* identities are usually, at best presumed, not worn publicly as theological banners. They no longer need to be. We may speculate here that one reason *Mu'tazilite* theology appeals to progressive and modernist *Muslim* feminists – enough to be announced publicly – is that it provides its defenders with an *Islamic* basis for resisting the traditional male dominant discourses about gender and equality that pervade the Muslim public sphere today. Beyond that, to underline a point made earlier, theological argument and interlocution requires and produces a more coherent world view than piecemeal and truncated discussion of scriptural verses and legal rulings. It allows the individual-thinking feminist to test specific commandments and practices against a larger coherent system of thinking and understanding that historically is Islamic and for a few centuries was a major school of theology. Although, it lost its place of societal and political dominance to the *Ash'ari* school as the official school in Sunni Islam and was even proscribed and labelled a heresy after its heyday in the ninth century, a library of *Mu'tazili* scripturally based arguments against *Ash'ari/Hanbali* interpretations of Islam has partially survived the ravages of time. With Rhouni, we may wonder if progressive and modernist Muslim feminists are reviving ninth-century *Mu'tazilism* in order to transform it into a twenty-first-century expression of Islamic rationalist theological ethics in the new cosmopolitan environment in which Islam now finds itself. However, the *Ash'arite*s and *Mu'tazilite*s did not and could not agree to disagree in pre-modern Islam. How useful will it be, then, for feminists to invoke *Mu'tazilism* as a progressive understanding of Islam?

Can Conflict be Resolved or Managed through Argument?

Can dangerous antagonism between what Akeel Bilgrami calls 'absolutist' Muslims and liberal and progressive Muslims (or within and between any religious communities) be turned into useful conversations about global Islamic justice and human rights, particularly among Muslim feminists who have established Islamic identities from these very different perspectives and commitments. The problem with participating in dialogical reasoning among secular, religious and Islamist feminists is that the objective of dialogue on, say, human rights and social justice is not the same for each of them. Those differences must be defined and negotiated. The challenge to successful dialogue is that participating feminist groups do not automatically have equal access to the conversation and debate. That is a difficulty that is not easily overcome.

Fundamental to this project is whether or not there are Islamic discourses and models that may serve these ends – or other models that might be useful in the present moment? This chapter has argued that debating theological differences by Muslim feminists has produced a tradition of discursive practices that go beyond scripture and law. In ninth-century Baghdad and elsewhere, Christian, Jewish and other religious leaders also participated in such debates, and they, too, referred to their discourse as *kalam*.[41] The argument is that this was a form of pre-modern public theology, which was a discursive practice that allowed diverse religious communities living under Muslim rule through dialectical argumentation to manage their doctrinal differences.

My own interest in this medieval cosmopolitan period of theological discourse and debate goes back several decades. For a 1991 conference on 'Islam and the History of Religions' at the University of Cape Town in South Africa I presented a paper on the role of *kalam* in medieval Islamicate society, titled 'Was There a

Public Theology in Medieval Islam? The Role of *Kalam* in Conflict Definition and Resolution'.[42] The comparison of medieval Islamic discursive practices with contemporary Western theological discourse in the public sphere was inspired in part by conversations with my former colleague Linell Cady, whose *Religion, Theology, and American Public Life* I read in pre-published draft as I prepared the conference paper cited above.[43] The 1980s and 1990s were a time of 'culture wars' in South Africa as well as in America, but they were also a time when more voices were trying to be heard in the public sphere. In 1991, however, South African Muslim modernists and progressive youth movements were seeking to join other religious and secular groups in ending Apartheid and building a civil society. The more notable conflict for the Muslims engaged in opposing Apartheid was not with other religious communities, but rather with an established older generation of Muslim leaders who had accepted a co-opted state of political quietism in Apartheid society. The 1991 paper 'Was There a Public Theology in Medieval Islam?', made the case that liberal theologians in the West made theological arguments in public for causes such as social justice and an end to racism, and that Islamic theologians, particularly the *Mu'tazila*, in the ninth to eleventh centuries had similarly engaged their ideas in public debates.

Since the Cold War ended in 1991, global conflict has revolved around a presumed clash of civilizations in which Islam is often seen to be the vortex, especially by a growing chorus of Western critics. It is in that global political context that the progressive Muslim feminists discussed above seek to address the conflicts they face with opponents within Muslim societies as well as with non-Muslim critics of Islam *per se*. Their project also includes arguments for public goods such as social justice for Muslim women (and all women) and ending the violence of war. Although proponents of public theology have mainly theorized about the role of theology in Western public spaces, Muslim intellectuals, including feminists, in the age of the internet and international conferencing, are increasingly able to bring their causes out of their religious communities into the public sphere.

In the postmodern world, is there a model for scholarly reasoning among liberal Muslims, Islamists, secular intellectuals and organizational leaders? Although a rigorous investigation of this problem lies beyond the scope of this essay, I conclude with some thoughts on possible avenues to pursue and their present limitations whose boundaries must be explored further. These afterthoughts are forethoughts for the continuation of this project; they arise from the belief that scholars of religion in the twenty-first century must theorize how they will reason and communicate with global conversation partners in the Academy. Critical theorists, such as Talal Asad, have demonstrated the weakness of post-Enlightenment theories of religion, which have usually been applied uniformly to all species of religion in human society, past and present. Such criticism is a labour of deconstruction in order to understand, say, Islam as it understands itself, in terms of its own discursive practices. Yet, critical theory, so far, has been less helpful to theorize discursive practices appropriate for the public spaces in which Islamists and secular and liberal Muslims, as well as non-Muslims, try to engage each other. Such goals are judged and too quickly dismissed as thinly disguised liberal and secular attempts to persuade radical Islamists to adopt Western values and ideas.

Jürgen Habermas in his many writings has tackled the problem of reasoning in the modern, global and pluralistic public sphere. For Habermas, also a critical theorist but of the later Frankfurt School, modernity is not a failed project as it is for critical theorists who lean more towards post-modernism and post-colonial theory. Although, in his numerous writings Habermas has not failed to criticize many of its failings, particularly in light of European political and intellectual history since the eighteenth century. Rather, Habermas sees modernity as an unfinished project as, indeed, are all post-Enlightenment philosophies and institutions. What he proposes is to learn from the failures along the way but hold on to the *intentions* of modernity.[44] The intention of modernity has been to theorize successful communication within society in its modern, polarized state through what he calls *communicative reasoning/rationality*. In the current unfinished condition of modernity, cognitive–instrumental rationality, which is characteristic of reasoning and problem-solving in the modern technological age, is *monological*. It has proven to be inadequate; insofar as it only deals with the subject—object relation. He proposes instead that the requirement of dialogue between different religious and cultural backgrounds calls for a concept of communicative rationality, which is intrinsically dialogical. Habermas holds that modernization and rationalization involves not only purposive rationality, as for example, in higher-critical readings of a scriptural text, but also communicative rationality, which is oriented towards establishing consensuses within opposing points of view that can be the basis of critique and progress.

The problem a theory and practice of dialogical communicative reasoning must face head on, as indicated above, is that Islamic 'radicals' often seem to be on the margins of dialogue among more liberal and secular Muslims because: (1) they do not arrive at the conversation on an equal footing with their opponents thus, they suffer from insufficient leverage to advance their positions; and (2) they tend to participate in their own intra-Islamist dialogues and debates outside the orbit, and on the margins of secular, liberal and progressive Muslim conversations. Can communicative reasoning and communicative action produce radii of common interest between the centre and the periphery? This chapter argues that the question should not be closed. As cited above, the dialogue reported by Fatima Sidiqi in 2006, shows that communicative reasoning, based on partially shared goals for social transformation, can take place between secular and religious feminists in a traditional society like Morocco.

Is *communicative rationality* a viable project for Islamic feminists and other religious social movements that seek to find and share common goals with other religious and secular groups in the modern public sphere? Habermas and his critics have left us with some very enticing but abstract ideas. What would communicative rationality look like on the ground, and how would it work as distinct from ninth-century *kalam* discursive practices in the context of twenty-first-century struggles among groups to define Islam, and to define Islamic feminism? At this point, Muslim intellectuals and activists living in the West may find the challenge of public theologising and developing communicative reasoning more practical with liberal Western religious and secular groups than engaging absolutist Islamist Muslims. Margot Badran was pessimistic about the possibility of productive conversations between Islamist feminists on the one hand, and both secular Islamic feminists and Islamic (religious) feminists on the other. Nonetheless, Akeel Bilgrami's warning that the near deadlocked conflict between absolutist Islamists and liberal Muslim understandings of Islam implies that it is a condition of the moment and thus is potentially subject to change. The appeal to *Mu'tazilite* theology on the part of a few Muslim feminists as a way to engage Muslim and non-Muslim opponents over social matters of vital importance in the public sphere presents itself as a discursive practice that worked, sometimes imperfectly, a millennium ago. It was their 'intention' to find a way to communicate across factional and theological boundaries within a broad cultural and political ethos they shared with their opponents that makes their case interesting for the contemporary historian of religion. The potential of neo-*Mu'tazili* ideas for contemporary Islamic feminist discourses remains an open question.

Notes

1. I would like to thank Manuela Ceballos for helpful criticism and useful suggestions.
2. Richard C. Martin, 'Public aspects of theology in Medieval Islam: The role of *kalam* in conflict definition and resolution', *Journal for Islamic Studies* 13 (1993), pp. 101–20.
3. Richard C. Martin, Mark R. Woodward and Dwi Atmaja, *Defenders of Reason in Islam: Mu'tazilism from Medieval School to Modern Symbol* (Oxford: OneWorld, 1997).
4. Ziba Mir-Hosseini, 'Muslim women's quest for equality: Between Islamic law and feminism', *Critical Inquiry* 32 (Summer 2006), p. 632.
5. Anne Sofie Roald, 'Feminist reinterpretation of Islamic sources: Muslim feminist theology in the light of Christian tradition of feminist thought' in Karin Ask and Marit Tjomsland (eds), *Women and Islamization: Contemporary Dimensions of Discourse in Gender Relations* (Oxford and New York: Berg, 1998), pp. 17–44.

6. Akeel Bilgrami, 'The clash within civilizations', *Daedalus* 132/3 (2003), p. 88.

7. Ibid.

8. See Richard C. Martin and Abas Barzegar (eds), *Islamism: Contested Perspectives in Political Islam* (Palo Alto: Stanford University Press, 2010), introduction and chapter one by Donald Emmerson.

9. Bilgrami, 'The clash within civilizations', p. 89.

10. Ibid.

11. Fatima Sidiqi, 'Morocco's veiled feminists', *Project Syndicate* (2006). Available at http://www.project-syndicate.org/commentary/morocco-s-veiled-feminists (accessed 1 June 2011). Reference suggested by Manuela Ceballos in personal communication (30 May 2011).

12. While the goal of most Islamist feminists is an Islamic state guided by the Shari'a, other Islamic feminists support more liberal and pluralist visions of Muslims living in society with non-Muslims, as argued elsewhere in this chapter.

13. Margot Badran, *Feminism in Islam: Secular and Religious Convergences* (Oxford: OneWorld, 2009), pp. 2–3.

14. Badran, *Feminism in Islam*, p. 6. For a different view, see Azza Karam, chapter 9, this volume, 'Religion, women, and peaceful revolutions: Perspectives from the Arab Middle East.'

15. Fatema Mernissi, *Islam and Democracy: Fear of the Modern World*, transl. Mary Jo Lakeland (Reading, CA: Addison-Wesley, 1992), pp. 32–3.

16. Edward W. Said, 'Opponents, audiences, constituencies, and communities', in W. T. J. Mitchell (ed), *The Politics of Interpretation* (Chicago: University of Chicago Press, 1983), p. 7.

17. Khaled Abou El Fadl, *Speaking in God's Name: Islamic Law, Authority, and Women* (Oxford: OneWorld, 2001).

18. Ibid., p. 128.

19. Ibid.

20. Martin, *Mu'tazilism*, p. 16.

21. El Fadl, *Speaking in God's Name*, pp. 93–94; italics added for emphasis.

22. Fazlur Rahman, *Islam and Modernity: Transformation of an Intellectual Tradition* (Chicago: University of Chicago Press, 1982).

23. Fazlur Rahman, *Major Themes of the Qur'an* (Minneapolis: Bibliotheca Islamica, 1980), p. xi.

24. See, for example, Rahman, *Major Themes of the Qur'an*, pp. 48–49.

25. Amina Wadud, *Inside the Gender Jihad: Women's Reform in Islam* (Oxford: OneWorld, 2006), p. 207.

26. Ibid., p. 187; italics added for emphasis.

27. Ibid., p. 200.

28. Kecia Ali, *Sexual Ethics and Islam: Feminist Reflections on Qur'an, Hadith, and Jurisprudence* (Oxford: OneWorld, 2006), p. 149.

29. Ibid., p. 192, note 48.

30. Raja Rhouni, *Secular and Islamic Feminist Critiques in the Work of Fatimah Mernissi* (Leiden: Brill, 2010), p. 267.

31. Mir-Hosseini, 'Muslim women's quest for equality', p. 629.

32. Ibid., p. 632.

33. Ibid.

34. Ibid., p. 633.

35. Ibid., p. 633, note 6.

36. Ibid.

37. Rhouni, *Secular and Islamic Feminist Critiques,* p. 268.

38. Richard W. Bulliet, *The Patricians of Nishapur: A Study of Medieval Islamic Social History* (Cambridge: Harvard University Press, 1972), p. 33.

39. Ibid., pp. 76–81.

40. Ibid., p. 33.

41. Sidney H. Griffith, *The Church in the Shadow of the Mosque: Christians and Muslims in the World of Islam* (Princeton: Princeton University Press, 2007).

42. See Martin, 'Public aspects of theology'.

43. Linell Elizabeth Cady, *Religion, Theology, and American Public Life* (Albany: State University Press of New York, 1993).

44. Jürgen Habermas, 'Modernity versus postmodernity', transl. Seyla Benhabib. *New German Critique* 22 (1981), p. 9.

PART 2

INTERVENTIONS: CLAIMING PUBLIC SPACE

CHAPTER 4

WOMEN, ISLAM, TRANSNATIONALISM: 'POLITICS OF LOCATION' AND OTHER CONTENTIONS IN WOMEN'S ORGANIZING IN BANGLADESH

Elora Halim Chowdhury

As a feminist activist and scholar interested in women's transnational organizing in Bangladesh, I have followed with curiosity a sudden soar of reports over the last several years in the Western media depicting the country as alternatively 'the site of the next Islamist revolution' and a model developing nation. The first of these reports of Bangladesh was tied to a series of attacks on non-governmental organizations (NGOs), women clients of NGOs, progressive intellectuals and leaders of a secular-leaning political party. Ostensibly, these attacks were by Islamist groups, many of whom claimed transnational allegiances with growing networks of extremist organizations in the region.[1] The second report was associated with the globally acclaimed Grameen Bank and Professor Muhammad Yunus, its founder, and the winner of the 2006 Nobel Peace Prize. More recently Dr Yunus was one of 16 to be awarded the

2009 Presidential Medal of Freedom by President Barack Obama. The Presidential Medal of Freedom is America's highest civilian honour extended to individuals who have made a 'contribution to the security or national interests of the United States, world peace, cultural or other significant public or private endeavours'.[2] In a ceremony in Washington DC in 2013, Professor Yunus was awarded the Congressional Gold Medal for his efforts to fight global poverty and praised for being the first Muslim and first Bengali to have won the distinction of receiving not one but all three of these prestigious prizes. Professor Yunus was particularly lauded for helping to launch Grameen style micro-finance programmes integrating women in Afghanistan into the monetary economy. Even as Professor Yunus is celebrated and admired in Washington, DC for his pioneering work on poverty alleviation through investment in poor women, at home in Bangladesh he has come under fire recently from the current government; and has been removed from the post of Executive Director of the Grameen Bank.

Discourses around the empowerment of poor 'brown' Muslim women through micro-loans, with Dr Yunus as their moderate 'brown' Muslim male voice, have gained prominence.[3] These discourses emphasized an alternative to the stark contrast between Western 'civilisation' and Islamic reticence to join it. Several questions come to mind in response to these categorical representations of the third largest Muslim majority nation. First, why the shift from a developing nation status to that of a moderate/ violent Islamic country? Second, in what ways are women perceived to be the measure of development or lack thereof? Third, in the age of transnational feminism, what kinds of mobilizations and alliances are possible, as women activists in Bangladesh face the multiple challenges of neoliberal development, patriarchy and rising religious extremism regionally, as well as resurgent Orientalism globally? Fourth, how do transnational constructions of gender violence in a Muslim-majority country articulate with local feminist responses? Fifth, what conditions are necessary for an equitable, peaceful society that involves addressing inequalities based on class, gender, ethnicity, religion and nation?

In this chapter, I discuss the interface among women, religion, development and peace by investigating women's transnational organizing efforts in Bangladesh. If we understand the praxis of peace as an epistemological, analytical and political vehicle to the creation of conditions conducive for equitable development and democratization across the social categories mentioned above, how does its application aid in strengthening and improving local, regional and global feminist activism around gender violence?[4]

By looking at Bangladeshi women activists' responses to gender violence within a climate of rising national and global religious extremism – as well as within the constellation of dependent relationships spanning the state, international aid organizations, women's NGOs and their 'clients' – I wish to deepen our understanding of more effective transnational analysis and organising at local and global levels. Like the 'NGOisation' of women's activism, another force that is increasingly important to address is the rising religious extremism in Bangladesh and its consequences for feminist mobilization. This conversation is not de-linked from what the world has been witnessing in the post 9/11 climate in which discussions about women's emancipation in the Muslim world have taken on a new kind of intensity. The agendas of women activists organising on the ground and transnational feminist scholars critiquing the various forces shaping activists' responses and strategies can be at odds and create a chasm between the feminist transnational activists and scholars. For instance, the concerns of transnational feminist scholars located primarily in the North can be perceived as overly 'academic' (focussing on important and vigorous debates over location, privilege, colonial legacies and neo-colonial relations), which can derail the practical and exigent issues on the ground (such as mobilizing global awareness and resources for constituencies in immediate need of assistance).

As a feminist scholar, occupying multiple and often contradictory locations in the North American academy and Bangladeshi activist circles, I fully understand the importance of scholarly concerns problematizing Orientalist framings of gender violence in non-Western locations. Yet I am equally cognisant of the difficult conditions in which local activists organize. They are conditions involving time and resource constraints, working with recalcitrant state services and international aid agencies, and making use of transnational networks which can perpetuate one-dimensional images of women's oppression under indigenous patriarchy. These conditions may render irrelevant or suspend the pertinence of scholarly concerns that in theory should inform activist agendas.

Neither do I mean to reify the activist/academic binary, nor do I intend to suggest that activists are not aware of complex global power configurations shaping local contexts. Instead I suggest that: (a) these debates may very well be more pressing for academics located in the North than for activists or academics in the South; and (b) in the process of instigating urgent action and advancing complex negotiations, they may lose pragmatic relevance. My purpose is to open up a more nuanced discussion around transnational feminist praxis that addresses the troubling yet real disconnect between criticism and urgent action. I also seek to shed light on the question of feminist complicity in, and mounting dissent against, the interlocking hegemonies of neo-imperialism, fundamentalism and patriarchies.

Feminist sociologist, Amina Jamal has urged feminist theorists to 'reject the division of the world into zones of traditionalism and modernity, particularly in questions related to women, religion and the postcolonial nation-state'.[5] She argues that 'we need intensely nuanced accounts of the relationships among Islam, women and modernity in a manner that highlights the specificity of Muslim women's appropriation of modernity in different contexts of struggle'.[6] She encourages feminists to engage with the strategic value universal principles of enlightenment and modernity may bring in countering right-wing religious groups' culturalist agendas, whether at the local or transnational levels. The engagement of feminists with modernity in post-colonial contexts is, Jamal says citing Gayatri Spivak, 'catachrestic' or 'wrested from its proper meaning', and it takes into account differences in national origin.[7] Both Islamization and feminism in this analysis are located within processes of nation state formation and globalization. Secular feminist rhetorical practices make use of universal human rights ideals in a counter-hegemonic move against the Islamization of law and society to the detriment of equal citizenship for women and minorities.

Jamal's theoretical insight, I believe, is useful in understanding the connected ways feminism and Islamization have co-developed amidst the specific historical and political backdrop of Bangladesh. The available literature on Islamization in Bangladesh has focussed little on its relationship to the national women's movement, which historically has been aligned with the nationalist movement for liberation. The nationalist movement has remained secular in orientation as a means to create a distinct identity from the colonizing West Pakistani State ideology of 'authentic' Islam.[8] In fact, the very visible urban-based progressive movements in Bangladesh have collectively taken a strong stance against Islamization, perhaps at the expense of attention to the complex ways in which the contemporary social and political landscapes have shifted since 1971 and led to a strengthening in national- and local-based Islamist politics. Post-independence, the women's movement has been equally influenced by 'modernizing' forces of international development initiatives. The secular–nationalist stance of the women's movement, then, generally understands Islamists as a force external to the nation. In turn, progressive movement activists in Bangladesh believe that Islamists are bolstered by those factions in society who collaborated with the West Pakistani State in 1971, which unleashed genocide on the Bengali peoples whom they considered not properly Muslim. These factions have gained prominence in the political life of the nation over the years and are in leadership positions particularly within the Islamist political party, Jamaat-e-Islami. At the same time, a certain conservative strain of religious ideology has also burgeoned among Bangladeshis as a consequence of their increased labour migration to the Middle East. That is, labour migrants who travel to the Middle Eastern states tend to return and propagate a more rigid form of religious identity and values that are different from the historically plural and syncretic nature of Islam practiced in the Bengal region. Furthermore, financial support and the attendant spread of a more 'puritan' value system and understanding of Islam, from Gulf Arab states leading to proliferation of religious institutions and social organizations have also contributed to the changing landscape in Bangladesh where newer meanings of Islam and Islamism are in motion.[9] At the same time, regional conflicts involving India, Pakistan and Afghanistan, in particular, and global processes of Islamophobia have all fed into reactionary movements across South Asia. A conflux of all of these elements – a strengthening of Islamist political parties at the national level, the increasing presence of religion-based social organizations at the local level and the ripple effects of regional and global politicized religion-based conflicts – are interactively shaping the current forms of Islamization in Bangladesh.

The question I engage in here is how the women's movement has responded to these social and political changes in the nation. The Liberation War and women's important role in it, is undoubtedly an inspiring legacy for women's activism in Bangladesh. However, framing all contemporary feminist struggles in that light – as the women's rights leaders often do – leads to the marginalization of other struggles incommensurate with the politics of Bengali nationalism and development.[10] Some feminist struggles – as I will discuss later in this chapter – may not be fully encompassed or served by the nationalist–secularist framework. The challenges that the women's movement in Bangladesh currently confront require an analysis that goes beyond the Islamist/secular–nationalist binary and engages a more self-reflexive lens to acknowledge the linkages that connect disparate power structures, including feminist ones that have differential implications for differently-located women.

It is important to acknowledge that the landscape of contemporary Bangladeshi politics is such that divisions like nationalist, secularist and Islamist are often contingent and in flux. Historians Sugata Bose and Ayesha Jalal encourage understanding 'regional dissidence' in the subcontinent, as it is manifested in secular democratic as opposed to authoritarian and Islamic government, in terms of the 'historical dynamics of the transition from colonialism'.[11] That is, the relationships among seemingly oppositional discourses have to be understood in the context of the colonial past and its legacies in the subcontinent. They point out that historically these apparently contradictory modalities of governance – democracy, authoritarianism, secularism and religion-based – 'have co-existed if not been thoroughly imbricated' within the nation.[12]

Too often the women's movement (and feminist politics generally) in Bangladesh is uncritically coupled by its participants with the secularism of the civil society or the NGO sector. These groups in turn are deemed to be the progressive voice in the backdrop of a weak State that has dubious allegiances to Islamist parties. Both the State and the civil society, however, are implicated in donor-driven modernization and 'nation-building' initiatives with contradictory consequences that are not always entirely 'emancipatory' for women. In such an intricate web of relationships, it is difficult to tease out autonomous agendas for any of these constituencies. Nor is it easy to understand the specific constraints that the women's movement must negotiate, constraints that might involve confronting instead of aligning with so-called secular–modernizing forces of NGOization. Indeed, in my view, the women's movement's attention needs to be shifted precisely to the interface of globalization, national development and rising militant Islamic politics. Therefore, in this chapter I argue for a more nuanced analysis of Islamist–secularist politics in Bangladesh with a focus on the class-based women's movement's responses to the perceived dichotomy between the two. Moving beyond this dualistic framework, which I argue serves a narrow and elitist agenda, we must call for more serious attention to the actual and potential links between Islamist and secular agendas. We must begin to imagine feminist dissent that is more accountable to those constituencies, such as poor women, that seemingly 'benefit' from, yet are also abjectly affected by, the promise of secular development.

Women's NGOs: Complicit and/or Dissident?

Women's NGOs, like mainstream NGOs, occupy a complex position in Bangladesh as they frame their organizational agendas and visions within the neo-liberal development policies of donors and the State while pushing their boundaries too. It is at the intersection of this complicity and dissidence that the possibility lays of a more autonomous space for women's organizing, which I discuss in this section.

As feminist scholar Najma Chowdhury's account of implementing women's rights in Bangladesh shows, the impetus behind women's organizing post-1971 reflects the merging interests of the State and its economic development initiatives supported by international organizations such as the United Nations, other donor agencies and global corporations that bring capital into the country in the form of direct foreign investment.[13] Chowdhury points out that some women's organizations distinguish themselves from NGOs because their service is not salaried but voluntary. Nevertheless, they too solicit donor funds for projects and often partner with NGOs who provide them with the infrastructure to access subjects of development, namely poor women. Hence, even women's organizations that do not strictly identify themselves as NGOs, nevertheless operate within an NGO paradigm. One of the major challenges for the women's movement is to carve out an autonomous space from colonial discourses of donor-driven development agendas, the State's conflicting ideologies and practices subscribing to these agendas and the Islamist visions of a moral society.

Women-specific NGOs, as well as those with a major focus on women, are an important part of the national women's movement in Bangladesh.[14] These NGOs, however, tend to have specific class-based characteristics. In Bangladesh the headquarters for women's NGOs are primarily concentrated in urban areas and are largely led by Western-educated urban elites who advocate women's rights within a secular–modernist framework. This class-based women's movement – a legacy of the secular–nationalist politics of the Independence movement that is integrated in to the cultural underpinning of the progressive urban ethos – is highly visible and active in the public arena. On any given day if one were to look through the national newspapers, there would be a plethora of seminars and workshops on topics related to women, gender and development that feature the familiar names of professors, lawyers, researchers, NGO advocates and professionals who circulate with high frequency at national and international conferences.

To complete the picture of the background against which Bangladeshi women's organizing takes place, we should emphasize that women have been heavily implicated in the nation-building project, and they play important roles in government. Leaders of the two major political parties are women. The position of the Prime Minister has been held alternately by these two women from 1991 until present. Bangladesh has a Ministry of Women's Affairs, Women in Development (WID) focal points, a National Policy for the Advancement of Women, reserved Parliamentary seats, non-professional, clerical and custodial posts for women and a national umbrella women's organization entrusted with improving conditions faced by women. However, these opportunities for government service continue to come from and benefit mostly certain sectors of the population, namely educated and urban-based women.[15] Outside of the urban centres, the large rural population in Bangladesh is mostly poor, illiterate, unemployed/underemployed and alienated from the nation-building project.

Women's NGOs in Bangladesh have been able to exploit the globalizing force of human rights and women's rights ideology by taking on the mandates and implementation of the Convention on the Elimination of All Forms of Discrimination against Women (CEDAW).[16] While Bangladesh is a signatory to international treaties and, therefore, obligated to protect the human rights of all its citizens, the various successive governments remain ambivalent regarding policy on gender and are ineffective in operationalizing gender mainstreaming.

Chowdhury reports, in preparation for the UN's World Conference on Women in Beijing in 1995, women leaders in Bangladesh participated in the formulation of national plans of action, monitoring tools and measurable targets for gender mainstreaming with tremendous enthusiasm even though the implementations of these have been met with a tepid response by the government. The Bangladesh National Preparatory Committee Towards Beijing, a coalition of over 200 individuals and organizations encompassing civil society, women activists, researchers, professionals, workers, development organizations, grassroots-workers, cultural organizations and human rights groups engaged in awareness raising and mobilizing for nearly 18 months previous to the conference. The main agenda items of this committee included lobbying the government to withdraw reservations pertaining to CEDAW and spotlighting violence against women. Post-Beijing, national workshops and taskforces were formed, which broadened access to government-level policymaking for civil society advocacy groups.

The tangible outcomes of these alliances have included strategies to strengthen the capacity of law-enforcement authorities and agencies to deal with crimes of violence against women, but there has been minimal intervention in the social arena that inhibits the majority of the population's access to such legal machinery.[17] Critiquing the festival-like organizing stimulated by transnational forums, such as the Beijing Conference, Suzanne Bergeron, citing Gayatri Spivak, likened the UN-sponsored World Conferences on Women held in Beijing in 1995 to a kind of 'global theatre', where a show of global unity is produced in spite of continuing colonialist power relations, and where subaltern women remain invisible.[18] Bergeron notes that according to Spivak, these conferences further the image of global unity while obfuscating the premise of the conferences, which is the 'unspoken assumption of the U.N. that the South is not capable of governing itself'.[19] Women's groups at the conference rallied around issues identified by the global platform instead of allowing for issues to be defined by local groups based on their specific situations.

Urban-based women's rights organizations in Bangladesh are using the UN mandate for gender mainstreaming and international human rights treaties to put pressure on the government to implement more gender sensitive policies. Moral-shaming of the government in the global community by pressuring it to comply with the international treaties has been an effective mobilizing tool for women activists in the global South even as it means integrating gender mainstreaming as an 'external' discourse rather than an organic 'internal' one to define movement agendas. As International

Relations scholar Liz Kelly has suggested, mainstreaming a gender perspective into development and human rights discourse, and practice has been more of an exercise in mainstreaming activists than ensuring gender mainstreaming's methodological incorporation at all levels.[20] It implies a 'rhetorical absorption of a gender perspective' rather than meaningful infusing of gender discourse and transformation of gender relations.[21]

Transnational organizing thus often follows the mandates of global feminist advocacy, and is further shaped by the way these mandates figure into national government priorities instead of identifying diverse local concerns. This point emerges more clearly when we take into consideration Najma Chowdhury's observation that as the time for submission of the Bangladesh report to the CEDAW drew closer in 1995, the government surreptitiously withdrew some of its reservations to Article 2 (those having to do with equal enjoyment of family benefits and guardianship and custody of children).[22] This decision was most likely made by the government to appear in sync with global women's rights mandates and therefore project a progressive front internationally. However, by not publicising the withdrawal of reservations and keeping it out of a public debate, the government also chose not to trouble its ties with local groups – such as religious political parties – and, presumably, to protect itself from appearing inconsistent.[23]

The point above is an example of the way that the Bangladesh Nationalist Party (BNP) government has manipulated the 'religion card' while simultaneously projecting modernist and Islamist identities for State politicians' own political agendas. So, for example, the Islamist political party Jamaat and the secular-leaning Awami League (AL) participated in the parliamentary election in 1986, breaking a promise to boycott it because it was held under martial law. The election helped give constitutional cover to the military regime of President Ershad. However, in 1990, Jamaat again joined the AL along with its rival, the BNP, and the leftists in an urban uprising that took down the Ershad government. In 1991, the BNP formed a government with Jamaat's support. By the mid-1990s, Jamaat had once again allied with the AL in a series of street protests against the BNP government. These shifting allegiances demonstrate the contingent ideological positions – secularist, Islamist, nationalist – embraced by dominant political regimes in the interest of jockeying for power. As Bangladeshi feminist scholar and activist Meghna Guhathakurta has suggested, Islamization has tended to influence restrictions on women's rights in the legal arena to a greater extent than in the mainstream political and economic spheres, which are more heavily determined by the flows of the political economy than by Islamist ideology.[24] On the one hand, official policies espoused the Beijing Platform of Action and passed the National Women's Advancement Policy (NWAP) crafted with progressive feminist and human rights groups. On the other hand, in 2004 the BNP government secretly introduced changes to NWAP that undermined its previous progressive elements without discussing it either in Parliament or with women's groups.[25]

Curiously, adds Dina Siddiqi, the Western donor-endorsed Poverty Reduction Strategy Paper (PRSP) still reflects the principles of the 1997 document.[26] She also notes that a group of 35 women's and other social-justice-based organizations have formed a coalition, the Shamajik Protirodh Committee, to protest the underhanded revisions to the NWAP. This coalition protests the BNP government's secretive alliances with Islamists. However, it is not equally critical of the limited ways that gender mainstreaming has translated within economic and social arenas for diverse groups of women.

Moving away from the principle of equality stated in an earlier 1997 document formulated under the AL government – historically more secular in policy and outlook – the revised policy under the BNP government, which came into power in coalition with Islamist political parties, restricts women's rights to inheritance and control over resources, employment and political and economic autonomy. Siddiqi suggests that, 'in terms of employment, the new policy calls for efforts to employ women in "appropriate" professions. What constitutes appropriate is left open to interpretation.'[27] Furthermore, women are barred from holding the highest positions in the judiciary, the diplomatic corps and key administrative bodies. The government has neither formally endorsed nor rejected the revised documents, but the common understanding is that these changes were brought on by directives from the Islamist parties with which the government was in alliance. Most recently, in its 2008 election manifesto, AL removed all references to the Beijing Platform for Action, which it previously used as the basis for its policies for eradicating gender inequality. However, AL maintained that it would not act in contradiction to the Qur'an or *Sunnah* (the second source of Islamic jurisprudence after the Qur'an detailing the way Prophet Muhammad lived his life) but made feminist interventions to reform family law quite challenging.[28] One cannot make too much of the differences between these two main political parties' (the AL and the BNP) stances in regard to women's rights, because when it comes to gender policy, they cannot be significantly differentiated. The BNP has overt ties to the Islamist political party, and that alliance makes it more susceptible, according to progressive activists in Bangladesh, to enact stricter policies with regard to women's rights. Both parties, however, have trodden a fine line in navigating the competing ideologies of modernization and Islamism, and the attendant interests of the constellation of actors they collaborate with who espouse these seemingly divergent views.[29]

In a recent conversation with a women's movement activist in Bangladesh, I learned that the emphasis on PRSP by the then BNP government reflects its class-based top-down approach. The PRSP, which was developed by member countries along with the World Bank and the International Monetary Fund (IMF), is an imposed agenda – one that is not grounded in country-specific needs and realities. Together with the implementation plans of Millennium Development Goals (MDGs), donor-driven gender mainstreaming overlooks differential realities of women by class, ethnicity and religion. While the national government historically laid out programme goals for development in five-year cycles, that strategy was replaced by gender mainstreaming through MDGs and the PRSP mandates.[30] This shows a supplanting of the State's development agenda by that of the international development apparatus. Not to mention that matters are further complicated by the competing versions of women's rights initiatives espoused within donor-driven documents (PRSP and MDGs), individual political party manifestos, the Constitution and family law.

Lamia Karim and Elora Shehabuddin have criticized the urban-based women's movement for either exploiting unequal social relations with their clients or having little understanding of women's realities in rural Bangladesh.[31] These scholars bring to our attention the fact that women who staff and run NGOs lead vastly different lives from the women who are their clients. While not intending to lessen the very important work that women's rights organizations do, it is nevertheless critical to acknowledge that privilege based on religion, ethnicity and class result in the perpetuation of the clientelist social structure of Bangladesh and hinder feminist alliances.

The consequences of unacknowledged privilege are brought up through the example of the women in the Chittagong Hill Tracts (CHT) of Bangladesh by Meghna Guhathakurta.[32] Guhathakurta uses this case to illuminate the contested ways violence and victimization have been understood by the mainstream women's movement, the State and indigenous community struggles for citizenship. Guhathakurta's work reinforces the idea that the dominant women's movement ignores ethnic and class differences in thinking about violence. While the State conceptualizes violence against women primarily in its physical manifestation, the national women's movement has also located its causes in patriarchal and culture-based structural inequalities. The indigenous women's movement, however, has integrated more nuanced intersectional analyses of gender, ethnicity, militarism, nationalism and class when thinking about violence. A critical reading of the writings of Kalpana Chakma, the organizing secretary of the Hill Women's Federation (HWF) — an organization that mounted a powerful response to the state brutalization of the Jumma people — reveals the multiple challenges facing indigenous women against 'politico–military' interventions of the Bengali State such as patriarchy, poverty and struggle to retain cultural identity.[33] Guhathakurta surmises:

Kalpana's feminism also differs sharply from that of her middle-class Bengali sisters because unlike them her life struggles force her to confront and engage military and ethnic/racial domination in a way that is not easily comprehensible to the privileged Bengali.[34]

Chakma's writings also frame struggles for gender and ethnic justice within the broader struggle for Bengali democracy, nationalism and freedom, which demonstrates that her ethnic identity does not exclude her from Bangladeshi nationalism: 'we are part of the students' movement who had created '52, '69, '71, and '90!'[35] Although the Jumma struggles were perceived as a threat to the sovereignty of the Bengali nation by the State, this statement casts them as part of the democratic movement for self-determination within the nation of Bangladesh.

Despite the flourishing civil sector in Bangladesh, very few organizations expressed interest in the CHT issue. Nevertheless, following the abduction and alleged murder of Kalpana Chakma in 1996 and the subsequent organising among the Jumma people, as well as various human rights reports in the mainstream media, the women's movement joined the indigenous women's group, albeit not using the conceptualization of the larger struggles so eloquently defined by Kalpana Chakma. The HWF participated in the International Women's Day Rally in 1994 and participated in the NGO Forum of the Women's Conference in Beijing in 1995 with their slogan 'Autonomy for Peace'. (Kalpana Chakma could not go because of lack of funds.) Yet, a description of their struggles barely appeared in the summary of the official NGO report. Guhathakurta's study shows that indigenous women would have benefited from global feminist networks to promote visibility of their struggle for autonomy and to promote cross-border coalitions, but their agenda was not prioritized in the mobilizations led by the national women's movement. Middle-class Bengali organizations are so driven by the development discourse and its narrow conceptualization of gender mainstreaming that there are serious limitations to engaging more critically in questions of ethnicity and nationality as they intersect with gender. While showing support to the Hill women around generalized notions of human rights violations by the State, the same women's organizations failed to interrogate notions of citizenship, nation, self-determination and ethnicity – the very ideals upon which the Bengali nationalist movement was started.

This blind spot regarding the Jumma struggle and history is built into the country's constitution, which recognizes only the singular Bengali national identity that encompasses religious and ethnic minorities. For the Bengali majority, acknowledging ethnic–linguistic difference or autonomy of the minorities is perceived as oppositional to their national cohesion because of the particular history of the Liberation struggle, which asserted the right to claim linguistic, religious and cultural autonomy from West Pakistan. Yet, this category remains contentious, particularly with regards to the recognition of Jumma people's right to self-determination. Bengali Muslims find it threatening to acknowledge their own repression of the Hill peoples over the years because it challenges the sacrosanct space the Bengali Nationalist movement occupies in the nation's imaginary. This point was driven home to me recently at a forum on human (in)security in South Asia that was hosted in the USA at the University of Massachusetts Boston where two scholar-activists spoke on the convergences and divergences of Bengali nationalism, feminism and indigenous rights in Bangladesh. Kabita Chakma, a prominent Jumma activist related the story of Kalindi Rani, a queen regnant who ruled the Chittagong Hill Tracts in the nineteenth century and who defied British colonial administration and the patriarchal and patrilineal Chakma society. She was especially known for her use of non-violent means and the court system to negotiate her position of power within the Chakma Kingdom and the British colony. Interestingly, Kalindi Rani died in 1873, seven years before the birth of Begum Rokeya Sakhawat Hossain, who is known as the first Bengali Muslim feminist, and celebrated for her work as an educator, writer and social worker. Yet, Kalindi Rani remains obscure in South Asian feminist and historical discourses.

When Kabita Chakma criticized the transmigration policies of the Bengali State for allowing Bengali populations to settle sections of the Chittagong Hill Tracts in tandem with deployment of military cantonments in disproportionately large numbers compared to the rest of the nation, her comments met with indignant furore from members of the Bengali community in the audience. (Since independence, the percentage of Bengali settlers have increased from 9 per cent to 50 per cent.) One elderly male academic launched into a long explanation to the (American) audience how he had taught at an institution where Kabita Chakma had studied in Bangladesh and thereby asserted his authority over her. Secondly, he took grave offence to Chakma's rendering of the marginalization of the Jummas by the Bengali State as an instance of cultural genocide. Since this man was a member of a nation that prides itself for having fought for the right to language, yet at the same time denying that same right to its own minorities, it was ironic to witness his loud and outright dismissal of Chakma's argument. Further, the same gentleman subsumed the oppression of indigenous women of which Chakma spoke at length about, emphasizing the layered oppression by militarism, nationalism and patriarchy into the fold of 'universal patriarchy' that affects all women in Bangladesh thereby flattening the differences and hierarchies between Bengali and indigenous women.

Another young Bengali gentleman in the audience who identified himself as a member of the AL youth society offered a benevolent response to an audience member's query about ordinary Bangladeshis' perceptions of the indigenous. He said, 'I hail from Chittagong, which is adjacent to the Hill Tracts. In my eyes, there is no difference between us. We, you (pointing at Kabita Chakma) and I are the same'. He then urged Kabita Chakma to 'tell the audience' how the current AL government should be commended for signing the 1997 Peace Accord, which outlined important steps towards securing the rights of the Jumma community. When Kabita Chakma pointed out the recent and egregious violent attacks on Jumma land and villages by Bengali settlers despite the existence of the high number of military cantonments in the area, the elderly gentleman responded in a patronizing tone, 'This government is still better than any other we have had. If you were in the seat of the Prime Minister, you would understand how difficult her job is.'[36] This exchange was a microcosm of the pervasive double-standard in Bangladesh with regard to ethnic minorities, to which the feminist community is also a party. In such a context, argued feminist scholar Bina D'Costa at the same forum, the idea of peace is not only elusive, but more accurately termed as a time of 'violent peace'.

Like the stance taken by the AL youth society member, feminist organizations in Bangladesh are also polarized along party lines, and this seriously influences the kinds of responses they mount towards other important campaigns such as those advocating a Uniform Family Code and female students' movements against sexual harassment. There is a tendency for women's organizations to follow the general trend among civil society and to line up alongside the AL or the BNP – the two major political parties who have ruled the nation for much of its 40 years of independence. Although policies regarding gender do not differ in any great detail from one political platform to another, they do capitulate to alliances with the Islamist parties to varying degrees thereby consolidating the Islamic–secular bifurcation. The AL was the political party that led the secular–nationalist independence struggle, and while both parties have embraced secular–modernist development initiatives for nation-building, the BNP has made more overt alliances with Islamists over the years. The AL's more recent support of Islamist platforms has been met with harsh criticisms from progressive constituencies including women's groups. These continuing alliances are demonstrative of a politics of convenience, which has once again erupted in 2013 in recent strikes in Bangaldesh involving massive protests over the adjudication process in the War Crimes Tribunal, the Jamaat-Shibir (the student wing of Jamaat) backlash, the government crack-down and the emergence of the Hefazaat-e-Islam, a *madrassah*-based Islamic group, as a player in the national political scene. The AL government has been criticized for turning the Tribunal into a personal vendetta against Jamaat and BNP leaders and for stoking nationalist sentiments in the interest of regaining power in the upcoming elections. The BNP and Jamaat have allied yet again to castigate the opposition as anti-Islamic and the citizen uprising for justice of 1971 perpetrators of genocide as the voice of the non-believers. Amidst the national unrest, the Jamaat was barred from participating in the 2014 elections, and Hefazaat (backed by BNP) unfolded its own manifesto of demands including gender segregated educational institutions and work spaces, and banning of 'free-mixing' between sexes.

These vacillations clarify the intricate co-dependencies between various State and non-State actors, and the need for analysis that recognizes the cross-currents in discourses of religiosity, secular development and global feminism shaping women's organizing strategies in Bangladesh.

Brahmanbaria Rally – Vying for Social Control

The complex position of NGOs and their contradictory relationships to their constituencies are crystallized in two competing representations of a women's rally led by the NGO Proshika in Brahmanbaria, a district in east-central Bangladesh, in December 1998. Namely, one of these representations is furthered by the political science scholar, Ali Riaz, and the other by feminist scholar, Lamia Karim. Riaz describes the events of that day as an attack by Islamists on women who took part in an NGO-led rally to celebrate the liberation of Brahmanbaria from the Pakistani Army in 1971 (the local police failed to intervene).[37] In contrast, Lamia Karim's account of the same event exposes how democratizing impulses of women's NGOs are in conflict with the clientelist relationship they have with their constituencies, whom they profess to empower.[38] Here, the secular–progressive underpinnings of NGOs, which are frequently heralded as democratic and modernizing forces in Bangladesh, have come to be seen as making poor women particularly vulnerable to physical and structural violence.

The attack on the women's rally needs to be contextualized within a spate of violence in the late 1990s against NGO staff and women clients, as well as poor women in general. Most media reports portrayed the acts of violence during this time as symbolic of the threat modernization projects posed to more orthodox factions of society, namely Islamists. Anthropologist Dina Siddiqi's analysis of *Eclipse*, a film made by women activists in Bangladesh in response to *fatwa*[39]-related violence against women in the 1990s, demonstrates how similar ideas were reflected within progressive organizing as well.[40] She argues in *Eclipse*, that Islam is seen as an 'external threat' to the nation and its women, and 'Islamist violence' is carried out in the film by those groups who opposed the nationalist struggle of Bangladesh. The film places Islam in a stark binary against both Bangladeshi nationalism and modernism. Analysing the attack on the Proshika-led women's rally in December 1998 will shed further light on this particular debate pitting Islam against nation while framing women activists' agendas as secular–nationalist.

In December 1998, Proshika, one of the biggest NGOs administering micro-credit in Bangladesh, organized a *Mela* (village fair) for its women members in Brahmanbaria. The location is significant because it is the place of a historic victory won by the Bengali Liberation forces against the Pakistani army in 1971. Moreover, it is known for its concentration of conservative Islamist political groups and of *Qwami madrassahs*, religious schools that offer free education for poor students. *Melas* and folk theatre, historically associated with Bengali Hindu culture, and often used as tools of grassroots-organizing and consciousness-raising by NGOs, were considered blasphemous by the Islamist groups in the area who issued a *fatwa* against Proshika. Subsequently, Proshika changed the *Mela* into a public rally to commemorate the 1971 Liberation War, thus setting in motion an implicit challenge to Islamist groups. As Proshika symbolically invoked the memory of 1971, it strengthened their secular–progressive positioning, which is not an uncommon strategy in Bangladesh among the progressive communities.

Approximately 10,000 impoverished women and men attended the rally. At this rally, *madrassah* students and clergy launched an attack on the NGO staff and the women participants in particular. Women were beaten, their clothes were torn-off and they were called insulting names for daring to gather in public despite the *fatwa*. In the days following the rally, NGO offices, schools and staff homes were looted, burned and torn down. The police were notably absent despite existing laws against issuing *fatwas*.

Ali Riaz and Lamia Karim see the attack and the subsequent fallout as a result of conflicts between very different forces.[41] Riaz sees the event as a clash between Islamists and secular–progressives. According to him:

> Their [NGO workers'] only crime was that they didn't heed the warnings of the Islamists not to join a gathering deemed 'un-Islamic' [...]. The NGO activists in particular were forced to flee the city. Thus, twenty-seven years after independence, Brahmanbaria returned to the media spotlight, once again as a battleground, this time between the secularists and the Islamists. And this time, the secularists had to take cover, at least for that day.[42]

In contrast, Lamia Karim emphasizes the disconnect between the NGO staff of Proshika and their poor women clients. She notes, not without irony, that the leaders of the NGO, rather than staying to support the local victims of the attack, fled to the capital 'in their imported SUVs', and began holding seminars to raise awareness and support to mobilize against Islamism.[43] She further comments that feminist leaders in Dhaka also responded by blaming the gradual Islamization of society as the source of violence against women, while the NGO complicity in stoking the fire in this particular conflict remained unquestioned.

Following the rally, Karim interviewed men and women who had borrowed from Proshika. They revealed that they had little choice in the matter of attending the rally in the first place, as they believed their loan approval depended on it. What is more, the attendees were unaware of the *fatwa* issued by the Islamist group against potential attendees and they did not know that the *Mela* had been changed to a rally by the NGO. Karim further argues that the Islamists' aggressive reaction towards women – particularly poor rural women – was class-based, since a women's rally attended by middle-class women activists from Dhaka a few days earlier had gone unchallenged. In a climate of increasing socioeconomic disempowerment of both men and women, and the loss of employment and underemployment of men, 'modernizing' forces of NGOs represent a layered threat. The NGOization of society within the context of globalization is perceived at the grassroots-level to go hand-in-hand with Westernization and even Christianization.[44]

NGOs have become a powerful symbol of change in the domain of gender relations and the social structures of Bangladesh and elsewhere. As Dina Siddiqi has argued, the hierarchical gender practices that Islamist parties seek to protect, overtly clash with the seemingly modernist ideologies of NGOs.[45] Women NGO staff members, in particular, have been attacked by religious extremist groups, as have NGO schools and offices. Ironically, points out Karim, despite the anti-Christian rhetoric, neither missionary schools nor the more radical NGOs with overt feminist agendas have been attacked.[46] It is the large NGOs of Bangladesh (such as BRAC, known globally as a model development organization whose education and health programmes have been replicated worldwide, and Proshika) that have borne the brunt of most Islamist attacks.

Siddiqi connects BRAC's iconic position and visibility to these attacks. She observes that 'this kind of movement [Islamist] must ultimately be located within the specific predicaments of modernity, in particular the tensions of the postcolonial nation-state and the contingencies of global capitalism.' In the context of Bangladesh, she concludes, politicization of Islam has been State-sponsored rather than a 'fundamentalist' people's movement.[47] In other words, the allegiances forged between ruling political parties and Islamist parties at the national level have emboldened Islamists at the local levels, and increased their power.

Like NGOs and State-sponsored development initiatives, Islamist political groups are also invested in mobilizing poor women to bolster their group support. Ali Riaz suggests that these Islamist groups accuse NGO education programmes of spreading atheism, and they see Western development aid organizations as continuing colonial era structures by transforming existing gender relations to the detriment of the family.[48] Digging deeper, Riaz also reveals that the rural power structure in Bangladesh, patron–clientelist in nature, is grating against shifting gender dynamics.

On the one hand, the State too is complicit in maintaining the rural power structure as a means to secure its own link to the rural population. Developmentalist agendas of the NGOs, on the other hand, have relied on the active participation of women in credit and educational programmes that have directly confronted the rural power structures' assignation of proper female behaviour. As Dina Siddiqi has argued, the advent of NGOs has actually reconstituted local power structures.[49] The patronage system run by religious leaders and other formations of local elites, like rural moneylenders and large landowners, is in the process of being replaced by NGOs providing low-interest loans. Simultaneously, these different elite formations are strengthening their alliances in opposition to the shifting social and economic tides in rural society. At the same time, *madrassahs* are losing students to NGO education programmes. The prominent presence of NGOs and their perceived ties with Western institutions in a context where large segments of the rural population feel disempowered, creates conditions for a certain type of Islamist rhetoric to thrive.

The State and NGOs have failed to protect poor women citizens and have left them vulnerable to physical violence emanating from power struggles among various interest groups whose existence is legitimized precisely by invoking the rights of poor women. While Proshika depicted women's participation in the *Mela* as democratization, and the religious groups saw it as un-Islamic, the women involved saw it as simply meeting the conditions of their NGO contracts. In this instance, integrating gender into development required their visibility, in the form of participation in a public rally, without ensuring the social and economic empowerment needed to make this participation a real choice. Furthermore, it hinted that the vehicles of women's empowerment, in this case NGOs, are just as interested in self-promotion in a fashion that is ostensibly recognizable by international development structures (galvanizing bodies of poor, brown, Muslim women in the public space) as in attaining goals of gender mainstreaming. As Liz Kelly points out, the turn to gender mainstreaming has resulted in increased donor support for NGOs, although not always for feminist ones.[50] Intergovernmental organizations have become major players in choosing large NGOs over smaller, long-standing feminist ones to be their service providers, thus entrenching new hierarchies.

Feminist scholar Chandra Mohanty has argued that although much of the literature on globalization has marked the centrality of race, class and gender in critiquing global capitalist development, racialized gender still remains a largely unmarked terrain.[51] In this case the poor women who are the constituencies of State, NGO and Islamist group-led social mobilization are subject to racialized patriarchal marginalization in the context of globalization. Furthermore, the political economy of capitalist development brings into sharp focus the intersections of colonialism, capitalism, race, class and gender as they discipline labour, and the public and private lives of the poor in the Third World, and of other women of colour disproportionately. The abject victimization of the impoverished women and men at the Brahmanbaria rally is an instance where we see the intersecting forces of global capitalist development and religious patriarchy through NGOs who are integrating poor women into the market through micro-credit initiatives. Rising religious extremism itself is a complex phenomenon that is inseparable from the particular dynamics of modernization and global capitalism. It is this uncomfortable intersection that global feminism, in its resolute allegiance to the so-called belief of progressive development, may not have given sufficient attention to.

The Brahmanbaria example brings home the point that while Bangladesh has been portrayed by international and national groups as a site where tension manifests violently between modernism, nationalism and Islam, the less-discussed chasms between elite and poor and NGOs and their clients are equally palpable here, and push us to go beyond the secularism–Islamism binary, as we try to explain the dynamics of violence against women. These intra-nation and intracultural tensions stemming largely from class-based inequalities help us understand how the women's movements' responses to gender violence cannot be effectual unless they are more fully confronted.

This confrontation would require a deeper understanding of the linkages between discursive, physical and structural violence as well as everyday and extraordinary violence. Anthropologist Veena Das argues that 'violence is actually embedded in sociality and could itself be a form of sociality'.[52] The violence that society deems spectacular or extraordinary is neither set apart nor aberrant from sociality, rather it is part and parcel of the structural relations of power. Civil society organizations ostensibly fighting against the forces of the global economy are also connected to and benefit from their operations. Within such arrangements of power certain bodies are subjected to more insecurity, more management and more wilful neglect. The machinery of international humanitarian aid, the State and patriarchies work together to reify these invisible linkages marking the vulnerability of 'other' women. The two examples I offer in this chapter, that of the indigenous minority and the poor rural women, work to illustrate how, while they might be the 'subject' of feminist interventions, they are also othered by the very mechanisms by which women's rights activists mobilize.

Conclusion

In 2000, I was in the audience of a forum in Dhaka where women activists were presenting an appraisal of the 1995 Beijing Platform for Action, five years after its declaration. Speakers and audience included representatives from prominent national and women's NGOs. Also in the audience were staff and clients of NGOs, many of whom had travelled long distances to be part of a ceremony, which clearly had a celebratory tone. Following a presentation by a representative of BRAC, a member of the audience identified himself as an ordinary citizen of Bangladesh who worked hard to provide for his family and who had travelled from Kishoreganj to hear the 'national development plan' for Bangladeshis. He said, 'I did not come here to listen to a progress report from BRAC. I want to know what plans the NGOs have to improve the lives of the poor (*gorib manusher jonno apnara ki korchen?*)'. This man did not get an answer that day, and the stir he momentarily created in the room was quickly suppressed as the facilitator stepped onto the platform and moved on with the programme.

As an inside–outsider, I have often wondered about the relative absence of critique by scholar–activists in Bangladesh of development and social mobilization in Bangladesh. I have seen first-hand the difficult challenges of transnational organizing that feminists face in Bangladesh, even as they sometimes depend on framing issues in essentialist terms to mobilize disparate communities to take urgent action. The NGOs occupy such a powerful social space in Bangladesh that they seem to have appropriated the space of dissent even among progressive intellectuals and activists. In fact, much of the organizing, production, dissemination of knowledge, and social mobilization now occur through NGOs and not against them. The NGOs contract professionals as consultants and researchers; organize national, regional and local forums; employ increasing numbers of graduates interested in grassroots-development work and mobilize constituencies for social and political action. How do we have conversations in this context that can engage the particular ways in which NGOs have become the vehicle of neo-liberal governance, control and the disciplining of post-colonial subjects even as they produce new identities and meanings that, on a smaller scale, disrupt the global order?

I raise here the question again of recent conceptualizations about women and Islam in Western academia, and South Asian women at home and in the diaspora, which begs for an analysis of the politics of location. Afiya Sherbano Zia, a researcher based in Pakistan, has recently raised this question in connection to Western donor-funded research initiatives on religion and women. She asks if development policies based on such research, which she sees as introducing a 'creeping theocratisation of formerly rights-based approaches to gender', will lead to any kind of liberation? While not questioning the value of research, she is leery of projects targeting institutions and developmental or educational joint ventures between Western governments and international, and local institutions. As an example, she describes how the US Agency for International Development (USAID) funded a 2007 initiative on 'Respecting the

Veil' in Pakistan, which purported to assist husband–wife teams by providing gender-specific assistance for women to carry on home-based work like embroidery and for their husbands to act as the sellers. While the men benefited at the expense of their wives, this project compensated the women well-below minimum wage and did little to challenge or disrupt traditions barring women's social or economic mobility.

Zia asserts, Muslim women, including feminists, face very different identity issues in the West when compared to South Asia. Therefore, when South Asian feminist researchers become implicated in projects that foreground religion in their home contexts, the secular indigenous possibilities and spaces become more vulnerable and are even deemed 'culturally inappropriate'. She is particularly concerned about the shift from earlier 'rights-based' advocacy for gender equality (as propagated by organizations in the global South like Women Living Under Muslim Law) in the 1980s, and an approach of 'rescuing the oppressed Muslim woman' which presently inheres liberal methods to women's empowerment. Further, she sees the growing academic interest in Islam as useful in helping boost careers of some academics and consultants who have jumped onto this bandwagon, and think that it should not divert from the very real political challenge presented by localized analysis, debate, contestation, understanding and struggle. She sees this research as 'academic exercise' far removed from the complex realities of the ways in which religious identities play out in Muslim majority countries. She concludes such research needs more rigorous scrutiny in terms of its methodology and politics before it starts informing policy and development interventions. The link between Western donor initiatives on education and foreign policy intervention particularly in the contentious field of women's empowerment (which fuelled jihadis and misogynist ideologies in Afghanistan in the 1980s) has been cogently made through the discussions of USAID-funded textbooks.[53] As recently as 2003, the Department for International Development (DFID) funded initiatives in the North Western Frontier Province of Pakistan where the religious political alliance in government then imposed Shari'a (Islamic law) legislation and severely curtailed women's participation in social, political and economic arenas. Such double standards, by which Western donors support repressive agendas and tout Muslim women's emancipation as their party line, convey a troubling message, and shrink spaces for progressive organizing.

Another example would be the DFID's Pathways of Women's Empowerment project in South Asia that is also funded by the Norwegian and Swedish governments. In contrast to Zia, Firdaus Azim, who is one of the leaders of the Pathways Initiative in Bangladesh, and a leading feminist activist researcher, suggests:

> In South Asia as elsewhere in the world, religion has come to play an increasing role in shaping and reshaping women's lives. This process is a particular challenge to people like myself, a feminist who 'grew up' intellectually and politically via involvement in the women's movement of the 70s and 80s in Bangladesh. The activism of that period was explicitly secular; its main priorities were the issues of rights, inequalities and violence prevalent in a young state which had achieved independence only in 1971. Today, we are addressing a different set of issues.

In the context of Bangladesh where the secular nationalist stance of the women's movement has arguably created its own hegemony, Azim's engaged reflection over the changes in Bangladeshi society that calls for a rethinking of feminist politics is commendable. The question, however, remains whether a donor-driven Islam will engender the kinds of conversations that addresses the cleavages *between* (the question of politics of location) and *within* nations (gender-based inequality, but also ethnic- and class-based inequalities).

Azim explains that the new research is centred on urban women as opposed to the historical and dominant focus on rural women's advancement. She further concedes that while urban-based women's emerging public roles illuminate changing notions of sexuality, marriage and employment, the negotiations women engage in are mired within patriarchal structures, namely religion. And, while these negotiations can be considered practical, they are hardly transformative. A publication of the Pathways Women and Religion initiative reveals high participation rates in *dars* classes (Arabic recitation, translation and discussion classes) and women's desires to 'authenticate' their religious knowledge through textual readings. The information was gleaned through focus group discussions with women living in university dorms, hostels for working women and low income urban areas. This bulletin noted that *dars*-goers claimed for themselves an identity based on 'True Islam' and that those who attend *dars* are intolerant of other Islamic belief systems associated with *Sufism*, which historically has had a strong influence in South Asian Islam. A desired outcome of this research is stated as 'the potential to influence policymakers in formulating policies that are sensitive to women's religious sensibilities. It could also affect development practitioners in re-evaluating the liberal values and goals that underlie much of their initiatives.'[54] In a study that problematizes the zealous attention to the concept of 'Muslim women's rights' as it circulates in different global and local networks, Lila Abu-Lughod has criticized donor-funded initiatives that focus on women and religion in Egypt. Abu-Lughod argues that these initiatives further a cosmopolitanism among urban elite women that engenders conversations about identity, which are not necessarily connected to larger historical, political or structural inequalities in Muslim majority countries.[55] Like Zia, while I do not dismiss the value of this new research trend, I agree with her that the question of such Western donor-funded research initiatives bleeding into development policy, and the resultant shift in policy agenda remains a contested terrain.

I return to the question of what kinds of mobilizations for peace are possible as women activists in Bangladesh confront the scattered hegemonies of rising religious extremism in the region, neo-imperialism, global Islamophobia and neo-colonial development initiatives that make use of poor Bangladeshi women's participation to bolster their own sustainability. Although, I agree with much of Karim's analysis of the unequal power relations between NGO-based urban feminists and poor rural women clients of NGOs, I am not comfortable in dismissing urban women's activism as wholly uninformed and clientelist.[56] The struggle here is to deal with injustices that are embedded in sociality without negating relationships that may be supportive. Ideas for justice, peace and empowerment are often rooted in grassroots experiences women have within their own communities, and the challenge for women's rights activists then is to draw from these community-based practices and values and infuse them in advocacy work from the ground-up. Nevertheless, recent research has shed light on ways to conceptualize women's activism outside and beyond the narrow frame of nationalism. These include: (1) Naila Kabeer's research on how women participants of social development organizations contest injustice in the domains of family and kinship redeploying normative ideas of responsibility, obligation and honour; (2) Fauzia Ahmed's research on how poor women (re)interpret and (re)define religious principles to their own advantage in order to avail economic opportunities; and (3) Elora Shehabuddin's similar research regarding poor Muslim women's political participation.[57]

The urban-based women's movement in Bangladesh has flourished as a result of transnational networking and availing itself of global feminist instruments. At the same time, such alliances hinder a more nuanced engagement with the diversity of women's realities on the ground. This contradictory consequence of global women's organizing efforts, whereby new kinds of hierarchies emerge, and only certain kinds of organizing are visible, has been noted by Elisabeth Freedman as an example of 'transnationalism reversed'.[58] Anthropologist Sally Merry's ethnographic work on the making and implementing of human rights policy on gender in the UN reveals how participants seem to perpetuate an image of an unchanging essential national culture in which women's status is embedded in order to maximize the impact of their own claims on behalf of women.[59] Instead of explaining how culture is used in struggles over class, kinship and ethnic or religious identities, global feminist activists often invoke an essential culture as detrimental to women's emancipation. Sally Merry writes, 'in the context of an international setting and universal principles, acknowledging such complexity would diminish the political impact of her [the woman activist's] statement.'[60] International documents and country reports on Bangladesh are rife with such simplistic 'progress narratives' where women are perceived to be victims of culture and indigenous patriarchy, deflecting attention from other kinds of analysis.

Even if feminists use essentializing discourses of gender and culture consciously and strategically, we must persistently ask about the implications for transnational solidarity and praxis. Saba Mahmood observes that feminism is both an analytic and a political project, and while the two certainly inform one another, they ought not to be collapsed into one approach.[61] There is value in keeping the possibilities of the analytic project open in the interest of thinking beyond immediate or urgent political action. The expediency of mobilizing campaigns under difficult circumstances may lead to silencing critical voices, as we saw happen in organizing related to the Beijing Conference, as well as, the constructing of a nationalist identity to counter an Islamist 'threat'. Nevertheless, ongoing reflection and dialogue are essential if NGOs are to effectively serve and integrate their constituencies into peaceful development initiatives.

In order to understand women's experiences more clearly, feminism and fundamentalism must both be viewed as part of modernity instead of as opposing discourses. In Western discourses, the idea of Islamic fundamentalism is linked to the racialization of Muslims as a people without history, the demonization of Islamic masculinity as barbaric and Islamic femininity as victimized and subordinate. Western egalitarian feminism, on the other hand, is tied to the feminist progress narrative of women's emancipation from backward tradition (often associated with patriarchal religion) to enlightened modernity. This dichotomy disallows an understanding of the complexities of women's experiences as both Muslim and feminist.

Feminist scholar Minoo Moallem sees overlap between feminism, fundamentalism and co-complicity in:

> perpetuating power relations, either by sustaining the
> boundaries of a totalistic ideology (in the case of

fundamentalist feminists), or by creating restricted boundaries through a replacement of patriarchy with matriarchy, or by limiting women's issues to only one set of relations, and thus putting an end to any constructive sociological discussion.[62]

Sometimes feminists and fundamentalists alike can be intolerant of other perspectives on women's status, yet they can function as rivals. However, they can also act in similar ways in their rigidified positions and categories of analysis. Subject positions emerging from such fixed formations remain cut-off from historical and geopolitical contexts. Several scholars have proposed a transnational discourse that is based on intersecting and interlocking positionalities, and power relations. Further, feminism must disrupt its own complicity with perpetuating rigidified analysis of women's oppression within transnational spheres of mobilization. Following this line of thinking, NGO-based organizing, important as it is as a venue for social change, must interrogate this rigid dichotomy between secular development and religious oppression and find more nuanced causes of conflicts, such as the one that unfolded in Brahmanbaria.

Binary analysis of women's organizing as secular/Islamist or modern/underdeveloped freezes up conversations that recognize the heterogeneous ways in which women activists negotiate their environments. Instigating action within the structure of global UN-based feminism is imbricated within the culture of such a field that inhibits multi-axial analysis of diverse women's positionalities and realities. Sociologist Raka Ray suggests that organizations are embedded in and respond to a set of unequal socially-constructed structures and relations which ought to be understood 'both as configurations of forces and as sites of struggle' that perpetuate yet disrupt existing dynamics.[63] She presents the term 'protest fields' to imply subgroups and networks that oppose the logic of power relations in the larger political field even as they are constrained by them. Organizations act, not as free agents, but rather within the context of asymmetrical power relations within a given field. Ray's analysis of women's movements juxtaposed with Moallem's assertion of Western egalitarian feminism's (one that appears to dominate global feminist scripts of fashioning 'other' women's needs and desires in the image of the liberated western subject) complicity in furthering imperialist discourses of modernity and development opens up an important dialogue.

My work here illuminates intra-movement tensions in the context of Bangladesh in an attempt to theorize and imagine feminist alliances that are more equitable, peaceful and just across borders of nation, class and community. As feminist activists, scholars and practitioners we need to be more attentive to the protest-field conversations that rupture the asymmetrical plane of political fields and open up more productive dialogue for effective transnational praxis.

Notes

1. Researchers have contended these attacks in actuality were orchestrated by religious, as well as other elite groups, whose positions were undermined by the emergence of newer patronage systems of the development NGOs.

2. The White House Office of the Press Secretary, 'President Obama names medal of honour recipients', (July 30, 2009). Available at http://www.whitehouse.gov/the_press_office/president-obama-names-medal-of-freedom-recipients/ (accessed 24 May 2009).

3. A term widely used to describe South Asians as a racialized community in the West.

4. Paul Rogers, 'Introduction to the special issue of Peace, Conflict & Development', *Journal of Peace, Conflict & Development* 18 (December 2011), pp. 1–6.

5. Amina Jamal, 'Transnational feminism as critical practice: A reading of feminist discourses in Pakistan', *Meridians* 5/2 (2005), p. 58.

6. Ibid.

7. Ibid.

8. In the context of Bangladesh, secular at the nation's founding and as defined by 'father of the nation' Mujib, implied coexistence and tolerance of plural religious beliefs and practices as opposed to a strict separation of religion from state. Subsequent regimes, however, as a result of complex global and regional social, economic and political forces dropped secularism from the constitution and declared Islam as the state religion. Increasingly, and particularly in relation to current global politics, it is important to keep in mind for any discussion on Islam vs. secularism the ways in which the latter has been deployed in the service of imperialism by idealising a linear narrative of

progress and development in opposition to the term religious—Islamic. Gil Anidjar quotes Talal Asad and says, 'the "religious" and the "secular" are not essentially fixed categories' but gain in prominence and hegemony by the culture – more specifically, 'Western Christendom'. See Gil Anidjar, 'Secularism', *Critical Inquiry* 33/1 (2006), pp. 57–8. Furthermore, Ashis Nandy has argued that the birth of secularism as an ideology in modernity makes it deeply intolerant because modernity undermines faith in favour of secular values of rationality and development, which is achieved by abandoning or devaluing 'traditional' belief systems. A belief in secular development, constructed as the opposite of traditional belief systems, overlooks the accommodating ways faith systems have coexisted historically. See Ashis Nandy, *Time Warps: Silent and Evasive Pasts in Indian Politics and Religions* (New Brunswick: Rutgers University Press, 2002).

9. Nazli Kibria, 'Muslim encounters in the global economy: Identity developments of labor migrants from Bangladesh to the Middle East', *Ethnicities* 8/4 (2008), pp.539–56.

10. The term Bengali has an ethno-linguistic or cultural connotation, whereas Bangladeshi has a more nationalistic connotation. While Bengali nationalism emphasizes a more plural culture, recognising the syncretic Hindu and Muslim traditions of the region, it too can assume hegemonic characteristics.

11. Sugata Bose and Ayesha Jalal, *Modern South Asia: History, Culture, Political Economy* (London: Routledge, 1998), p. 203.

12. Ibid.

13. Najma Chowdhury, 'The politics of implementing women's rights in Bangladesh', in J. H. Bayes and N. Tohidi (eds), *Globalisation, Gender, and Religion: The Politics of Women's Rights in Catholic and Muslim Contexts* (New York: Palgrave, 2001), pp. 203–30.

14. Ibid., p. 212. The leadership of women-focussed NGOs is provided by women while most of those that are not women-focussed are led by men with women serving at middle and lower levels.

15. Lamia Karim, 'Democratising Bangladesh: State, NGOs, and militant Islam', *Cultural Dynamics* 16/2–3 (2004), p. 301.

16. The State of Bangladesh has ratified CEDAW with reservations to Article 2, which has to do with the implementation of Shari'a law in personal—family matters.

17. Chowdhury, 'The politics of implementing women's rights in Bangledesh', p. 217.

18. Suzanne Bergeron, *Fragments of Development: Nation, Gender, and the Space of Modernity* (Ann Arbor: University of Michigan Press, 2006).

19. Ibid., p. 161.

20. Liz Kelly, 'Inside outsiders: Mainstreaming violence against women into human rights discourse and practice', *International Feminist Journal of Politics* 7/4 (2005), pp. 471–95.

21. Ibid., p. 472.

22. Chowdhury, 'The politics of implementing women's rights in Bangledesh'.

23. Ibid., p. 226.

24. *Eclipse* [motion picture] (Dhaka: Ain O Salish Kendro, 1994).

25. Dina M. Siddiqi, 'In the name of Islam? Gender, politics, and women's rights in Bangladesh', *Harvard Asia Quarterly* 10/1 (winter 2006).

26. Ibid.

27. Ibid.

28. Sohela Nazneen, Maheen Sultan and Naomi Hossain, 'National discourses on women's empowerment in Bangladesh: Enabling or constraining women's choices?' *Development* 53/2 (2010), p. 243.

29. In this chapter, I use the term Islamist or Islamism to refer to the political actors and organizations who are acting to establish an Islamic state in Bangladesh based on their interpretation(s) of Shari'a. For a discussion of the AL, BNP and Islamist political parties, as well as Jamaat-e-Islami positions regarding women as reflected in their election manifestos (2008), please see, Nazneen et al., 'National discourses on women's empowerment'.

30. Halim, personal communication.

31. Karim, 'Democratising Bangladesh' and Elora Shehabuddin, 'Contesting the illicit: Gender and the politics of fatwas in Bangladesh', *Signs: Journal of Women in Culture and Society* 24/4 (1999), pp. 1011–44.

32. Meghna Guhathakurta, 'Women negotiating change: The structure and transformation of gendered violence in Bangladesh', *Cultural Dynamics* 16/2–3 (2004), pp. 193–211.

33. The ethnic nationalities of the CHT are collectively known as Jumma people.

34. Guhathakurta, 'Women negotiating change', p. 201.

35. Ibid., p. 202. 1952, 1969, 1971, and 1990 are all significant dates in the struggle for autonomy and democracy in pre- and post-independent Bangladesh. Known as the Language Martyr's Day, on 21 February 1952, then East Pakistanis revolted against West Pakistan's declaration that Urdu would be the official language of both wings of Pakistan. This was a controversial declaration as Bengali was the predominant language of East Pakistan. In 1969 a mass uprising broke out in East Pakistan in protest of West Pakistan's martial law regime and the killing of students. In 1971 Bangladesh became an independent nation after a nine-month long Liberation War fought in East Pakistan. In 1990 the democratic parties in Bangladesh cooperated to end 15 years of military rule. A democratic government came into power through an election process.

36. See Amnesty International Public Statement, 'Indigenous land dispute turns deadly in Bangladesh', (20 April 2011). Available at http://www.amnesty.org/en/library/asset/ASA13/003/2011/en/0e39431c-934e-4fb8-8c23-efa1e42a3cf5/asa130032011en.html (accessed 13 July 2013).

37. Ali Riaz, *God Willing: The Politics of Islamism in Bangladesh* (Lanham: Rowman & Littlefield Publishers, Inc., 2004).

38. Karim, 'Democratising Bangladesh'.

39. A legal opinion or ruling issued by an Islamic scholar. In the case of Bangladesh, rulings have been issued by religious leaders leading to communities carrying out sentences based on rigid interpretations of the Qur'an. These rulings are not recognized by the State and have been banned by the government after a series of cases of gender-based violence against women.

40. Siddiqi, 'In the name of Islam'.

41. Riaz, *God Willing*, and Karim, 'Democratising Bangladesh'.

42. Riaz, *God Willing*, p. 90.

43. Karim, 'Democratising Bangladesh', p. 306.

44. Karim, 'Democratising Bangladesh'.

45. Dina Siddiqi, 'Taslima Nasreen and others: The contest over gender in Bangladesh', in H. L Bodman and N. Tohidi (eds), *Women in Muslim Societies: Diversity Within Unity* (Boulder: Lynne Rienner Publishers, 1998), pp. 216–17.

46. Karim, 'Democratising Bangladesh'.

47. Siddiqi, 'Taslima Nasreen and others', pp. 212–13.

48. Riaz, *God Willing*, p. 123.

49. Siddiqi, 'In the name of Islam'.

50. Kelly, 'Inside outsiders'.

51. Chandra Mohanty Talpade, *Feminism Without Borders: Decolonising Theory, Practicing Solidarity* (Durham: Duke University Press, 2003).

52. Thomas Cushman, 'A conversation with Veena Das on religion and violence, suffering and language', *Hedgehog Review* 6/1 (2004). Available at *http://virginia.edu/iasc/hedgehog.html* (accessed 10 June 2012).

53. Shafqat Hussain, 'Of tea and snow leopards', *Counterpunch* (8 April 2011). Available at http://www.counterpunch.org/hussain04282011.html (accessed 3 May 2011).

54. Pathways of Women's Empowerment, 'Women and religion in Bangladesh and Pakistan: Pathways South Asia case study', (2010). Available at http://www.pathwaysofempowerment.org/Bangladesh_Pakistan_religion.pdf (accessed 6 May 2011).

55. Lila Abu-Lughod, 'The social life of "Muslim women's rights": A plea for ethnography, not polemic, with cases from Egypt and Palestine', *Journal of Middle East Women's Studies* 6/1 (2010), pp. 1–45.

56. Karim, 'Democratising Bangladesh'.

57. Naila Kabeer, 'Between affiliation and autonomy: Navigating pathways of women's empowerment and gender justice in rural Bangladesh', *Development and Change* 42/2 (2011), pp. 499–528; Fauzia E. Ahmed, 'Hidden opportunities: Islam, masculinity and poverty alleviation', *International Feminist Journal of Politics* 10/4 (2008), pp. 542–62; and Shehabuddin, 'Contesting the illicit'.

58. Elisabeth Friedman, 'The effects of "transnationalism reversed" in Venezuela: Assessing the impact of UN global conferences on the women's movement', *International Feminist Journal of Politics* 1/3 (autumn 1999), pp. 357–81.

59. Sally E. Merry, *Human Rights and Gender Violence: Translating International Law into Local Justice* (Chicago: University of Chicago Press, 2006).

60. Ibid., p. 18.

61. Saba Mahmood, 'Feminist theory, agency and the liberatory subject', in F. Nouraie-Simone (ed), *On Shifting Ground* (New York: Feminist Press, 2005), pp. 111–52.

62. Minoo Moallem, 'Transnationalism, feminism and fundamentalism', in C. Kaplan, N. Alarcon and M. Moallem (eds), *Between Woman and Nation: Nationalisms, Transnational Feminisms, and the State* (Durham: Duke University Press, 1999), p. 325.

63. Raka Ray, *Fields of Protest: Women's Movements in India* (Minneapolis: University of Minnesota Press, 1999), p. 7.

CHAPTER 5

AGENTS OF PEACE: AN EXPLORATION OF THREE ACEHNESE WOMEN LEADERS

Asna Husin

The issue of women's active participation in social life is sometimes regarded as a secular value infiltrated into Acehnese and other Muslim societies through Western influence. Yet, the active role of Acehnese women reflects entrenched Acehnese cultural norms, as well as deeply embedded teachings of equality in Islam. Culturally Acehnese women have always been very assertive. Describing their involvement in the wars against the Dutch occupation, H. C. Zentgraaff commented in his work on Aceh: 'Acehnese women are extremely courageous [. . .]. When they have to fight, this task is carried out with full energy, fearless of death, and [they] are often superior to men.'[1] The Dutch Orientalist and colonial official Snouck Hourgronje in his classic study *De Atjehers* (*The Acehnese*) included an interesting image of women and men vendors in the marketplace – a condition that continues to this day. The image was probably taken prior to, or during his station in Aceh (1891–2). Elsewhere in the two volumes of his work Hourgronje confirms that women were active members of society, especially as *teungkus* (religious teachers) and as advocates of their own rights in marriage, property and child-custody. Women's involvement in the day-to-day management of communal life was natural in the context of Aceh's social reality, plausibly driven by the common sense of sharing tasks and burdens between household members, as well as, in the community with its social norms that treated women and men as equals. The testimony of these two Dutch authors characterized the position of Acehnese women across classes and social status, and underlined that their engagement in society was a continuation of the traditional Acehnese style of men–women partnership; this was demonstrated in the early period of Acehnese Islamic history, and which to a certain extent still persists to the present day.

From this perspective, the men–women partnership or gender equality was enacted as part of the normal fabric of human existence and was never a matter of discursive debate, as is the case in the modern era. In ordinary practice, women and men could not think or behave otherwise. In fact, questioning or acting against this widespread general custom of gender–relational fairness was deemed unworthy of dignified men and women. This analysis of men–women collaboration in Aceh does not imply that the two sexes shared the same ratio of equal rights and responsibilities, nor does it suggest that social practices of women and men in Aceh exhibited the universal rights' principles of gender equity eventually adopted by the United Nations in the twentieth century. The reality remained one of obstacles facing both women and men, and discouraged movement beyond established social norms. Rather, it is to indicate that men–women partnership was enacted because it reflects the tendency of human nature to act in mutual association to achieve common goals of family and society where men and women are equal members. This statement should also emphasize that Aceh's established social norms recognized the constructive role of women far beyond their domestic tasks in the *dapur, sumur dan kasur* (kitchen, wash room and bedroom). This positive condition was reflected in the long history of Acehnese women's engagement in the domestic, economic, political and educational dimensions of human existence. Furthermore, the unquestioned acceptance of gender involvement as an *act* rather than a *discourse* was shared across all segments of Acehnese society and was never viewed to be the privilege of a specific class. This legacy stands in sharp contrast to modern feminist movements, which remain predominantly an upper- and middle-class phenomenon.[2]

Similarly, the effort to locate gender concerns within Islamic classical teachings signals the reality that the issue of female representation and women's rights constitute a praxis or an activity rather than a mere conceptual discourse. An example of such praxis can be seen in the case of Umm Salamah, beloved wife of the Prophet Muhammad, who subtly complained to God's Messenger regarding the fact that divine *wahy* (revelation) was addressed solely to male believers. Her direct challenge led to the revelation[3] of Qur'an *Surah 33 al-Ahzab* verse 35: '*Surely the Muslim men and women and the faithful men and women* [. . .]',[4] wherein 11 virtuous qualities referring equally to both men and women are specified. Similarly, Arwah (known as Umm Musa), wife of the second 'Abbasid Caliph al-Mansur (rg. 754–75), demanded a written marriage stipulation from her husband that he would neither take a second wife nor have a concubine while she was still alive. When the Caliph subsequently regretted his agreement and sought it annulled, Arwah appealed to the chief justice whose verdict ruled in her favour.[5] Umm Salamah's sponsorship of equal representation of men and women in Allah's revelation, as well as Arwah's effort to not share her husband with other wives, may be understood as gender-oriented advances advocating women's rights and gender equity.

These examples indicate that these two Muslim women figures might never have recognized the term 'gender' nor promoted gender discourse, but that gender was acted upon in an orthopraxic way. Understanding gender as an act rather than a discursive idea is very important in any discussion of women's rights and responsibilities in an Islamic context including in their promotion of peace. The same attitude had been demonstrated in Aceh and other Islamic societies throughout history. This further suggests that gender concerns are as old as Islam itself, and as such gender is a human concept rather than a Western import, even though the very word and modern discursive advocacy may have its origins in Europe. In other words, to better comprehend gender-equity aspirations and the promotion of women's rights in Muslim societies, such as Aceh, requires us to look at actions and the active social engagement of women in their respective communities.

This chapter surveys the activities and roles of women in Acehnese society by looking at the lives and experiences of three leading Acehnese women who are active agents of peace. I narrate the story of their agency as they engage with their families and society. The narrative demonstrates that their gender consciousness occurs as a natural process of life action and social activism without a conscious awareness of the notion of gender discrimination and social inequity. Their access to education began with community-based Islamic institutions, and their involvement in Islamic youth organizations was a very important foundation for developing their social awareness. Family support was an essential dimension that shaped their agency of peace. Similarly, the backing of their husbands in their mature life was also necessary. Exploring the experiences of these women assists our understanding of both Acehnese Islamic culture and women's active engagement.

Similar to the case of Sudan and Nigeria[6] women in Aceh play a central role in peacemaking using both Islamic and cultural approaches. This, in turn, empowers them to be leaders for change in their country. No doubt, women's success is limited, but the exploration of the strategies and methods offer a gateway to understand women's peace-building roles in developing societies within the Muslim world. This is significant within the context of real issues of political problems that stand in the way of the development of peace and women's participation in these communities. This study is divided into three sections. The first part looks at the emergence of gender consciousness as these three women journey through their growth and social engagement while reflecting relatively positive attitudes of Acehnese culture towards women. The second part gives a brief overview of the conflicts they experienced and their growing involvement in promoting peace and reconciliation. This features the importance of social institutions and collective partnerships in nourishing gender consciousness and fulfilment of their agency for change. The final section assesses the role of these women in post-conflict Aceh and focuses on their professional and sociopolitical activism to promote gender equity and sustainable peace.

Gender Consciousness and Social Activism

A strong sense of complementarity between men and women in Acehnese society is reflected in its history. Seven women ruled three different Acehnese Islamic kingdoms[7] – four ruled the Aceh Sultanate for 59 consecutive years (1641–99). The famous woman admiral Laksamana Keumalahayati controlled the Sultanate's maritime security in the late sixteenth and early seventeenth centuries. She was noted for designing naval tactics to repulse outside encroachments from rival powers. Such prominent figures were the high point of women's public engagement in Aceh. Women royal guards were also known throughout the Sultanate beginning with Sultan Alaidin Riayatsyah al-Mukammil (rg. 1589–1604) and Sultan Iskandar Muda (rg. 1607–36) with his famous female royal division Keumala Cahaya. The heroic engagement of women, such as Cut Nyak Dhien (d. 1908), Cut Nyak Meutia (d. 1910) and Pocut Meurah Intan (d. 1937), as revolutionary leaders against the Dutch further underlines the high position of Acehnese women in their society. Just as significantly, Acehnese women, including the well-known *Teungku* Cutpo Fatimah (d. 1912) and *Teungku* Fakinah (d. 1933), were involved in the development of the earliest educational institutions known as *dayah* (from Ar. *Zawiyah* (prayer corner or study lodge)).

These historical leaders inspired the women selected for this study. The three represent different professional backgrounds: (1) Rosmawardani Muhammad is a religious high judge; (2) Naimah Hasan is a lecturer turned bureaucrat; and (3) Adiwarni Husin is a businesswoman turned politician. Yet all three are active members of women's religious networks. The first two came from the same geographical area of North Aceh, which has a strong *dayah* environment.[8] Yet they had distinctive upbringings. Muhammad first learned religion (*mengaji* (religious education)) by attending *dayah* courses whose teachers were primarily men, while Hasan received early religious education in her village from a female *teungku buet* (religious village teacher).[9] Husin came from a different district, Pidie, and received early childhood religious education from her mother before joining a village *bale buet* (religious teaching institution) that was also run by a woman. Although all three are politically conscious, Muhammad has never joined any political party. Hasan, however, independently ran for the national senate in 2004 but lost; this action cost Naimah her university position. In contrast, Adiwarni was a deputy for Indonesia's Islamic Bulan Bintang (PBB) party in the province of Aceh and briefly was a member of the provincial parliament. Husin married a businessman some time after secondary school and never enrolled in university until after her children had grown up; Muhammad and Hasan married their seniors in college (who later became professors) right after finishing their bachelor's degrees.[10]

Coming from a large family of ten children, the sixth child Naimah Hasan lost her father when she was only ten-years-old. Raised by her widowed mother and older siblings, Hasan attended the local Islamic *madrasah* (school) where she impressed her teachers as very intelligent. As a semi-orphan, Naimah was once forced to marry the son of a wealthy family, but she protested by going on a hunger strike, which led to the cancellation of the planned matrimony. Her rejection made her family realize Hasan's ambition for education. Besides attending school, she attended *mengaji* in her village *bale buet* led by *Teungku* Asiah (known as *Miwa*). The *teungku* taught her to read the Qur'an and the basic principles of religion, while Asiah's husband instructed the young woman in reading religious books written in *Jawi*. The *Miwa* was an influential teacher who cared for her pupils and their character development. As one of her best students Hasan gained access to *Teungku* Asiah's leadership circle and became an active and leading member in her village.

Naimah confessed that her *Miwa* and the *bale buet* unconsciously helped her to become active in community building, which raised the youth's sense of gender consciousness. Along with her friends, she and her teacher observed that other villages celebrated Islamic holidays, such as the *maulid* (birthday of the Prophet) and *isra' mi'raj* (the Prophet's night journey), with public sermons (*ceramah*) and feasts; her village had never done it. In about 1968 Naimah, assisted by her friends, led the organizing committee to hold the first ever *maulid* ceremony for her village. They invited a female *'alim* (religious scholar), *Teungku* Sapiah and her eight-year-old daughter Mardiana, to give public sermons in a well-publicized and attended *ceramah*. According to Naimah, 'this event was unique. It was a women's initiative, since everyone involved in organising and performing was female; yet it was attended by both men and women.'[11] The initiative celebrating the *maulid* became a habitual practice in her village repeated for years to come. For Hasan this was just the beginning of her community activism and gender awareness.

At almost the same time of this *maulid* celebration Naimah became involved in the youth organization of the Indonesian Muslim Student Association (PII). She attended its training and leadership workshops that instilled in her the idea of an Islamic mission for a just society and increased her desire for social engagement. Upon completing secondary school Hasan was adopted by her older brother, and she moved to the capital Banda Aceh to attend *'aliyah* (Islamic high school). Being in the provincial capital, Naimah blossomed further. Her affiliation with PII expanded her horizons as she became acquainted with other students from different areas of Aceh. When she entered University in 1973 at the IAIN Ar-Raniry State Institute for Islamic Studies (now the Ar-Raniry State Islamic University), Hasan had already become a mature young adult. Here she joined the Muslim University Students Association (HMI) that further advanced her experience of Islamic activism, cultural diversity and leadership skills.[12] Naimah excelled in both her academic and extracurricular activities, and she climbed the ladder to become the leader of the HMI Women's Corps in 1978. She was also active in the Ar-Raniry student body where she met her future husband who later supported her activism unconditionally. It was as the head of HMI Women Corps that Naimah experienced the authority and responsibility of leadership. She states that PII and HMI helped develop 'in me a sense of identity as a woman and a Muslim'.[13]

She notes that her awareness of gender equity also emerged from reading books on history: 'I learned about Cut Nyak Dhien and Cut Meutia early on in the context of Indonesia's struggle against the Dutch'.[14] Since she did not understand gender discrimination and did not feel that she had been discriminated against, she stated that her 'reading of Cut Nyak Dhien and Cut Meutia was neutral'.[15] However, the youth trainings as well as her university education changed her perspective when reading history: 'I realized the great contribution of Acehnese women towards Indonesian independence and for the development of Islam. I also discovered that Aceh was once ruled by our queens for well over a half century'.[16] Naimah continued, 'the current [official] version of Indonesian history projecting the struggle of the Javanese woman Raden Adjeng Kartini [d. 1904] was different from the Acehnese female experience'.[17] She became enlightened and realized that unlike Javanese culture, which restricted women down to the early twentieth century, 'Acehnese women were liberated by Islam long before the arrival of the Dutch, and there were sultanas, palace guards, admirals, freedom fighters, and educators'.[18] This awareness made her proud but sad at the same time – sad over the predicaments of women in contemporary Aceh. Therefore, reading history reinforced her notion of women's social engagement and strengthened her Acehnese Islamic identity.

Like Naimah Hasan, judge Rosmawardani Muhammad also comes from North Aceh, but from another village. The two met at the same *madrasah* in their area. According to her own account, Rosmawardani 'was not an exceptionally smart student'. She continued, 'unlike Naimah, I was just average'.[19] In addition to schooling, she informally attended *mengaji* at a famous local *dayah*. She went there because the *dayah* was close to her house and one of her brothers, as well as her aunt, boarded students at this *dayah*. Muhammad said, 'I did not formerly register because of its policy banning pupils from attending [public] school' as students were not allowed to attend both.[20] However, being an informal student did not prevent Rosmawardani from learning and experiencing *dayah* culture. According to her own words, when she was in the village, she 'dressed as those registered students and learned along with them'.[21]

However, she also said 'when going to the Islamic school I dressed differently'.[22] Juggling between the *dayah* environment and the school culture made Muhammad aware of their distinct social dynamics and cultural peculiarities, which in a way had implications for her understanding of gender and its multiple social manifestations.

Supported by her parents who were both *madrasah* teachers and local leaders of the Islamic national organization al-Wasliyah (founded in 1930), Rosmawardani developed within herself a strong sense of responsibility and mission. Her comprehension of gender was augmented by the speech of the al-Wasliyah national female leader Ibu Umamah during its 1966 Mushawarah (assembly) in Banda Aceh. Although Muhammad was only 14-years-old at the time and had just entered secondary school, she was so moved by Umamah's words: 'Whosoever among you raises and educates two or three daughters well, then marries them off and treats them honourably, you will indeed enter Paradise'.[23] Rosmawardani continued:

> I was so touched by that speech and thus repeated her words over and over and remember them to this day. I did not know then that this was a tradition of the Prophet. It certainly made an eternal mark in my heart.[24]

Rosmawardani began to realize that education was her birthright, and it reinforced her understanding of another Prophetic tradition which she had long since memorized. That is, 'seeking knowledge is obligatory upon every believing man and woman'.[25] These two *Hadiths*, especially the first one as expressed by Umamah, forever changed how she saw herself. As she says, 'I recognise that I have a mission and fulfilling it must begin with my own spiritual and intellectual growth'.[26] Her experience at school and at PII contributed to her development. At one time, her school was organizing a speech competition for students with all candidates being boys. 'I like rhetoric and thus asked the *madrasah* principal if I could compete along with the boys. He welcomed my request and I won third prize'.[27] Muhammad was a brave student. She said, 'My courage led the school to entrust me to be the head of the student body'.[28] This leadership position was facilitated by her membership in PII whose trainings and workshops helped her 'understand leadership as trust' and expound principal human rights as God-given. When she moved to Banda Aceh to pursue her University education in Islamic law (Shari'a) in 1972, Rosmawardani continued her association with PII. A year later she became the head of the PII Women's Corps when her leadership skills were further sharpened. As leader, she understood her responsibility to realize 'the PII mission of Muslim unity and the empowerment of the youth'.

Rosmawardani also learned about women's rights through history books. She notes:

> I learn[ed] about Malahayati and other Acehnese figures early on during our history classes. But I did not then understand their role in the context of gender. I viewed them like any other national heroes who had to defend their country from colonial encroachment.[29]

However, her engagement with historical texts at a deeper level coupled with her enlightenment through the youth organization made her aware of these women's exceptional roles. 'Malahayati's strategic abilities to deter modern Western fleets at sea and her involvement in protecting Aceh's sovereignty were a true act of patriotism'.[30] Her knowledge about these great women leaders increased her sense of identity as an Acehnese and a Muslim. Muhammad attributed their activist role to Islam, a religion that she believes protects women's rights and honours their social, intellectual and religious manifestations. 'Ignorance and stupidity is the only argument placing us women in our current predicament'.[31] Like Naimah, Rosmawardani also found history classes to be empowering and strengthened her sense of responsibility and identity.

Our third informant, Adiwarni Husin, comes from Pidie. Her father was a merchant and an *'alim* who quit his studies to raise a family and became successful in his textile trading. Her mother was a talented woman from a wealthy family who only finished primary education, but she was proud to be the first and only woman from her village to have completed primary school. Even though her mother was intelligent, she could not continue her education due to the revolutionary and colonial wars. In a sense, both her mother's and father's longings for their own education was transformed in the way they raised Adiwarni and her siblings. Being the second of six children and the eldest daughter, Adiwarni became a second mother to her siblings. She assisted her mother who was involved in community work and Islamic studies. Husin received her initial *mengaji* from her mother and only joined the village *bale buet* when she started school at a local *madrasah* at the age of seven in 1958. She notes: 'I had already completed reading the entire Qur'an when I joined the *bale buet* to learn *kitabs* [religious studies]'.[32] Both her mother and teacher provided Husin with the 'first sense of women leadership; they were influential leaders in our community and their charitable contributions to the needy were their true act of leadership'.[33]

Adiwarni's experience at school was extremely positive. As the most intelligent student in her class, she received praise and attention. When the school organized festive events to celebrate certain Islamic holidays, she would ask for a stage role singing, reciting praises upon the Prophet (*salawat*) or reading poems she created for the event. Husin stated: 'Our school principle was glad that we [my female classmates and I] requested to perform'.[34] When she entered secondary school at the age of 14, Adiwarni also became acquainted with the PII youth organization, and she attended PII trainings with her older brother. Participating in PII evening activities was not easy at the time because there was no electricity, no public transportation and the roads were separated by jungle. The presence of her brother helped but was not enough to make their mother have confidence in the safety of her children. Their mother sent her female relative to escort Adiwarni, her brother and friends to PII trainings. Adiwarni states: 'I was grateful to the efforts of my mother and to the lady who always accompanied me to the night events'.[35] Adiwarni felt that PII trainings inculcated in her a sense of identity as part of the global Muslim community as demonstrated in her statement: 'PII enlarged my horizon not only on the issue of women's rights, but also on our connections and responsibilities to the Indonesian nation and the *ummah*'.[36] She discovered the importance of Islam as a social force for the betterment of men and women and the human family. Thus, PII broadened her view and provided an additional substance to the Islamic education she received from her school and the *bale buet*.

Adiwarni was engaged to a relative during her secondary school years, but the marriage was only to be consummated some years later. Upon finishing her secondary schooling in 1968 she wanted to enroll at a high school, especially as her older brother had now left Aceh for Medan in North Sumatra to enter university. Knowing that her parents had always supported her education, she was not prepared to hear otherwise. She was sad and disappointed that they did not let her go, but she understood the reasons: the absence of a high school in their area and the safety of a young girl living alone away from home. Her disappointment did not derail her ambition. With her mother's encouragement, Adiwarni began attending advanced Islamic courses offered by various *'alims*. As she excelled with one teacher, Adiwarni moved to another. In her quest for knowledge and opportunity, she became a teacher at her former primary school and taught *Bahasa Indonesia* (Indonesian Language). She remained in this position until she married in 1971 and moved to Banda Aceh with her husband. While teaching and studying she prepared for a high school exam that she passed with honours. During the course of her religious study an incident occurred that tested her gender consciousness. Her teacher was accused of impregnating a young student, which he vehemently denied. To defend himself, he took his case to the court. According to Husin: 'Many believed that the charge was made to undermine his credibility'.[37] Believing in his innocence, Adiwarni and her friends attended his court proceedings in the district capital about 16 kilometres from her village. As a bicycle was the only means of transportation, the journey was difficult. On the trial days Husin often arrived home at midnight, welcomed by her anxious mother who was very concerned for her safety. Both mother and daughter understood the principle of trust. Adiwarni noted that 'it was her trust in me that she permitted my going, and it was my trust in my teacher that I continued to be at the court'.[38] The accusation and the court proceedings taught Adiwarni about the fragility of social connections and the importance of one's honour. She believes that 'we must be vigilant of our actions and movements in order to block any room for allegations and doubts'.[39] As women, she says, 'we have to be even more watchful in order to keep ourselves in the right orientation and perspective'.[40]

As a student, Adiwarni loved history and poetry, and she had access to her father's books and journals. Her older brother who often brought books home was also a lover of Islamic literature. Additionally, her mother was a reader of traditional Acehnese narratives (*Jawi hikayat*s) and the well-known scriptural commentary *Tafsir al-Jalalayn*.[41] Her mother regularly discussed what she had read in her study circle, which Husin was sometimes part of; furthermore, Adiwarni's school library had a good collection of historical and literary works. Thus, when she became a teacher of *Bahasa Indonesia*, she taught by using history and literary works. She also requested that her students practice poetry writing and the transcription of *Jawi* works into *Bahasa*. She was fascinated by prominent female figures in Acehnese history, and she utilized such materials in teaching her *Bahasa* classes. Sometimes she picked out a chapter from a history book and asked her students to discuss or summarize it, or occasionally requested them to analyse its grammar and syntax. She also asked her students to write a poem on famous female or male historical figures and then present their poems to the class. Regarding her own history study, Husin stated:

> I never read history works from a gender perspective, since I thought it was natural for women just as for men to engage in their society. One of the benefits of our history study at the time was its gender neutrality which to a certain extent honoured women.[42]

Adiwarni referred to local authors, such as Ali Hasjmy (1914–98), Haji Abdul Malik Karim Amrullah or Hamka (1908–81) and

Mohammad Said (1905–95), who were genuine supporters of women. History taught Adiwarni the naturalness of women's leadership, the contrary of which is against nature. 'Aren't women *khalifat ul-Lah fi al-ard* [God's deputy on earth] just as men are?' stated Adiwarni[43] – referring to the Qur'an *al-Baqarah* 2:30 which portrays the divinely-granted responsibility of human beings on earth.

These fascinating stories about the lives of Adiwarni Husin, Rosmawardani Muhammad and Naimah Hasan demonstrate that equal treatment and social justice is an instinctive human leaning that can only be achieved through proper understanding and assertive perseverance by both individuals and the community. The actualization of justice and peace are values whose practice remains as a quest and a challenge in Achenese society.

Conflict and Reconciliation

Aceh has always known conflict. However, the current violence began in late 1976 when the Aceh Freedom Movement (*Gerakan Aceh Merdeka*, GAM) was founded. The GAM demanded independence from Jakarta and waged an insurgency against the Indonesian military (*Tentara Nasional Indonesia*, TNI). The TNI sent a large military force to combat the small number of GAM fighters, but they also killed and abused many civilians. Initially GAM received only limited support from the people of Aceh. At that time conflicts were confined to certain areas, while many other places in Aceh remained vibrant and peaceful. However, as killings and torture spread, support for GAM increased and created new pockets of conflict. Once again Suharto's authoritarian government sent more troops and special forces to the province and placed Aceh under the Military Operational Zone (*Daerah Operasi Militer*, DOM) from 1989–98. The removal of Suharto by the reformation movement brought more political openness. In Aceh this unleashed information about ongoing DOM abuses, which raised outcries across the country, and Acehnese support for GAM skyrocketed. Many non-governmental organizations (NGOs), including those demanding a referendum, emerged while national and international civil society showed support for Aceh. All these developments were greeted by Jakarta with antagonism. In the midst of violence, Acehnese women convened an assembly (*duek pakat*) demanding a peaceful solution to the conflict shortly after the first peace negotiation known as the *Jeda Kemanusian* (Humanitarian Pause) was signed. The failure of the *Jeda* further escalated the conflict leading the government to multiply ground forces, which turned Aceh into a theatre of open war. This was followed by imposing martial law province-wide and an act of civil emergency from May 2003 to January 2005 when open battles, rapes, detentions, mass burning of schools and towns, as well as the destruction of houses and businesses, became a daily routine. The war traumatized the people and destroyed the very fabric of their social lives. This was the situation that Rosmawardani, Adawarni and Naimah faced during the height of conflict.

Adiwarni experienced conflict early on. When GAM was founded one of her brother's friends Teuku Asnawi joined the insurgency movement. As he fought in GAM's guerrilla war, Aswani occasionally sent messages to Adiwarni's family. Several years later when Asnawi was captured and detained in Banda Aceh's prison, Adiwarni regularly visited him and sent food to his prison cell. As a woman, she had leeway without being accused of supporting GAM. It was during this period that Adiwarni became familiar with Jakarta's unjust economic and social policies against Aceh that had triggered the rebellion. Adiwarni stated: 'It was difficult not to sympathize with our own Acehnese aspirations; yet I was also aware of the danger of associating oneself with GAM'.[44] When the conflict escalated dramatically during the DOM period, Adiwarni encountered it as she travelled across Aceh with her women colleagues. By then she had already become the head of the Wanita Islam national organization in the province and the deputy of the Council of the National Forum for Majelis Ta'lim headed by the wife of Aceh's vice governor. These two are in addition to her affiliation with other institutions, such as the Women's Organization Cooperative Body (BKOW), led by Naimah Hasan. These organizations became Adiwarni's channels to serve those affected by the conflict. She accompanied the wife of the vice governor across Aceh and experienced the tensions and distrust widespread in the community.

At the height of the conflict during the period of martial law sufferings increased, and the voices of moderation disappeared. As tensions escalated, the Acehnese people even became afraid of each other. Husin stated: 'The most difficult was to be neutral. As Acehnese no matter what we did we were considered GAM [by TNI]. Yet, we were also afraid of our Acehnese fellows [GAM]'.[45] As a business family Adiwarni and her husband had to watch their company's dealings. According to her, 'financial extortions in the name of one or the other party were common. It was an impossible moment for business'.[46] Husin further stated: 'We tried to survive even in the most difficult situation'.[47] As part of her peace efforts in 1994 Adiwarni began a scholarship fund from her family's *zakat*, which later extended to supporting the livelihood of conflict victims. She collected thousands of dollars from her family and relatives in Indonesia and abroad, and travelled to conflict zones to assist victims. As the scale of the need was far greater than what she could give, she felt humbled by 'grief for those who had lost everything to war'.[48] Realizing that material assistance alone would not resolve the root causes of the conflict, Adiwarni and her women colleagues embarked on the next level of their peace efforts.

It was in early 1999 when Adiwarni first contemplated rallying women against violence. Upon returning from a peace assembly in Jordan and learning about the Women in Black network, she discussed the issue with her colleagues. 'We should protest against abuses in front of military offices and public institutions and demand the end to this war', she said.[49] Adiwarni and her friends did not yet have a chance to protest, but this was part of their search for a solution. Discussions on how to respond to violent conflict materialized during the women's dialogue initiated by BKOW in December 1999. The women called for a Consultative Assembly of Acehnese Women (*Duek Pakat Inong Aceh*, DPIA) to be convened in February 2000. The DPIA was a difficult undertaking amidst the polarization of Acehnese women. Nonetheless, 476 women representing a variety of organizations and interests attended. In

spite of efforts to hijack this assembly, the women stood firm on
their neutrality. They demanded that the Aceh conflict be solved
non-violently.[50] Adiwarni was involved in the DPIA from the start of
its preparations. On its opening day before Banda Aceh's historic
mosque *Baiturrahman*, she and Rosmawardani led a public *du'a*
(supplication) before several thousand participants, invitees and city
dwellers who had come to support the women's initiative. The
deliberations during the *Duek Pakat* were not always easy. Husin
acknowledged: 'As the Acehnese were torn between the demands for a
referendum [on independence] and re-integration, so were the
participants'.[51] Threats against and support for these two choices as
well as walk-outs coloured the deliberations, but overall 'the DPIA
was a success'.[52]

   Neither the *Duek Pakat* nor the *Jeda Kemanusian* that was signed
shortly after stopped the violence, but with the voices of women
and efforts of numerous civil society groups, solving conflict
through compromise now became a viable alternative. Nonetheless,
the failure of the *Jeda Kemanusian* further intensified violence with
the swelling number of internally displaced persons (IDPs).
Frustrated by this situation Adiwarni engaged the *ulama*, as she
now became an executive member of Aceh's *ulama* Consultative
Body (MPU).[53] She argued for action, but Husin was aware that
'everyone [*ulama* or otherwise] was really afraid to act;
psychological fear and emotional trauma overwhelmed all of us
[Acehnese]'.[54] Once again she contemplated a women-in-black-type
protest, but according to her, 'this proposal also received limited
support due to the common dread of martial law'.[55] In spite of the
lack of concrete results, 'we continued to search for a solution', said
Husin. As the situation became more fearful, Adiwarni stated
further that 'even bringing humanitarian assistance could become a
problem if we were accused of partiality'.[56] It was during this
highly traumatized period that Adiwarni became involved in her
sister's peace education project and assisted at its trainings and
workshops. Husin stated: 'Peace education was the anticipation for
emotional and social healing, and through it I glimpsed the
shining lights'.[57] The terrible conditions in the wake of the

December 2004 Tsunami finally brought peaceful change to this violence-torn province.

The University lecturer Naimah Hasan gained her master's degree from the Philippine Women's University in 1985. Naimah first learned about the Aceh conflict in the early 1980s but did not experience it directly. She noted that 'life was still normal in most places in Aceh. Activities on campus took place without security concerns'.[58] However, the situation changed during and after the 1990s when violence became widespread. 'We were afraid of both GAM and the military, and felt we were under their surveillance. The news of killings and disappearances were extremely fearful'.[59] Yet the Acehnese could not do much. However, the new era of reformation after the fall of Suharto brought a drastic change. The revelation of these previous atrocities led Naimah and her friends to establish the Human Rights Forum in 1998 in order to properly document them. Enlisting over 100 students and activists, they uncovered numerous abuses across Aceh that reached the national headlines. This forced Jakarta to repeal DOM, but it did not improve the situation. According to Hasan: 'Student activists were pursued, and when they went out of their houses they were prepared never to return. Accused of being *cuak* [conspirator] led to disappearances and killings. The conditions were extremely destructive'.[60] Naimah continued on to say, 'we were all frightened; when our friends were seized and killed we remained silent. Our religious teachers were accused and then murdered, and we also were silent. We were frightened of both sides of the divide'.[61] As IDPs became more numerous and widespread, Hasan collected food packages from colleagues in Jakarta. When the food stuffs arrived in the military plane, Naimah was accused of poisoning the IDPs. She then received personal threats and intimidation as well as 'accusations of being a spy for Indonesia'. Her house was infiltrated, compromising her personal and family safety. She recounts that 'strangers would sometimes arrive to terrorize us with guns. Fortunately, they still respected my husband and called him *Teungku* [*'alim*]. Yet my personal life became very precarious, especially when other leading citizens were being killed'.[62]

Fear for her life did not stop Naimah from thinking of Aceh. Informal and formal discussions were convened in Jakarta, Medan and Banda Aceh that all explored possible solutions. Hasan stated: 'One of our meetings in Jakarta was attended by Bang Nur [Muhammad Nur Husin or Adiwarni's late brother] when we discussed the role of academics and the business community in resolving conflict'.[63] Thus, the *Duek Pakat*, initiated by women, was 'one of the many initiatives' in the making. It was about 'the role and position of women in politics, the economy and the implementation of Shari'a'.[64] As the head of BKOW where the ideas for DPIA were conceived, Naimah was indeed its true initiator. Therefore, when the controversy over a referendum slipped into the *Duek Pakat*, Hasan felt responsible and stated: 'we would all be killed by the military had we accepted the referendum choice'.[65] She tried to convince the participants to 'support neither re-integration nor a referendum, but to focus instead on a peaceful solution to conflict'.[66] In the heated chaotic debates over the two alternatives, Naimah took over the chairing and recited the *salawat* (praises upon the Prophet) to relax the atmosphere. When the situation became slightly calmer, Naimah repeated the disputed choices, and then quickly gavelled in favour of 'a peaceful solution'. Outcries and anger were expressed, but 'the decision was made'. Dissatisfaction was also expressed by spectators outside the hall, and the call quickly spread to harm Naimah and several others. Fortunately the women of the *Duek Pakat* had good internal security, and all were safe while the DPIA was concluded with integrity.

One of the recommendations of the *Duek Pakat* was to create an umbrella organization called *Balai Syura Inong Aceh* (Consultative Council of Acehnese Women), which selected Naimah as its leader. With the *Balai Syura* and BKOW as channels, she embarked on a two-front programme: a legal framework and women's participation. The task at hand was to create laws and regulations supporting direct elections in Indonesia and Aceh that would accommodate the 30 per cent quota for women candidates. Therefore, Hasan lobbied the Indonesian Parliament during its debates on Aceh's *Special Autonomy Law* to help promote both Aceh and women's agendas. She focussed on policies affecting women and argued for their proper implementation. An important policy dimension was proper distribution of Indonesian public funds designated for Aceh. Joining the national monitoring team, Naimah travelled across the province to evaluate the national government's projects. 'This monitoring showed what conflict had done to these projects. Money was wasted and numerous projects could not be completed'.[67] Security problems, extortion and corruption were the main factors compromising the projects. 'Everyone knew the problems, yet no complaints were filed'.[68] War and conflict had caused the Acehnese to 'lose their values and integrity, for everyone has now become greedy and self-concerned'.[69]

On the issue of women's participation, Naimah and her colleagues spoke of their involvement in the peace process and beyond. When the *Jeda Kemanusiaan* was signed she served on the Committee leading its humanitarian action. Even when the *Jeda* conditions continued to be devastating, Naimah carried out her responsibility often at great personal risk. When the *Jeda* broke down in 2002 the conditions further deteriorated as both sides became more extreme. 'The *Jeda* made GAM stronger', stated Hasan. Aceh was boiling, and the attacks on Hasan increased. Obviously perpetrated by GAM, the threats to kill her, or to bomb her house, as well as the written harassment 'stop selling Aceh', became a daily routine. Her 'husband had to negotiate with GAM' for her personal safety. When the security became very worrying, the Indonesian Government offered to police-guard her house, which she rejected. She did, however, accept an offer of bodyguard protection from friends in Jakarta. Even then her life was at risk; Hasan was then exiled to the capital for two months to protect her own life. This was followed by imposition of martial law and a civil emergency when the violence and brutality peaked. Notwithstanding the deteriorating situation, attempts for peace continued, but to no avail until the Tsunami when new efforts led to the Peace Agreement signed on 15 August 2005. Although women were not directly involved in this peace negotiation, the agreement itself was a fulfilment of their call for a peaceful solution to this long, drawn-out conflict.

Rosmawardani Muhammad also went through the same negative effects of the conflict. She experienced violence first-hand since the early 1980s. Her husband's village, Cot Lureng, in Bireuen was a hot spot in the conflict. Her father-in-law secretly supported GAM. One of her nephews was also a GAM member who was often followed by the security forces. In addition to her family's leaning, Muhammad experienced conflict through another manifestation. While living in Banda Aceh where violence did not manifest until the late 1990s, she and her husband regularly returned to their villages to visit elderly parents since their marriage in 1980. 'We did so even during the height of the conflict', she said.[70] They sometimes arrived in Cot Lureng during the course of open fighting and 'saw the dead bodies being carried away'.[71] They experienced detentions and body searches, and they saw villages and towns burnt down with flaring fires. Her affiliation with the court and her husband's professorship helped them when they argued for neutrality. When life in Cot Lureng was no longer bearable, her in-laws moved to another village and left their house behind damaged and looted. 'This was the price of war'. Rosmawardani observed that 'being always at gun point made us less afraid, although we had to be very careful'.[72]

Although Muhammad herself had become immune from the fear of war, the damage she saw 'broke [her] heart'. Her village had been a prosperous farming area with all varieties of fruit and crops, but 'it is now all left fallow, causing poverty and hardship'.[73] Feeling depressed by this situation, she searched for a solution and reached out to the *ulama*, the Provincial Secretary and to her women colleagues. When the call for the *Duek Pakat* emerged, she embraced it with an open heart. Rosmawardani was part of its planning committee and attended its preparatory meetings in Jakarta, Medan and Banda Aceh. Not aware of donors' financial assistance, Muhammad helped raise funds to support the DPIA. Although she did not secure much, the fact that many donated showed 'how much women and the people of Aceh wanted peace'. The energy manifested during 'the *Duek Pakat* was phenomenal, and the controversy surrounding a referendum was a natural manifestation of a divided society caused by war'.[74] The fact that the *Duek Pakat* was concluded with integrity demonstrated the maturity of its women participants and organizers.

Rosmawardani believed strongly that political actors and public institutions were critical to conflict management. In 2000 she consciously supported a candidate for governor believing that he would bring peace to Aceh. When her candidate lost, Rosmawardani was disappointed, yet she realized 'that was the reality of the elections: one won and the other lost'.[75] She then tried to work with the elected governor to promote peace. Rosmawardani and several of her friends formed a secret group to search for a solution. They quietly brought the new governor and the GAM leader together to explore the possibility for a compromise. While this meeting was constructive, it did not materialize its intended objective. However, it showed to 'both sides the wish of the Acehnese'. People were indeed tired of war and this initiative was one of many promoted by different Acehnese groups. When the situation 'was extremely frightening with bloodshed and coercion', she returned to the head of the *ulama* arguing for action. Muhammad stated: 'I had a huge disagreement with him because I wanted the *ulama* to do more'.[76] In the midst of uncertainty and fear, martial law was instituted causing Rosmawardani to think '*ka kiamat* [sign of the end hour]'.

Martial law was seen to be a sign of *kiamat* by the Acehnese. Civic work and activism were put on hold, and all NGO foreign workers were forced to leave. Activist citizens were put under surveillance. One of the very few NGOs that remained active was the Peace Education Program (PPD)[77] and Rosmawardani had been involved in this initiative since 2001. She assisted in its workshops and teacher training and attended a PPD mediation workshop where she was exposed to contemporary mediation skills for the first time. Reflecting on her experience, she stated: 'I found peace education to be empowering. At the time [of martial law] when no other activities were possible, PPD became a place of refuge'.[78] Indeed at this time when civic education promoting Indonesian national values and State ideology was banned, PPD's peace manuals were used in schools to inculcate universal Islamic teachings on human rights, pluralism and social justice. As admitted by the teachers involved in this effort at that time, 'our peace manuals were considered neutral by both GAM and the military'. The experience of these Acehnese women leaders during the conflict and their unceasing efforts at reconciliation highlights the human need for communal integrity and societal harmony in the midst of violence.

Sociopolitical Activism and Sustainable Peace

Rosmawardani's exposure to modern mediation skills strengthened her capacity as a religious judge. The Tsunami that swept away over 150,000 Acehnese created a massive inheritance problem. Daily, she witnessed gender insensitive verdicts at the religious court: 'There was an assumption that men were breadwinners. So the assets of those men who had died in the Tsunami went straight to their families, giving female widowers only a small share of their legal inheritance'. If the victims were female, all their assets went directly to the surviving husbands leaving nothing for the wives' relatives. 'This was un-Islamic'.[79] She protested against such verdicts and argued that women could have been the breadwinners, and thus it was the responsibility of the judges to investigate and search for this information. In spite of her protests, these decisions were made, and banks paid the claims. She brought the issue to the attention of her superiors, the National Bank, the local parliament, the *ulama* and many others. Finally, the idea of a workshop to explore this matter emerged in late 2005. This workshop recommended that the rights of women should be given a priority and the issue of *hak bersama* (rights to mutual earnings) – a customary practice sanctioned by religious authority – should be examined. 'This workshop was an eye opener for many religious judges, and it changed their understanding of the Islamic legal injunctions they sought to implement'.[80]

This unusual gathering led to two other important initiatives that Rosmawardani conceptualized: gender training and a mediation workshop. Supported by the Asia Foundation, the three-year gender project aimed to 'empower religious judges with gender perspectives in order to help them deal with court cases with fairness and sensitivity'.[81] This project trained all 300 religious judges from

Aceh's 18 religious courts. It was successful, and many participants felt empowered by this new perspective. It also generated envy on the part of certain court leaders who regarded that 'Rosmawardani has usurped [their] ploughing land'.[82] Despite this, with the support of her superiors in Jakarta, she continued her work, which resulted in her promotion to the rank of High Judge, a promotion she had long deserved; 'as women we were not given any priority'.[83] Her active engagement changed the inattention of her superiors. Upon completing the gender project, Rosmawardani received another grant for mediation workshops. Her own experience with the PPD trainings, as well as her mediation trip to Australia in 2006, helped her see the importance of resolving court conflicts in a peaceful manner. She found it in accord with the Islamic principle of legal justice. Unfortunately, before Rosmawardani could complete her mediation project, news of her transfer to Pekan Baru in central Sumatra arrived. Her 'wish to empower all Acehnese religious judges in mediation skills was shattered by this transfer', but the decision was irreversible.[84]

Rosmawardani has since been retransferred to the high religious court in Medan, the capital of North Sumatra. 'Neither Pekan Baru nor Medan is the same as my homeland of Aceh. New places with new people and fresh challenges required time to adjust. It was very difficult, so I could not do like I had done in Aceh'.[85] This challenge opened up a new opportunity, for she indeed found a fresh, broader role in her legal service. Her contribution will now benefit not just Aceh but the entire country. Currently, Rosmawardani is working on a number of legal projects. One concerns the right of women to appeal their divorce cases all the way to the highest national court of appeal – the *Mahkamah Agung* (Supreme Court). This jurisdiction is now part of the Indonesian legal system, but parliament is currently contemplating a new draft law that would remove this issue from the jurisdiction of the *Mahkamah Agung*. Rosmawardani opposes its removal, and along with other advocates she seeks to keep this issue as part of legal protection for women. She has met with members of the Supreme Court, the national parliament and the Women's Human Rights Commission to enlist their support for its preservation. The second case is that Rosmawardani is now contributing a module for a manual being developed by the Supreme Court. Her 'module focusses on gender issues that can empower religious judges in their court dealings', and it is based on her research and her personal reflections.[86] These are only two examples of Rosmawardani's commitment to gender fairness in her relentless effort for women's empowerment as an essential ingredient for sustainable peace.

Adiwarni, who only enrolled in college for a degree in Islamic law in 1989 at the age of 38 after becoming a successful business woman in property, continues her charity work in the aftermath of the Tsunami. Having earlier become a member of PBB, she was then selected as one of its deputies. Her interests in politics began from childhood as her family was a strong supporter of the (now dissolved) Islamic party of Masyumi. Her career in current politics began in 2001, and she ran for Aceh's parliament in the 2004 election – the single seat PBB won went to her male colleague. During his term this man angered his party for not supporting their agenda, and PBB resolved to remove him and to put Adiwarni in his place. She rejected this on moral grounds and said, 'if we bring someone down, God will bring us down. I will never accept a seat at the expense of friendship'.[87] She often argued that 'politics should be based on legal principles and sincerity, and only then can we honestly represent our constituents'.[88] Her principled ethics and absence of political selfishness marks Adiwarni's quality as a public servant. In the meantime she served as a member of the Governor's Advisory Team. When the male colleague left his seat to run for a higher office, Adiwarni was appointed as a new member by means of the mid-term replacement. Although her parliamentary services were brief, she made an impact by focusing on three major issues: education, women's empowerment and the implementation of Shari'a. 'These matters are extremely critical for gender justice', she stated.[89] She was among those politicians who inaugurated scholarships, which are now still offered to hundreds of young Acehnese to pursue masters and doctoral degrees overseas in Egypt, America, Australia and Germany.

Outside of Parliament, Adiwarni assists female political candidates and has repeatedly been asked to join another party since PBB was disqualified to stand in elections in 2010 for not meeting the required threshold. Since morality and integrity are her guiding principles, she is extremely selective. She turned down a number of offers including an invitation to run as a candidate for Vice Governor in 2011. She has now joined the newly emerging National Democratic Party (Nasdem) because of the issues it espouses. This party's view of women and its concern with gender restorative justice are attractive to Adiwarni. Nasdem is listed as Number One on the electoral ballot across Indonesia for the 2014 elections, and Adiwarni is assigned as Nasdem's number one candidate for the Aceh Parliament representing the areas of Banda Aceh, Aceh Besar and Sabang. She has also served on the *Dewan Syariah* of the *Baitul Mal*, a State-owned institution governing *zakat* and *sadaqah* (obligatory and voluntary charitable contributions). The *Baitul Mal* has provided financial aid to hundreds of poor children, the elderly, handicapped and to small vendors. It has restored the houses of poor families across Aceh and helped build new ones. Her work with the *Baitul Mal* allows Adiwarni to assist many poor women, since 'most poor families are run by women and most elderly are also women'.[90] Adiwarni who is now pursuing her master's degree sees both the *Baitul Mal* and 'politics as instruments to perform good in fulfilment of her responsibility as *khalifat ul-Lah fi al-ard*'.[91]

Like Adiwarni and Rosmawardani, Naimah is also a woman of mission. The Tsunami destruction of Aceh was so enormous that its reconstruction required both local and international support, which gave birth to the Reconstruction and Rehabilitation Body (BRR). Naimah served on BRR's Consultative Board (BC), which she later led. This was a weighty responsibility given that the BC was responsible to ensure the proper implementation of BRR's projects funded by both Indonesian and international donors. With a total budget of roughly 7 billion US dollars in the four years of BRR's existence (2005–9), the recovery effort in Aceh was 'one of the largest humanitarian programmes in history'.[92] While the actual implementation was the responsibility of BRR executives, Naimah as the head of BC oversaw its effectiveness, its goals and its implementation standards as the agency struggled to restore livelihoods, strengthen communities and rebuild infrastructure. With nearly 700 funding agencies and over 1000 implementing partners, both local and international, the work of BRR was quite complex. Coordination and duplication was daunting, yet with the existence of BC as an internal mechanism 'such weaknesses could be minimised'. As BRR recognized the importance of local community participation in the reconstruction efforts, Naimah and BC strove 'to ensure that such participation be maximised'. Furthermore, she oversaw that women victims received an equitable share and that their needs were properly met. 'Though we recognised some limitations, BRR with its BC contributed to the reconstruction of Aceh and the rehabilitation of our community', Naimah emphasized.[93]

Besides BRR, Naimah has served a few other important institutions at the local and national levels. Since 2011 she has been a member of the Advisory and Assistancy Board for the economic development of Sabang Free Port. This board is the Aceh government's economic institution to negotiate the rights of Aceh vis-à-vis Indonesia in the progress of Sabang Free Port and its overall role in Aceh's economic development. In addition, Naimah has also served the *Kemitraan* (The Partnership) since its foundation in 2000. This is a multi-partnered non-profit organization working with government institutions, international organizations and civic society to advance the reformation of Indonesian State bureaucracy. Initiated by the powerful institutions of the United Nations Development Program, the World Bank and the Asian Development Bank in the aftermath of the 1997–8 economic crisis, The Partnership was established by 20 influential citizens of Indonesia including current President Susilo Bambang Yudhoyono (SBY) and Vice President Boediono. Naimah Hasan is a founding member who has since served on its Executive Council. As a high-profile organization, its work has received praise as well as criticism. Some of the positive claims for The Partnership refer to its insistence on good governance and anti-corruption. In contrast, criticism of The

Partnership reflects the conventional distrust by many Indonesians of foreign aid and UN agencies. Their chief concern is the perceived promotion of the global capitalist agenda for the benefit of powerful nations and their local collaborators. Naimah is not apologetic about such criticisms. She openly states that 'any intervention of this kind carries strengths and weaknesses, and The Partnership is no exception'.[94] Her association with it was 'motivated by [her] wish to assist Aceh'. In so doing she is now able to help both Aceh and the rest of Indonesia. Her active concern with women's issues may be better addressed if 'government [of Indonesia] practices good governance, and this is the interest of The Partnership'.[95] In short, the *Kemitraan* for Naimah is a venue for continuing her 'struggle against corruption and injustice'. Finally, Hasan is now a candidate for the 2014 national parliamentary elections listed on ballot number six for the SBY-founded Democratic Party representing the North East Aceh region. Similar to the *Kemitraan*, Naimah's engagement in politics is an integral 'part of her active exertions for good governance and social and gender justice'.[96] All of these may be regarded as our women's holistic effort to create sustainable peace in their community and nation.

Conclusion

This survey of the lives of three contemporary Acehnese women activists demonstrates that fairness and equity is a natural human inclination requiring recognition and nourishment. These women have fought hard to actualize these in practice, albeit with limited success. Their efforts, however, strengthen the claim that the ideal and real is a continuous negotiation for becoming. The potentials are there and efforts make one move forward in a journey for continuous improvement. The role of religious and social institutions, family environment, and the overall flexible posture of Acehnese culture, as well as the dynamism of an individual's personality, are important factors for the activation of gender consciousness. Acehnese legacies and positive female experiences provide certain advantages for the nourishment of women's active agency. The prototype of the

Sultanahs and Admirals of the past still reverberates within the Acehnese psyche, as does the heroic participation by women opposing colonial oppression. Although this legacy has not been fully emulated, contemporary Acehnese women seek to implement it through differing manifestations as they respond to the challenges of today's cultural and social reality. Their response to the demands imposed by violent conflict and civil war, their promotion of peace and of gender empowerment and their fulfilment of social and ethical obligations are contemporary manifestations of the historical women's legacy. The present study has not discussed the post-conflict challenges affecting Acehnese women, including an emerging trend of religious and political conservatism; matched by the attraction of materialist and permissive lifestyles, which is indeed a real concern. Both of these opposing tendencies could impact negatively on women as they engage in socially-conscious activism and promote sustainable peace.

Notes

1. H. C. Zentgraaff, *Aceh*, transl. Aboe Bakar, (Jakarta: Beuna, 1983), p. 78.
2. Consult Margot Badran's study on the emergence and evolution of the feminist movement in Egypt in the first half of the twentieth-century in her *Feminists, Islam and Nation: Gender and the Making of Modern Egypt* (Princeton: Princeton University Press, 1996).
3. Those unfamiliar with the 'causes of revelation' of the Qur'an (the exegetical genre known as *asbab al-nuzul*) should be mindful that among the many occasions of Qur'anic revelation were events provoking answers and responses to requests by the Muslim community of the time – which of course included prominent women. Thus, the complaints and veiled protests by the Prophet's wife Umm Salamah fall within this category.
4. Wahbah az-Zuhayli, *Al-Tafsir al-Munir fi al-Aqidah wa al-Shari'a wa al-Manhaj* [A Clear Exegesis about the Doctrine, Law, and the Path], Vol. 22 (Beirut: Dar al-Fikr, 1411/1991), p. 17.
5. See narratives of courageous women in Islam recounted in Wiebke Walther's *Women in Islam: From Medieval to Modern Times* (Princeton: Markus Weiner Publishers, 1993).
6. Souad Ali, 'The Role of Muslim Women in Engendering Peace: Bila-d al-Sudan (Sudan and Nigeria)', Chapter 6, this volume.

7. Aceh's Islamic Kingdom of Tamiang was ruled at one time by Queen Lindung Bulan (rg. 1353–98) who acted as Prime Minister to her Royal Father; and the Kingdom of Samudra Pasai was ruled by Queen Nur Ilah (d. 1380) and Queen Nahrasiyah Rawangsa Khadiyu (rg. 1400–28).

8. *Dayah* or Islamic boarding school is known by different names, including *pesantren* in Java and Kalimantan, *surau* in West Sumatera and *pondok* in other regions of Southeast Asia. In Aceh it was also called *rangkang* 'hut'. For the development of *pondok* or the Islamic traditional school in modern Malaysia, see the chapter 'Pondoks, madrasahs and the production of "Ulama" in Malaysia', in William R. Roff, *Studies on Islam and Society in Southeast Asia* (Singapore: National University of Singapore Press, 2009), pp. 116–30.

9. *Teungku buet* directs a *bale buet* (village religious teaching institution) found in almost every Acehnese village, which provides basic religious instruction and religious education for young children. There are thousands of *bale buets* across Aceh, and most are run by women.

10. I have known these three women for over 25 years, and one is in fact my older sister. In addition to watching their roles in their families and in society, as well as their professional careers, I conducted five interviews with each of them in August, September and October 2012. I also had two telephone interviews with Rosmawardani in November 2012, and three telephone interviews with Naimah: two in November 2012 and one in November 2013; I also conducted one Skype interview with Adiwarni in December 2012.

11. Naimah Hasan, Personal Interview (August, 2012).

12. Both HMI and PII were born in 1947 during Indonesia's final phase of colonial revolution and its early state of nation-building as a free country. The former is affiliated with school students and the latter with those studying at university. The two organizations were major players not only for reinforcing Indonesia's Islamic character but also for safeguarding the new nation from political and social confrontations. Both PII and HMI have produced some of the finest intellectuals and officials who dominated the country's academic, social, political and religious scenes from the 1960s down to this day. While their torch has now faded by the emergence of modern NGOs, HMI and PII remain significant players in Indonesian youth development.

13. Naimah Hasan, Personal Interview (August, 2012).

14. Ibid.

15. Ibid.

16. Ibid.

17. Ibid.

18. Ibid.

19. Rosmawardani Muhammad, Personal Interview (August 2012).

20. Ibid.

21. Ibid.

22. Ibid.

23. Rosmawardani believed that neither she nor her parents received a written text of Umamah's speech, but the speaker's words were remembered by many, and our quotation is given as memorized by Rosmawardani.

24. Rosmawardani Muhammad, Personal Interview (August 2012).

25. Ibid.

26. Ibid.

27. Ibid.

28. Ibid.

29. Rosmawardani Muhammad, Personal Interview (September 2012).

30. Ibid.

31. Ibid.

32. Adiwarni Husin, Personal Interview (August 2012).

33. Ibid.

34. Adiwarni Husin, Personal Interview (September 2012).

35. Ibid.

36. Ibid.

37. Adiwarni Husin, Personal Interview (October 2012).

38. Ibid.

39. Ibid.

40. Ibid.

41. As its title indicates, this Qur'anic commentary was written by two *Jalals*: Jalaluddin Muhammad b. Ahmad al-Mahalli (d. 864 H) and Abu al-Fadl Abdur Rahmah b. Abi Bakr b. Muhammad Jalaluddin al-Suyuti (d. 911 H). The *Tafsir al-Jalalayn* continues to be famous among religious teachers and Islamic schools in Indonesia.

42. Adiwarni Husin, Personal Interview (August 2012).

43. Ibid.

44. Adiwarni Husin, Skype Interview (3 December 2012).

45. Ibid.

46. Adiwarni Husin, Personal Interview (August 2012).

47. Ibid.

48. Ibid.

49. Adiwarni Husin, Personal Interview (September 2012).

50. Although participants in non-violence workshops conducted by Michael Beer and Karim D. Crow of Nonviolence International in 1999 may have been the first group in Aceh to promote a non-violent solution for the Aceh conflict, these women were the first to popularize the demand by making it central to daily discourse.

51. Adiwarni Husin, Personal Interview (October 2012).

52. Ibid.

53. Even before the arrival of Adiwarni, many *ulama* members had always discussed the possibility of solving the Aceh conflict peacefully, and Adiwarni, along with her female colleagues, provided an additional energy and flavor to an already existing idea for a non-violent solution to Aceh tensions.

54. Adiwarni Husin, Personal Interview (September 2012).
55. Ibid.
56. Ibid. and October 2012.
57. Adiwarni Husin, Skype Interview (3 December 2012).
58. Naimah Hasan, Personal Interview (October 2012).
59. Ibid.
60. Naimah Hasan, Telephone Interview (16 November 2012).
61. Naimah Hasan, Personal Interview (October 2012); Telephone Interview (16 November 2012).
62. Ibid.
63. Naimah Hasan, Telephone Interview (17 November 2012).
64. Ibid.
65. Ibid.
66. Ibid.
67. Naimah Hasan, Telephone Interview (16 November 2012).
68. Ibid.
69. Ibid.
70. Rosmawardani Muhammad, Personal Interview (October 2012).
71. Ibid.
72. Ibid.
73. Rosmawardani Muhammad, Telephone Interview (3 November 2012).
74. Rosmawardani Muhammad, Personal Interview (October 2012).
75. Rosmawardani Muhammad, Personal Interview (August 2012).
76. Rosmawardani Muhammad, Personal Interview (October 2012). Muhammad's view reflects the frustration of Acehnese leaders *during* the height of the conflict, rather than any lack of action by the *ulama*. This author has worked closely with the Acehnese *ulama* for over 12 years and knows they also pursued several initiatives, but the destructive situation mitigated their efforts.
77. PPD was founded by Asna Husin in October 2000 as an independent affiliate of the Washington-based Nonviolence International. It executed two projects: peace education for high schools and for the *dayah*. In the first project PPD cooperated with the government of Aceh, the second with the MPU. Its close association with the government and Asna's Acehnese connections were the main reasons PPD was allowed to operate during this challenging period. Nevertheless, it experienced great difficulties.
78. Rosmawardani Muhammad, Personal Interview (September 2012).
79. Rosmawardani Muhammad, Telephone Interview (5 November 2012).
80. Ibid.
81. Ibid.
82. Ibid.
83. Rosmawardani Muhammad, Personal Interview (October 2012); Telephone Interview (3 November 2012).
84. Ibid.
85. Rosmawardani Muhammad, Telephone Interview (3 November 2012); Ibid.

86. Ibid.
87. Adiwarni Husin, Personal Interview (September 2012).
88. Ibid.
89. Adiwarni Husin, Skype Interview (3 December 2012).
90. Ibid.
91. Adiwarni Husin, Personal Interview (September 2012).
92. Naimah Hasan, Personal Interview (August 2012); Telephone Interview (17 November 2012).
93. Ibid; Telephone Interview (17 November 2012).
94. Naimah Hasan, Personal Interview (September 2012).
95. Ibid.
96. Naimah Hasan, Telephone Interview (7 November 2013).

CHAPTER 6

THE ROLE OF MUSLIM WOMEN IN ENGENDERING PEACE: BILĀD AL-SUDAN (SUDAN AND NIGERIA)

Souad T. Ali

Theoretically, many Muslim women and feminist scholars approach the concept of peace in Islam from the perspective of its original sources, the Qur'an and *Hadith*. Nimat Hafez Barazangi's approach on education and empowerment using Qur'anic pedagogical dynamics can be considered as a tool for peace. She uses Qur'anic pedagogical dynamics as the philosophical basis for Muslim women to develop an integrative curriculum that proposes a shift in learning, knowing and teaching, and the application of the Islamic world view. In this project, the learner is placed at the heart of the curricular process, and these same Qur'anic dynamics become the medium through which the learners move towards the intended gender revolution as an integral part of the Qur'anic principle of social and economic justice while simultaneously balancing the tension between pluralism and secularism.[1] Comparatively, advocates of religious education for women can be found in other parts of the world as reflected in the emergence of the International Institute of Islamic Education for Women (Al-Huda) in Pakistan. Founder and director Dr. Farahat Hashmi established Al-Huda as a small academy for women in Islamabad in 1994, and it eventually branched into an organized movement in many other Pakistani cities and abroad. According to Faiza Mushtaq, the primary activity offered by Al-Huda is education in religious subjects intended to supplement rather than replace secular academic education.[2] At Al-Huda attending classes held in mosques, cooperating with other women and adhering to specific forms of dress and comportment are important ways of developing a Muslim consciousness. There are several other theoretical approaches to Islamic education for women in developing Muslim consciousness, including the Gülen movement in Turkey. Founded by Fethullah Gülen, the movement is simultaneously traditional and progressive. It focusses on Qur'anic principles of peace and recognizes women's freedom of choice as an integral part of rejecting all forms of oppression. Such freedom allows women to exercise their leadership roles in society. Gülen's main contribution in the context of empowering women has been his focus on education. 'With education women in the movement have been assigned a tool which they always will carry with them and which will help them define and negotiate their role in society'.[3] These movements provide a diverse theoretical understanding of how Muslim women approach the subject of an Islamic-centred education for a renewal of faith and how they engage in peaceful transformations in these different societies. Educating women on the principles of peace in Islam is meant to lead to greater focus on social justice, to include women towards peaceful action and to help them endeavour towards these qualities in their educational approaches.[4]

This chapter draws on two African examples from Sudan and Nigeria to address the theological and social principles of peace in Islam. I emphasize the role women can play to facilitate members of their communities to negotiate and practice peaceful coexistence. This analysis suggests that the seeds of peaceful social coexistence can be integrated into society by women who can use this knowledge to instil a culture of peace particularly in raising new generations of citizens. Another question this study addresses is what new approaches and methods are required to understand and evaluate women's agency in peace-building politically and socially in everyday life.[5]

A Focus on Two African Examples from the Sudanic Belt

Two African examples from the Sudanic Belt of the East African country of Sudan and the West African country of Nigeria highlight the role of Muslim women in engendering peace in the region. The position of Sudanese women religious scholars and preachers are a part of an old tradition in Islamic history in which women played a unique role in the transmission and dissemination of Islamic knowledge. The Qur'an makes no distinction between men and women in this regard, and the Prophet Muhammad in a famous *hadīth* advised his companions[6] to 'learn half of your religion from that woman', in reference to his wife 'Ā'isha who transmitted 'some 2210 *hadīth*'[7] narratives to the 'foremost early Muslim traditionists'.[8] Sudanese written sources such as *Kitāb al-Tabaqāt* by Muhammad al-Nūr Wad Daiffalla briefly discuss some women preachers as prominent figures and cite Fatima bint Jābir as one of the earliest women educators in the Sudan.[9] Drawing on the wealth of this historical background, today many categories of female preachers can be cited in the Sudan. The first part of this chapter discusses four categories and what role these women played within these brackets.

Another interesting example is the unique experience of Nana Asma'u, a nineteenth-century Nigerian Muslim scholar and peace advocate who used her faith as basis for the pursuit of her knowledge and who was dedicated to promoting peace among conflicting groups in her community. Raised in the *Qadriyya* Sufi order, Nana Asma'u was devoted to promoting reconciliation, education and justice through peaceful means based on her knowledge of the Qur'an and the prophetic *Sunna* tradition. In the midst of warfare, in the West African part of the Sudanic Belt, currently Nigeria, Asma'u's teaching greatly and positively helped change the culture in which she lived. She was an eyewitness to battles about which she reported in her written works. During the period of the Sokoto jihad[10] (this is a reference to a series of battles in a campaign to reform Islam between 1804–30) and thereafter, Asma'u's personal and peaceful jihad was a jihad of knowledge that focussed on the education of women as primary mentors of future generations and the promotion of reconciliation and peaceful coexistence among conflicting groups in her community.[11] Asma'u thus assumed the role of an active teacher of both men and women and did not confine herself to teaching students in her immediate community. Instead, she reached out through other teachers to engage women in isolated rural areas, as is further explained below.

Sudan

The role played by Sudanese women in the field of Islamic education has been documented by several scholars and commentators. Figures such as Shaykha Khadijah al-Azhari, Zeinab Muhammad Ahmed, Fatimah bint Jabir and Khadijah Omer Kashoi are among early Sudanese women educators that this chapter references. While reflecting on the experiences of these early women, the chapter will simultaneously focus on and discuss more closely the current situation where at least four categories of female preachers and Qur'an teachers can be found in the Sudan: Independent, Islamist, *Ansār al-Sunna* and Republican Sisters. Although the latter groups are relatively new to Sudanese society, Independent women preachers have deeper roots in Sudanese life.

Historically, since the fifteenth century Sudanese women were active participants in *khalāwī* (religious seminaries – singular *Khalwa*) as teachers of the Qur'an and Islamic education. Women's *khalāwī* specialized in female education in order to eliminate their religious illiteracy and to teach them elementary religious sciences. Women used to memorize the Qur'an and learn *tartīl* (the art of recitation) and *tajwīd* (perfection of recitation) in addition to some of the Shari'a principles.[12] By the eighteenth century many women preachers were as famous as their male counterparts. Among those preachers were Shaykha bint Ata, Shaykha Rogaia bint Abdul Qadir and Shaykha Khadijah al-Azhari. Khadijah, the sister of Ahmed al-Azhari, was one of the highest ranking *fuqahā* (jurists) in the Sudan during the *Turkiaya* (1820–85). Khadijah and Ahmed were the son and daughter of Sheikh Ismail al-Wali, the founder of the Ismailia Sufi path in Kordofan in western Sudan. Khadijah directed her seminary and provided religious instruction for women in their homes.[13] Other women teachers included Shaykha bint Abd al-Rahim, from the city of El-Obeid in western Sudan, who worked with many other women from the household of the al-Mahdi family and his successor. Besides directing her *Khalwa*, Shayka bint Abd al-Rahim used to visit women in their own homes to educate them.

However, despite the efforts of women like Khadijah and Shaykha, the situation for women was not significantly affected during the Mahdiya (1885–98) period, and the presumption was that women 'were followers of men'. Accordingly, a system was enforced that deprived women of their independence and dictated that they should be protected by men. Nonetheless, women continued their personal efforts to maintain their Islamic educational endeavours.[14] One of the positive outcomes of the women's personal efforts was reflected in the fact that such educational activism helped to establish the basis of women's educational work, as many of the pioneering women received their education from those *khalāwī* sources. The first inspector of girls' education, Mrs Medinah Abdallah, received her elementary education, or part of it, at the hands of Shaykha Khadijah bint wad ab Safiya. And the first Sudanese woman physician, Dr Khalda Zahir, received her elementary education, or part of it, at the *Khalwa* of al-Faki Hassan in the Mourada neighbourhood in Omdurman.[15]

In Eastern Sudan, and by the standards of that early time, a plethora of women's *khalāwī* flourished given that many religious families, including the al-Mirghani family,[16] were settled in that area. The al-Mirghani family and other prominent families in the East were concerned and made sure that 'the Muslim woman learned the basics of her religion'. Hence, they paid utmost attention to women's *khalāwī* and opened several of them after 1890, a move 'which accorded the woman a high status'.[17] This was the basis of a tradition that continued throughout subsequent decades in Eastern

Sudan. In 1945, a group of women, including Zeinab Muhammad Ahmed, Khadijah Omer Kashoi and Hania Ibrahim, established women's *khalāwī* that are still in operation in such cities as Toker, Port Sudan and Sawakin. In 1950 a group of the Eastern Sudanese Hadandwa tribe, led by Sheikh Ali Bitai, was active in establishing women's *khalāwī* in the regional city of Aroma.

Unfortunately, the concept of the *Khalwa* itself, as a form of national education in general, faced not only negligence but was also fought by the colonial British administrators. Such antagonism and inattention were reflected in different forms as a way to discourage them, including the refusal to pay salaries or to support those who maintained *khalāwī*. Other forms involved 'the shutting down of some of the *khalāwī* based on weak justifications, simultaneously activating Christian missionaries and establishing a sub-grade school system to totally eliminate the *khalāwī*.[18] However, in 1938 with the establishment of the Sudanese Graduate Congress, some of these *khalāwī* were re-established in a clear reaction to the British government and in an attempt to strengthen national work and the activities of women's *khalāwī*.[19]

To contextualize Sudanese resistance against colonial attempts to eliminate the *khalāwī*, and Sudanese efforts to claim a space of autonomy of the mind, it is interesting to look at arguments made by scholars in the field of 'subaltern studies'.[20] Post-colonial approaches regarding tensions between private and public spaces in colonial India examine how the private space, a space of female power, have held on to traditions and religion as a form of autonomy. To better understand the structure of class relations in India, subaltern studies focus on the undefined label of citizens. Post-colonial scholars, such as Gyanendra Pandey and Partha Chatterjee, have discussed the way in which gender and race have served as the basis for and have infused class differentiation. Focussing on gender differences, women in particular were deprived of privileges that were accessible to their male counterparts. Specifically, due to the historic division of labour prevalent in India, women were relegated to roles within the household and denied opportunities to participate in public society, particularly the opportunity to get an education. In this sense, there was a separation between private and public spaces.[21] From this perspective, Sudanese women can be identified as 'subalterns'; they had to find ways to gain and help other women achieve an education and become literate as the discussion has shown.

The Islamic educational tradition continued throughout the centuries, and today a good number of female preachers are active participants in daily preaching in Sudanese society. Leila Sayyed Khidr – aka Leila Jābir (b. 1938) – is an independent preacher in Khartoum who began preaching in mosques in 1980. Khidr holds a Bachelors degree in psychology from Cairo University, Egypt. She preaches in four major mosques, seven times a week, in the affluent 'Amārat and Riyād neighbourhoods of Khartoum. She began her preaching in discussion groups with only a few women in attendance. Over the years an increasing number of women began attending her sermons, and she moved to bigger mosques to accommodate larger audiences. Khidr related that her decision to become a preacher followed a severe illness she suffered that confined her to bed for over a year. It was during that time that she began reading religious texts and became deeply inspired by them. She is critical of 'doom and gloom' preachers who tend to frighten women. Her intention is to make women more aware of their rights under Islam and to instruct them in their duties in a positive tone. These women's detractors are often criticized for being non-specialists in the religious sciences and, therefore, not being qualified to preach. Their defence is that they are only preachers, and they do not issue *fatwa* on matters of juristic *fiqh* (Islamic jurisprudence).[22]

The second category of women preachers revolves around the Islamist Muslim Brotherhood movement. 'Ā'isha al-Ghabshāwī (b. 1947) is a well-known religious scholar/preacher in Sudan. She received a PhD in 1986 in Theology and Islamic Philosophy from Omdurman Islamic University, Sudan, where she is currently Professor of Islamic Studies. Al-Ghabshāwī gives lessons to women's groups on subjects related to religion and life. Her lessons, which began in the 1970s, were initially given in response to invitations she received from various women's groups. She then started her public appearances on Sudan's national TV when she interviewed the late

Egyptian Islamist, Zeinab al-Ghazali, in 1978. Al-Ghabshāwī then began her own TV show, 'The Muslim Family', that aired for ten years. In 2000 she began anchoring her new TV programme, *Risālah Khāssa* (A Special Message), that continued until 2004 when it was transformed into a TV lecture series entitled *Majālis al-Humairā* (Councils of *al-Humairā*). The new programme included segments on advising women on social issues such as marriage, raising children and family life. Other women Islamist preachers/scholars include: Suad al-Fatih, member of the National Congress ruling party; Umm Kulthum Ismail, dean of the College of Family Studies and Society Development at the University of Sudan; Fatima Abdul Rahman, Dean of the Students Centre of Qur'an University in Omdurman; and Fathiya Mirghani, professor at Omdurman Islamic University.

It is worth noting that the women mentioned above have been considered as part of the current Islamist regime that assumed power in the Sudan on 30 June 1989 through a military coup that overthrew a democratically elected government. Some questions may legitimately be raised regarding the manipulation by the regime of these women to serve the regime's agenda. Al-Ghabshāwi and some of these women have turned a blind eye to the atrocities the regime has committed against not only women, but the Sudanese people at large. The oppressive nature of the Sudanese regime and the crimes it has committed against the people of the Sudan across the country have been widely documented by the United Nations, and international Human Rights organizations such as Amnesty International and Human Rights Watch. Further, the regime is primarily accused of overthrowing the democratically elected government to stop a serious peace process that would have halted the war in southern Sudan.[23] The logical criticism that should be addressed to the Islamist women leaders of this group concerns their failure to use their knowledge of Islam to foster peace and peaceful coexistence. Instead, these women continue to follow the political agenda of the ruling party that has clearly been acting against Islamic principles of peace.

The third group of Sudanese female Qur'an instructors and preachers is the *Ansār al-Sunna*, to which Mariam 'Abbādi (b. 1954) belongs. 'Abbādi gives lessons on Islamic studies to women's groups in their homes in the Khartoum North neighbourhoods. Having studied *tartīl* and *tajwīd* in Saudi Arabia, she focusses on teaching women how to correctly recite the Qur'an and to avoid making mistakes in pronunciation.[24] However, some professional members of this group, especially some female medical doctors, have been engaged in such practices as female genital[25] circumcision (FC) in the Sudan. One well-known medical doctor (name withheld) is widely known for using her practice to perform FC on five- and six-year-old girls, with the consent of their families, in a clear violation of these girls' human rights. Although FC has been banned in the Sudan since 1946, it has been performed illegally since then. To add insult to injury, the Islamist regime recently made legal what they erroneously call '*Sunna* FC' and falsely claiming an Islamic basis for this act, which has further encouraged these medical doctors to openly practice this heinous crime. Neither the Qur'an nor the authentic *Hadith* spoke of FC, apart from a discredited unauthentic *Hadith* narrative that was published. Such practices are clearly a form of violence against innocent children based on harmful and inhumane traditions.[26]

The fourth category of female preachers developed as part of the Republican Brotherhood movement. Mahmoud Muhammad Taha established the Republican Brothers Party in 1945. However, women did not become active preachers until the 1970s when *al-Akhwāt al-Jumhūriyāt* (the Republican Sisters) was formed and 'women members participated fully in all [...] activities' through their roles as leaders of activist groups on university campuses, public parks and even street corners preaching and distributing party booklets.[27] However, the execution of Taha in 1985 by the military rule of Ja'far Nimeiri was a severe blow to the party and both its male and female activism.

A question that arises is how can the women who are involved in Islamic education for peace move from theory to practice. In other words, how can they use their knowledge of the principle of peace in Islam and their educational experiences to help their society move from conflict and war to reconciliation and peace? As previously noted, a significant point that is worth considering relates to my critique of Sudanese political parties' manipulation of some of their female members to serve the party agenda, which does not necessarily focus on women's issues. Further investigations should be sought of why these women continue to allow this manipulation. Having said that, it is very important to discuss all this in a separate project within the historical context of the political situation in the Sudan given the fact that the country has not only been afflicted by the longest civil war on the African continent, but also by subsequent dictatorial regimes that continue to hamper attempts for peace.

Nonetheless, it is worth noting that the peace agreement signed by general Nimeiri in Addis Ababa in 1972 with Southern Sudanese rebels secured self-determination for the South, through which the war stopped and the South enjoyed peace for ten years. Ironically, the same dictator rescinded and repealed that agreement when he conspired and collaborated with the National Islamic Front (NIF) – the name of the Muslim Brotherhood then – to implement his distorted version of Shari'a laws in September 1983, and war broke out again. Sentiments of rejection against Nimeiri were on the rise until he was ousted by a popular uprising on 6 April 1985. The country then witnessed democratic elections, and the Sudanese people freely voted in a democratic government that lasted only three years, and until Omer al-Bashir, the current Sudanese dictator, supported by the NIF overthrew that democratically elected government through a military coup that implemented the longest dictatorial and brutal rule in the history of the Sudan (24 years; 30 June 2013). It is this regime that has witnessed the ongoing separation of the South and has instigated the ongoing bloody and ugly situation in Darfur.

In the midst of this complex situation, would any of the theoretical female frameworks discussed above work? Before addressing this question, it is important to look at another African scene in Nigeria in relation to women and peace-building.

Nigeria: Nana Asma'u

Nana Asma'u (1793–1864) was the daughter of 'Osman dan Fodio, who established the Sokoto Caliphate following several battles and tribal conflicts in what is currently known as Nigeria. The Sokoto Caliphate was one of the most influential kingdoms in the northern part of the African Sudanic Belt of the time. Asma'u was an example of a highly-educated woman who was considered a leading scholar in the Islamic sciences of the Qur'an and *Hadith*. Most importantly, Asma'u used her knowledge of Islam's original sources to educate women of the conflicting tribes against violence and to foster a culture of peace following the Fulani Jihad (1804–10) when Dan Fodio defeated his enemies. Another tool that Asma'u skilfully used in her instruction of both men and women in the Caliphate was her remarkable collection of poetry. As Beverly Mack and Jean Boyd have documented, Asma'u was quite influential and played a major role in the field of women's education when she organized groups of female instructors and teachers that travelled throughout the country to educate women.[28] These *Jaijis*, the local name for such teachers, employed Asma'u's writings and books of verses in addition to other Sufi manuscripts to train women of all tribes, conquered and victorious, in a culture of peaceful coexistence. Based on this well-established educational tradition, Asma'u eventually became a model for African women in the fields of education, poetry and peace-building.

As was the case with her family, Nana Asma'u was a Sunni Muslim who was raised as a follower of the *Qadriyya* Sufi order (founded by Abdul Qadir al-Jeilani of Baghdad (d. 1166)). Records on her Fulani family indicate that they had been Muslim scholars for at least ten generations. As traditionally known with *Sufis* in general and with the *Qadriyya* order in particular, material life and comfort were not part of their primary concerns. Asma'u's views of the world were hence shaped by classical Islamic education that transcended the traditional education of memorizing the Qur'an. Her education included a rigorous programme of study that was comprised of Islamic philosophical texts on prayer, *Sufism*, legal issues and *fiqh* that deals with religious behaviour and conduct in addition to *Tawhid* or monotheism. Islam thus constituted the foundation of Asma'u's experience where she learned from her family's library of hundreds of handwritten manuscripts on Islamic studies as well as her own poetry. She eventually maintained her family's aim in teaching and transmitting Islamic knowledge to subsequent generations.[29]

Through education, this wealth of Islamic knowledge helped Asma'u deal with the tribal conflicts that her community was afflicted with.[30] Inspired by her father's devotion to Islam and the Prophet's *Sunna*, Asma'u's personal and peaceful jihad focussed on preserving all that her people held, which constituted the backbone and basis for her efforts towards reconciliation, peaceful coexistence and the education of women as primary mentors of subsequent generations. In addition to being a gifted woman in Islamic and poetic studies, Asma'u's linguistic skills (based on her being well-versed in major languages such as Arabic, Hausa and Greek, among other local dialects) earlier encouraged her family to entrust her with the organization of her father's volumes of manuscripts following his death. It also significantly helped Asma'u in playing a major role in assembling his library, which she eventually used as a rich resource to educate women and other members in her community.[31] The training and education of these women in the principles of Islamic teaching on peace instilled in them a strong belief of peace that played an important part of reconciling the conflicting tribes. Instilling those principles of peace was also made easier by Asma'u's Sufi and pious qualities that rendered her personality admirable among her people. Her charismatic nature complimented her literary, linguistic and poetic skills, which together made her instruction quite effective. Accordingly, Asma'u became a famous teacher not only among the Muslim scholars of her community and beyond, but she was the beloved of the ordinary, as well as, the uneducated villagers. At such a grassroots-level, the great admiration Asma'u enjoyed among the villagers stemmed from her ability to communicate with them in languages and dialects they could understand and comprehend easily. As Mack and Boyd have commented:

In addition to religious instruction and enlightenment, Asma'u's poetic works offered views on recent history, with which they were familiar, and practical tools for their participation in a community newly unified under Islam.[32]

An interesting aspect of her instruction that appealed particularly to women was the clear absence of gender bias in Asma'u's teaching. In keeping with the percepts of *Sufism* relating to the equity of the position of men and women, she emphasized the belief that 'the soul has no gender', despite the fact that in later and other works she focussed on the importance of women's unique roles, where appropriate.[33] Such a significant awareness has only surfaced recently in the scholarship of Muslim American feminist scholar Amina Wadud, as is discussed within the course of this chapter.

Thus, Asma'u's role and place in a society torn apart by warfare was the respected teacher who aimed to unify a community with diverse cultural backgrounds through a religious philosophy that emphasized and encouraged the obligation to practice generous social welfare and the education of every soul regardless of gender or social position. She drew attention to what Islam had to say about peace. Largely, Asma'u's teaching sent beacons of knowledge throughout society. The messages it carried promised the dissemination of education, and mutual aid aimed at attaining a higher knowledge of Islam, whose very name is a celebration of peace.[34]

Given this early awareness of Islamic knowledge in general, and on peace in particular, it becomes quite ironic to see grave misinterpretations in Northern Nigeria today among several groups including Boko Haram and others with their severe abuse of women in the name of Shari'a and Islam.

Recent Female Scholarship on Education and Peace in Islam

To address the earlier question of new approaches and methods that are required and needed and to understand and evaluate women's agency in peace-building politically, socially and in everyday life, it is useful to look at some recent studies by Muslim American female scholars who emphasize Islamic education as a possible approach towards effecting positive and peaceful change in Muslim societies. Syrian American scholar Nimat Hafez Barazangi has suggested one such model through her 'Self-Learning of Islam' (S-LI) educational project that she proposed in her book, *Women's Identity and the Qur'an: A New Reading*.[35] The central issue in Barazangi's argument is reflected in her questions. She asks why the authority to interpret 'religious' texts has been exclusive to male religious elites? She believes that nothing will change the condition of Muslim women and the Muslim society, unless the authority to interpret the Qur'an is equal among men and women. Her strategy to achieve this objective is manifested in her proposal of S-LI's curricular framework as a means of self-realization and self-identity grounded in the Qur'an. Barazangi's stated purpose is not only to speak in a Muslim/feminist voice, but also 'to create a new venue for exploring and engaging the sources of Islamic education and Islamic higher learning within the framework of the Qur'anic mandate and call to self-identity'.[36] Her work also attempts to stimulate discussion about the Qur'an in the community as a whole. Within her discussion of what she perceives as educational objectives and the framework of learners' needs and interests, Barazangi advocates an approach based on interest 'such as a current event, in the form of a problem or an issue that begged a solution or a discussion'.[37] This is in contrast to the mere accumulation of facts, unsynthesized and unconsidered. She focusses on engaging the mind and spirit in intellectual discourse as she believes that 'Muslim women who are trying to recapture their own agency in the textual interpretation process need to move one step farther'.[38] Such agency, Barazangi believes, is linked to the notion of autonomous morality in Qur'anic terms. Within her pedagogical redefinition of Islamic religio–morality and its potential impact on Muslim attitudes towards women's morality and education, Barazangi critically analyses the works of three Muslim women scholars: 'A'isha 'Abd al-Rahman, Amina Wadud and Aziza al-Hibri. She maintains that the lack of leadership initiative in affirming a woman's autonomous religio–morality, as represented in the works of these women, contributes to the separation between the formative and perceptive, even when these women discuss the favourable Qur'anic status of women. Barazangi sees these women as succumbing to the 'interpretation of complementarities', and she argues that this reflects their 'unwillingness to question the prevailing social structure, or their inability to self-identify with the Qur'an in a pedagogical sense'. Moreover, the Qur'anic assertion that the female is an autonomous moral being with a direct relationship with God as her only guardian should not be compromised but asserted even if it leads to controversy. Only then, Barazangi maintains, can the Qur'anic social revolution involving gender justice be practiced.

We have already seen examples of women moving 'one step farther', as was the case with Nana Asma'u in a nineteenth-century African situation. While Barazangi's model of 'Self-Learning of Islam' is largely theoretical as it seems to be addressed to highly educated women engaged in the task of interpreting the Qur'an, moving from theory to practice is what will not only effect change in the society, but motivate women to play a role using their knowledge of the theological and social principles of peace in Islam to help members of their communities negotiate and practice peaceful coexistence.

Clearly, the issue of Muslim–American women's discussion on education becomes particularly important to this study within the context of the two African examples that I have addressed above. It is also significant given the current conflict between religion and culture in most of these Muslim societies, especially in areas of conflict and war. This discrepancy is largely blamed on a misinterpretation of Islam and specifically the Qur'an. Amina Wadud's discussion on the misinterpretation of the Qur'an is crucial to this study. She discusses three categories generally used to interpret women's rights in the Qur'an: traditional, reactive and holistic. She argues that traditional *tafsir* (interpretation) provides construal of the entire Qur'an, from classical to modern times, with specific objectives in mind: legal, historical, grammatical, rhetorical or esoteric. However, while *tafsir* may be different based on each of these objectives, all objectives share an atomistic methodology. This includes interpreting each verse of the Qur'an separately beginning with the first and ending with the last. What Wadud sees as problematic of this particular traditional interpretation is that neither does it look at the Qur'an thematically nor discuss in detail the relationship between these Qur'anic verses. Given that this *tafsir* was written exclusively by male interpreters, only men's perspectives and experiences were taken into consideration to the exclusion of women's experiences and perspectives. A major point that Wadud draws attention to is that the lack of women's voices, in this context, is perceived as female voicelessness reflected in the Qur'an itself.[39]

The second category of the Qur'an's interpretation that Wadud discusses is the reactive interpretation. This is primarily expressed by some modern scholars who may be opposed to Islam in general or the Message of the Qur'an, in particular, and who use the poor status of women in some Muslim societies as justification for their negative reactions. She maintains that such reactive understandings have also failed to draw a distinction between text and interpretation. Wadud further argues that although some feminist ideals and rationale might contribute to this reactive interpretation, this can be overcome through the demonstration of the link between liberation and the primary source of Islamic theology.[40]

The last category discussed by Wadud is the 'holistic interpretation' that reconsiders the whole method of Qur'anic exegesis with respect to different social, economic, moral and political concerns, including the issue of women. It is on this category of interpretation, which is relatively modern, that Amina Wadud grounds her book, *Qur'an and Woman: Rereading the Sacred from a Woman's Perspective*.[41]

In the absence of an interpretation of the Qur'an that emphasizes gender equity, one of the most shocking events that took place at the closing of the twentieth century occurred when the former Taliban of Afghanistan came to power during the early 1990s.[42] The first action widely documented that the radical extremist group did was to close girls' schools throughout the country and to deprive the entire population of women of their legitimate right to education. Although the Taliban example was extreme, it is by no means unique. The irony is that those who commit such acts claim that their decision to deprive women of education is based on Islam; hence, the irony demonstrates importance of these women's scholarship and activism to correct such grave misconceptions. However, such claims are easily refuted by numerous examples in the Islamic tradition both from the Qur'an and *Hadith*.[43]

The efforts of such women as Nana Asma'u and the early Sudanese women religious scholars discussed are deeply rooted in the Qur'anic tradition of supporting women's attainment of knowledge. The juxtaposition alluded to earlier also resides in the fact that the experiences and works of many of the women discussed in this chapter cannot be separated, in a broader sense, from how feminist criticism in Islam aims to deconstruct patriarchal interpretation of women's roles in Islam. Despite the historical gap between the works of such early women religious scholars as Nana Asma'u and the early Sudanese examples, on the one hand, and the works and scholarship of such recent Muslim feminist scholars as Nimat Hafez Barazangi and Amina Wadud, on the other hand, the parallel is unmistakable given that they all emphasize the identity of women, promote women's issues/education and demand rights for women rooted in the religion rather than borrowed from other traditions. As Margot Badran has noted in her insightful article, 'Feminism and the Qur'an', 'in developing their feminist discourses, women have looked to the Qur'an as Islam's central and most sacred text, calling attention to its fundamental message of social justice and human equality and to the rights therein granted to women'.[44]

These important studies can open greater avenues for women from around the world to direct their education towards emphasising a culture of peace and to share their experiences on how to move from conflict and war to reconciliation and peace. They also instruct on how to further instil concepts, beliefs and themes of social justice and solidarity, and to simultaneously acknowledge and value these peaceful means while reducing the negative impact of harmful cultural and traditional practices on the society. Principles of democracy, tolerance and openness are obvious prerequisites for a successful implementation of these endeavours.

Notes

1. Nimat Hafez Barazangi, *Women's Identity and the Qur'an: A New Reading* (Gainesville: University Press of Florida, 2004), pp. 86–111.

2. Faiza Mushtaq, 'Al-Huda and its critics: Religious education for Pakistani women', *ISIM Review: International Institute for the Study of Islam in the Modern World* Vol. 22 (2008), p. 30.

3. Patrick Hällzon, 'The Gülen movement: Gender and practice', *Gülen Conference in Washington* (15 November 2008). Available at http://fgulen.com/en/gulen-m ovement/conference-papers/gulen-conference-in-washington/26438-the-gulen-movement-gender-and-practice (accessed 13 July 2013).

4. It is worth noting that, in attempting to answer the question of how peace can be understood in an Islamic context, the US Institute of Peace scholar, Qamar-ul Huda, suggests that four interrelated contexts be considered, including the metaphysical-spiritual where peace (as one of the names of God) is seen as an essential part of creation and assigned substantive values. Another context is the philosophical-theological, within which the question of evil is addressed as a cosmic, ethical and social problem. Other contexts discussed by Qamar-ul Huda focus on the political–legal, the proper locus of classical legal and juristic discussions of war, rebellion, oppression and political order/disorder; and the sociocultural context that reveals the parameters of the Muslim experience of religious and cultural diversity in communities of other faiths and cultural traditions. See Qamar-ul Huda (ed), *Crescent and Dove: Peace and Conflict Resolution in Islam* (Washington, DC: US Institute of Peace Press, 2010).

5. As a background to understanding the concept of peace in Islam, it is important to mention that, linguistically, the root of the Arabic word Islam is *silm*, which denotes the English meaning of peace. The word Islam also means submission to the will of God and peace to all humanity. Several verses in the Qur'an discuss and promote peace including, '*Let there be no compulsion in religion*' (Q 2:256). In addition, in the context of dealing with the enemy, in a war or conflict situation, the Qur'an states, '*And if they {the enemy} incline towards peace, do thou {also} incline towards peace, and trust in Allah, for He is the One who hears and knows best*' (Q 8:61). Similarly, the concept of peace runs in the Prophetic *Hadith* tradition, which is the second source of Islamic Law after the Qur'an. For example, the Prophet Muhammad is quoted to have advised his followers to salute people of all faiths with peace before beginning any discussion, '*al-Salaam Qabl al-Kalam*' (Peace before Speech).

6. Souad T. Ali, 'Religious practices: Preaching and women preachers (Sudan)', *Encyclopedia of Women and Islamic Cultures*, Vol. 5 (Leiden: Brill Academic Publishers, 2007), p. 346.

7. Plural *Ahādīth*.

8. Leila Ahmed, *Women and Gender in Islam: Historical Roots of a Modern Debate* (New Haven: Yale University Press, 1992), p. 73.

9. M. A. Wad Daiffalla, *Kitāb al-Tabaqātfī Khusūs al-Awliā al-Salihīnwa al-'Ulamāwa al-Shu'arāfī al-Sudan* [The Book of Stratifications of Holy People, Scholars, and Poets in Sudan], 3rd edn (Khartoum: University of Khartoum Press, 1985), p. 46.

10. It is important here to explain that the concept of jihad in Islam primarily reflects the meaning of struggle, striving and exertion; a just war in self-defence. Jihad, however, has largely been misinterpreted by Westerners and some radical Muslims as 'war against non-Muslims'.

11. Beverly B. Mack and Jean Boyd, *One Woman's Jihad: Nana Asma'u Scholar and Scribe* (Bloomington: Indiana University Press, 2000), p. 6.

12. Haja Kāshif-Badri, *Al-Haraka al-Nisā'iyyafī al-Sudan* [The Women's Movement in Sudan] (Khartoum: University of Khartoum Press, 1984), p. 58. (The original texts were in Arabic, and all English translations from this text are mine.)

13. Ibid., pp. 7–8.

14. Ibid., p. 8.

15. Ibid.

16. In reference to Muhammad Uthman al-Mirghani (1793–1853), founder of the Khatimiyya Sufi path in Sudan.

17. Kāshif-Badri, *Al-Haraka*, p. 59.

18. Ibid., pp. 58–9.

19. Ibid., p. 50.

20. To understand Subaltern Studies and how the term was created, it's important to note that the term 'subaltern' was created from the word 'proletariat'. Famous Italian writer and politician, Antonio Gramsci, while imprisoned for allegedly attempting to take Mussolini's life, wrote about the proletarian class. However, because he was confined behind prison walls, his writing was censored and the term 'subaltern' was implemented to replace 'proletariat'. Gramsci, a very important Marxist thinker during the twentieth century, focused on cultural analysis. While in prison he was writing about the subaltern class division in Italy at the time; however, this was very relevant to the class separation then and now in India. Similar to the situation in Italy, much of India was divided between industrial workers and agrarian farmers. See Moyukh Chatterjee, 'Reflecting on 30 years of subaltern studies: Conversations with Professors Gyanendra Pandey and Partha Chatterjee', *Cultural Anthropology Online* (1 December 2011). Available at http://www.culanth.org/curated_collections/6-subaltern-studies/discussions/14-reflecting-on-30-years-of-subaltern-studies-conversations-with-profs-gyanendra-pandey-and-partha-chatterjee (accessed 5 June 2012).

21. Ibid.

22. Ali, 'Religious practices', p. 347.

23. A few months before this regime staged its military coup in 1989, a major Peace Agreement had been signed by the Southern Party, the Sudan People's Liberation Movement (SPLM), the political wing of the Sudan People's

Liberation Army – that was fighting for the freedom of Southern Sudan – and one of the major political parties in the northern part of the country, the Democratic Unionist Party (DUP). The remarkable Peace Agreement was signed by the two leaders of the SPLM, the late John Garang, and Muhammad Uthman al-Mirghani, the leader of the DUP. Although the southern problem had existed since before the independence of the Sudan in 1956 and continued unresolved throughout subsequent governments after independence, this Islamist regime introduced an offensive, so-called 'jihad' war against the South that was unprecedented in the history of the Sudan.

24. Ali, 'Religious practices', pp. 346–7.
25. Although Female Circumcision, an ancient Egyptian/African harmful act is coined in Western literature as "Female Genital Mutilation (FGM)", Muslim activists utterly reject using FGM as a Western imposition that they find provocative and hindering their campaigns to eliminate and eradicate this brutal act.
26. The *Ansār al-Sunna* group, for the most part, has focused on the *Hadith* more than the Qur'an.
27. An-Na'im (1987), p. 6.
28. Mack, *One Woman's Jihad*.
29. Ibid., pp. 6–7, 9.
30. Several verses in the Qur'an discuss and promote peace, see footnote 5.
31. Mack, *One Woman's* Jihad, pp. 46–7.
32. Ibid., p. 61.
33. Ibid., p. 81.
34. Ibid., p. 11.
35. Nimat Hafez Barazangi and her 'Self-Learning of Islam' educational project that she proposed in Barazangi, *Women's Identity in the Qur'an*.
36. Barazangi, *Women's Identity in the Qur'an*, p. 18.
37. Ibid., p. 100.
38. Ibid., p. 105.
39. Amina Wadud, *Qur'an and Woman: Rereading the Sacred from a Woman's Perspective* (New York: Oxford University Press, 1999), pp. 1–2.
40. Ibid., p. 2.
41. Ibid., p. 3.
42. Souad T. Ali, 'Women in Islam and civil society: An overview of the disparity between religion and culture', in Sibel Halimi (ed), *A Lecture on Gender Issues* (Prishtina: Kosovar Centre for Gender Studies, 2009), p. 109.
43. Examples include Qur'an 96:1–6 among several other verses promoting education, and *Hadith* narratives such as: 'seek knowledge from the cradle to the grave'.
44. Margot Badran, 'Feminism and the Qur'an', in *The Encyclopedia of the Qur'an*, Vol. 2 (Leiden: Brill, 2002), pp. 199–203.

PART 3

FORMATIONS: ENGENDERING PEACE DIALOGUES

CHAPTER 7

IN PURSUIT OF PEACE: MUSLIM WOMEN'S INVOLVEMENT IN PEACE-BUILDING

S. Ayse Kadayifci-Orellana

Peace-building is a long and complex process involving many different segments of the society. Women's engagement and full participation in all aspects of society, including peace-building, is fundamental in this process. Today, many women in Muslim majority countries such as Egypt, Palestine, Afghanistan, Kenya, Yemen, Somalia and Iraq, among others, are taking up proactive roles in response to conflicts and working toward establishing just and peaceful societies. Despite formidable challenges and social inequalities, these women have been working tirelessly to address conflicts and build peace. Although each conflict is unique with its own history, issues and dynamics, they often create space for women to assume new roles in their societies.[1] While some women become victims of these conflicts, others take up hands-on roles in response to what they experience. In many cases becoming breadwinners in their families, women are more involved in making decisions and finding ways to address trauma and resolve conflicts.

Muslim women are playing critical peace-building roles either by organizing to stop violence and end the conflict, by reaching out to the 'other', by rebuilding relationships, by healing the wounds of others in their societies, by addressing the needs of the widows, orphans and other victims of war, or educating women and girls. They are active as both founders and leaders of civil society organizations and advocates for peace. Each woman has different experiences, needs and concerns and often faces significant challenges. The experiences of women during conflicts frequently lead them to develop unique approaches to address the needs of their communities.

While their context, needs and priorities may differ, peace-building efforts of women in Muslim communities also share certain characteristics. By examining these characteristics through case studies and stories of women this chapter will explore their strengths, highlight success stories and discuss challenges women in the Muslim world face in their efforts to build just and peaceful societies. In addition to contributing to a scholarly understanding of these efforts, this analysis will also support more effective and productive partnerships and cooperation among Muslim women, as well as inform external actors who are interested in supporting their work.

Muslim Women Peace-Builders

Women's active participation and leadership during the uprisings of 2011 in the Arab World shed a new light on the role Muslim women play in peace-building. From Tunisia to Egypt to Yemen, women were the organizers, the protesters and the leaders.[2] Tired of unjust social, economic and political systems and oppressive regimes, they called for transformation of their societies. One such woman is Tawakkul Karman of Sanaa, Yemen, who, for her role in the non-violent struggle for peace, democracy, human rights and justice in 2011, was the first Arab Muslim woman to receive the Nobel Prize.[3] Karman is a journalist, a human rights activist and a prominent leader in her community. Karman founded the Women Journalists Without Borders and published the Semi-Annual Press Freedom Report on violence against journalists in Yemen. Despite the fact that she was arrested many times, she adamantly criticized widespread corruption and killing of civilians, and as a journalist continued to report human rights abuses in her country. She also organized weekly sit-ins and led rallies protesting unjust policies of the government during the Yemeni uprisings.

Although Karman is one of the most well-known Muslim women peace activists today, she is neither the only one nor the first one. Women's involvement in the Muslim world dates back to the formative years of Islam, and throughout centuries women have taken up active roles to further peace and justice in their communities.[4] More recent times, women like Asmaa Mahfouz and Israa Abdel Fettah of Egypt, Lina Ben Mhenni and Radhia Nasraoui of Tunisia, Najla Emmangoush and Amina Mogrebi of Libya, Dekha Ibrahim of Kenya, or Ibtisam Mahameed of Palestine, Soraya Jamhjuree of Thailand and Asha Hagi of Somalia, among many others, have long worked to build a more peaceful world, inspired and motivated by their faith. As founders or key players in civil society organizations, these women continue to inspire and become role models for other women in their communities and beyond.

Each of these women has significantly different experiences, needs, opinions and priorities, and they respond to their unique social, historical, political and cultural contexts. Despite these differences, it is possible to identify various common characteristics of peace-building efforts of women in the Muslim world. It is worthwhile to analyse these characteristics as they shed light on the strengths and successes of their efforts.

Characteristics of Muslim Women Peace-Builders

1. Islam as a Source of Inspiration

Many Muslim activists argue that Islam emerged as a revolutionary movement that aimed to emancipate both men and women from oppressive systems.[5] They argue that Islam was the first Abrahamic religion to articulate and ensure women's right to divorce, right to inherit, right to choose their own husband and right to participate in social, political and economic life, among others. Focussing on the religious texts, scholars argue that Islam clearly emphasizes social justice and peace. Familiarity with this content provides a basis for understanding women's actual, as well as potential, contributions to peace-building in Muslim societies.

Islamic sources such as the Holy Qur'an and *Hadith* are the main sources of legitimacy in Muslim communities, providing criteria for what is moral conduct and for what relations are permitted. It is important to note that there are a variety of different interpretations among Muslim women, some more progressive and others more conservative. While the secular nationalists address women's rights within the frameworks of modernization and secularization, many religiously motivated women seek to steer a course between emulation of Western societies, and a reactive celebration of 'pure' traditional norms deriving their legitimacy from these Islamic sources.[6] Islamic texts provide a moral compass and inspire women to work for peace while providing the legitimacy to challenge unjust systems and patriarchal structures. In fact, armed with Islamic teachings and inspired by the countless role models throughout history, Islamic texts are reclaiming a space of authority to promote principles of justice, equality and peace in their communities.[7] For example, Zainah Anwar, the project director of the *Musawah* (Equality) movement for justice in the Muslim family stated at the 'Global Meeting for Equality and Justice in the Muslim Family' that 'we are here because we believe that Islam upholds the principles of equality and justice. We are here because we believe that there is hope and possibility to reconcile the teachings of Islam with human rights, with women's rights, with democracy'.[8]

Similarly, locating their work within the Islamic tradition was an important aspect of the Sixth Clan Movement. Elmi and others in the movement effectively utilized Islamic texts and history, and consciously avoided connections to feminist movements. Women involved in the movement also had very high levels of Islamic education and knew the Shari'a quite well. Thus, they were able to vehemently reject any language that contradicted Islam during discussions and meetings. They chose to adhere to the Islamic code of conduct and modes of dress.[9] They gained credibility through their religiosity and alliances with moderate Islamic groups. Along with their allied groups, they supported the perspective that adherence to Islam should not be an obstacle to competent women who want to take leadership roles.[10] Opposition groups could not criticize them for lack of religion or for posing a threat to Islamic identity. Additionally, their legal agenda focussed on gaining total equality with men beyond Wahhabi conceptions and the Somali contexts used by *Shafii* jurists.[11]

Sakena Yacoobi, the founder and director of Afghan Institute for Learning (AIL), is another Muslim woman inspired by Islam to rebuild her country. Empowered by her faith, Yacoobi established AIL in Peshawar in 1995, which was the same year the Taliban came into power.[12] This period was particularly restrictive for Afghan women, as the Taliban practiced one of the most radically conservative understandings of Shari'a law in the Muslim world. Yet, AIL persisted and developed programmes focussing on health and education of Afghan women and children.[13] AIL's work includes teacher training programmes, preschool education, advanced classes for children whose education was interrupted by war and violence, women's learning centres and grass-roots community-based support programmes. Additionally, AIL established a university for women and publishes a magazine.[14]

Islamic teachings played a significant role in AIL's work. As a result of strong cultural traditionalism, legitimacy and authority in Afghanistan are based on religion (Islam), tribal codes and customs. Born and raised in Afghanistan, Yacoobi understands that while the culture of Afghan society constrains efforts to improve the status of women, it also provides possibilities for transformation. By teaching women to read the Qur'an, Yacoobi equips her students with the knowledge of Qur'anic principles of equality between men and women and their rights derived from Islam. In addition to teaching women their rights, her programmes include training on how to negotiate on the basis of shared values such as diversity, equality, fairness and justice.[15] She views education as a sacred duty that is consistent with the Islamic emphasis on justice and protection of the poor, weak and needy. She also supports the needs of the oppressed by dedicating herself to attitudinal change through education and working on local development projects that promote hygiene and sanitation. By integrating religious values with her educational priorities, she empowers women to become effective leaders in their communities.

Islamic sources of peacemaking are also a wellspring of inspiration for Soraya Jamjuree – the founder of Friends of Victimized Families and a lecturer at Prince Songklah University in Pattani province of South Thailand. Jamjuree works to establish harmony between Buddhists and Muslims through interfaith dialogue, reconciliation and mediation. Like Yacoobi, Jamjuree derives a strong sense of responsibility from the Islamic principles of vicegerency and justice. She invokes Islamic ideals of forgiveness, apology and compassion to prevent militants from creating hate between Muslims and Buddhists.[16] Jamjuree faces significant threats to her life, but she gains courage and motivation from her faith. She states, 'we believe God will protect us, because we do good things to help the people'.[17]

Basing their arguments on the Islamic texts and the Prophet's examples enables Muslim women to respond to conservative interpretations much more effectively than secular arguments urging democratization and Westernization. Understanding these religious sources is extremely important in transforming current patriarchal and tribal systems that often discriminate against women. Additionally, Islam provides concepts, language and terminology that are familiar and meaningful to Muslims. Therefore, the Islamic framework makes it more meaningful to Muslims and provides sources of legitimacy that empower women to take an active role in the social, political and economic aspects of their societies.

2. Use of Islamic Principles of Peace-Building

Certain fundamental Islamic ethical principles and moral values provide coherence to Muslim peacemaking across cultures and historical periods. Many of these principles continue to inspire Muslim women in their efforts to establish a just and sustainable peace. Key principles and values are derived from the Qur'an, *Hadith* and *Sunnah* (the collections of sayings and actions of the Prophet

Muhammad). While war is permitted under very strict rules to defend a community or to correct an injustice, many verses of the Qur'an and other Islamic sources give preference to values such as peace (e.g. *salam, silm* and *sulh*), forgiveness, patience, compassion, mercy and love. Some of the Islamic principles that play an important role in peacemaking of Muslim women include: *tawhid, fitrah, khilafah, adl, rahmah and rahim, afu, sabr and hubb.*

Tawhid (Principle of Unity of God)

Tawhid is the principle of the unity of God and all beings. It calls for submission to the One who transcends all duality and plurality, and who embraces all diversity and multiplicity.[18] Through the principle of *Tawhid*, Muslims are reminded of the connectedness of all beings. In particular, all human communities are called to work toward establishing peace and harmony amongst themselves. *Tawhid* recognizes unity irrespective of religious, ethnic or racial origin, or gender. It asks Muslims to establish harmony between all of humankind – men and women – based on mutual understanding and cooperation. Hence, it is the basis of Islamic universalism, tolerance and inclusivity as everything emanates from God, and everything is part of His creation.

This principle has been a strong motivator for Muslim women peacemakers such as Jamjuree in her work to promote an understanding between Muslim and Buddhist women in southern Thailand, where 'more than 2300 people have been killed in insurgent violence and government counter-attacks'.[19] Similarly, this principle prompts Cemalnur Sargut, a well-known Muslim sheikha from Turkey, to say to her followers, 'let us unite and let us be committed to spread the message of Allah: of His love, compassion, peace and tranquillity to humanity at large which is now reeling under hatred, violence, wickedness'.[20]

Fitrah (Original Constitution of Human Beings)

Closely linked to *Tawhid, Fitrah* is the original constitution of human beings. According to Islamic tradition, every human being is created in the form and image of God and Divine Names or Qualities, which are manifested in their entirety in the human form.[21] This perspective holds that every human being is created 'innocent, pure, true and free, inclined to right and virtue and imbued with true understanding about [. . .] his [or her] true nature'.[22] *Fitrah* rejects notions of innate sinfulness and recognizes that all humans are related and derive from the same pure origin (Q4:1; 6:98). *Fitrah* recognizes the goodness inherent to each and every human being at birth, regardless of religious, ethnic, racial or gender backgrounds (Q17:70, 95:4, 2:30–34, 33:72). It reminds Muslims that only God knows the heart of a human being. Therefore, he is the only judge (*Hakeem*), and at any point in his/her lifetime, each individual, regardless of his/her actions, has the potential to repent and turn to God. As such, it is a safeguard against dehumanising the 'other'. As Nobel laureateTawakkul Karman noted in her acceptance speech, the Qur'an urges: 'O ye who believe, enter ye into the peace, one and all' and warns that 'whosoever killeth a human being for other than manslaughter or corruption in the earth, it shall be as if he had killed all mankind'. *Fitrah* reminds us that, irrespective of gender, religion or race, all human beings are created in the image of God; therefore, they are all sacred.

Khilafah (Principle of Stewardship)

Meaning stewardship or 'vicegerency', *Khilafah* has been an inspiration for many Muslim peace actors. As vicegerents of God, humans are armed with reason to distinguish between moral choices of right and wrong. It is through faculty of reason that individuals can choose to follow the path of God as stewards on earth and strive to bring justice, harmony and peace, and thus perfect their humanity; or they can choose their egos (*al-nafs*) and follow their own interests.[23] The Women's Shura Council's declaration states, 'as vicegerents of God, we must struggle to make life on earth safe and peaceful, resisting violence in all its manifestations'.[24] According to Islamic theology, each individual is a representative of God on earth (*khilafat Allah fi l-Ard* Q2: 30) and is responsible for the order thereof[25] and for bringing all creatures to equilibrium and harmony.[26] Therefore, irrespective of their gender, ethnicity and race, humans are responsible for the order on earth. Muslim peace-builders such as Sakena Yacoobi of Afghanistan and Soraya Jamjuree of Thailand were inspired by a strong sense of responsibility derived from the Islamic principles of vicegerency to establish a more just and peaceful society.[27]

Adl (Principle of Justice)

Adl, meaning justice, is another key Islamic principle that informs Islamic approaches to peace. A strong sense of justice has been a central tenet of peace for many Muslim women peace-builders because absence of justice is a source of conflict and disorder. In many Qur'anic stories and narratives, God warns believers against oppression and injustice and explicitly urges Muslims to treat everyone fairly as is shown in the verses (Q4:135 and 5:8): 'o ye who believe! Stand out firmly for justice as witnesses to Allah even as against yourselves, your parents or your kin, and whether it be (against) the rich and poor'; and 'to fair dealing, and let not the hatred of others to you make you swerve to wrong and depart from justice. Be just for it is next to piety'. Pursuing justice is not only the responsibility of Muslims as vicegerents of God, but it is also a divinely ordered command.[28] Therefore, every Muslim must pursue justice in order to establish the Islamic ideal of harmony and peace (Q4:135; 57:25; 5:8; 2:178; 2:30; 16:90). This principle is invoked in the preamble of the Women's Islamic Initiative in Spirituality and Equality (WISE), which states that 'justice, fairness and equality are core values of Islam'.[29]

Rahmah and Rahim (Principles of Compassion and Mercy)

The Islamic call for justice is balanced by the twin principles of Rahmah (Compassion) and Rahim (Mercy), which are invoked by every Muslim by reciting 'Bi Ism-i- Allah al-Rahman al-Rahim' (i.e. 'In the name of Allah Who is Compassionate and Merciful') before they take any action. The Qur'an states that God's mercy is infinite and asks Muslims to be forgiving and compassionate to all creatures. For instance, one verse reads, 'to be one of those who believe and urge each other to steadfastness and urge each other to compassion.

Those are the Companions of the Right' (Q90:17–18). The concepts of *Rahmah* and *Rahim* indicate that Muslims cannot be insensitive to the suffering of other beings (physical, economic, psychological or emotional); nor should they be cruel to any creature.[30] Accordingly, a true Muslim must be merciful and compassionate towards all of God's creations, irrespective of external distinctions such as ethnic identity, religious origins or gender.[31] The organization WISE recognizes that peacemaking in Islam seeks compassion, mercy and justice and invokes the Qur'anic verse, 'my mercy extends to everything' (Q7:156) to argue that mercy is rendered as the principle law of all creation.[32] Other Muslim women peacemakers such as Sheikha Sargut, Dekha Ibrahim Abdi and Soraya Jamjuree also emphasize the centrality of *Rahman* and *Rahim* in their work.

Afu (Principle of Forgiveness)

This key Islamic principle of forgiveness is viewed in the Qur'an as more important than maintaining hatred. Believers are urged to forgive when they are angry (Q42:37) and to reconcile (Q42: 40). The Prophet himself demonstrated the centrality of forgiveness when he forgave all those who persecuted and fought him when he entered Mecca, and stated, 'there is no censure from me today on you (for what has happened is done with), may God, who is the greatest amongst forgivers, forgive you'.[33] This attitude of forgiveness was the basis of reconciliation efforts to establish peace between the Muslims and the Meccans, which allowed him to make friends amongst his former enemies, to build up the Islamic community peacefully, and to do away with the desire for revenge.[34] Forgiveness is a central concept for peace and is best reflected by Sheikha Cemalnur Sargut who states that 'Muslims make peace by sharing mercy, love and forgiveness towards themselves and their neighbours'.[35] Thai peacemaker Jamjuree also emphasizes the centrality of forgiveness, apology and compassion in her work to create harmonious and peaceful relations between the Buddhist and Muslim women of South Thailand.[36]

Sabr (Principle of Patience)

Meaning patience, *Sabr* is another important Islamic principle for peace, and has inspired many non-violent resistance movements against oppression and injustice throughout history. Non-violent leaders, like Ghaffar Khan of India in the 1940s and Jawdat Said of Syria today, have argued that *sabr* is the antithesis of violence from an Islamic point of view.[37] *Sabr* was also advised repeatedly to the Prophet Mohammed in the early years of Islam when establishing the community in Medina. During these difficult times, the Prophet and his followers held firmly to truth without retaliating violently or retreating as the ultimate submission to God's will, which is also the true meaning of Islam.[38] The Islamic principle of patience should not be equated with inaction. On the contrary, the Qur'an asks Muslims to work hard and strive to ensure justice for all in active, creative and non-violent ways that would restore harmony amongst God's creations. In this process, justice, compassion, mercy and forgiveness should be central to the way Muslims deal with current problems and conflicts. Dekha Ibrahim Abdi and others have often emphasized patience as a core principle of Islamic peace-building.

Hubb (Principle of Loving Kindness)

Another important principle of peace in Islam is love, as God is love (*Allahu muhibba*). Also, al-Wadud which means 'loving kindness', is one of the 99 names of God. Love is the source and cause of all creation. The source for humans to love one another and all creation is rooted in the loving nature of God Himself. The Sufi poet Rumi alludes to the significance of love in his famous *Mathnawi*, as the attraction that draws all creatures back to reunion with their Creator.[39]

Love comes from God. It is often associated with peace, mercy and forgiveness and is a sign to be reflected upon. For example, the verse Q30: 21 reads:

And among His Signs is this, that He created for you mates from among yourselves, that ye may dwell in tranquillity with them, and He has put love [*mawadda*] and mercy between your [hearts]: Verily in that are Signs for those who reflect.

Transforming enmity into love is a sign of the mercy of God and emphasizes the importance of transforming hostile relations into love and friendship. The verse Q60:7 states that: 'it may be that Allah will grant love (and friendship) [*mawadda*] between you and those whom ye (now) hold as enemies. For Allah has power (over all things); and Allah is Oft-Forgiving, Most Merciful'. Linkages between peace and God's love are also clear in other verses that call for restraining anger, forgiveness and justice – key components of peace according to Islamic tradition (Q3:134; 5:96; 60:8).

The Islamic concept of love has often encouraged Muslim women in their work for peace and justice. For example, Sheikha Cemalnur Sargut stresses in her work the need for love. In one of her inspirational speeches, she summarized the Islamic perspective of peace rooted in Divine Love:

> We should be in a state to forgive and love others, then Allah will not be leaving us alone and He will shower His choicest blessings on us [...]. Let us unite and let us be the one committed to spread the message of Allah; of His love, compassion, peace and tranquillity to humanity at large which is now reeling under hatred, violence, wickedness.[40]

3. Context Specific Approaches to Peace

In the context of modern conflicts, many Muslim women have adjusted their approaches creatively to their particular cultural, historical and political contexts. Even though Islamic values and principles inform peace-building traditions in the Muslim world, local realities push Muslim women to address real-life challenges in new and creative ways. The story of Asha HagiElmi, who played a critical peace-building role in her country of Somalia, is illustrative. Elmi founded and chairs Save Somali Women and Children (SSWC) and the Sixth Clan Movement in Somalia. Established in 1992, SSWC supports women to overcome marginalization, violence and poverty in Somalia. Through empowerment, advocacy, awareness and mobilization, SSWC works to advance women's rights, to help them realize their full potential and to promote child welfare and peace.[41]

The Sixth Clan Movement is a women's political network that strives to include women's voices in the peace process. Founded by Elmi during the Arta Peace Talks in 2000, the Sixth Clan Movement invited women to the negotiation table as equal partners in decision-making. In addition, their work helped establish the Ministry for Gender and Family Affairs. The Sixth Clan was able to secure a 12 per cent quota for the representation of women in the Transitional Federal Parliament and a 30 per cent quota for women in district and regional councils, national commissions, local committees and conferences. The movement also introduced fair gender formatting (he/she) in the charter language. Finally, Elmi became the first woman to be represented in the peace process in Somalia. Elmi's success represents the achievements of Somalian women during the 13 years of civil war. Her achievements are particularly impressive considering the challenges women faced during this period.

Traditional patriarchal practices in Somalia excluded women from economic, social and political power structures and mostly restricted the role of women to the private domain of the home. Although they had some economic power over their property and could voice their opinions in the household, women were excluded from public affairs and official decision-making processes.[42] In the context of Somalia, the obstacles to women's political participation stem from the traditional interpretation of the Jurists and the clan system.[43] As the most influential structure in the society, the clan system was based on a male-dominated system that excluded women.[44] Decision-making power within the clan system was based on respect according to age and gender with older males having more power than younger men and men having more power than women.[45]

The long civil war in Somalia had a detrimental impact on the society, particularly on women, as it destroyed traditional kinship ties.[46] It also shattered traditional household structure, which forced women into the uncharacteristic role of breadwinners.[47] Dissolution of the clan system left women unprotected, and violence against them increased significantly. Frustration from watching the violence and their loved ones fight helplessly led a group of Somali women to join together to provide basic needs for their families. They organized traditional credit and savings schemes called '*shollongo*'.[48] Initially, women from Northern Somalia raised funds to establish and manage a police force to ensure security. The next step was to organize and empower women in peace-building. In their efforts for peace-building, they used various traditional approaches. One key tool, for example, was the traditional poetic verse called '*buranbur*', which was sung by women to show the suffering of women and children during the war.[49] It was important for Somali women like Asha Hagi Elmi to develop a strategy built on Islamic principles and practices. This strategy and their strict adherence to cultural and tribal customs provided them with a platform to engage different religious groups and leaders. Utilizing their family and clan networks, they made alliances with moderate Islamic groups that supported women's participation in decision-making processes. They were effectively and creatively able to use poetry, their clan ties and networks to strengthen their alliances.[50] Eventually, their efforts bore fruit; they gained the trust and respect of the community and were invited to participate in the official peace talks.

Another powerful story relates the efforts of the late Dekha Ibrahim Abdi who founded the Wajir Peace and Development Committee (WPDC) to address the violence that erupted after the 1992 drought in the Wajir District of Kenya. Since they were frustrated by constant violence, arms smuggling, refugee migration, kidnappings and mistrust among clans, Abdi and a group of women invited women from different social strata to discuss the situation. They soon established the Wajir Peace Group, which later became WPDC, with the main objective to restore peace by involving all stakeholders, especially women and youth groups. Through a variety of different approaches, such as interfaith dialogue, forming early warning teams and engaging all stakeholders in the peace process, WPDC has proved quite successful in reducing and preventing violence.

Women for Peace, founded by Dekha Ibrahim Abdi and her colleagues in the Wajir District of Kenya, was born out of necessity as Abdi explains.[51] Their approach creatively combined different strategies to respond to the unique challenges of their context.

In fact, Ibrahim stressed the nature of their approach and stated, '[o]ne has to design context-specific action that is informed by the analysis, but that is also linked to the wider conflict system'.[52] In order to transform the conflict, women in Kenya recognized the need to include all stakeholders in the peace-building process. They invoked traditional Somali laws, which required an entire clan to be involved in resolving a conflict. They made a significant effort to include all warring factions in negotiations to create a sense of ownership of the peace process.[53] Drawing on traditional precedents, they convened peace festivals to publicly honour and financially reward major stakeholders and gave peace awards to police chiefs who had previously incited violence.[54] In this way, the group transformed how some major players viewed their power and legitimacy, which encouraged them to regard themselves as the peacemakers.

Wajir's approach was particularly sensitive to the region's cultural values and was derived from its faith traditions. Traditional Wajir culture accorded women only a minor role in the public sphere. Therefore, although they maintained direct influence, they took specific measures to ensure that male elders and young male leaders of the community were also represented in the leadership of their peace initiative. Similar to the Somalian women's experience, this strategy helped them develop alliances with the men in their communities and gave them credibility. By doing so, their non-violent movement was accepted as mainstream and legitimate.[55] In the long run, however, by providing successful examples of reducing violence and by involving religious leaders and elders, the women of Wajir were able to challenge and change traditional perceptions of women's roles in society and in peacemaking in particular.[56]

4. Informal and Ad Hoc

As a result of various convergent factors, Muslim Women's peace-building efforts are often ad hoc and informal. Some of these factors are a result of the status of Muslim women in their society. Others are a result of organizational differences between Western and Muslim understandings of civil society institutions in general and peace-building institutions in particular.[57] Since Islam influences all aspects of life in Muslim societies, it is usually not possible to separate the religious from the non-religious.[58] Therefore, men and women who work to reduce violence and resolve conflicts may not feel the need to articulate or emphasize the role of Islam in their work. In other cases, they have not organized into particular non-governmental organizations or institutions. Islam nonetheless reinforces their motivation to work towards peace, and Islamic principles and values stated in the Qur'an and *Hadith* are among their key resources for solving conflicts.

Furthermore, even though Muslim communities have old traditions of social services, community assistance and charitable work, they have not typically organized institutions devoted solely to peace-building.[59] Peace work is regarded as a collective responsibility, and those who know the Islamic history and tradition, such as elders and religious leaders, are perceived as natural peacemakers.[60] This view is supported by Abdulaziz Sachedina who states that the Qur'an 'promotes social responsibility and positive bonds between people because of their common ethical responsibility towards one another'.[61]

Resolving conflicts, preventing violence and addressing sources of conflict, such as injustice, are important components of Islamic ethical life and communal responsibility. Traditionally, religious leaders and clergy assume this role as part of their responsibility. As Abu Nimer and Kadayifci-Orellana note:

> Traditionally, ad hoc bodies consisting usually of religious leaders intervene (either upon a request by one of the parties or on their own initiative) to resolve conflicts in their communities both between Muslims and between Muslims and non-Muslims. Often it is the local imam and sheikh who undertake the role of interveners as part of their leadership role and religious obligations.[62]

These individuals often work informally when their services and expertise are required. Peacebuilding organizations in the Western sense, with established staff and offices, are a recent phenomenon.

Absence of established organizations renders informal peace-building actors and their activities invisible.

The situation is compounded for Muslim women who work in the area of peace-building because traditionally women do not have official religious leadership roles. Mainstream definitions of peace that focus on official, governmental peace-building approaches obscure the constructive role women play in peace-building processes. In traditional patriarchal Muslim communities, official negotiation and peacemaking efforts are mostly undertaken by men who occupy official political and religious positions. Although there have been exceptional women, such as Asha Hagi Elmi from Somalia and Amina Rasul from the Philippines, who have participated in the official peace processes, Muslim women's contribution has been mainly at the local community level.[63] One reason is that patriarchal norms and structures tend to hinder women's participation in public decision-making and prevent the recognition of women's participation when it occurs. Especially in religious peacemaking, women are marginalized because Muslim women are rarely recognized as clergy. While there are many influential Muslim women religious and spiritual leaders, religious scholars and woman-led organizations, traditional clergy in the Muslim world is exclusively male. For that reason, religious peacemaking initiatives, such as interfaith dialogues that bring together clergy, rarely include Muslim women leaders.

Since Muslim women's work has been mostly informal and at the community level, their contributions have been largely unrecognized or neglected. Their absence and invisibility have limited their influence in official negotiations and decision-making processes, as well as their ability to impact agendas. Subsequently, formal negotiations and peace processes are shaped by men and rarely reflect women's priorities and concerns. Women do not benefit from financial resources, training opportunities in negotiation, mediation or interfaith dialogue available to men.

Still, Muslim women are becoming more active in civil society and organizing amongst themselves to end violence and injustice in their communities. Since they do not have access to official channels, they tend to create informal, mostly ad hoc, peace-building processes and mechanisms at the grass-roots level. The majority of their work focusses on providing social and economic services and assistance to the needy and marginalized. For example, in Thailand though the present violence between Muslims and Buddhists is a relatively recent phenomenon, militants, mostly from outside the country, have been fighting to create a separate state since 2004. The conflict originates in discriminatory policies of ethnic Thai Buddhist governments in Bangkok since the beginning of the last century[64] and the extremely heavy-handed policies of Prime Minister Thaksin Shinawatra in the 1960s. As a result of this conflict, Buddhist and Muslim families have suffered tremendous losses. Nevertheless, in 2005 Soraya Jamjuree of Thailand founded Friends of Victimized Families.

Supported by the Canadian government, the organization focusses on reconciliation between Muslims and Buddhists.[65] Her work uses an informal approach at the grassroots level – rather than a formal/official reconciliation process – to focus on traumatized families who have lost loved ones, particularly husbands and fathers.[66] The programme aims to build healthy relationships and bonds between Muslims and Buddhists and address the needs of survivors of violence, to improve families' coping skills and to establish a database of victimized people. Jamjuree's goals are to bring together the women from both sides and to reduce their pain and to avoid a vicious cycle of revenge and hate between the two communities. To address the needs of these women and their children, Jamjuree and her student teams visit them at their homes and help them meet their basic needs by bringing them small gifts, food and job opportunities. They also offer psychological and emotional support. The programme now extends to 50 families in the region.

It is important to note that this informality is not seen as an obstacle for Muslim women, but as a strength. In reality, Muslim women have been successful in shaping religious motivations, interpretation and behaviours by putting pressure on religious leaders, and by educating and influencing their families and communities. Women have a significant impact on their children's education and development of their world view. Consequently, women, as mothers, have a greater influence than clerical leaders in the development of their children's perception of other faiths. Since they do not represent a particular faction or group, they are not restricted by political constraints or discourses, allowing them more flexibility in relationship building and giving them more mobility to go to areas where official representatives may not be able to go to.

The experiences of Bilkisu Yusuf – founder of Federation of Muslim Women of Nigeria (FOMWAN), a non-profit and non-governmental civil society umbrella body for Muslim women associations in Nigeria – reflect the ability of women to reach out even within set hierarchies and thus to bring in new ideas:

> For a long time the women of FOMWAN have spoken on behalf of Muslims when there was some issue the government wanted to address, because it was easier to work with us than with the men's organizations, where there is so much bureaucracy they can't respond promptly. The men do not have a rapid response like we have, so the government has turned to us to speak for Muslims [. . .]. The male leaders are under the Supreme Council, the highest Islamic body. The group is led by the Sultan, the emirs and the clerics. Bureaucracy has made them not as effective as they ought to be, and they don't seem to be implementing projects in their communities. All they do is just meet and discuss the sighting of the moon for the month of Ramadan and the start of Eid al-Fitr, and when to break your fast [. . .]. In times of building communities, it is FOMWAN who will look out for you. Increasingly we have been invited to take up positions in government committees and have input into policies, because the government recognizes the work we are doing – building hospitals, addressing development issues, etc.[67]

5. Focus on Relationship Building

Derived from these Islamic principles and values, and adjusted to their unique cultural and political contexts, peace-building efforts undertaken by Muslim women take different forms that include advocacy, intermediary, observation, education, transnational justice and interfaith–intrafaith dialogue.[68] The majority of these efforts have been in relationship building. Even though they may not have access to resources available to male religious leaders and training in specific skills, women rely on the resources and skills they have.

It is likely that the social construction of gendered roles for women as nurturers, care givers and centre of the family endow them with skills central to interfaith dialogue such as sociability, hospitality, empathy, good listening, sensitivity, non-adversarial attitudes, and the ability to create a cooperative atmosphere.[69] As mothers, sisters and wives, they are often expected to play integrative roles in the family to link different points of view and encourage empathy. Thus, they habitually focus on relationship building and bringing parties together. They often understand the needs of widows and orphans, among other victims of war and violent conflict. They are inclined to make use of their informal networks and connections to reach out to women from different groups. They are comfortable working with emotions and many of their efforts focus on healing and addressing traumas. They have, therefore, developed particular communication skills that are helpful, especially in reconciliation and dialogue processes.

Ibtisam Mahameed, founder of Women's Interfaith Encounters (WIE) and a member of Jerusalem Peacemakers, notes that coexistence and dialogue are areas where women have been particularly masterful due to their sociocultural context. She states that 'there is no solution [to extremism] other than spreading the culture of coexistence and dialogue, skills that women master and possess' and adds, 'women are able to see many things at the same time and have a vision of future based on mutual understanding'.[70] As a programme of the Interfaith Association, Mahameed established WIE programme[71] the perspective to promote mutual respect and understanding by encouraging each community to learn about each other's religion and culture.[72] By focussing on the principles and values of peace-building and non-violence in each religious tradition, WIE brings people together to change stereotypes and create conditions for peaceful relations between different faith groups in the region.

Similarly, FOMWAN aims to respond to conflict in its communities by building relationships between Muslim and Catholic women. The group seeks peaceful coexistence between Christians and Muslims in the country and has been involved in interfaith dialogue with their Christian counterparts, the Catholic Women Association of Nigeria.[73] The Leader of FOMWAN, Hajia Maryam Idris Othman, noted that establishing working relationships and programmes to facilitate peaceful coexistence became necessary as attacks by Boko Haram increased.[74]

Muslim women combine interfaith work with women's empowerment in other Islamic peace-building activities as well. For instance, the Islamic Foundation in the UK ran a six-week course entitled Women in Faith to assist women who wanted to get involved in interfaith work or to enhance the capacity of those who were already working in this area.[75] Tayyibah Taylor, the founding editor-in-chief and publisher of *Azizah Magazine* in the USA, sought to amplify Muslim women's voices and empowerment. To do this, she focussed on interfaith initiatives with various groups of Buddhists, Jews, Christians and Muslims.[76] Other initiatives, like the Mindanao Commission on Women, established in 2001 by Muslim, Christian and indigenous women leaders of Mindanao, Philippines, attempted to influence public policy and public opinion about peace by focussing on mobilization, education, persuasion and lobbying.[77]

Challenges in Muslim Women's Peace-Building Initiatives
Muslim women have been resourceful, creative and dedicated actors of peace-building and justice, individually and communally. However, these success stories should not lead us to ignore real barriers they have to overcome which affects their ability to contribute to peace-building efforts. In addition to a lack of security and safety, especially in countries like Afghanistan, Iraq and Somalia, Muslim women continue to face enormous challenges in gaining access to the decision-making processes, education and training facilities.

For instance, conservative interpretations of Islamic texts continue to undermine the efforts of many Muslim women. Islam as a discourse refers to a body of thought and writing that is united by having a common object of study, a common methodology and a set of common terms and ideas that are linguistically and culturally specific.[78] Islamic discourse makes it possible for all Muslims who have been socialized under its authority to speak and act together with a universal source of Islamic teachings (i.e. the Qur'an and the recorded sayings and deeds of the Prophet Mohammed) and basic tenets of Islam.[79] It creates a unified *ummah* (community) and provides Islamic approaches to peace with common vocabulary, values and principles. Although this discourse enables the emergences of various different narratives, it also constrains Muslim agents of peace by drawing the borders of what they can legitimately say or do in the name of Islam.

However, 'Islam, like every other religious tradition, is the product of both its heritage – itself the synthesis of ideas, beliefs and the concrete lived experience of the earlier Muslims and the way that heritage is interpreted by every generation'.[80] However, the Qur'an is revealed in the context of seventh-century Arabia, it requires human interpretation to respond to new conditions, problems, needs and questions facing Muslims. Sacred texts must be reinterpreted based on the ever-changing needs and social contexts of society. This naturally leads to multiple perspectives/truths that compete with one another, especially in the absence of a central religious authority that can legitimately derive meaning from the texts for the community of the believers.

The diversity and tension among interpretations is a result of the interplay between cultural, socioeconomic and political contexts and their influence on how religious texts are understood to address contemporary issues. Islamic discourse contains what Viviene Jabri calls 'a complex array of memory, myth, symbolic orders and self-imagery come to constitute the life-world of the situated individual'.[81] Contextual factors go through meaning systems that are shaped by religio–cultural constructions and institutional and discursive structures that enable the emergence of multiple interpretations that claim to hold the *Islamic Truth*.[82] Consequently, there are different interpretations of Islamic texts and what it means to be a Muslim. These different interpretations range from conservative to progressive with different shades of each. Both conservative and progressive Muslims derive their legitimacy from the Islamic texts and examples. Diversity of interpretation of Islam points to the interplay between cultural, socioeconomic and political contexts, and their influence on how religious texts are understood to address contemporary issues including the role of women in the society.

Another barrier that impacts women's peace-building efforts is the culture of patriarchy. Although not unique to Muslim communities, historically, the culture of patriarchy has conditioned the interpretation of Islamic sources and has impacted the status of women in society. Patriarchal cultures contain an inherent preference for male authoritative rule, and often exclude women from decision-making processes. In Muslim contexts such a gender-selective approach to authority restricts access of women to intellectual, religious and political institutions, and limits opportunities for women. The modern era further brought new challenges for the Muslim world and for its women in particular. For instance, a perceived threat from globalization – often associated with Westernization and secularization – at times has led to reactionary attitudes towards Western influences. Especially within the context of the power disparity between the Western and Islamic communities, globalization is equated with cultural, economic and political hegemony of the West, and is seen as an existential threat to the Islamic culture and identity.

Reactions to the process of globalization cannot be understood without understanding the traumatising and disempowering impact of colonization. Associated with control and exploitation by foreign powers, the experience of colonization and subjugation has also been interpreted in the historical context of hostile Muslim – European relations during the Crusades. Experiences of civil war and invasion often reinforce modes of religious thought that highlight insecurity and downplay the importance of tolerance and dialogue. These elements contribute to a defensive attitude that rejects 'Western' norms and holds on to an idealized past that is defined in narrow and fundamentalist terms.[83] Any form of intervention, whether it is a peace-building or a human rights initiative, is considered as a direct attack on Islamic culture and identity. As a result, many Muslims are resentful towards the West and are thus easily influenced by aggressive and radical interpretations of Islamic beliefs and core values. This is particularly felt in relation to women's issues. Issues and activities related to empowerment and rights of women are associated with the colonization experience and therfore are strongly rejected.

Colonialism was facilitated through the Orientalist process of abstraction of the 'Muslim other'. Based on the assumption that there was an ontological and epistemological distinction between the 'Orient' and (most of the time) the 'Occident',[84] Orientalism depicted the Orient as alien, unusual, irrational, deprived and childlike, whereas the Occident was seen as rational, mature, virtuous and normal.[85] Through the Orientalist process of abstraction, essentialization and reduction, the Muslim other was stereotyped, judged and conquered. This image of the 'Muslim other' continues to influence relations between the Western and the Muslim worlds.

Especially since 9/11 and the rise of violence in the Muslim world under the name of Islam, the image of the 'Muslim' as the irrational, violent, barbaric and despotic other has amplified. Women's status plays a central role in this image of the other as many Western scholars, governments and activists argue that Muslim women are oppressed because Islam demands it. In order to 'rescue' Muslim women, the culture must be modernized by reforming Islam or secularizing the Muslim world. This provides the backdrop of the current day reactions to Western interventions under the rubric of democratization, women's emancipation, human rights and peace-building.

As a reaction, an essentialized self as a Muslim, rooted in the fundamentals of the faith is constructed to restore a secure sense of self or 'ontological security' as Giddens, a well-known British sociologist, calls it.[86] Within this idealized Muslim identity, purity and image of Muslim women play a significant role. Any behaviour or action that contradicts the image of the 'ideal Muslim self' is considered a Western influence that threatens Muslim identity. This view is supported by the Moroccan writer and sociologist Fatima Mernissi who observes that fundamentalist movements in the Muslim world represent an attempt to affirm Muslim identity in the face of rapid social changes, which threaten traditional social organization and elicit a reaction to the boundary problems created by intrusions of colonialism, new technology, consumerism and economic dependency.[87]

Furthermore, the discourse and attitude of Orientalism was internalized by the secularized elites in many Muslim countries. Elites of these countries have blamed Islam for the demise of their societies and have attempted to de-Islamize their societies by borrowing scientific, legal, political and cultural structures from the West. Among these elites, Islam is associated with backwardness, barbarism and ignorance. Many of the first feminist approaches in the Muslim world also reflected this Orientalist and colonial attitude that depicted Muslim women as victims of an oppressive religion who needed to be saved. The subtext of many women's organizations that came to operate in the Muslim world was that Islam as a religion was fundamentally oppressive, and Muslim women could only be saved by either conversion or secularization. For instance, Marnia Lazreg, a Professor of Sociology at the Graduate Center and Hunter College, observed that 'not only do US feminists often assume that in order for Arab women to become real feminists they must dissociate themselves from Arab men and their own culture but their attitude is often informed by an unmistakable bias against Islam'.[88]

Additionally, the introduction of secular/modern educational institutions – either by colonial powers or by secularist elites – has uprooted the traditional educational institutions that provided broad and elaborate education in Islamic sciences and topics. Consequently, many *imams* (religious leaders) lack the proper education and training to critically engage with this historical legacy. In present Muslim majority contexts, strong perceptions of gender-based injustice stemming from these experiences create adversarial (and stereo-typically male) readings of religious sources. As Deniz Kandiyoti, scholar in the fields of gender relations and developmental politics in the Middle East, notes that the status of women becomes a 'hotly contested ideological terrain where women were used to symbolise the progressive aspirations of a secularist elite or a hankering for cultural authenticity expressed in Islamic terms'.[89]

All these factors impact women's peace-building efforts in the Muslim world adversely, as this environment contributes to the rise of more conservative interpretations of religious texts and disempowers Muslim women, making it harder for them to challenge the patriarchal structures and interpretations of the texts. Increasingly, women's participation in public decision-making has been curbed and women's peace-building initiatives have been limited to the private realm. Western peace-building interventions, as well as women's rights and empowerment, were considered a Western cultural encroachment that must be prevented at all costs. In fact, political scientist Francois Burgat observed that 'the social status of women constitutes one of the terrains on which the invasion of Western references has disturbed the dynamics of the internal evolution of the universe of Islam'.[90]

Additionally, such an attitude is quite offensive to many Muslim women who find Islamic values and traditions liberating and a safeguard against patriarchal and tribal social structures. They argue that authentic and genuine Islamic teachings are not the source of discrimination and injustice against women. Many Muslim women contend that Islam was a revolutionary movement that recognized their right to inherit, to divorce and to work, among others, and it aimed to emancipate women from oppressive systems, such as killing newborn girls. Therefore, many Muslim women are reclaiming their faith by calling for a critical methodology focussing on the understanding of the process of interpretation itself and a re-reading of the Islamic history and sacred texts.[91] This methodology of Qur'anic interpretation calls for reconciliation between the eternal and temporal dimensions of God's revelation by going back to the Qur'an and re-reading it from a gender-sensitive perspective.

In the final analysis, as the stories and case studies presented in this chapter indicate peace-building work within the context of Islamic values and principles, deriving inspiration from Islamic texts and influential women in Islamic history is an approach that helps Muslim women reclaim agency and gain legitimacy as leaders and role models in their peace-building efforts. Consequently, it adds to their strengths and effectiveness in their work.

Conclusion

Increasingly, the diverse roles played by Muslim women in building long-term peace are being recognized internationally and locally. While recognizing the diversity of their contexts, opinions, priorities and needs, this paper argued that various distinct characteristics of peace-building efforts of women in the Muslim world can be identified. In addition to exploring these characteristics, the chapter also examined various challenges they face.

This chapter showed that, in their efforts, Muslim women are inspired by their faith and have found a set of Islamic values and principles that affirm and encourage them to resolve conflict and build sustainable peace. While these Islamic values and principles inform their peace-building efforts, local realities and their specific contexts push Muslim women to address real-life challenges in new and creative ways. The majority of the women's involvement in peace-building is informal and ad hoc, although there have been occasions in which Muslim women participated in official and formal peace-building processes. Women have been involved in diverse activities ranging from mediation, observation and advocacy; however the majority of their peace-building efforts focus on relationship building.

The chapter also discussed various challenges women face and concludes that locating their peace-building initiatives within the context of religio–cultural texts, traditions and history helps Muslim women overcome many challenges in their communities. Women creatively engage in a process of rediscovery in which they find new meanings within Islamic tradition and new ways of perceiving historical or archetypal Muslim women figures whose stories inspire courage in modern-day peacemakers. Positioning their peace discourse and initiatives within the Islamic religious sources and history provides Muslim women with the necessary legitimacy that makes it easier to be accepted by more conservative segments of the society. Drawing on these textual and historical experiences empowers them to stand up against patriarchal interpretations and gives them a sense of ownership that is so critical for the sustainability of their efforts. By critically engaging religious texts and traditions, Muslim women such as Asha Hagi Elmi, Sakena Yacoobi, Soraya Jamjuree, Dekha Ibrahim Abdi and many others are attempting to redefine what it means to be a Muslim woman in a conflict situation. By invoking Islam as a mandate for gender equality and peacemaking, they are stepping beyond more discrete ways of influence behind the scenes such as using informal networks to relay information and attempting to persuade male members of the household to support and join peacemaking efforts. In the process, they are drawing upon and extending the range of resources within Islam for peacemaking and adding new examples of empowered women to those provided in Muslim history. Their experiences move us away from the stereotypical image of the Muslim woman and help us understand the diverse roles they play, and the contributions they make as powerful, creative, proactive agents of social transformation and peace-building.

Notes

1. See S. Ayse Kadayifci-Orellana and Meena Sharify-Funk, 'Muslim women peacemakers as agents of change', in Qamar-ul Huda (ed), *Crescent and Dove: Peace and Conflict Resolution in Islam* (Washington: USIP Press Books, 2010), pp. 179–204.
2. See S. Ayse Kadayifci-Orellana, 'Muslim women's peacebuilding initiatives' in Katherine Marshall and Susan Hayward (eds), *Women, Religion and Peace: Exploring the Invisible* (Washington: USIP Press, forthcoming).
3. As also discussed by miriam cooke in 'Ungendering peace talk', Chapter 1 of this volume.
4. Kadayifci-Orellana and Sharify-Funk 'Muslim women peacemakers as agents of change'.
5. See Kadayifci-Orellana and Sharify-Funk, 'Muslim women peacemakers as agents of change'; Fatema Mernissi, 'Muslim women and fundamentalism',

Middle East Report 18/153 (July/August 1988), pp. 8–11; Gavin R. G. Hambly, *Women in the Medieval Islamic World: Power, Patronage and Piety* (New York: Palgrave MacMillan, 1999); Riffat Hassan, 'The role of women as agents of change and development in Pakistan', *Human Rights Quarterly* 3/3 (August 1981), pp. 68–75.

6. Kadayifci-Orellana and Sharify-Funk, 'Muslim women peacemakers as agents of change'.
7. The Global Muslim Women's Shura Council, 'Violent extremism: A violation of Islam', *American Society for Muslim Advancement* (2012). Available at http://www.wisemuslimwomen.org/pdfs/shura_council_violent_extremism_digest.p df (accessed 15 July 2013).
8. Carla Power, 'Muslim women demand an end to oppressive family laws', *Time* (17 February 2009). Available at http://www.time.com/time/world/article/ 0,8599,1879864,00.html (accessed 15 July 2013).
9. Interview with Asha H. Elmi in Abdurrahman M. Abdullahi, 'Women and constitutional debate in Somalia: Legal reforms during reconciliation conference (2000–2003)'. Available at http://www.scribd.com/doc/ 15421298/Women-and-Constitutional-Debate-in-Somalia (accessed 15 July 2013), p. 13.
10. Ibid.
11. Ibid., p. 14.
12. David Little, *Peacemakers in Action: Profiles of Religion in Conflict Resolution* (New York: Cambridge University Press, 2006), p. 391.
13. See Afghan Institute of Learning, *Creating Hope International* (CHI). Available at http://www.afghaninstituteoflearning.org/dr-sakena-yacoobi-bio.html (accessed 15 July 2013).
14. See Afghan Institute for Learning. Available at http://www.afghaninstituteofl earning.org/learning-centers.html (accessed 15 July 2013).
15. Little, *Peacemakers in Action*, p. 392.
16. Aaron Goodman, 'Thailand: Women for peace-offering solace to victims of conflict', *PBS Frontline World* (9 August 2007). Available at http://www.pbs. org/frontlineworld/rough/2007/08/thailand_women.html (accessed 12 May 2008).
17. Ibid.
18. Meena Sharify-Funk 'Peace and the feminine in Islam', in Abdul Aziz Said, Nathan C. Funk, and S. Ayse Kadayifci (eds), *Peace and Conflict Resolution in Islam: Precept and Practice* (Lanham: University Press of America, 2001), p. 278.
19. Goodman, 'Thailand'.
20. Zafar Alam Khan, 'There are different paths to the Kaabah: Cemalnur Sargut', *The Pioneer* (25 November 2011). Available at http://www.sufinews.org/paths-to-the-kaabah/ (accessed 15 July 2013).
21. Suad Al Hakim, 'Islam and peace', Tara Aziz and Karim Crow (transls.). Paper presented at the symposium Islam and Peace in the 21st Century, February 1998), p. 5.

22. Cited in Sharify-Funk, 'Peace and the feminine', p. 279.

23. S. Ayse Kadayifci-Orellana, *Standing on an Isthmus: Islamic Narratives on Peace and War in Palestinian Territories* (Lexington: Lexington Books, 2007), p. 103.

24. WISE, 'Jihad against violence: Muslim women's struggle for peace', *Women's Islamic Initiative in Spirituality and Equality* (July 2009). Available at http://www.wisemuslimwomen.org/images/uploads/Jihad_against_Violence_Digest (color).pdf (accessed 15 July 2013).

25. Kadayifci-Orellana, *Standing on an Isthmus*.

26. William C. Chittick, 'The theological roots of peace and war according to Islam', *The Islamic Quarterly* 34/3 (1990), p. 156.

27. Kadayifci-Orellana and Sharify-Funk, 'Muslim women peacemakers as agents of change'.

28. Ibid.

29. WISE, 'Jihad against violence', p. 4.

30. S. Ayse Kadayifci-Orellana, 'Exodus in the Qur'an: Mercy, compassion, and forgiveness', in *Freedom Journeys: The Tale of Exodus and Wilderness across Millennia* (Woodstock: Jewish Lights Publishing, 2011), pp. 210–16.

31. For more information on these see Ralph H. Salmi, Cesar Adib Majul and George K. Tanham, *Islam and Conflict Resolution: Theories and Practices* (Lanham: University Press of America, 1998); and Majid Khadduri, *Islamic Law of Nations: Shaybani's Siyar* (Baltimore: John Hopkins Press, 1966).

32. WISE, 'Jihad against violence'.

33. Cited in K. G. Saiyidain, *Islam: The Religion of Peace*, 2nd edn. (New Delhi: Har Anand Publications, 1994), p. 93.

34. Karl-Wolfgang Troger, 'Peace and Islam: In theory and practice', *Islam and Christian Muslim Relations* 1/1 (1990), p. 17.

35. Asna Husin 'Summary of the conference: Islam, women and peace building', Centre for the Study of Religion and Conflict, Arizona State University, Tempe, Arizona (10–12 March 2011). Available at http://nonviolenceinternational.net/wp-content/uploads/2011/03/Islam-Women-Peacebuilding-Asna-Husin.pdf (accessed 15 July 2013).

36. Aaron Goodman, 'Thailand'.

37. See Kadayifci-Orellana, 'Exodus in the Quran'.

38. See Robert C. Johansen, 'Radical Islam and nonviolence: A case study of religious empowerment and constraint among Pashtuns', *Journal of Peace Research* 34/1 (1997), pp. 53–71; Khan Abdul Ghaffar Khan, *My Life and Struggle: Autobiography of Badshah Khan* as narrated to K. B. Narang (Delhi: Hind Pocket Books, 1969); N. Pyareral, *Thrown to the Wolves: Abdul Ghaffar* (Calcutta: Eastlight Book House, 1966).

39. The first 18 verses of *Mathnawi* by Rumi.

40. See the interview with Cemalnur Sargut during the International Conference on Sufism in Bhopal, India (18–20 November 2011): Khan, 'There are different paths to the Kaabah'.

41. See SSWC information at http://wiserearth.org/organization/view/
    607d00e8ab5b98a7c8824a56a622b829 (accessed 27 June 27 2012). For
    more information on SSWC see also Somali Report at http://www.somaliarep
    ort.com/index.php/post/486/Somali_Aid_Group_Assists_Women_and_Chil
    dren (accessed 8 July 2013).

42. Debra Timmons, 'The sixth clan – women organize for peace in Somalia: A
    review of published literature', *University for Peace* (2004), pp. 1–30. Available
    at http://www.africa-upeace.org/Uploads/Publications/de99de80-057e-47c3-
    995d-318423d93a72/de99de80-057e-47c3-995d-318423d93a72.pdf
    (accessed 15 July 2013).

43. Abdullahi, 'Women and constitutional debate in Somalia', p. 12.

44. For more on the social and cultural traditions of Somali society, see Timmons,
    'The sixth clan'.

45. Timmons, 'The sixth clan', pp. 6–7.

46. Ibid.

47. Ibid., pp. 10–11.

48. Ibrahim Nur, *Gender Sensitive Programme Design and Planning in Conflict-Affected
    Situations-Annex 5: Somali Case Study* (London: ACORD, 2002) p. 7. See also
    Timmons, 'The sixth clan', p. 14.

49. Timmons, 'The sixth clan', p. 17.

50. Abdullahi, 'Women and constitutional debate in Somalia', p. 13.

51. Emma Dorothy Reinhardt, 'Kenyan women lead peace effort', *National Catholic
    Reporter Online* (26 April 2002). Available at http://natcath.org/NCR_Online/
    archives/042602/042602p.htm (accessed 5 July 2012).

52. Berkley Center, 'Interview series: Women, religion, and peace', Berkley
    Center for Religion, Peace and World Affairs (February 2012). Available at
    http://repository.berkleycenter.georgetown.edu/1202WomenReligionPeace
    InterviewSeries_webversion.pdf (accessed 15 July 2013).

53. USAID, 'Alternative Nobel Prize goes to Kenyan peacemaker', *USAID East
    Africa* (2 December 2007). Available at http://eastafrica.usaid.gov/en/Article.
    1117.aspx (accessed 24 November 2009).

54. Reinhardt, 'Kenyan women lead peace effort'.

55. Ibid.

56. Mohammed Abu-Nimer and S. Ayse Kadayifci-Orellana, 'Muslim peace-
    building actors in the Balkans, Horn of Africa, and the Great Lakes Regions',
    Salam Institute for Peace and Justice (23 May 2005). Available at http://salamins
    titute.org/MuslimPeacebuildingActorsReport.pdf (accessed 15 July 2013).

57. Ibid.

58. Ibid., p. 11.

59. Abu-Nimer, 'Muslim peace building'.

60. Ibid.

61. Abdulaziz Sachedina, *Islamic Roots of Democratic Pluralism* (Oxford: Oxford
    University Press, 2001), p. 76.

62. Abu-Nimer, 'Muslim peace building', p. 11.

63. It is important to note that although these women have participated in official negotiations and peace-building activities, their efforts initially started as a grassroots movement.

64. International Crisis Group, 'Southern Thailand: Insurgency, not jihad', *Asia Report* no. 98 (18 May 2005).

65. Goodman, 'Thailand'.

66. Goodman 'Thailand'.

67. Katherine Marshall and Susan Hayward, *Women, Religion, and Peace: Exploring an Invisible Force* (Washington: Berkley Center for Religion, Peace, and World Affairs and the United States Institute for Peace, 2010), p. 21.

68. For more information on examples of different formats of Muslim women's peace-building initiatives, see Kadayifci-Orellana, 'Interfaith dialogue' and 'Islam and peacebuilding' in *The Oxford Encyclopedia of Islam and Women,* Series Editor Natana J. DeLong-Bas (Oxford: Oxford University Press, 2013), pp. 474–9 and 507–13.

69. Fatheena Mubarak, 'Women's interfaith initiative in the UK: A survey', *The Inter Faith Network for the United Kingdom* (2006). Available at http://www. interfaith.org.uk/publications/womenssurvey06.pdf (accessed 15 July 2013), p. 7.

70. Robin Morgan, 'Women of the Arab Spring', *Ms. Magazine* (spring 2011). Available at http://www.msmagazine.com/spring2011/womenofthearabspring. asp (accessed 15 July 2013).

71. Ibtisam Mahameed, "Ibtisam Mahameed: Complete interview", *Youtube* (25 February 2009). Available at http://www.youtube.com/watch?v=L93qTw8_v0s (accessed 15 July 2013).

72. Jerusalem Peacemakers, 'Interview with Ibtisam Mahameed'. At http://jerusal empeacemakers2008.jerusalempeacemakers.org/ibtisam/ibtisam-projects.html (accessed 15 July 2013); see also: Ibtisam Mahameed, Global Oneness Project at: http://www.globalonenessproject.org/library/interviews/role-women-p eacemaking%C2%A0 (accessed 15 July 2013); content of the document can be found at http://www.c-r-t.org/content/newsarticles/IbtisamMahameedGOP. pdf.

73. Akure Babatope Okeowo, 'FOMWAN, CWAON collaborate on Muslim-Christian ties', *Nigerian Compass* (25 March 2012). Available at http://www. compassnewspaper.org/index.php?option=com_content&view = article& id = 1310:fomwan–cwaon-collaborate-on-muslim-christian-ties&catid = 35: headlines (accessed 15 July 2013).

74. 'Nigerian Muslim and Catholic women's groups unite to promote peace', *Ahlul Bayt News Agency* (28 March 2012). Available at http://abna.ir/data.asp?l ang=3&Id=304955 (accessed 15 July 2013).

75. Mubarak, 'Women's interfaith initiative', p. 6.

76. See Saudni, '77. Tayyibah Taylor (Editor-in-Chief, Azizah Magazine)', *Muslim Heroes* (25 November 2010). Available at http://muslimheroes.org/2010/11/25/ 77-tayyibah-taylor-editor-in-chief-azizah-magazine/ (accessed 15 July 2013).

77. See the Mindanao Commission on Women. Available at http://www.mindanaowomen.org/mcw/ (accessed 15 July 2013).

78. Kadayifci-Orellana, *Standing on an Isthmus*, p. 29.

79. Ibid.

80. Farid Esack, 'The contemporary democracy and the human rights project for Muslim societies', in Abdul Aziz Said, Mohammed Abu-Nimer and Meena Sharify-Funk (eds), *Contemporary Islam: Dynamic not Static* (London: Routledge, 2006), p. 119.

81. Jabri Vivienne, *War and Transformation of Global Politics* (New York: Palgrave Macmillan, 2007), pp. 45–6.

82. For a discussion of different Islamic narratives of peace see Kadayifci-Orellana, *Standing on an Isthmus*.

83. For modern day Islamic movements and fundamentalism see Kadayifci-Orellana, *Standing on an Isthmus*.

84. Edward Said, *Orientalism* (New York: Vintage Books, 1994), p.2.

85. Ibid., p. 40.

86. David Steele, 'An introductory overview to faith-based peacebuilding', in Mark M. Rogers, Tom Bamat, and Julie Ideh (eds), *Pursuing Just Peace: An Overview and Case Studies for Faith-Based Peacebuilders* (Baltimore, MD: Catholic Relief Services, 2008), p. 32; Iver Neumann, *Uses of the Other: The 'East' in European Identity Formation* (Manchester: Manchester University Press, 1999).

87. Fatema Mernissi, 'Muslim women and fundamentalism', *Middle East Report* 18/153 (July/August, 1988), pp. 8–11.

88. Marnia Lazreg, 'Feminism and difference: The perils of writing as a woman on women in Algeria', *Feminist Studies* 14/1 (Spring 1988), pp. 81–107.

89. Deniz Kandiyoti, *Women, Islam and the State* (Philadelphia: Temple University Press, 1991), p. 3.

90. Francois Burgat, *Islamic Movement in North Africa*, transl. Austin Dowell (Austin: University of Texas, 1993), p. 104.

91. Amina Wadud, 'Muslim women as citizens?', in Nissim Rejwan (ed), *The Many Faces of Islam: Perspectives on a Resurgent Civilization* (Gainesville: University Press of Florida, 2000), p. 207. See also Isobel Coleman, *Paradise Beneath Her Feet: How Women are Transforming the Middle East* (New York: Random House, 2010).

CHAPTER 8

CRIME AND RECONCILIATION: WOMEN'S PEACE INITIATIVES IN THE ISLAMIC REPUBLIC OF IRAN

Arzoo Osanloo

In the immediate aftermath of the 1979 revolution, the Islamic Republic of Iran was forged on a set of compromises by politically diverse actors. Since 2005, many Iranians have been confronted with the State's increasing authoritarianism, and the dismissal of rights and republican values. A renewed politicization of rights-based claims by the Iranian government has pushed activists to formulate new strategies to assert demands, seek redress and be heard.[1] In doing so, Islamic values appear to re-emerge, but they take shape through hybrid Islamic and civil – State institutions that have materialized in the post-revolutionary era.

This chapter highlights the work of groups and individuals who have reframed the discourse of redress based on Islamic principles of mercy, justice and compassion, as well as the idea of humanity. With specific attention to the Iranian penal code and the criminal sanctioning provisions that permit *gozasht* (forbearance), I show how social workers, lawyers and even State officials draw from Muslim sacred texts and practices in the pursuit of restorative justice, peacemaking and reconciliation. In doing so, I also demonstrate how debates in Iran have moved beyond questions of the compatibility between Islam and human rights. Instead much on-the-ground activism consists of the pragmatic mobilization of the State's regulatory mechanisms, in tandem with the cultivation of local values in a new era of rights politics. Women, I argue, are at the forefront of this sort of activism for a number of reasons. The first is due to the long tradition of activism on behalf of women going back to the early twentieth century.[2] In addition, because of the reformulation of the legal system after the Revolution, women have had to learn to navigate the legal system in ways that men have not. This engagement with judicial institutions has given women much more experience with the legal system.[3]

Women at the Vanguard of Reform

The pragmatic mobilization of discourses that are local and not based on rights has been at the forefront of activism in Iran since the 1979 revolution, and women have been at its vanguard ever since. One reason that women play key roles in activism is that women in Iran have been fighting against discriminatory laws for several generations now. As the State marriage laws delegate greater control and ownership over family matters to males, women have literally become legal actors in marriage dissolution, custody and other family law issues. This is because the main avenues for seeking redress for family or marital grievances rest with the court system. As a result, women have become increasingly savvy players who have not only learned how to make use of their none-too-explicit nor broad civil and family rights, but have, through necessity, forged the legal avenue for reform. Because of this, many commentators on Iran have argued that women, and women's rights activists are the vanguard of reform. However, unless we understand the underlying political and ideological logics of the discriminatory laws and discursive nature of women's roles in the Islamic republic, it is hard to understand how women advocate for improvements in their lives, where advocacy is coming from, or indeed, how we identify advocacy when we see it.

Immediately after the 1979 Revolution, the politicization of 'women's rights' discourses – as Western, hyper-individualized and un-Islamic – engendered new ways of approaching discriminatory or unfair practices towards women in family or marital situations. Over two decades of reintroduction of civil family laws through Islamic verification, however, the re-juridicalization of women's status seemed to sanction women's appeals for redress through a discourse of Islamic and civil (or Islamico–civil) rights. The use of Islamico–civil rights discourse was most prominent during what is now referred to as the 'reform' period under the presidency of Mohammad Khatami, 1997–2005. Grievances were markedly couched in rights claims. Women's rights and human rights concerns were the concerns of an increasingly vocal civil society and a president who sought to participate in the international community.

During this time, we also saw the formation of rights groups that challenged government agencies on their promises, constitutionally based, and thereby Islamically validated, to address the people's grievances. This was a period when President Khatami had mounted a campaign to build civic, legal and regulatory support with the aim of growing the participatory nature of an Islamic democracy. He spoke unabashedly of rights – women's rights and human rights– because for his administration there was no conflict there with Islamic principles. And where the laws of the Islamic Republic were not in accordance with human rights laws, his government supported research and debate on how to go about changing the laws of the Islamic Republic. One example I have written about elsewhere is the Center for Women's Participation (CWP), a ministerial-level office within the executive branch, whose legal scholars studied the concordance between Islamic principles and the Convention on the Elimination of Discrimination Against Women (CEDAW).[4] Members of the CWP then briefed and lobbied the Iranian Parliament to ratify it. Although the CWP succeeded in its objective to have the Iranian Parliament ratify CEDAW, the Council of Guardians, the oversight body that evaluates whether laws passed by Parliament satisfy Islamic strictures disagreed with Parliament and dismissed the ratification.

Despite such seeming failures on the part of Khatami's reformists, Khatami's activities were important because he changed the discursive position of rights, which, in the aftermath of the 1979 Revolution, took rights-talk to be part of a broader project of Western imperialism. What was striking in the period from 1997 to 2005 were the growing networks of groups and individuals – to say nothing of the non-governmental organizations (NGOs) and independent newspapers – that sprouted up throughout the country to mount challenges based on women's rights and human rights without any debate on the compatibility between human rights and Islam. 'There is no question that they are in accordance,' a lawyer in Iran's Islamic Human Rights Commission told me back in 1999, 'our Declaration of Human Rights in Islam simply confirms that we have verified this'. Thus, during the Khatami era, discourses on women's rights and human rights flourished as activists did not need to anchor their claims on the question of compatibility with Islamic values. Khatami's rule of law approach became the subject of challenges by more conservative groups.

Beyond Rights Activism

Profiting from the 2006 US announcement of support for regime change in Iran, the Ahmadinejad government (2005–13) once again invoked the revolutionary-era association of rights discourses with imperialist threats and targeted domestic rights groups for their local activities. Since that time, Iranian human rights activists have come under new kinds of governmental scrutiny and surveillance. Today such activists are viewed by some government officials as threats to national security, and they fall under an ever-expanding definition of that term.

Iranian activists meanwhile continue advocating, increasingly at great personal risk, for change under these new conditions. Many take the position that their advocacy is based on Iranian laws and simply call for enforcing the existing legal codes. Even so, such activists risk falling under suspicion of having a political allegiance with the West and regime change policies, even with the new US administration.

While governmental crack-downs since June 2009 further dampened hopes for reform, activities continued. As a result of government scrutiny of rights-based activism, moreover, they have multiplied in form and scope. However, this is not a chapter on government responses to activism. Instead, this chapter focusses on non-state actors who operate in the context of the government repression of human rights-based activism. That is to say, this chapter explores on the nature of humanity and what it means to be human in a context where redress does not take shape solely in the form of human rights-based discourses.

Human rights theories contend that rights precede the state because humans possess dignity, and solely because of that quality, human beings have certain inalienable rights. The puzzle that international human rights laws present is that the primary entity available for guaranteeing that humans have rights is the state.[5] Indeed critiques of human rights laws, theories and practices find that human rights enforcement requires or depends on States and State recognition of the humanity of individuals inside their borders.[6] However, by moving beyond human rights to humanity, especially in the context of authoritarian States, I ask whether it is possible to recognize the humanity of another person when the State, as the grantor of rights, might not. In a sense, the question that my research poses is whether we can move beyond the human rights framework as our sole index for humanizing others. As a result, in my work, I am increasingly interested in patterns or practices that do not name human rights, but at the same time seek to broaden and deepen the terrain of what it means to be human, and to seek a sort of recognition based on that quality of humanity.

Humanity's Appeal

'At first they would throw stones. But then we would reach them with appeals to their humanity', recounted Sepideh, a social worker at the The Society for Protecting the Rights of the Child (SPRC), a Tehran-based NGO.[7] Sepideh worked with a larger network of NGOs, lawyers and social workers to assist in what largely amounts to anti-death penalty activities in Iran – the country with the highest per capita rate of execution. Sepideh was describing her attempts to talk to bereaving families of victims who had lost a son, a daughter, a brother, or other family member through a homicide. Iran's criminal justice system allows next-of-kin to pursue their cases through *qisas* (retributive punishment), but it also allows for the possibility of *gozasht* (forbearance).

In 1994, the Iranian government ratified the United Nations Convention on the Rights of the Child, which was approved by the governmental body that vets all laws for their conformity with Islamic principles, the Council of Guardians.[8] In tandem with the country's ratification of this convention, the Islamic Republic licensed the creation and operation of organizations to support underage defendants in death penalty cases. Among them was the SPRC, which also came into being in 1994. The main goals of the SPRC are to:

> Publicize and promote the principles of the International Convention on the Rights of the Child. With the help of its volunteer members, the Society strives to introduce, convey and promote these rights to the Iranian public in order to remove subjective and objective obstacles to the fulfilment of the rights of children. The Society strives to take effective steps towards establishing a suitable basis for the improvement of the general living conditions and the physical, mental, emotional and social growth of the children of this land.[9]

The organization works in three primary fields of advocacy for children: including legislation, enforcement and social.[10] While the SPRC sponsors many activities to foster the rights of children,[11] one of the areas of involvement that I focus on here is that of protecting juvenile offenders, sometimes from the death penalty.

Sepideh recounted her advocacy work with the organization that uses the very word 'rights', but avoided using this language in describing her approach to speaking with families of victims. When I asked her about this, she reflected on the notion of rights and noted that these grieving families are thinking about their own right of retribution. They are not thinking about the right of the defendant to live, and if she starts talking about rights in a purely legalistic way, it seems 'to distance or sterilize the issue at hand'. I asked her what she meant by that, and she continued:

> When we talk about rights, we are referencing individuals, but it seems to take them out of the context of their social lives, their problems and what led to the incident. If we talk instead about how the mother of the victim lost a child, and if she pursues retaliation, there will be another mother who loses a child, it seems to address the humanity of the other person. Something that for us seems to be more persuasive because it shows that this mother has something in common with that other mother.

Sepideh's description of her efforts at advocacy fit well with SPRC's overall emphasis on the broad goals of the welfare of children. Her strategy for this advocacy, however, drew from an approach that centred on the human connection between the victim's and defendant's mothers and sought to touch upon the human connection of a mother's sympathy for another mother.

In some cases, such as in the one above, organizations might send social workers to speak to members of victims' families to attempt to negotiate their forbearance – forgoing their right to exact in-kind punishment. Defence attorneys and even government agencies have also come on board to form a sort of 'cottage industry' of groups and individuals working against the death penalty through the logics of Islamic principles of forgiveness, as well as, the international human rights conventions. In the increasingly politicized context in which hardliners gain support by aligning their political opponents with Western human rights defenders, many activists have taken a different tack, one which aims to highlight the Muslim nature of the forbearance, moving away from a discourse of rights towards one of humanity. As Samira, an attorney, told me in November 2007:

> We cannot explicitly talk about ending the death penalty. This is why the CRC has proven useful. We start with juvenile

defendants and can refer to Iran's own normative legal structure and its ratification of the CRC as a part of this.[12]

In this context, activists deploy Islamic principles both embedded in the Iranian legal system and in the minds of pious Muslim families to address sociocultural and economic problems that might otherwise yield harsh criminal sanctions or complete societal neglect. One key consideration in this chapter is to understand how activists and legal practitioners use the Islamic mandate of forgiveness in their advocacy, especially in light of the politicization of the language of human rights in Iran today. Iranian restorative traditions may offer the site for internal reform as well.[13] Iranian activists and leaders make reference to their restorative justice traditions as part of a wider trend to reduce over-criminalization and work towards *solh* (reconciliation).[14] Such alternatives to penal sanctioning include informal mediation and discretionary remedies, such as financial reparations that aim to be compensatory and rehabilitative. Such practices are bound up with Islamic sacred texts as well as local customs that sometimes even pre-date Islam. However, it is significant that these local practices possess a strategic importance in a context where there has been a governmental backlash of mobilization around human rights concerns. Local activists seek other ways of approaching the issue of the death penalty. This may in part be a pragmatic approach to addressing an issue of human suffering, but it is also an attempt to call attention to and to cultivate indigenous belief systems.

Sepideh went on to explain that the most difficult part of her job was to gain access to the families of victims, many of whom did not want to be persuaded to forgo their right of retribution. 'At the beginning, they are too hot', she explained, 'so we have to wait until some time passes and they have a chance to grieve'. When some time would pass, often after several attempts, Sepideh would be able to see the families. She would tell the victims' families that while they have a right to retribution under the law, forgiveness is the will of God and that the peacemakers forgive and leave the rest to the judgment of God. I tell them that they can be merciful, this is what God commands, that being merciful will bring about peace'. This peace is not just a peace that aims to bring about reconciliation between parties, she told me, but 'peace in the heart of the individual'.

Mercy in Islam

According to Muslim scriptural texts, two of God's main qualities come from the words for mercy, *Ar-Rahman* and *Ar-Rahim*, meaning 'The Most Gracious' and 'The Most Merciful'. These two attributes are mentioned in the phrase recited at the beginning of 113 chapters of the Qur'an: 'In the name of God, the Most Gracious, the Most Merciful.' For Muslims, this phrase, known as the *bismillah*, is a constant reminder of God's never-ending mercy and the vast rewards awaiting the followers of the 'right path'. It also makes up the first *ayat* (verse) of the Qur'an, which is referred to as *Sura al-Fatiha*, translated as 'The Key Chapter' or 'The Opening Chapter'. Over 35 verses of the Qur'an employ the *bismillah* that serves as a reminder to Muslims of the obligation to be just and compassionate in their dealings with one another.[15] While mercy and forgiveness are not entirely interchangeable concepts, Islamic mercy encompasses forgiveness.[16]

Mercy has deep roots in the sacred texts that compel Muslims to forgive, to turn the cheek and not to seek revenge or retributive punishments. In the context of retaliation, one of the most significant verses of the Qur'an that speaks to forbearance is:

> We ordained therein for them: 'Life for life, eye for eye, nose for nose, ear for ear, tooth for tooth, and wounds equal for equal.' But if any one remits the retaliation by way of charity, it is an act of atonement for himself. And if any fail to judge by (the light of) what Allah hath revealed, they are (no better than) wrong-doers (Q5:45) (Yusufali, trans.).

The first sentence recognizes the harm done and that the penalty is retaliatory punishment. If, however, the person wronged remits, this itself will be a form of reparation for the injured party. However, in the same verse, the injured party is admonished not to go too far astray of exact punishment, as this would render the injured party an offender as well. Thus, the point of this verse is to show that there is a limit on punishment – it must never exceed the harm done. By not exacting in-kind punishment, there are rewards as well. Another of the most often quoted verses from the Qur'an associated with the act of forbearance is:

> O ye who believe! The law of equality is prescribed to you in cases of murder: the free for the free, the slave for the slave, the woman for the woman. But if any remission is made by the brother of the slain, then grant any reasonable demand, and compensate him with handsome gratitude, this is a concession and a Mercy from your Lord. After this whoever exceeds the limits shall be in grave penalty (Q2:178) (Yusufali, trans.).

In this verse as well, the right of in-kind punishment is confirmed, but again with the encouragement of forbearance. It is also here, in this verse, that the wrong-doer is encouraged to seek reconciliation with reparation and appreciation. In the final line, again the Qur'an warns against punishment or compensation that exceeds limits. Scholars who have studied this verse, taking it together with the whole of the Qur'an, have suggested a deeper meaning.[17] Indeed it references a period in which tribal warfare induced a never-ending cycle of violence. In such contexts, where one act of injustice was met with another, often greater act, the response was never in-kind, but far beyond. Religious scholar Abdulaziz Sachedina suggests that when taken in its context, this verse compels a remission of violence and counsels proportionality that aims to end the cycle of violence. Thus, in his interpretation of 2:178, Sachedina states:

> Reconciliation flows from forgiveness and willingness on the part of the victim to forego retribution as an end in itself. From the Koranic admonition to forgive and accept compensation, it seems retributive punishment is worth pursuing only to the extent that it leads to reconciling (*shifa' al-sudur* = 'healing

the heart') the victim and wrongdoer, and rehabilitating the latter after his or her acknowledgement of responsibility.[18]

Taken together, these as well as numerous other verses of the Qur'an compel Muslims to forgo the right of exacting punishment. Indeed throughout the Qur'an, believers are compelled to forgive others for transgressions, even the ultimate one, the killing of a loved one, as the above verses reflect.

The issue of forbearance in such contexts cannot be separated from compassion, mercy, and the ultimate objective in Islam, justice. Scholar of Islamic mysticism, *Sufism*, and *Shi'ism*, Reza Shah-Kazemi, links the values of compassion and mercy with justice in stating, '[T]he capacity to act with compassion in no way conflicts with the demands of justice; rather it is an intrinsic aspect of justice, conceived ontologically'.[19] Shah-Kazemi conceives of the ontological relationship between compassion, mercy and justice in his reading of one of the most sacred *Hadith*, the complied works of 'Ali ibn Abi Talib, whose words and letters were collected in the tenth century CE by Sayyid Sharif al-Radi in one volume entitled *Nahj al-Balaghah* (Peaks of Eloquence). 'Ali, as the Prophet Mohammad's cousin and son-in-law, is considered by Shi'i Muslims to be his rightful successor and first of the 12 Shi'i *Imams*.[20] He was also an important figure for *Sunnis*, as the fourth caliph. Among the hundreds of letters and writings that make up the *Nahj al-Balaghah*, one letter stands out for its contemplation on justice. This is the letter 'Ali ibn Talib wrote to Malik al-Ashtar appointing him governor of Egypt. This epistle, number 52, is regarded by Muslim scholars as a source of inspiration for the ideal Islamic governance and ethical principles, not only ideal for a ruler, but as a guideline for all Muslims.

Shah-Kazemi suggests that the letter expounds on the nature of justice and governance in Islam. In a section entitled, 'The Compassion of Justice', Shah-Kazemi argues that to act with compassion is inherent to justice. After a discussion of several key Qur'anic verses dealing with mercy, Shah-Kazemi shows that while the Qur'an recognizes that anger is present when one has been wronged, a leader must master that fury in order to achieve the higher purpose of justice – 'the wrathful side of the nature of things is not denied here, but it is clearly subordinate to the higher ontological purpose of mercy'.[21] Shah-Kazemi continues:

> One is therefore more 'real' insofar as mercy predominates over wrath, spiritually, within one's own soul and morally, in one's conduct; and it is in the very nature of justice, conceived in this sacred manner, to tend towards compassion wherever possible, even though there must also be a place for rigorous application of corrective penalty where this is unavoidable.[22]

Building on Imam 'Ali as a source of understanding, justice and mercy, scholar of Islam, Leonard Lewisohn focusses on the issue of forbearance in the same volume. Since 'Ali is such a significant figure for Shi'i Muslims and over 90 per cent of Muslims in Iran are Shi'i, it is no surprise, then, that 'Ali's *Nahj al-Balaghah* is a key text for Iranians. Lewisohn finds, moreover, that the notion of forbearance has deep roots in the Persian Sufi tradition[23] related to the Persian spiritual *futuwwat* (chivalric tradition) for whom 'Ali is the founding father. In the *futuwwat*, 'Ali is 'celebrated as being the incarnation of God's mercy, tolerance, forgiveness and generosity' and 'the epitome of courage, generosity and selflessness'.[24] The *futuwwat* were not a mere sect; the *futuwwat* were an indivisible feature of the sociocultural history of the *Sufis* throughout the Middle East.[25] Lewisohn states that numerous stories from the Persian chivalric tradition feature 'Ali as 'an expert in conflict resolution'.[26] Lewisohn notes that there was a significant difference of opinion between the chevaliers of the Sufi order and the Muslim jurists, especially on the application of the laws of retribution, in which the chevaliers held a more 'relaxed attitude toward its application'.[27] 'Ali's moral qualities are highlighted as virtues worthy of emulation because his conduct reflects 'a finer justice based on love'.[28] Lewisohn recounts several stories of how 'Ali forgave offenders and granted mercy over punishment. These anecdotes of a higher justice, he suggests, are stressed by Persian Sufi scholars. Citing a set of anecdotes by one such scholar, Suhrawardi, Lewisohn explains that 'Ali's idea of retribution

as in the verse from the Qur'an quoted above (2:178), advises a
'"healing of the heart" rather than a lust for punishment'.[29] In Iran,
thus, we can trace the lineage of the legal formulation of forbearance,
which takes its modern form through a legal mechanism in the penal
codes as *gozasht*, not only to the sacred text of the Qur'an, but also to
Imam 'Ali and the Persian Sufi tradition.

Iranian Criminal Sanctioning and the Principle of Forbearance

According to the penal code, certain crimes permit forbearance on the
part of the victim or victims' families. Thus *gozasht* is the legal
expression of the Islamic mandate of forgiveness that might have
consequences for peacemaking and forms of advocacy that we may not
be aware of if our focus is solely on human rights-based activism. In
classical Shi'i *fiqh* (jurisprudence), crimes are divided into three
categories of punishment: *hudud*, *qisas* and *diya*. *Hudud* are 'crimes
against God' for which amnesty is effectively impossible.[30] Crimes of
homicide and bodily harm against individuals are separated
according to appropriate punishments – those subject to retributive
punishments (*qisas*) and those corresponding to financial compensation (*diya*). Such crimes include battery, assault, murder and
manslaughter. In a shift from Western legal frameworks, these crimes
and their corresponding punishments are classified as crimes against
individuals as opposed to crimes against society.[31]

In crimes subject to the punishment of *qisas*, Shi'i *fiqh* and the
corresponding Iranian legal code affirms reciprocal death for
homicide in intentional deaths or *diya* in unintentional homicides.
The Iranian Penal Code stipulates that the surviving heirs of a
murder victim may also decide whether to demand in-kind
retribution or forgo this right (*gozasht*).[32] In cases where the victim's
next of kin does permit the offender's life to be saved, thus offering
gozasht, the offender will not be automatically freed. The offender
may still be subject to a criminal sentence as a sanction in
conjunction with the public prosecution.[33] In the 1991 revisions to
the Iranian Penal Code, a section was added to recognize that there is

harm, not only to the individual plaintiff, as the earlier revisions to the Penal Code acknowledged, but now, there is recognition that the public is also harmed. Thus, in addition to the private harm, for which *qisas* or *diya* may be appropriate depending on intent, there is also a public harm, for which the State prosecutor may pursue a remedy on behalf of the general public.[34] *Gozasht* is possible in multiple kinds of sanctioning, not only murder, and it can affect the outcome of a separate State prosecution, including leniency in sentencing.

The involvement of victims' families in the enforcement of retributive punishments confirms the State's concerns with victims' interests.[35] Thus, unlike the US and other Western legal systems in which private tort claims are settled separately from criminal sanctions, in the Iranian Penal Codes, prosecution of murder by the State and an unlawful death suit by the family of the victim occur together. When the family of the victim has the right to seek retribution, *qisas*, there is technically no *diya*. These are two separate causes of action, the former based on intent, the latter on an unintentional harm. However, the parties often make financial arrangements, but in the view of the courts, these are extra-legal arrangements. *Gozasht*, then, is codified forbearance, which can be seen as, and may even become, a form of private forgiveness.

Thus, one of the questions I have in mind in this chapter is what conditions have to be present for someone who has been wronged to give up or remit this right of retaliation? Of course, this depends on what we take forgiveness to mean. Philosopher Charles Griswold has considered the depth and breadth of the concept of forgiveness.[36] While Griswold sees forgiveness as an elusive subject, he also sees it as a moral relationship between a person wronged and a wrong-doer. His central argument is that forgiveness comes with terms attached; it is not unconditional, but 'is governed by norms'.[37] In this context, forgiveness can have a formal or official quality, perhaps like the codified forbearance discussed earlier. Forgiveness, moreover, is the elimination of revenge.[38] According to Griswold, traces of resentment may still be present, but this does not block an act of forgiveness. Instead, Griswold states, in forgiveness, one gives up the need or urge to seek revenge. I take Griswold's argument to apply in the case at hand. Forgiveness may be the elimination of revenge, or as is the case here, foregoing the right of retaliation. Griswold explores six conditions that make forgiveness possible: (1) acknowledgement of wrong-doing; (2) repudiation of the action; (3) communication of regret or apology; (4) rehabilitation; (5) understanding of wrong-doing; and (6) a narrative explaining the act in question.[39] There is plenty of debate on the nature of forgiveness, which may be beyond the scope of this chapter.[40] There is, however, some agreement that forgiveness may bring about reconciliation between two parties. And, for a person who forgives, it may bring the consolation of personal peace.

Face and Forgive

Maryam had a decision to make. Her brother, Behrouz, had been killed. They lived near *Yaft Abod* in an area called, *Shadabod*, not far from *Maydun-e Azadi*, Freedom Square. Maryam was a school teacher in her mid-30s when her youngest brother died at the age of 21. She was married and had her own three sons. However, as the only daughter in the family, she had grown into a nurturing and mothering role to her brothers because their own mother had passed away six years earlier. As Maryam described it, theirs was a 'traditional family', and 'our family is very much with feelings and I took care of my brothers when my mother died'.

Maryam had to decide whether to forgive her brother's assailant who was now awaiting either death or her forbearance. Although the Penal Code requires the entire family to reach accord for retribution, Maryam explained to me why it was, in the final analysis, up to her: 'I am very important in this family. The decision about what to do was mine. To be happy in a family, you have to make the woman *ghaneh* (satisfied).' However, it was not just her role in the family that made her the final arbiter of whether the family forgave her brother's assailant. In fact, her father and brothers looked to her for comfort after they had lost their mother. They also looked to Maryam to do what a mother would do. Maryam explained as much. 'Because we had lost our mother, this gave me a lot of influence; I was the one who made all the decisions.' However, because Behrouz was so young when their mother died, Maryam's relationship to her youngest brother took on even more of a mothering role. She felt the pressure, not just of her own pain of loss, but also that of having to represent their deceased mother's wishes. 'I became sick and my father saw that my illness was making me suffer, and my father did not want me to be sick.' Initially, the family was in agreement, Maryam related:

> At first, all of my family wanted execution. We all wanted *qisas* and nothing more because my family is very religious and we believe in God. We believed that the Qur'an stated that if someone kills, then *qisas* is the just punishment.

Maryam then recounted how little by little, her brothers and fathers began to change their minds. Members of the community in which they lived, from which both the deceased and the assailant hailed, came and talked to the family, as did members of the *ulama* (Islamic scholars). Maryam continued, 'over time, my brothers and father, who were all religious, began to feel that opting for *qisas* could influence our *ruh* (soul), and make us angry, and influence us to teach our children to be vengeful.'

Soon, Maryam became the lone holdout in the decision to forgive her brother's murderer. 'My father said "if Maryam is satisfied, then I forgive"'. Yet, she could not reconcile herself with the advice and the pleas of their wider relations. At this time, she told me, she hardly went out or spoke with anyone because she felt that everywhere she went, people were always trying to get her to change her mind, 'they would say, "your father is satisfied to forgive", and then they would ask me to do the same'. She went on, 'even to our extended family, I would say, "You don't feel the pain and suffering that I do; my brother was about to get married; his voice is still in my head." And it would make me mad – their insistence that I forgive. Then my father saw that I was so angry and he would say no, "I just want the law"'.

Indeed the case went on this way until the day of the planned execution. Maryam was the sole member of her family who did not agree to forgive, and the family was going to go ahead with their legal right to retributive punishment. Maryam went with her father to the prison. Iran's Penal Codes require the family of the victim to be present at the execution. Such executions are carried out just before dawn with crowds usually gathered outside the prison walls. Maryam went with her father that day because she was the sole person who wanted the death sentence carried out and thus played an important role in what was about to happen. She described the scene to me. 'Just outside of Evin [prison], there were many, many people because they were going to execute four people, so about one thousand people were there.' Maryam then described in painstaking detail the way in which another mother's wails gave her pause for the first time since her brother's death:

> I heard the scream of a woman. It is in my ears still. There were many women screaming and crying, but one stayed in my mind. I asked my brother who was outside the prison grounds who that was. He said this is someone who is going to lose her son, someone like you is going to execute her son.

The mother's wails continued as Maryam approached four large, athletic men. Maryam said, 'I asked them, "Why are you here?" and they said "We want to execute the murderer of our brother."' Maryam responded instinctively: 'What? That's so sad! His mother is really crying in a bad way and they said, "Our mother is also crying – and the pain really hurts. And a mother is not really like a sister."'

However, the grief and raw pain of the woman she heard was getting to Maryam. Now inside the prison yard, Maryam could still hear the wails. She suddenly began thinking about the possibility of relieving that woman of her pain. And as they brought out the defendants, she saw how small and youthful they appeared. 'Ali, her brother's assailant was crying as he held a picture of Behrouz to his chest. The scene that lay before her became heavy and she was starting to see the scenario differently. Now, when she considered the other families and other defendants, she started to think outside of her own personal desire for revenge and began to feel a sense of pain for the defendants, too. She went to the brothers and said if they agree to forgive, then she would as well. At first they were hesitant, but she would not stop pleading with them and discussing the importance of forgiveness and how she could see that they would never feel ease and calm or peace after killing someone, even if that person killed their brother. She said that she would forgive and that is what would bring peace, not just to her mind, but to her family and community. In the end, both Maryam and the brothers gave in and decided to forgive. Both families also accepted a financial settlement in exchange.

It was in seeing and feeling the humanity of the others, the mothers crying, that made her question, for the first time in many months, her desire to seek retribution. 'She is a mother and I am a mother. Suddenly I became aware of how she must be suffering too, maybe even more than me.' Maryam's reflection, raised once she faced the suffering of another, made her conscious of the effect her action was going to have as well. Up until then, she did not want to see or think about the pain of others, those whose suffering she would intensify by seeking retaliation. She recalls: 'I was in pain. I could not think about them. Not until I heard that mother's screams.'

Maryam's sudden reflection of herself in the mother of the boy about to be executed signified a consideration on her part for the humanity of the other. In order to be able to forgive, the person forgiving needs to be able to imagine himself or herself in the place of the other, which is what Griswold states is 'the recognition of the shared nature of humanity'.[41] Maryam's attitude similarly reinforces what Levinas has referred to as being conscious of the face of the other in your actions, 'the face speaks to me and thereby invites me to a relation'.[42] For Levinas, it is in the face of others that humans can see themselves and be compelled into action, '[T]he other faces me and puts me in question and obliges me.'[43] In one relevant section, Levinas speaks of the religious commandment against murder:

> The first word of the face is the 'Thou shalt not kill'. It is an order. There is a commandment in the appearance of the face, as if a master spoke to me. However, at the same time, the face of the Other is destitute; it is the poor for whom I can do all and to whom I owe all.[44]

For Levinas, the human face encompasses the living presence of the other. A person as social and ethical entity creates a bond with another. This connection is an appeal to a relational ethics, 'the face presents itself and demands justice'.[45] It was not until Maryam literally faced the pain of the other that she was able to understand her actions because she was now enveloped in the totality of another's living presence, which she had the power to deny.

Conclusion

Forgiveness is a foundational value in Islamic societies. Forbearance, moreover, is the responsibility of the individual. That is, religious teachings encourage victims of tortious acts to forgive rather than to seek revenge. In some societies, this supplication has moved beyond mere scriptural entreaty to legality. For instance, in the Islamic Republic of Iran, where European criminal codes were adopted as part of the government's State-building processes almost 100 years ago, this religious entreaty was codified. Today some scholars in Iran's academic and theological communities are making use of the scriptural values of forgiveness to engender new debates and to construct avenues towards an epistemology of humanity with an emphasis on Irano–Islamic principles.

Critics may find that while such values encourage individuals to play more proactive roles in furthering the core humanitarian commitments of human rights, as long as forgiveness is conceived as a praiseworthy virtue and not an enforceable obligation, it plays an ambivalent role with regard to human rights, just as the pardon does in Western Judeo-Christian law. This chapter explored the foundational Islamic principle and the history of its codification and legal rationalization to consider whether forgiveness in a different context may engender individual action in line with humanitarian values and perhaps even human rights.

Notes

1. In June of 2013, Iranians elected a seemingly more moderate president, Hassan Rouhani. Whether the new administration will be able to provide a more moderate political agenda and a shift in the government's stance on human rights, however, remains to be seen.
2. Janet Afary, *The Iranian Constitutional Revolution, 1906–11* (New York: Columbia University Press, 1996).
3. Arzoo Osanloo, *The Politics of Women's Rights in Iran* (Princeton: Princeton University Press, 2009).
4. Ibid.
5. Arzoo Osanloo, 'The measure of mercy: Islamic justice, sovereign power, and human rights in Iran', *Cultural Anthropology* 21/4 (2006), pp. 570–602.
6. Hannah Arendt, *The Origins of Totalitarianism* (New York: Harcourt, 1973), pp. 267–304.
7. The names of most interlocutors are pseudonyms. The interviews excerpted here took place on 18 November 2007, 8 September 2009 and 13 July 2010.
8. Upon ratification on 13 July 1994, Iran took a general reservation stating that it 'reserves the right not to apply any provisions or articles of the Convention that are incompatible with Islamic laws and the international legislation in effect'. Available at http://www.icrc.org/ihl.nsf/NORM/301345982738E9FB C1256402003FCA24?OpenDocument (accessed 11 January 2014).
9. SPRC brochure. Translation by the author. See also, http://www.irsprc.org/abou tsociety/mainpage.aspx?lang=En (accessed 18 December 2013).
10. Accordingly, in these three contexts, SPRC attempts to support the creation of new laws, to advocate for the reform of existing laws that render Iran in conflict with the CRC, to work towards the enforcement of existing laws that protect children, and to train and educate families, organizations and individuals about child protection. See note 8.
11. The SPRC partakes in activities that are directly referenced by the CRC, including education, information, training, health care and consultative services for families, as well as practical assistance for children injured as a result of social and natural disasters and living under difficult conditions such as poverty.
12. Samira, Personal interview, (21 November 2007).
13. Firouz Mahmoudi, 'The informal justice system in Iranian law', in Hans-Jorg Albrecht, Jan-Michael Simon, Hassan Rezaei, Holger-Christoph Rohne and Ernesto Kiza (eds), *Conflicts and Conflict Resolution in Middle Eastern Societies: Between Tradition and Modernity* (Berlin: Duncker & Humblot, 2006), pp. 411–28.
14. Hussein Gholami, 'Restorative traditions in violent conflicts in Iran', in Hans-Jorg Albrecht et al. (eds), *Conflicts and Conflict Resolution in Middle Eastern Societies*, pp. 457–70.

15. Mohammad E. Shams Nateri, 'Formal and informal means of conflict resolution in murder cases in Iran', in Hans-Jorg Albrecht et al. (eds), *Conflicts and Conflict Resolution in Middle Eastern Societies*, p. 404, n. 22; Reza Shah-Kazemi, *My Mercy Encompasses All: The Koran's Teachings on Compassion, Peace and Love* (Berkeley: Counterpoint Press, 2007).

16. Khaled Abou El Fadl, Joshua Cohen and Deborah Chasman, *Islam and the Challenge of Democracy* (Princeton: Princeton University Press, 2004).

17. Some scholars have argued that attention to reading of the Qur'an should rest on its broad aims. Such scholars suggest that the *maqasid*, or the higher goals of Islam, are justice, and that a comprehensive study of Islam requires a reading that is consistent with this highest-of-all-objectives. See, for instance Mohammad Hashim Kamali, *Maqasid al Shariah Made Simple* (Herndon: IIIT Books, 2008).

18. Abdulaziz Sachedina, *The Islamic Roots of Democratic Pluralism* (New York: Oxford University Press, 2001), pp. 111–12.

19. Reza Shah-Kazemi, 'A sacred conception of justice: Imam 'Ali's letter to Malik al-Ashtar', in M. Ali Lakhani (ed), *The Sacred Foundations of Justice in Islam: The Teachings of 'Ali ibn Abi Talib* (Bloomington: World Wisdom Inc., 2006), p. 83.

20. A *Shi'ite* is literally a partisan of 'Ali. The designation of *Imam* in Shi'i Islam is very different from that in Sunni Islam. *Imam* among the Shi'i is a beatific title given only to the leaders considered to be the rightful spiritual and political successors of the Prophet. *Sunnis*, in contrast, use the term *imam* to refer to a person with religious training and in a leadership position such as in a mosque.

21. Shah-Kazemi has also published a compilation of the verses from the Qur'an that deal with mercy; see Shah-Kazemi, *My Mercy Encompasses All*. In this chapter, he cites the following verses from the Qur'an: *My mercy encompasseth all things*, 7:156; *The Lord has prescribed for Himself mercy*, 6:54. See Shah-Kazemi, 'A sacred conception of justice', p. 83.

22. Shah-Kazemi, 'A sacred conception of justice', p. 83.

23. Lewisohn notes that *Sufis* are generally not *Shi'is* except in Persia (now Iran) after the rise of the *Mujtahid*s in the Safavid era in the late sixteenth century CE.

24. Leonard Lewisohn, ''Ali ibn Abi Talib's ethics of mercy in the mirror of the Persian Sufi tradition', in M. Ali Lakhani (ed), *The Sacred Foundations of Justice in Islam*, pp. 117–18. The term selfless is also a reference to a person who forgoes his or her right. One who forbears, or takes an exception from his or her self/right, is thus selfless and self-excepting.

25. Lewisohn, ''Ali ibn Abi Talib's ethics of mercy', p. 119.

26. Ibid., 120.

27. Ibid. On this point, see also Henri Corbin, *Traites Des Compagnons – Chevaliers: Recueil de sept 'Fotowwat-Nameh'* (Teheran: IFRI, 1973), p. 5. Corbin notes that the term, *futuwwat* (chevalier) is the Arabic equivalent of the term *javanmardi* in Persian. Writing in 1973, Corbin makes the point that the ideas associated with the *futuwwat* seem to bring about a renewed interest in Iran ('*semblent connaitre un regain d'interet en Iran*').

28. Lewisohn, 'Ali ibn Abi Talib's ethics of mercy', p. 126.

29. Ibid., 127.

30. Iran's Penal Code lists eight crimes subject to *hudud*: sodomy, drinking alcoholic beverages, adultery, falsely accusing someone of adultery, lesbianism, pandering, special cases of theft, and crimes against the State, such as unlawful rebellion. It should be noted that these crimes are rarely prosecuted.

31. In most modernized legal systems, including the Western, codification of private tort or personal injury law arises from the tribal customary laws of earlier periods.

32. Iranian Penal Code, Article 258.

33. Iranian Penal Code, Article 612.

34. This was actually a reversion back to the 1925 Penal Code. From 1983–90 there was no possibility of public prosecution.

35. Mashood A. Baderin, *International Human Rights and Islamic Law* (Oxford: Oxford University Press, 2003), p. 83.

36. Charles L. Griswold, *Forgiveness: A Philosophical Exploration* (New York: Cambridge University Press, 2007).

37. Ibid., p. xv.

38. Ibid., p. 20.

39. Ibid., pp. 49–51.

40. The literature on forgiveness is vast and spans numerous disciplines. Some important works in the context of politics and crime include Martha Minow, *Between Vengeance and Forgiveness* (Boston: Beacon Press, 1998); Desmond Tutu, *No Future without Forgiveness* (New York: Doubleday/Image Pub., 2000).

41. Griswold, *Forgiveness*, p. 5.

42. Emmanuel Levinas, *Totality and Infinity: An Essay on Exteriority*, transl. Alphonso Lingis (Pittsburgh: Duquesne University Press, 1969), p. 198.

43. Ibid., p. 207.

44. Emmanuel Levinas, *Ethics and Infinity: Conversations with Philippe Nemo*, transl. Richard A. Cohen (Pittsburgh: Duquesne University Press, 1985), p. 89.

45. Levinas, *Totality and Infinity*, p. 294. Given Levinas's contention of the face as a living presence, it is important to consider that the Iranian criminal justice system requires victims' families to be present before the offender whose life they seek to take.

CHAPTER 9

RELIGION, WOMEN AND PEACEFUL REVOLUTIONS: PERSPECTIVES FROM THE ARAB MIDDLE EAST

Azza Karam

On Faith, Religion and Politics

'Please, please don't say anything negative or critical about Islam. It is your faith!'

Such were the words of my late mother, with whom my relationship was never the easiest, as I decided to embark upon the journey of studying for my doctorate the tensions in my part of the world – the Middle East – within religion, governance and human rights. These three issues structured the dynamics of our lives in terms of local and international politics, social issues and even economics. Whether it was within our micro family or the entire region, religion, in this case Islam, was *it*. Having worked on and with non-governmental organizations (NGOs), I dealt with the extremely tricky subject of human rights for several years. I felt it was inevitable that at one stage I would critically examine why it is that religious arguments seem to be the ones that all protagonists – whether governing or in opposition – bandy about and why it is that women are symbolic as a terrain of contention between diverse opponents.

Events in many Arab countries today highlight the complex interplay between women's rights activism, political Islam in its various hues (Islamisms), socioeconomic dynamics and geo-political tensions. Too often, however, the presentation of events can be overly simplified. Islamisms, for instance, are seen through a limited prism of either religious fundamentalism or terrorism, while feminisms are often seen as anti-Islamist and usually a variation of some Western forms thereof. While some elements of the above are true to some extent, the reality is far more complicated, and often the dividing lines between ideology and action are far less clear-cut – especially when seen through the realities of women's lives. This complexity is what this paper will attempt to present and discuss.

I continue to come across some academics and policy advisors in diverse organizations, particularly European and North American ones, who are far more comfortable defining the Middle East as a single cultural unit and to lump people and ways of thinking into certain simplistic categories such as 'fundamentalism' (e.g. 'Islamic fundamentalism' as part of religious fundamentalism). Some of my activist colleagues, on the other hand, are equally attracted by this simple process of categorization – or naming – which makes 'the enemy' easier to label and distinguish: religious fundamentalism is anti-democratic and anti-women; therefore, religious fundamentalists are enemies of democracy and women's rights; and *therefore* anyone arguing about/for religion is against democracy and women's rights. So, the solution is not to engage with religion at all. Religious people, as 'non-democrats', cannot be engaged in the struggle for democracy. The solution to all the world's ills is, if you must have religion, then keep it personal.

When it comes to faith, why is that 'just' personal? By rendering faith non-political, are we not also allowing those who speak in the name of religion to be the sole spokespersons for the entire faith? For how can we challenge what faith means in people's lives – including one's own – if one is to be silent? In addition, those who speak in the name of religion do not do so 'personally', they create entire agendas of governance, economics, culture and social interaction based on their understanding of what religious is. Millions are swayed by these agendas; indeed, millions vote on the basis of such 'religious agendas'. Surely, that voting is an act of democracy, so how can one afford not to engage? Can we become non-democrats by – in the name of fighting for democracy – excluding millions and what sways them?

Such a 'secularist' approach to religion and politics utterly fails to comprehend and engage the diverse ways Islam, as a personal faith, can and does inform peace and social justice. This approach also ignores the rich diversity of interpretations and ways of being Muslim in the world. It is significant to first appreciate the verse in the Holy Qur'an (49:13) that indicates that God created us in all our diversity, not that we should sit in judgment of each other, but that we should *know* one another – that is and thereby know ourselves. And again, I think, to be a Muslim is also to read and learn that the term 'Muslim' is used in the Holy Qur'an to reference people who existed even before the advent of Islam as we know it today. Indeed, is it not used to refer to Abraham and consecutive prophets and people who were believers?

At best, many feminists see a confluence between their secular rights and their faith-based ones; they believe that the faith is about tremendous inclusiveness of and humility towards each other. At worst, many Muslims seek to remind ourselves that nothing is so clear-cut for our judgment, but everything bespeaks an ambiguity that in itself is a miracle of our creation and existence.

Studying the efforts of women of faith who represent different religious traditions and who work with communities of faith, teaches a number of important lessons.[1] Not only are women of faith the bulwark of faith-based services, in some instances they form over 90 per cent of basic service providers in religious communities.[2] However, whether traditional African, Chinese, Buddhist, Hindu, Jewish, Christian, Muslim or Baha'i, these women of faith see a huge difference between the spirit of their faiths and the practices done in the name of their religions. Many of these women, through their remarkable intellectual endeavours and activism in both public and private domains, seek to reclaim their religious heritage and reinterpret the understandings of religion such that faith becomes central to practice rather than the current paradigm in which the religious institution is the focus of the practice and is its sole interpreter. Part of the significance of this work is the affirmation of the fact that far from being solely a tool of women's oppression, religion is a fundamental aspect of the struggle for human emancipation and, with it, for women's rights. There is no way that this process of reclaiming the religious can take place by ignoring religion, by castigating or alienating those who would speak in its name or, certainly, by assuming that only the religious institutions represent the 'religious'.

In addition, there is an increasing body of literature that points to the realization that one can be a person of faith and a feminist at the same time.[3] Religious feminism is not merely a concept but a reality born of the struggles of women of faith for their rights – with their faith as a constructive part of that struggle. There is no question that with the access of Islamist parties to leadership in Tunisia and Egypt and with their considerable political influence across the Arab region from Yemen to Libya, it is imperative that we arrive at a clear, nuanced and realistic appreciation of the nexus of religion, women's lives and political dynamics.

While the United States has boasted the Christian Coalition, mainland European countries in the 1990s and first two years of the twenty-first century hosted a re-emergence of rightist political thought – the kind championed by France's National Front Party, the Le Pen family and Geert Wilders, founder of the Dutch Party for Freedom.[4] Even though the stardom of these respective figureheads has faded, much of their political rhetoric, which has appealed to some of their economically disgruntled populations, has now been incorporated into mainstream political discourse.

It is at best a risk to believe that control can be exerted once individuals have espoused an ideology about the implementation of 'God's rules' or any absolutist values. And yet it is remarkable how many regimes and individuals will do just that to either gain or consolidate power, whether locally or internationally – including several US administrations. The formation of Jerry Falwell's Moral

Majority in 1979, which was the formalization of what is referred to as the Christian Coalition or the religious right, and signalled a situation where the entrance of the religious into the political fray became common practice in contemporary and supposedly secular US dynamics. However, George Marsden reminded us:

> For better or for worse, mixes of religion and politics have always been one part of the American political heritage [...]. The recent fundamentalist and evangelical political ventures can be best understood as a revival of one of the nation's major political traditions.[5]

Terence Samuel has written about the USA in a 2002 article entitled 'The Peak of Political Power':

> [T]he evangelical movement is firmly entrenched in the nation's political life, lobbying and leveraging like any of the hundreds of other pressure groups in Washington out to advance their causes and promote their issues. The Christian Coalition's Web site is a beehive of political advocacy and not just on traditional issues like abortion and school prayer [...] the Coalition worked doggedly on behalf of GOP candidates during the last election and might well take credit for swinging the Senate.[6]

Martin Marty, American religious scholar and author of *When Faith Collides* succinctly summed up the phenomenon in the following lines:

> Division of life into spheres worked better when religion was more credibly viewed as a private affair. Today, while it certainly has not lost its personal and private appeal, religion is highly public. It is evident in the prosecution of war and peace, in violence and reconciliation. One confronts its images in the arts and entertainment world. In any case, it certainly is no stranger to politicians in a world where 'faith-based' enterprises are not confined to the United States.[7]

So where does this leave us? It clearly leaves us with a need to re-evaluate the ways in which religion is understood, to reassess the varied protagonists thereof and to ascertain the actions that need to be undertaken to deal with terror. But to concretize what is argued here, let us use political Islam, or Islamism, as an example.

Political Islam/Islamism – An Arab Case Study

Islamism's emergence in the 1980s in the Arab world appeared to grab Western headlines with events such as the assassination of the Egyptian President, Anwar al-Sadat and variations of kidnappings, bombings and armed conflicts in Lebanon, Egypt and Algeria – to name but a few. Almost since then, political Islam was perceived in the Western public consciousness as synonymous with violence. This impression has almost been stamped by a searing rod in Western collective perception by unfolding events in the Arab world together with ongoing bombings and attacks elsewhere (i.e. the Paris subway bombings, US Embassy attacks in Nairobi and Dar El Salam, World Trade Center in New York and the Pentagon in Washington, followed by Bali, Madrid, London, Glasgow and so on). Needless to say, the conflict between the two Palestinian factions of *Hamas* and *Fatah* as it unfolded in the occupied Palestinian territories has done nothing to enhance the image of political Islam.

Islamism is only one stream of politics within and outside the Muslim world. In fact, this is but a fraction of the different forms of social and political mobilization that take place among Muslims in general – and certainly amongst Muslim communities in the western hemisphere.[8] Repeated statements by members of the US administration immediately after the events of 9/11 and then echoed by other leaders such as Britain's former Prime Minister Tony Blair highlighted that the 'war against terrorism' has nothing to do with Islam. And yet, 'Islamic extremism', 'Islamic terror', 'Islamic militants' and 'Islamic violence' have become mainstream lexicon.

Various authors have analysed political Islam; often, individual terms such as *Islamic fundamentalism*, *Salafi*, *jihadi* and *Islamic radicalism* have been used to explain the roots and objectives of a diversity of political and social movements.[9] Much debate took place, particularly in the late 1980s and the 1990s, about appropriate nomenclature. I posit the term Islamism as a continuum of movements which have a quintessentially political orientation that revolve around Islamising (rendering more Islamic) the structures of governance and those of the overall society. Shari'a, or the compendium which is Islamic laws, are considered by many Islamists to be a key way of bringing about this envisioned Islamization.

An Islamist needs to be distinguished from her/his fundamentalist counterpart, in that the Islamist is not literal in his/hers interpretations and understanding of text and, in fact, can be quite creative in the manner in which they implement their 'religious' understanding. Also unlike a fundamentalist, Islamists see religion as a primary motor for their public political work. Whereas a fundamentalist may or may not become engaged in political thought, debate and activism, an Islamist, per definition, does. *Political engagement of some sort is a sine qua non of being an Islamist.* The latter distinction also clarifies the difference between an Islamist, a Muslim fundamentalist and an average Muslim. In other words, it is the involvement in a movement or a group that advocates or struggles for political change – specifically to render more 'Islamic' *the social and political* governing principles (or government) – that is the principal hallmark of an Islamist.

For many Islamists, Islamization as a political agenda *is a means to bring about justice* – politically, economically and socially. To be an Islamist, it is by no means enough to be a Muslim, nor is it even sufficient (or even necessary) to be a fundamentalist. Rather, an Islamist must be committed to active public engagement in the quest for a more Islamic (read: just) society. All Islamists will share this ultimate aim.[10]

What constitutes an 'Islamic' (or just) society or Islamic governance? And what methods should be used to achieve this aim? These are amongst the most important questions around which Islamists will differ (often radically and violently, as we see in present-day Afghanistan and Iraq) from each other. There is no homogenous Islamist entity. Thus, not all Islamists are alike, and there is a serious misrepresentation when they are all lumped as either 'fundamentalists', 'fanatics' or 'terrorists'. The latter obscures the significant differences within Islamist political thought and praxis.

'Moderate' Islamists, perhaps best exemplified by the Muslim Brotherhood, maintain that change will come about only through long-term education, social and economic engagement and constituency building and advocacy, whereby increasing numbers of people becoming 'followers', and eventually espouse the political ideology-cum-social action package.[11] Moderates will generally advocate for and participate in elections, and in several majority Muslim countries and societies where this is permitted, they will register as political parties and organize themselves as such.[12] One notable difference between Islamist parties and other political entities is that the moderate Islamists tend to have relatively well-defined social agenda(s) often exemplified by their provision of important social services (e.g. schools and clinics) in their respective communities. The latter lends them credibility and support among the various social classes (particularly the larger poorer ones) and thus constitutes an important factor in their political outreach and popularity. Moderate Islamists will generally not condone violence as a means to an end. However, depending on the situation (e.g. the Palestinian struggle for self-determination), they may well refrain from outright condemnation of suicide bombings with the proviso that the targets should be military and not civilian, and the act is considered to be self-defence.

The picture of moderate Islamism is rendered even more complex, however, with the emergence of relatively 'new' Islamist actors on the block, particularly in Egypt – that is the *Salafis*. Previously thought to abhor political engagement or to studiously avoid appearing to be politically active, the *Salafis* emerged after the January 2011 events in Egypt and Tunisia as a breed of devout Muslims with a political agenda firmly grounded in Islamic values. And, they appear on the political space precisely as part of an emerging Islamic political consciousness which Egypt (and other Arab countries namely Tunisia and Yemen) witnessed. Almost as an alter ego, the Salafists – who are also diverse – are juxtaposed against the Brotherhood; and whereas the latter made several promises (to field limited candidates for parliamentary elections and then not to field a Presidential candidate), and then proceeded to break them, the Salafists on the other hand, only articulated social justice and God-driven commitment. Compared to the Brotherhood's litany of errors during their very brief tenure in governance, the Salafists appear relatively more 'clean' (read untarnished by the exigencies of political governance) and astute about their consistent mistrust of the military (which the Brotherhood's political party – the Freedom and Justice – initially sought to accommodate). Salafists are clear about denouncing violence as a political means, which positions them on the 'moderate' end of the spectrum. Yet, unlike other political parties, the political moderation of the Salafists, as the next section will show, does not extend to their positions on women.

Contrarily, 'radical' Islamists may be so named precisely because, to most of them, the Machiavellian refrain 'the ends justify the means' is popular. Violence thus becomes a means to what they perceive as a 'necessary' or 'holy' end. Nevertheless, some 'radical Islamists' may veer towards the moderate end of the continuum on specific issues or during certain times. An example of this is the Lebanese *Hizbullah* (Party of Allah), which has a history of anti-Israeli struggle and became particularly infamous during the 1980s for the kidnapping of Westerners in Beirut. In the 1990s, *Hizbullah* coalesced into a legitimately recognized political party, ran for elections and won seats in the Lebanese parliament. Their decision to participate in electoral politics was certainly based on *real politik*, but it was also a choice for a relatively moderate strategy – selectively installed.[13] Such a shift has implications for whether or not (and how) shari'a should be applied.[14]

Appreciating the Specificity of Women's Roles

Assessing where various parties stand on the 'question of women in the Muslim world' also provides an important political and social insight. The parliamentary elections in Egypt at the beginning of 2006, which despite government harassment and intimidation, witnessed a rise in the presence of the Muslim Brotherhood to approximately a fifth of the parliamentary representation. The achievements of the Muslim Brotherhood and the success of *Hamas* in the Palestinian legislative elections have been attributed to – among many things – the roles of the women in these parties.

Although the Egyptian Muslim Brotherhood did not boast about having women in its *shura* (consultative) council (its main decision-making body), women are nevertheless a key part of its outreach, informal decision-making and constituency. The same applies to *Hamas*, which boasts a wide popularity among women, as well as their representation in the newly formed Palestinian Assembly. As articulators and disseminators of the ideology and as voters, women have provided the edge to the ascent of the Islamist parties in these two countries. In fact, elsewhere I have noted how it took one woman and her team of women to 'rescue' the Egyptian Muslim Brotherhood from annihilation by the Nasserist regime in the 1960s.[15] All of these dynamics have repercussions on the extent that these parties formulate their policies on a range of critical social issues, which will undoubtedly play a role in the interaction they have with those in the Western world who are so concerned for Arab and Muslim women's well-being.

In fact, the decision-making and activist roles attributed to and played by women in these parties is a significant marker in distinguishing between moderate and radical Islamists. Moderate Islamists have women members; who are active in the various echelons of the party structure (and different parties have differing numbers of women in various positions within the hierarchy). These women are not hidden from view; but on the contrary, they play visible and public roles.

This should bring to mind the public commitment of former President Mursi of Egypt when newly elected, which he articulated at the very outset of his acceptance speech in June 2012 that he have a woman and a Coptic Christian as Vice Presidents. While many detractors dismissed this as a ploy of some sort, the fact remains that as a Muslim Brotherhood representative, a veteran of several years, and as a popularly elected (first ever in modern Egyptian history) president, President Mursi did not need to gain popularity by compromising on any deeply held principles of moderate Islamism. Indeed, he was not compromising on any such principles precisely because the *Ikhwan*, and moderate Islamism more generally, tends to be politically savvy and religiously astute. In practice, as far as gender dynamics are concerned, this means that many Islamists realize the critical role women play in public and private life, and base their very own successes of mobilization, indeed of the revolutionary experience of the Arab Spring itself, on the active presence and contributions of women – both those within their own party echelons and those on the outside.

Where do the Salafists stand on women's rights? While they have women adherents, they have neither sought to issue a manifesto stating their position on women, nor have they fronted any women in any leadership positions. When questioned, many Salafists will, at best, voice various iterations of the 'complementarity' of women and men's roles in society. Most are unequivocal in indicating that they do not see women as leaders of any particular sphere beyond the home. Their narrative on gender roles is conservative to the extreme, and it remains challenging to see any of their women members as active and articulate about women's rights.

Radical Islamists as a rule, rarely have women in their decision-making structures (and if they do, it would be anything but publicly done). Radical Islamists have not shied away from recruiting women to carry out acts associated with violence, whether to carry and deliver arms or even as suicide bombers. The distinction becomes far less clear-cut, however, in the complex Palestinian context where *Hamas* too has been alleged to recruit women suicide bombers.[16]

Today, many spokespersons of the diverse array of political Islam, or Islamism, find themselves at best, on the defensive (about their diversity and their aspirations) and at worst, cornered – and fighting.[17] This may often translate into the women protagonists 'going more underground' or becoming less visible while nevertheless working tirelessly to promote the Islamist causes by mobilizing and serving their communities socially and politically. It is this tendency to vilify, or alternatively to attempt to marginalize, Islamists that I warn against; it requires serious self-reflection and pause on the part of researchers and policymakers alike, as the paragraphs below also discuss.

Feminisms in the Middle East

With this nuanced picture of Islamisms in mind, we now tackle another feature of the ongoing regional dynamics which are part and parcel of the competing political narratives: women's rights. More specifically, what do feminism and gender mean in this context? To many, feminism, insofar as it is an attempt to struggle for more rights for women (whether the right to vote, to earn equal pay, or to divorce and retain custody of children without the legal harassment currently in store for many women), has become a permanent feature of the social, cultural and political landscape. Although the first modern feminist movements (as opposed to feminist discourse which was, in some instances, attributed to men in Egypt and Tunisia) are often spoken of as appearing in the late nineteenth and early twentieth centuries, students of religious history (whether of Islam or Christianity) are quick to unearth examples of much earlier champions of women's rights. As indicated earlier, reclaiming this history (or 'herstory') has gained credibility as a legitimate scientific enterprise in Arab academe. Indeed, I would argue that this reclaiming of a voice in history and present-day public life, and the subsequent change in the consciousness of both women and men, while immeasurable, is precisely what made the Arab revolutions that erupted in 2011 possible.

'Feminism' as a term, however, is far from widespread. With no equivalent in the local languages, the word itself contributes to the misperception of the entire movement as 'foreign'. Few women activists feel comfortable with the term and those that do are not necessarily consistently vocal about it as a self-definition. It is not uncommon to find researchers referring to feminism – or to certain activists as feminists – while the activists themselves balk at the reference. At the same time, however, an alternative mode of reference to these women and men has yet to arise. Some have toyed with the Arabic term *niswiyya* or *nisa'iyya*, which acts as a translation of the word feminism, but such terminology has simply not become popular.

Similarly, the term 'gender' does not have an equivalent in local languages and is more often used by feminist groups, and sometimes social scientists as a descriptive or analytical category. Gender is still seen as synonymous with 'women' and a widespread or popular appreciation of the nuances of the term – whether semantic, actual or both – remains lacking. At the same time, the social construction of masculine and feminine roles, and identities is central to an understanding of the social oppression and the cultural constructions of violence that affect women in the Middle East.

The Continuum of Feminism

For the sake of clarity in this chapter, a broad definition of the term feminism is used with two key components: a consciousness that women are oppressed in many ways and actual attempts to rectify or deal with this oppression.[18] This working definition is inspired by the extensive research carried out by women researchers such as Leila Ahmed, Mahnaz Afkhami, Haleh Afshar, Fatma Göçek, Yvonne Haddad, Mervat Hatem, Deniz Kandiyoti, Lila Abu Lughod and Valentine Moghadam, to mention but a few.

With the above definition, it is possible to identify three main feminist streams in the Arab world. These streams clearly align along a continuum: secular (herein understood as non-religious discourse); religious (largely, but not only, couched in Islamic terms); and Islamist (framed within and advocating for political Islam). None of these streams is by any means homogeneous or generic. Each category is full of diversity (and ambiguity), and often the 'barriers' delineating one form of discourse from another are tenuous. Hence, there is the importance of imagining a range of qualities and strategy rather than a distinct discursive practice (as depicted below).

The Continuum of Feminism in the Middle East

← - →

Secular   Religious   Islamist

Secular feminists on the whole (such as the New Women's Research Centre in Egypt or the Association Démocratique de Femmes de Maroc (The Democratic Association of Women in Morocco)) tend to shun faith-based discourse. This does not mean that they disrespect religion or are themselves non-religious. On the contrary, some of them are devout (and are keen to describe themselves as such) in their personal lives.[19] However, when it comes to publicly framing their discourse on women's rights, many secular feminists will skirt religious issues, or argue that to bring in religion is to risk endangering women's rights. This is either because of the dominance of conservative religious establishments or because they fear creating a rift amongst their own ranks as they may not all share the same faith tradition. Secular feminists are generally comfortable with the term feminist, and many have strong connections with their feminist sisters from other countries. Secular feminists advocate for the implementation of all international legal human rights instruments and challenge all forms of discrimination, which is evidenced by their support for the Convention for the Elimination of All Forms of Discrimination against Women (CEDAW), the Beijing Platform for Action, and others.

Some secular feminists can be openly antagonistic about and towards religion. They maintain that religion itself is the cause for much of the oppression women suffer. Feminists at this end of the spectrum are thus unwilling to engage with their more 'religious' sisters because they see them as labouring under a 'false consciousness'. The more 'religious' the message of the social or political activists, the more suspicious the secular feminists tend to be and often for good reason. Rarely in the Arab world is there any praise from religious circles for those outside of religious frameworks who advocate for women's rights. Similarly, wherever there is an active Islamist movement (e.g. in Sudan, Algeria, Tunisia, Libya, Egypt, Yemen, Jordan or Lebanon), some of the strongest opposition will be from secular feminists who strongly believe that women's rights will be the first serious casualty of any Islamist regime.

On the opposite end of the diapason, Islamist feminists (sometimes the women's wing of the Muslim Brotherhood movements – albeit not defining themselves in 'feminist' terms) – to many, a contradiction in terms – have an important role to play. In the same way that not all secular women are feminists, not all women members of Islamist movements (which themselves exist right across the region) are feminists by any means. On the contrary, some of the most vociferous critiques of feminists and feminism emanate from men *and* women in Islamist circles. So who are Islamist feminists then? These are the activists within the movement advocating for political Islam who subscribe to the working definition of feminism used above. In other words, these are the women who acknowledge that women are oppressed and see the Islamist reality as an option to bring about a better world for both men and women.

Broadly speaking, for Islamist feminists the reasons for women's oppression are often explained in terms of society's lack of adherence to Islam (or to God) and the junctions of that faith in general. Since Arabs are not following God's laws (which can only be just), runs the argument, we confront the social, political and structural problems we have today. A society dominated by (an enlightened interpretation of) the Shari'a is one that, in these women's opinion, will guarantee justice for women, and thus improve Muslim women's conditions. These women see Islamism as an advocate for a more just society, and they perceive it as the means to achieve this end. Islamist feminists share two things with their secular counterparts: at best a sense of unease and, at worst, outright suspicion, vis-à-vis each other. They argue that international legal instruments are at best redundant and, at worst, problematic and foreign because all that Muslims need are the Qur'an, the *Sunna* and the *Hadith*.

Religious feminists fall somewhere in the middle of the continuum, and it is within this category that I situate Muslim, or Islamic feminists (many of whom are members of *Musawah* – an impressive umbrella network of practitioners, policymakers and grassroots women and men). They are, by and large, to be distinguished from Islamists in that they do not advocate for any one political philosophy or ideology. In fact, many of them can be uncomfortable with what they perceive as the homogenising tendency of Islamist feminists and their dogmatism with respect to interpretation and understanding of the Shari'a. They share with their Christian and Jewish counterparts the same discomfort with 'fundamentalist' interpretations of religion. With a healthy respect for the role of faith in empowering and liberating women and men, religious feminists are nevertheless keen to emphasize new and evolving interpretations of doctrine, and they advocate for the meeting point between international legal instruments such as CEDAW and the essence of all faith traditions.

Religious feminists stand apart from their secular counterparts by maintaining that no discourse of women's rights that rejects religion can achieve its objectives in contexts where such a religion is the pervasive *lingua franca* of the masses and the politicians. Religious feminists are as vehement in urging caution towards blind espousal of a religio–political cause (without a distinct women's rights agenda) as they are towards an outright rejection of religion as a framework for reference. For many of them, faith traditions (in this case mostly Islam) guarantee a context of infinite justice for women, but the way the religion is preached, interpreted and manipulated (politically) is highly problematic. In order to counter this manipulation, many religious feminists are keen to learn or advocate for a rereading of religious and non-religious history, and religious texts and traditions. Familiarity with, if not mastery of, the religious language is one of the strongest tools for rejecting religious dogmatism, political obfuscation, and the manipulation of religious rhetoric against women, as well as for developing constituencies that can engender social transformation.

As indicated earlier, women activists are not glued to or confined within these feminist categories. In fact, on some women's rights issues including the abolition of female circumcision, reform of family, and/or civil laws, and certain political dynamics, such as support for the Palestinian cause and calls for democratization, there is often an overlap of interests and a commonality of agendas amongst the otherwise different streams. Regardless of their position on the continuum, many of today's feminist organizations had some of their roots in charity work in the late 1800s and early 1900s. By the middle of the twentieth century charity work gave way to activities that ranged from promoting women's electoral participation and running for political office, to organizing and providing small grants for rural development projects (micro-financing) and income generation initiatives, to organizing and lobbying politicians, and producing some seminal academic research.

Lived Realities of Muslim Feminism

There are a number of issues on which one can see how several Muslim feminists tend to appreciate their advocacy and activism. Female circumcision is one of the most blatant and painful customs frequently practiced in the name of the religion and on which one can find clear positions of Muslim feminists. It is helpful to note the example of Azza al-Jarf, who was a female member of Egypt's short-lived Parliament in 2012 representing the Muslim Brotherhood. In al-Jarf's case, she actually argued to maintain the practice of female circumcision, but have it performed by medical officers. Muslim feminists, by and large, will be against the practice as a matter of principle since they question any religious backing or justification thereof.

Other issues include: questions of women's inheritance (men inherit twice what women do); testimony (two women's testimony equals that of one man); wife beating; polygamy for men (that it is not only permissible but advocated); and stoning (supposedly the Islamic 'thing'). These are also issues frequently cited as examples of how 'Islam' is inherently oppressive towards women. While there are indeed many interpretations claiming that the above notions are based on an inherent belief that women are 'less than' men in value, intelligence, capacity and so on, Islamic feminists would be quick to point out that many of these concepts also come with a wealth of alternative interpretations, which can in fact be perceived as empowering for and considerate of women. Below I cite some of these differing elucidations while stressing the importance of keeping in mind the context in which these ideas appear and the differing schools of thought prevalent even today.

Many Muslim feminists maintain that in pre-Islamic Arabia, women were considered chattels, or belongings, of men and the tribe. Women's ownership over anything was rare and was the experience of those, few and far between, who were protected by their male lineage. Property ownership was largely seen as a favour bestowed upon women by their fathers or husbands. Muslim laws that give women a legitimate right to inherit from any member of their family an amount equal to half that of their male brethren and allow them to keep their inheritance untouched and exclusively their own, while their male brethren are required to spend their inheritance on the welfare and protection of these women, were actually quite revolutionary laws. In other words, under the Muslim code, Muslim Arab women are entitled to inherit, not as a favour, but by law. At the same time, men who inherit double what women do are required to support all the women and children with that inheritance, while the women can keep their money and do with it as they please.

Similarly, Islamic/Muslim feminists maintain that the seemingly oppressive practice of legal testimony is more complex than it first appears. Some of them, such as those engaged within a global network of *Musawah*, argue that prior to the Muslim code at no point were women considered reliable witnesses to anything legal or significant, and a man's word would override that of any woman, if her voice was heard at all. But by urging that two women's testimony could equal that of a man, the Qur'an effectively makes it 'legal' for women to act as witnesses in the first place; simultaneously, two women testifying can act as a support for each other in a society dominated by men and thus protect each other from retaliation.

On the verse in the Qur'an that supposedly allows or urges husbands to beat their wives, Muslim feminists (e.g. Ingrid Mattson, Laleh Bakhtiar and Asma Barlas) often mention how the verse has come under heavy scrutiny and interpretive discussions (Surat Al-Nisa, verse 34). In a very rich language where one word can have several meanings in a given context, they uphold that one of the explanations concerns the varied meanings of the Arabic word for 'beat'. Some maintain the argument that the verb used for 'beat' or 'hit' is also the one for 'refrain', 'abstain' and/or 'leave'. If the verse were translated with this meaning in mind, rather than urge husbands to beat recalcitrant wives, it would seem to urge them to let women be, or leave them alone for a while. As for stoning, the practice is not mentioned in the Qur'an, but it was a practice existing in the wider region for some time as evidenced by the words of Jesus during a situation where a crowd wished to stone an adulteress. Once again, many Muslim feminists would argue that far from being 'Islamic', this is one of the legacies of older tribal ways.

Polygamy is by far the most controversial of the Islamic injunctions, and it has certainly received its fair share of discussions among Muslim feminists and their secular counterparts both within and outside the Muslim world. Many Muslim feminists maintain that the verse where polygamy is mentioned is frequently only partially quoted by pro-polygamy advocates. A detailed theological explanation is beyond the purview of this chapter, but suffice it to say here that Islamic feminists uphold interpretations of the text that oppose polygamy. Muslim feminists usually cite the fact that the call for polygamy is highly conditional (men have to be egalitarian to each of the maximum of four women they espouse) and is based in a context that no longer has validity for contemporary times. For example, it was based in times when wars that led to the deaths of many fathers and heads of households left women destitute and vulnerable to exploitation in male-dominated societies, so taking some of them in marriage would have been considered a way to offer them protection.

Wide disagreement on the rights, responsibilities and roles of women, and the significant diversity in the practice of all aspects of the Islamic faith are clear indicators that 'Islam' is not 'inherently' discriminatory towards women. For something to be inherent, it needs at least to be agreed upon by all those who believe and/or practice, and it should be deeply ingrained. This is very difficult to assert given the brief insight into the diversity of understandings, interpretations, laws and practices mentioned above.

Women, Religion, Violence and Politics

The predominant concern with the nexus of religion, violence and politics is overly dramatized and possibly has resulted in overlooking factors, which led to critical sea changes in attitudes and behaviours – that is, the Arab uprisings starting in 2011. We need to revise some critical parameters of women taking action. The following section outlines the most notable of these parameters and caveats: women are as culpable as men in threatening to commit violent acts, in inciting violence and in actually undertaking acts of brutality as cooke argues in Chapter 1 of this volume. They are also leaders of change and builders of communities as we see with the lives and teachings of Cemalnur Sargut and Daisy Khan in their dialogue summarized in this volume.

Far from assuming a more 'nurturing' nature for women, their experiences in political processes repeatedly indicate that it is the process – which remains largely male-dominated and operates with male norms – that structures the attitudes, responses, and acts undertaken by women in positions of decision-making authority.[20] Hence, it is not always to be assumed that women alone change politics, especially not if and when they remain in the minority.

A vivid example of how women can see the need to use violence, much the same way as men do, is given by Luisella Neubruger and Tiziana Valentini's interviews of Vincenza Fioroni (a member of the Italian far-left organization Prima Linea). In the answer to the authors' question as to why she decided to become active in the movement, Fioroni responded 'I think that for me it was a last resort after having seen first-hand our total impotence to change things without violence'.[21]

Even when women achieve a critical mass in any political or decision-making context, they do not always rise to support, overtly or covertly, other women or women's interests. This is due to several reasons, which vary from tactical calculations to downright disinterest (the latter more rare). Development experience thus far points to the critical need for women and men to work together as opposed to in separate interest-related camps.[22] This entails reassessing how challenges are defined in the first place, as well as re-evaluating the methodology of finding solutions, and making important allies across the political, and gender-segregated spectrum.

Further, there are current ideological fault lines between secular women's organizations and faith-based ones. Each 'group' tends to work in isolation from the other. This can and does constitute a fundamental stumbling block when it comes to much-needed strategic alliances. It remains overly simplistic to assume that one group of women (or men) from Europe and North America will be able to 'help' others in the non-Western world to overcome their challenges. The perspective of the West extending 'a helping hand', whether in the name of 'noblesse oblige' (otherwise known as 'White man's burden') or 'freedom' has already created centuries of resentment and failures, measured in human lives.[23]

Preventing misunderstandings, or even anticipating positive social change, requires that women ally themselves with men and with their counterparts in the faith-based movement to challenge stereotypes and create critical 'spaces of communication'. The creation of such strategic alliances requires clarity and distinctions to be made as to the precise nature of the terrorism in question (what specific tactics), the reasons behind its emergence, as well as who the protagonists are. Moreover, these strategic alliances have to be built on a level playing field and not, as can be evidenced in some literature, on the provision of handouts.[24]

Going Forward with Revolutions in Consciousness

Remarkably, even though we are now increasingly lamenting population increases in many debates about Climate Change and diminishing planetary resources, it has been possible to overlook the fact that part of this demography is a youth bulge, which many see as a predominant cause for concern. This concern was articulated variedly, but mostly in terms of the following (oversimplified) equation:

Unemployed youth + poverty + a healthy dose of sense of indignity and injustice = higher potential for terrorism, drugs and violence.

We failed to grasp the possibility of a radically different (and equally simplified) modern-day equation:

> 60 per cent of the population (youth — with a large majority of girls
> and women among them) + access to social media and cell phones
> + a healthy dose of a sense of indignity and injustice = revolution.

The Arab revolutions were spearheaded by the young, who used social media to ignite the revolutions. Yet there was a time, when some of the regimes in the desperate throes of survival, shut-off the internet and cell phones. Still the revolutions continued and grew beyond the national borders. How? Because the 24/7 satellite news coverage combined with the courage and creativity of young demonstrators – male and female – who risked their futures and sacrificed their lives. The anticipation of further degradation from poverty and austerity measures announced by despised regimes, in different ways, propelled remaining generations to revolt.

Western discourse about the revolutions and their varied outcomes are rooted in simplistic and essentialized assumptions that fail to acknowledge and understand the diversity of opinions and interests of Arabs and Muslims broadly. The predominate assumption following the collapse of the dictatorial regimes in Egypt, Libya and Tunisia, particularly, reproduced the knee-jerk fear of the Islamists (read: terrorists) as taking over and creating Islamic/shari'a-run states – that is, the Iranian Revolution revisited. While the Muslim Brotherhood did initially win a fully democratic election, the impact was far from being a clerical State as in Iran. This simplistic narrative is being harvested tenfold by militaristic regimes in countries as diverse as Egypt, Yemen and Syria. The reason this is frustrating is because it continues to portray developments in the Arab region through the same prisms that were used to sustain autocracy in the first place. Moreover, this perspective – and the authoritarianism it is justifying – also turns a blind eye to the *revolution in consciousness*, which has effectively taken place.

The Libyan electoral results did not favour Islamists with a victory. Instead, a coalition of largely – albeit not only – liberal political voices claimed the majority of votes. In Yemen, Islamists are struggling to retain popular legitimacy as the allegiances of the myriad political actors shift, and yet both the physical and cultural institutions of power seek to remain unchanged. The reasons for this are varied and beyond the scope of this article, suffice it here to say that these outcomes provide opportunities for comparison of women's rights' trajectories, which can only be instructive for students of women, religion and revolutionary politics as a whole in the region.

There is a very widespread concern among many liberal and secular activists, and even some Muslim feminists, that any Islamist regime will revoke hard-won legal and social–cultural achievements, particularly those relevant to gender equality. These fears are not groundless or limited to Muslims, but they are very much shared by the non-Muslim minorities across the Arab countries. The concerns are based on the rhetoric and actions of many Islamist parties inside and out of the Arab countries. Disturbing noises were in fact made by some women members of the Muslim Brotherhood (as noted earlier) in favour of female circumcision, which reinforced these worries. Actions undertaken by Tunisian religious fundamentalists in some academic campuses to allegedly persecute unveiled female members of the teaching staff, added fuel to the fires stoking these deep anxieties.

The emerging constitutional debates and dynamics in Egypt, Tunisia and Libya are highlighting considerable challenges including the need to learn how to disagree among civil society actors – women's rights actors included – while maintaining a certain degree of grace and civility. This is not an art that any one nation has mastered by any means. However, it is especially difficult for those communities who have learned how to cope with the deep social and political traumas engendered by cultures of fear and oppression. A great deal of this coping comes at the expense of learning how to differ, how to disagree, how to maintain distinct identities, and how to coexist without seeking to, at best silence and at worst, eliminate, the other within.

This challenge is further accentuated by at least four interesting features that now characterize the Arab uprisings: (1) the political violence that has unfolded along sectarian and religious lines; (2) the fact that in several instances, the very party most vilified by the former regimes as a means to legitimize themselves (i.e. Islamists) were the ones *elected* to political power; (3) the continued legacy of remnants of the old regimes (e.g. the military institutions) and their stranglehold over the economic lifeline and politics of these countries; and (4) (last but by no means least) the large majority of women themselves remain as divided about their future as their male compatriots.

At the same time however, a very real, yet significantly difficult to quantify, change, has already taken place in the entire region – a change in consciousness. An almost endemic sense of fear of power in its many guises, especially that of governments, military institutions and even of institutions that implement the rule of law, is no longer either determinant to sociopolitical behaviour or even palpable. Instead, as many of us now say, our feet have learned the walk of protest, and our hands and voices have learned how to communicate and articulate that protest through more ways than one. Indeed, there is a sense of dignity that has been retrieved in the process of overthrowing the yoke of fear. As a result, there is no going back to the fear-loaded impasses of intellectual and political stasis, which subsumed, silenced and rendered invisible ways of thinking, behaving and believing.

As the moderate Egyptian and Tunisian Islamists soon found out, some of the very same people who may have voted for them are also among the first to exercise their displeasure in clear ways – increasingly paying for their dissent in spilled blood and lost lives. And if those who were democratically elected can be demonstrated against, then any other authoritarian regime will be far less likely to curry favour with this 'new' public consciousness. This is the lesson that Syria's Assad regime and Egypt's military one, are adamantly refusing to accept. Instead, and with all due respect to the differences between these two regimes, they are each nevertheless becoming more draconian in implementing their (literal) firepower – in turn engendering a more radicalized opposition, especially among Islamists. This vicious cycle of violence is traumatising the region's already fraught social, economic and political fabric – with consequences that include rising tides of physical brutality and outright violence among the populace, from which women are by no means immune.

The fact remains that the culture of fear no longer dictates the terms of reference for many Arabs' lives – including those of women. Instead, the cacophony of voices and activism now even engenders a certain amount of confusion and difficulty of categorization of beliefs or ideas. Interestingly therefore, in finding our voices and our strength, we have also realized how diverse and polarized we are. But in the relative absence of fear, this realization of the polarization need not be paralysing given the current abilities to articulate, and the continuous learning and political evolution we are bound to encounter, with all that is no longer hidden. In other words, the concerns are important to acknowledge; they form a necessary part of the emerging kaleidoscope of political cultures and lived realities. Rather than shun them or seek to belittle or exaggerate their significance, these concerns must be seen as feeding into the processes of formation of new paradigms, which are an inevitable part of the next phase of Arab and feminist consciousness – phases which sadly, some will pay for in human rights abuses and with their lives.

Yet, it is precisely these new paradigms that are shaping the emerging Arab *demos* and its institutional formations.

Notes

1. See, for instance, Azza Karam (ed), *A Woman's Place: Religious Women as Public Actors* (New York: World Conference of Religions for Peace, 2000) and Isabel Apawo Phiri, Sarojini Nadar and Betty Govinden (eds), *Her-Stories: Hidden Histories of Women of Faith in Africa* (Pietermaritzburg, South Africa: Cluster Publications, 2002).

2. This figure is based on my own research after several years of culling information from various religious organizations around the world, and actual field observations from numerous communities in the United States, South and South East Asia, Latin America and the Caribbean.

3. See woks by Haleh Afshar, *Women In The Middle East: Perceptions, Realities, And Struggles For Liberation* (New York: Palgrave, 1993); Fatema Mernissi, *Islam and Democracy: Fear of the Modern World*, transl. Mary Jo Lakeland (Reading, CA: Addison-Wesley, 1992); and, Suzannah Heschel (ed), *On Being A Jewish Feminist* (New York: Knopf Doubleday, 1987).

4. See also for instance Diana L. Eck, *A New Religious America: How a 'Christian Country' has become the World's Most Religiously Diverse Nation* (San Francisco: HarperCollins, 2001); John Danforth, *Faith and Politics: How the Moral Values Debate Divides America and How to Move it Forward Together* (New York: Penguin Group, 2006).

5. George M. Marsden, *Understanding Fundamentalism and Evangelicalism* (Grand Rapids: William B. Eerdemans Publishing, 1991), p. 85.

6. Terence Samuel, 'The peak of political power', *US News and World Report*, 23 December 2002, p. 42.

7. Martin E. Marty, *When Faiths Collide* (Oxford: Blackwell, 2005), pp. 161–2.

8. For more on the transnational connections between Islamist ideology in Muslim countries, Europe and the USA, and the variations between Islamist positions on a range of issues, see Azza Karam (ed), *Transnational Political Islam: Religion, Ideology and Power* (London: Pluto Press, 2004).

9. Gilles Kepel, *The Prophet and the Pharaoh: Muslim Extremism in Egypt*, (Berkeley: University of California Press, 2003 (1985)); Olivier Roy, *The Failure of Political Islam* (London: I.B.Tauris, 1994); Fred Halliday, *Islam and the Myth of Confrontation: Religion and Politics in the Middle East* (London: I.B.Tauris, 1995).

10. This partly explains why the Egyptian Islamist party *al-Wasat*, at one time in 2008, boasted some Christian members.

11. The Muslim Brotherhood (*al-Ikhwan al-Muslimin*) came into existence in 1928 in Egypt as a social movement with a political agenda to struggle against British colonization and the incumbent social, cultural, political, economic and legal oppression and humiliation therewith. The Brotherhood's philosophy of embracing an Islamic identity and 'way of life' as a critical means of achieving social justice has since branched in different countries while being diverse in its structure and organizational method(s). Today's *Islah Party* in Yemen, the Palestinian *Hamas* and Tunisia's *Al-Nahda* are descendants of the *Ikhwan*.

12. Lebanon, Jordan, the Palestinian Territories, Algeria, Indonesia, Malaysia and Pakistan to name but a few.

13. This was an indication that the Israeli withdrawal from the South of Lebanon did in fact lead to a questioning of the longevity of *Hizbullah*'s claim to legitimacy. Needless to say, with the Lebanese-Israeli events of August 2006, the legitimacy of *Hizbullah* ceased to be an issue then, as it became an icon of Arab pride after the humiliation of the 1967 war. However, *Hizbullah* **has** lost considerable legitimacy as a result of the pro-Syrian regime position many see as having taken with the unfolding atrocities in the Syrian revolutionary – and now civil war – trajectory.

14. Commonly translated as Islamic law, it is worth noting that Shari'a is not one body of text or interpretation but rather the sum of various juridical interpretations collated over a certain course of time. Thus, there is no one Shari'a law but a whole set of man-made laws – some of which may differ according to the specific school of interpretation followed. This would also partly explain why certain applications of Shari'a differ from one Muslim country to another.

15. Azza Karam, *Women, Islamisms, and the State: Contemporary Feminisms in Egypt* (London: Macmillan, 1998).

16. See Barbara Victor, *Army of Roses: Inside the World of Palestinian Women Suicide Bombers* (New York: Rodale Inc., 2003).

17. Or 'resisting' as some, like *Hamas*'s Ismail Haniye (the Prime Minister in the former Palestinian ruling coalition), would have it. However, was this defensiveness more evident than when Essam El-Eryan, the spokesperson for the Egyptian Muslim Brotherhood, had to clarify in several media interviews exactly what their position is and would be, pending the Egyptian Revolution of 25 January 2011, thereby consistently 'minimizing' their role in the Revolution.

18. Azza Karam (ed), *A Woman's Place*.

19. Azza Karam, *Women, Islamisms and the State*; and see Azza Karam, ed., *Women in Parliament: Beyond Numbers* (Stockholm: International IDEA, 2004).

20. For an overview of women's ascendance to national legislatures and their impact within them, see Azza Karam (ed), *Women in Parliaments*, as well as the 2nd edn. of the same book with Jullie Ballington as co-editor (2006).

21. Prima Linea (Front Line) was founded in Lombardy in 1976 and was a communist worker and students' organization that carried out several violent acts, second only to the Red Brigades. Vincenza Fioroni was briefly a militant in this movement, was prosecuted and found not guilty in 1980. The authors interviewed her on 30 May 1990. See Luisella de Cataldo Neuburger and Tiziana Valentini, *Women and Terrorism*, transl. Leo Michael Hughes (London: Macmillan, 1996), p. 153.

22. See for instance, the UNFPA work on this at http://www.unfpa.org/gender/men.htm.

23. See for example of this critique Lila Abu-Lughod, *Do Muslim Women Need Saving?* (Cambridge, MA: Harvard University Press, 2013).

24. Curt Weeden for instance, in a book with a title which itself signifies a problem – *How Women Can Beat Terrorism: How Women in the U.S., Europe and Other Developed Nations can Empower Women in Poor Countries – and Move the World Towards a More Peaceful Tomorrow* (Mount Pleasant: Quadrafoil Press, 2003) – mentions three steps that women and men can take: (1) 'use foreign aid primarily to attack poverty and hopelessness at the grassroots level; (2) give women and women's programmes the highest priority when deciding how to allocate foreign aid; and (3) put the brakes on population growth in places where the addition of more people increases the probability of global problems', pp. 215–30.

PART 4

RELATIONSHIPS: BUILDING COMMUNITIES

CHAPTER 10

STRANGERS, FRIENDS AND PEACE: THE WOMEN'S WORLD OF ABDULLAH HALL, ALIGARH MUSLIM UNIVERSITY

Yasmin Saikia

The nineteenth century was a period of loss for Muslims in the Indian subcontinent. The end of the Mughal Rule (1526–1857) produced a foreboding sense of uncertainty, and the diverse Muslim communities were unable to conceptualize what lay ahead. 'Twilight', a metaphor used by Ahmed Ali, encapsulates the mood of the time as Muslims fumbled in anxiety within the structure of the Company Bahadur's rule.[1] It was a kind of anxiety that qualifies in the Heideggerian sense as a state of loss calling for change; Muslims had to find new directions to serve their communities. Anxious questions arose: would the Englishmen in India be friendly towards Islam given that they had deposed the Muslim rulers, the Mughals, from political power? Or, more precisely, would the Company Bahadur reduce the multitude Muslims into the reductive category of rebels and refuse to improve the Muslim condition? The Muslim psyche was deeply troubled, but Muslims could not imagine an independent and alternative vision for themselves. Like the other communities in India at that time, the Muslims treated the Company Bahadur as if it was a human being encapsulated in the term *mai-baap* (mother and father); thus, their relation with the Company Bahadur occupied a paramount position in their minds. Nonetheless, the basic desire to survive in these uncertain times, to avoid the existential threat of annihilation, meant a search for the 'Muslim self'. Given that the responses in the Muslim communities differed from one another, some turned to revivalist movements looking to the past for meaning in the present. Others searched for more dynamic and bold solutions looking forward to the future for Muslim development and progress.

It is the latter kind of response, which created a new consciousness of Muslim identity as progressive and forward looking, that I am interested in exploring in the chapter. In particular, I focus on the new vision of education for development of Muslims conceived by Sir Syed Ahmed Khan (1817–98; from here on Sir Syed as he is generally referred to by Aligarh graduates) under the auspices of the residential college called Mohammedan Anglo–Oriental College that later became Aligarh Muslim University (AMU). Sir Syed envisioned AMU as a space for new learning of secular knowledge taught in English. The educated Aligarh community in Sir Syed's dream was to serve as a beacon of a free-thinking, modern, Muslim community who would lead the Muslims of India from their state of colonization to their destiny as free and emancipated people. *Colonializability*, a term and concept advanced by the Algerian political thinker, Malik Bennabi, in Sir Syed's mission was meant to be overcome through modern education.[2] This emancipating vision was conceived as a development of human potential in which the capacity of being with different others in the residential communal living in the university was prioritized. This was combined with religio–cultural training in the residential halls, which he believed would improve both the individual and the community.[3] In the Islamic lexicon, this holistic approach qualifies as *Tarbiyya*, which stands for an inclusive system of education for refining a person in every aspect of life. The residential halls of AMU, the heart of the university, served as intimate spaces for the cultivation of individual students and the ethos of friendship for building a moral Muslim community. The residential lifestyle of AMU brought strangers together to form an ever-expanding 'Alig family'. Women's friendship in the lived environment of Abdullah Hall, the foremost women's hall of AMU and the seat of women's education in Women's College, is the focus of this chapter.

Friendship among women belonging to different religious groups, sects, classes and ethnic backgrounds that were nurtured in Abdullah Hall made the place into *darul aman*, a place of peace, and 'Abdullah girls' (this term is used for the residents and alum of the hall within and beyond AMU) became partners in developing a forward-looking, strong and peaceful Muslim community. Abdullah girls were not conscious of their role as peacemakers, but they accepted the capacity of peaceful-living within the hall as a way of being with others. The emphasis on friendship for improving Muslim community for peace is yet to be written, and the role of women in upholding this ethic is critical for our understanding of lived experiences of Muslim women within AMU. I present a narrative ethnography of the culture of friendship at Abdullah Hall to engage the issue of women's role in creating peaceful and resilient societies, albeit it may be a local and small effort, but this understudied field of friendship as a way of making peace is worth investigating for a renewed understanding of AMU's role in peacemaking in the Indian subcontinent. I suggest that the AMU's ethos of friendship among the students, particularly the way women actualized this in their day-to-day living in Abdullah Hall can serve as a model to overcome the challenges that arise from the proximity and differences, which is at the heart of violence in India as Ashis Nandy has argued.[4] The capacity to live and accept differences among the divergent religious groups in South Asia is vital for proper functioning of society today.

Background in History

Broadly speaking, there were three kinds of responses of Muslims to the traumatic changes of the nineteenth century. Sayyid Ahmad Sayyid Barelvi (1786–1831) organized a religious movement that he called *Rah-i-Nabuwwat* (misinterpreted as *Tariqa-e-Muhammaddiya* by the British) and assembled a '*Mujaheed* army' comprised of Bengali and

Hindustani soldiers to vanquish, in his estimation, the two enemies of the Muslims – the Sikhs and the British.[5] Sayyid Barelvi was killed in a campaign in 1831 in Balakot, present-day northern Pakistan. After his death the myth of his mystical powers and his return as *Amirul Momenin* (leader of the faithful) provided his followers the necessary impetus for continuing the struggle against the British in hope of freedom in the future.[6] Dubbed as the 'Hindustani fanatics' by the British colonial administration, Sayyid Barelvi's supporters were incessantly pursued and ultimately pushed out from British India to the 'independent territories' on the border of Afghanistan where they continued to operate until the mid-1930s.[7]

The roving religious preacher and political agitator, Jamalaldin Afghani (1838–97), offered another language of protest. He called upon the Muslims of India, which he approached as a singular body of oppressed and subjected people, to make unity with the Hindus for consolidating their strength to resist British colonialism.[8] Afghani's message made religion into a political agenda and some sense of a Muslim unity was offered by linking Muslim intelligentsia in India with Muslim intelligentsia in Egypt, Turkey, Iran and even Sudan.[9] This became evident during the *Khilafat* movement (1913–21) that combined an ethos of nationalism alongside pan-Islamism. The *Khilafat* leaders rallied the Indian masses to protest the dismantling of the office of Caliph after World War I, and the end of the Ottoman Empire. No doubt, it was a powerful historical moment setting the stage for the Indian freedom struggle under Gandhi's leadership, but curiously the *Khilafat* movement made Indian Muslims vulnerable and placed them in an uncertain position. Even today in India, six decades after independence, Muslims continue to exist as a hyphenated category – Indian-Muslims – and their loyalty as Indian citizens is suspected and menacingly used by fundamentalist Hindu political parties like the *Bharatiya Janata* Party (BJP) and *Vishwa Hindu Parishad*.[10]

Sayyid Barelvi and Jamaladdin Afghani's struggles can be read as revival movements looking to the past and the loss of Muslim political power that they hoped to revert. They used modern technology, a concept of 'national consciousness' and the discourse of violence to mobilize the masses.[11] Their religious appeal was not sufficient for achieving real and immediate changes for the development of the Muslims of India though.[12] Both these movements assumed that Muslims constituted one community (of believers) and urged for a unified response. Based on their assumption they called upon Muslims to assert their identity against the British through the use of force, which overlooked a foundational ethics enjoined by Islam on all Muslims to be hospitable to strangers and be at home with others in peace.[13] The Muslim identity that they hoped to reformulate mimicked the strategies of the colonizers combining fear and force. The reformation of multiple Muslim communities required a vision beyond the reach of colonialism for truly emancipating the people.

Sir Syed perceived the issue of colonializiablity of Muslims from a different perspective and offered a yet unthought solution for massive and positive change in the future. Instead of opposition against the British, which was a predictable strategy, Sir Syed promoted a positive relationship with the British/other for empowering a group of Muslims.[14] He adopted a moderate inclusive voice of reform focussing on education for Muslim identity formation under the watchful eyes of the British colonial government. The Muslims that Sir Syed's vision of education targeted was a selective group that represented the upper class, Urdu speaking northern India gentry. This was a small group when we take into account the vast numbers of Muslims who were dispersed throughout British India. It was also gender biased, exclusively focusing on men's education. Sir Syed's selective plan for Muslims was however envisaged as a launching pad to extend the benefits of education to a wider base and transform the self and community, which he believed were closely interlinked. The historical events of the time, the demise of the Mughals after the Revolt of 1857, the entrenched position of the English mercantile company in the Indian economy, and the reduction of Muslims to 'civilisational nothingness' by a 'concerted Orientalist discourse', were matters of great concern and anxiety that became the site on which Sir Syed conceived his new epistemological vision.[15]

Sir Syed's vision was based on the Oxbridge model and was actualized in the foundation of the Mohammedan Anglo–Oriental

College (MAO) at Aligarh in 1875. Despite the fierce opposition of the Muslim *ulema* who denounced Sir Syed as an apostate for introducing Western secular education, he tenaciously persisted on delivering the promise of a new and positive future for Indian Muslims through his reformed educational plan. In 1920, MAO College became a full-fledged autonomous university called Aligarh Muslim University (AMU). In the initial period of AMU's existence it was an all boys' university that catered almost exclusively to the upper class Muslim elite. Although selective in its appeal, the place became a dynamic site for an emergent and confident Muslim voice. This voice was represented within the residential life of the university by the students who combined the pursuit of Western knowledge with a grounded learning of religion and culture, keen interest in sports, rhetoric and debate, poetry and drama, and music and creative arts.[16]

The Aligs, as the student community of AMU became known, emblematized the modern Muslim. They were also seen as representatives of the *ashraf* class (the Urdu speaking gentry) who were now further empowered by Western education, and removed from the teeming and poor Muslim masses. For the Muslim masses AMU's education remained inaccessible. Notwithstanding this criticism against AMU (which seems to persist even today as a way of undermining its role in the general development of Indian Muslims), it is worth noting that although a small and select group, the Alig Muslim exuded an infectious optimism and confidence and a bold and hopeful outlook towards the future, which was radically different compared to the supporters of the revivalist movements, such as Sayyid Barelvi or Jamaladdin Afghani, that looked backwards. Aligs did not borrow the glory of the Mughal past for reassurance in the present, nor did they seek to purify Indian Islam through pan-Islamic and Arabic connections; they confidently claimed a place as Muslims of India–*Mussalman-e Hind* (term used by Sir Syed) based on self-worth and a sense of civic citizenship.[17] The term Muslims of India is worth further research to understand how Sir Syed imagined a single Muslim community to be constituted from the multiplicity of Muslims of India.

The unique feature of Alig identity that built community was a firm commitment to friendship that developed from the beginning as the hallmark of the residential halls. As the 'AMU family' kept expanding and growing, friendship continued to serve as the glue for Aligs and enabled them to see themselves as part of one complete whole. Multiple fractions existed within the Alig family, but the commitment to the place and vision of Sir Syed served as a hard glue to bind the diversity as the institution kept growing and including different varieties of students. This unique community of friends generated a peaceful environment of *darul aman*, that Sir Syed had envisaged as the future of Indian Muslims.[18] Alig friendship built on shared common values and lived experiences in the residential halls serves even today in crossing the divide between the so-called 'enemy' countries of India, Pakistan and Bangladesh, and functions across the border separating the private from the public.[19] Today, AMU serves some of the poorest Muslim students in India who cannot afford to live and study in the metropolitan educational hubs, such as Delhi, Poona, Bangalore or Mumbai. And, AMU is the only place of education for these disempowered marginal Muslim students. With the rapid expansion of the student body and the dearth of residential space within AMU, the art of communal living has been de-emphasized. However, in Sir Syed's time, his vision for the future of *Mussalman-e Hind* produced in the lived environment of AMU resulted in an unusual possibility of transforming Muslims into forward-looking citizens of India and friends of one another.

Women's College, the educational institution for Abdullah girls, was the product of Sheikh Abdullah (lovingly referred to as Papa Mian), his wife, Waheed Jahan (Ala Bi) and their daughter, Mumtaz Jahan's efforts. In 1906, several decades after the foundation of MAO College, Women's College and Abdullah Hall were established and quickly became the girls' campus of AMU. Abdullah Hall girls became the 'other-selves' of AMU boys, and AMU's emblematic friendship became Abdullah Hall's culture too.[20] Friendship as the foundation of a new Muslim identity manifesting peaceful living may seem intriguing and, simultaneously, a commonplace achievement – 'a simple point' in the words of Francis Robinson.[21] Is it so?

Arguably, friendship as a site for group identity, according to Western critical theory and the philosophical canon on the subject (going all the way back to the Greeks), is only possible in its absence; it cannot be actualized because it is corrupted by politics that is supposed to work outside of it. In other words, politics de-personalizes friendship, and becoming public like a business relationship, it must compete with what is understood as friendship; 'and thus *in the name of friendship*, we must conclude, alas ... "there is no friend"'.[22] In theory then, friendship as a shared experience and a site of identity is a promise, hoped for, but rarely actualized. Aristotle considered this rare possibility only among the most excellent of men whose virtue was mutually felt by the other, *the brother*, pursuing 'good' for the sake of the other.[23] The confined nature of friendship among virtuous men automatically excludes friendship between women and between women and men.

Reflecting on the above discussion, how are we to understand Alig friendship? How was it possible that strangers who came together at AMU became lifelong friends and were transformed into a 'family' seeking the development of self and community together? What did this community look like, especially when we are addressing women's friendship as a way of living peace in the everyday? Women's friendship suffers from 'double exclusion' in the Western tradition; Abdullah girls' friendship is not a simple point.[24] It is an exceptional happening that calls for careful engagement and placement within the context of Muslim identity in lived experiences. To understand both concept and experience of friendship for peace, in this chapter the focus is on a 'moment' within Abdullah Hall's history, during the 1980s, when I was a student and resided in the hall. The dialogical space of transformation that I experienced along with my Abdullah Hall family has produced a kind of certainty of this knowledge, to borrow Imam Ghazali's concept of *yakin* (conviction). Certainty is produced in understanding within a context. To convey this knowledge, the middle-voice of narration in history is crucial. Thus as an Abdullah girl I write this chapter not as a way of glorying AMU, but to bring into the site of conversation an understudied subject of friendship as an identity of being in the world with others in peace.

Respecting those who are not related by the ties of blood or association to a shared religion, and recognizing and fulfilling one's responsibility to those others, despite it, is the root concept of Islamic ethics for maintaining peace (Q60:8). The ability to live this responsibility speaks of a 'rooted cosmopolitanism' that is able to include multiple others without losing the sense of self.[25] Can the friendship that starts and blossoms among strangers and different others at Abdullah Hall serve as a model for Muslim women to forge peaceful methods for resolving difficult and critical issues today? By focusing on the subject of friendship we increase our knowledge of 'positive peace', which highlights the potential of human development, and directs our attention away from the fixated concern on conflict resolution and containing war between nations, also known as 'negative peace'. Adding to the scope of knowledge on positive peace and the role women's friendship can play in this process contributes to strengthening people's peace, and centre-stages the Humanities' contribution to peace within a wider context of peace studies.

Reading Friendship

The phenomenon of friendship has fascinated philosophers, literary figures and scholars for a long time. It has raised a wide variety of questions and responses. Are there different kinds of friendships? Aristotle ponders this and concludes that friendship is the rarest of human relationships.[26] Tolstoy, on the other hand, was concerned with the way friendship functions.[27] Augustine was concerned that if friendship develops as a process and is not inherent, how does friendship bear on the relationship between the human and the Divine?[28] Daniel Hruschka, a medical anthropologist, asks if friendship works for people at an emotional, psychological, social and neurological level.[29] In Ahmed Achrati's work, we become aware that friendship (like hospitality) is an ethical responsibility perfecting humans to reach their true potential.[30] Derrida's penetrating question urges us to consider whether friendship informs us for effectively realizing 'good' in a liberal democratic state.[31] Reading friendship as a tool for forging international relations is a way that Felix Berneskoetter sees to reduce the anxiety between States while maintaining the modern State's autonomy.[32] In short, friendship is a subject of intense scholarly discussion in multiple sites, including philosophy, literature and religious studies, and the discussion has spanned several centuries of thinking and deliberations. Although there are various perspectives on friendship, they do not define friendship. Definitely friendship is not a substitute relationship for filling up an empty space for other relationships like family, neighbours or kin. That friendship exists outside these bonds of relationships requires us to grasp the more fundamental question of how it emerges and what becomes revealed in consequence. It is a question of identity, how we are with others and how we come to know ourselves in association in a community.

The role of community and the need for belonging have been widely studied, particularly political community or nationalism. Friendship occupies an in-between space between the public (political–national) and private (intimate) domain. It is the space for developing belonging, as well as recognition, becoming part of something and receiving others, and becoming who we are. It is a space for sharing endeavour for hope. Friendship is the glue that creates a moral community of equals and nurtures peace as a way of being with one another. Thus, notwithstanding the deconstruction of friendship in Western literature, in line with Achrati's analysis (on hospitality), I think of friendship as the human-possibility-of-being, which is not an end in itself but a process for fulfilling human potentials in the company of others.[33] Specifically, I am interested in the space of dialogue between friends at Abdullah Hall that stands as witness to Sir Syed's vision of a Muslim community sharing a common endeavour for progress while recognizing interdependent relationships with others beyond AMU. This voice is politically relevant for peace-building and opens new possibilities for dialogue between Muslims and others.

Engagement with the human condition and advancement beyond the Hobbesian state is a central concern of friendship.[34] The relationship of the self to the other, Achrati suggests, is an ethical act of subjectivity requiring moral agency. (This explanation of subjectivity from an Islamic standpoint is very different from the Western postmodern approach.) In responding to the cry of the other, the Hobbesian behaviour of humankind is disrupted and the 'awakened' person becomes aware of his and the other's condition as human (limited but possessing moral consciousness for growth).[35] I understand the awakening of consciousness to be human, to become something beyond where one is now, as a space for ethico–politics, a place to connect to one's humanity and hear the appeal of the friend seeking unity.[36] Friendship in this perspective is the Nietzschian 'cork' saving us from narcissistic fixation of personal interests.[37] The humanistic turn of friendship de-emphasizes the instrumentalist outlook of group identity for fulfilling political goals of 'separatism', which Francis Robinson argues was the general outlook of Muslim politics in India.[38] The inspired relationship of friendship that brings together people seeking, finding and knowing oneself better and becoming *better* in relationship with others enables and promotes peace. Keeping this in perspective, I suggest Alig friends are Muslim peacemakers of the subcontinent.

The other issue of concern regarding friendship is reciprocity. This is a matter of identity requiring a sense of self as distinct in relation to others; significant 'others' are integral for friendship. Michel Foucault and Edward Said have convincingly argued that the construction of the 'other' during colonialism did not generate friendship between the encountering groups, but it served the assertion of power for the Western self to triumph over 'native subjects'. Said's study, in particular, provides an understanding of the construction of the Arab world as the subjected other that was developed as a historical and epistemological project in support of Western colonialism.[39] Samuel Huntington's reading of the Muslim other as a perpetual 'enemy' forecloses the possibility of positive recognition between the Christian and the Muslim worlds.[40] The disintegration of human interaction to a hierarchical scale, where the self is represented as 'good' and 'civilised', and the other as 'evil' and 'uncivilised' excludes reciprocity between humans. The something 'to-be-friendship' is killed and a fixed position of (mis)recognition is established. This is counter to the Islamic ethical position of unfolding and process that gestures to an invitation, an opening for exchanges and connections between humans, to be friends, as Achrati argues.

A certain positive sense of human relationship must precede the recognition of the worth of others for friendship to emerge and develop. Philosopher Emmanuel Levinas has elaborated on the moral imperative of emotional and human response for cultivation of this understanding.[41] Levinas calls it 'transcendence' whereby the ability to see the world from the position of the other enables the self to overcome self-interest, at least temporarily. It requires a movement towards the other beyond the level of the cognitive. This approach is also evident in Islamic Sufi philosophy of Jalaluddin Rumi and Sheikh Sa'adi.[42] One can say they are the thinkers on friendship. To them friends is not a group, like a herd, but people who presuppose and value others not for selfish agendas of personal benefit, but for living in awareness of the presence of the other. It is assumed to be an emotional experience that requires a certain measure of judgment based on knowledge of the intellect, or 'heart-knowledge' in Rumi's term to accept the other, the stranger, as a friend to-be.[43]

Friendship 'dialogues' serve as the gateway for enriched experience in which discovery and knowledge continue and transform self and other. This happens not with the intention of making others like the self or subservient, which Levinas warns against, but with the intent of allowing for unfolding, which is an ontological process.[44] Achrati defines the 'awakening' of self as a state of wilful submission to the great and infinite power of Allah (al-nafs al-mutma'inna or 'the soul at peace').[45] Its actualization is not dependent on conditions of external circumstances such as a perfect community or an empty horizon of desire for 'we'. It is an inward intentionality to move forward in the journey of knowing.[46] Enabling humans to actualize his/her humanization is a core Islamic concept of the progression to al-insan (a human person becoming human). This reading on friendship highlighting human virtue as an endeavour for realization of the human potential of being, is different from being human in the polis required for 'true' friendship according to Aristotle. Rather, in the context of the Islamic understanding on friendship that I am privileging, emphasis is on the process – strangers, outsiders and others joining the circle of friends for refinement – to be at peace with self and others. I probe this process at work in the space of Abdullah Hall in the rest of the chapter.

I am using the term 'peace' as the space of trust that progresses through continuous engagement with the Other without a pre-given map. I present Abdullah Hall as a space of peace that is continuously in process. Strangers and incoming students meet there alone and away from their familial and kinship groups, and they forge new relationships. In this place of communion they become friends and contribute to the well-being of one another. Friendship in this sense in Abdullah Hall is not about similar people finding reassurance in one another, nor of dissimilar people forced to know one another leading to mutual interdependency. The society of friends constituted at Abdullah Hall, one may say, does not submit to a definition of what it is; rather it is a way of life, an experience of being with others that enables those within the space to negotiate a mutual relationship. It is, in Maurice Blanchot's term, 'a place of relations'.[47]

To understand this place of relations, one cannot approach it as a temporal or historical question. Nor is it a question of definition of what makes the relationship or friendship between the Abdullah Hall girls qualitatively different from other kinds of friendships. Rather it calls our attention for appreciating the lived that one experiences in the space that shapes the individuals who become part of the community of Alig friends. Friendship at AMU is not what Derrida would qualify as 'teleiopoetic', loving someone from afar without the experience of interaction. It is instead a kind of friendship in an intimate space, a space that is so close to one's being that even after leaving AMU, the old boys and girls remain connected to the place.[48] It is an unbroken chain created by women and men that does not circulate in the sphere of economy of gains, but a kind of giving with a sense of responsibility to those with whom one shares the space as well as to the ones who were there before, and those who are not there, yet. This is similar to Shahla Talebi's observation in Chapter 11 in this book on mourning and remembering the martyrs in Iran that serves as an entry point into developing a human relationship between the dead and the living, the ones who were there before and ones who are here now and will be in the future. Friendship in this sense marks our humanity. The society of Alig friends is an excellent example of Muslim humanity in India.

To appreciate the lived experiences that I address in the next section requires a consideration of how anxiety works for producing conditions for friendship in the intimate space of Abdullah Hall. I read this anxiety as a consciousness of being in the presence of the other that guides the process of improvement and enables advancement of human potential. The formidable space of Abdullah Hall, which is often referred to as a 'fortress', is a world apart, a miniature self-contained city within a walled compound.[49] Physically and conceptually, the walled-in Abdullah Hall evokes multiple emotions from people within *and* outside its premises. Much depends on the capacity of negotiations, exchanges and connections to know this place and the people within. The anxiety that every incoming student experiences on entering this world is a useful opening to understand the initial practice of living there because it precedes will and desire. This experience creates the ontological awareness of inward reflection and the awareness of the self as a potential part of the Abdullah Hall family slowly develops in anxiety. The Heideggerian approach to conceptualization of being and becoming part of a community follows throughout the life of an Abdullah Hall Alig.[50] The growth is directed to be in the company of others and to become part of a whole. This requires cultivation of the self in ways that are deemed 'good' and 'meritorious', not in the scholarly or academic sense, but in human qualities. This is closer to the Aristotelian call for the development of virtue for amity and friendship between equals. At the heart of this development, the stranger–other is privileged because it requires the anxious stranger to see the potential of a friendship. Everyone arriving at Abdullah Hall is a stranger, but when they leave the place the individual is transformed into a friend. The experience of the individual becomes the process of creating a collective of friends. Thus, self and other continuously evolve in this space; and the memory of the space and people enable new developments in the future for sustaining the ethos of the AMU family.[51] At Abdullah Hall the question of friendship does not emphasize the issue of 'who is' but 'what is' a friend, as the girls are refined in relationship with one another. Friendship thus is no ordinary task. It is a living space for encountering one's own humanity looking out to the future to foster the creation of *darul aman*, a place of peace.

A question that may rise for the reader is how does the story of Abdullah Hall and Alig friendship illustrate women's peacemaking? How do we locate this narrative of peace within the existing studies on AMU and Aligarh women? The second question is addressed first because it is a historiographical issue. The study of Indian Muslim women's lives as a field of scholarship is very thin.[52] Gail Minault's *Secluded Scholars* is perhaps the only full-length study on the history of education and social development of Aligarh's Muslim women.[53] Minault's focus is on the process of education; she pays exclusive attention to the challenges and small successes of learning behind *purdah* in segregated spaces of modernising Muslim families, which led to the foundation of Women's College and Abdullah Hall. The role of male patriarchs supporting women's education within their private households is critical in the analysis of women's 'enlightenment' in education, she argues. This is an important issue to consider because the women of Aligarh in Minault's representation continue to be recipients of men's progressive efforts. However, David Lelyveld's very accessible and lively reading of *Aligarh's First Generation* does not include the story of Muslim women's education because women were not part of the original vision of Sir Syed's educational endeavour.[54] Likewise, Christian Troll's comprehensive book *Sayyid Ahmad Khan* and Hafeez Malik's carefully researched monograph *Life and Works of Sir Syed Ahmed Khan* do not include the story of Muslim women's lives at AMU; there was no story to be told.[55]

A recent article by Shadaf Bano, an Aligarh scholar, provides interesting insights into the intellectual activities in Sheikh Abdullah's family, the founders of Abdullah Hall.[56] Bano's essay is of particular interest because the protagonist in her narrative is Rashid Jahan, Sheikh Abdullah's daughter, who was actively involved in the *Angarey* group that led the Aligarh Movement (a scholarly intellectual project in the early twentieth century). Exploring the literary contributions of Rashid Jahan, the essay addresses her tireless struggle against the normative–conservatism of middle-class Muslim culture, and its repressed sexual anxiety and brings into focus the need for reform and social justice. Rashid Jahan inspired Ismat Chughtai, one of the most radical old-girls of AMU, who produced searing literature attacking head-on the duplicities of upper-class Muslim life. Chugtai's short story *Lihaf* is perhaps the first in the genre of lesbian love in a Muslim household.[57] How Chugtai saw women's friendship, possibly as a matter of sexual love remains to be explored with some thoroughness. Alig girls' lives have not been widely discussed in Urdu novels and short stories, although several of the well-known elite families of Aligarh produced some of the best-known women Urdu writers. Nazar Sajjad Haider, Akbari Begum, Qurratul-'ain Haider, Rashid Jahan and Zahida Khatun Sherwani, to name a few, were highly acclaimed Muslim women who wrote extensively on social issues and the struggles of modernization in the Muslim community.[58]

Returning to the first question of the rationale for studying Muslim women's friendship at Abdullah Hall as a way of rethinking everyday practice of peace is in my estimation a useful shift. It moves us away from stereotypical plots regarding Muslim society as violent and destructive, to a more nuanced exploration of another world inhabited by Muslims fostering individual and community growth through everyday human relationships. The desire to become better in association with others at Abdullah Hall and to contribute to positive human interactions must be recorded and remembered. As a place of peace, Abdullah Hall's story is worth knowing (as well, life in the residential boys' halls of AMU).[59] To me AMU's lived culture serves as a place of hope defying the Derridian skepticism of the impossibility of 'true' friendship for advancing human potential. It is a space created by Muslim women and men where the outsider–stranger is welcome to join the community of human-selves. The potential to sidestep individual egos of competition and produce emotions of care and concern for others that generate a moral community is an exceptional outcome happening at AMU, and it truly fulfils the call of education's mission for human development. The Muslim women's community at Abdullah Hall demonstrates the importance of being in the world as a friend that endows an ethically and politically meaningful life to humanity at large.

This leads us to a final question: can Abdullah Hall's ethos of friendship serve as a model for negotiating interactions in the real world? Muslim women's experiences within the marginal minority space of AMU seem like an unlikely place for envisioning a new discourse on peace in the post 9/11 world. Yet, as an old girl I remain hopeful that the way of living promoted at Abdullah Hall and AMU could serve as a kind of thinking on the possibility of friendship between different constituencies of people. It could offer a way forward for building relationships based on trust. This chapter is an invitation to participate in this dialogue. Friendship and justice must be proportional for imagining a peaceful world.[60] It is a promise; its possibilities are the witnessing we have to search in our times and in our efforts. Perhaps this view is starkly different from the Western deconstructivist theory that emphasizes that civic friendship is already absent, already perverted; its potential for peace cannot be actualized. This is not an Islamic approach. Abdullah Hall's story that I privilege in this chapter is an opening for improving the conduct of human relationship, the process of humanization, present and moving forward. It is a promise made by Sir Syed to the Muslims of Hindustan to become involved in their own advancement, and this promise has been lived by the Aligs for over 100 years and is still ongoing. Abdullah Hall is a ray within that beacon of hope generating an ongoing dialogue of peace led by Muslim women.

Lived Friendship and the Culture of Peace at Abdullah

One hundred miles southeast of Delhi is the town of Aligarh, whose name is synonymous with the university. Abdullah Hall, which was one of the 11 halls of AMU in the 1980s (since then new halls for both boys and girls have been constructed), is located in the area known as new Aligarh between Marris Road and Lal Diggy Gate. The high walls gave it a 'fortress-like' appearance (to outsiders). Inside the hall, however, a different reality pervaded. Abdullah Hall was an open space constituted by multiple welcoming spaces for the residents to enjoy (new constructions in these open spaces have changed the spatial geography of the Hall). The residents of Abdullah Hall were from the ages 6 to 21. They represented different social and economic classes, although it was generally assumed by those outside of AMU that it is a monolithic elite community within. In contrast to this assumed picture of elitism the everyday challenge of coping with diversity was real for each resident, and each boarder had to learn to live peacefully with different Others within the Hall. There were four hostels within Abdullah Hall. The elementary and middle school students lived in Rashid Jahan hostel; the pre-university) students lived in Wahidia hostel; the undergraduate students were residents of New hostel; and the Master's level students lived in Mumtaz Jahan hostel. The imagined and enclosed Abdullah Hall girl, that others perceived as the life inside the 'walled fortress', was and is not a weak and timid person. An Abdullah Hall girl learned to be purposeful and lively, fully engaged as a student and a person who is confident being in the world with others. The building of Abdullah girls' character and personalities was facilitated by the spatial arrangement that addressed their everyday needs. There were gardens, fields for sports, a student recreation centre, a library, a canteen, a general supplies store, a laundry service and multiple quiet spots shaded by large old trees creating an inclusive and communitarian place. The walls encircling the outside compound of the hall were irrelevant inside. Abdullah Hall was a gendered female space focussed on empowering girls to be meaningful participants in their immediate community and the world at large.

The dynamic relationship between the girls, administrators and workers in the hall was built on a vast array of reciprocal exchanges anchored on *adab* (civility). The Provost office served as the hub for facilitating these interactions and was the fountainhead maintaining and representing the *adab* of Abdullah to those outside the Hall. Its staff officiated, on one hand, as teachers, wardens and security personnel and, on the other hand, as mentors who cultivated relationships based on care and understanding of the girls who represented different cultural backgrounds and age groups. The forms of reciprocity and exchanges ranging from the contractual to the emotional, and from the hierarchical to the egalitarian guided the conduct of the girls within Abdullah Hall, and it prioritized human affinity. Since the residents in the hall comprised a small group (a couple hundred students when I was a student there from 1980–6), everyone became acquainted with one another. The emphasis on sociability was not simply a way of getting along; it was a way of cultivating association with others for improving knowledge of self to serve a higher purpose of being and building a moral community. The intimacy of association within this community was initially very challenging to most of the new students. I remember my elder sister's initial fear of living within the closed compound of Abdullah Hall with many other girls who she thought were 'utterly different' from her. She found herself incapable of communicating because she did not speak Urdu, the established language of communication in the hall, and had to undertake the painful process of learning a new language. In dress and mannerism, too, the girls appeared totally different from the known world of her Catholic convent schoolgirls that she was acquainted with in Assam, in northeast India, which was physically and culturally aeons away from the north Indian Urdu Muslim world. Although my sister thought she was an exception, she was not at all unusual. In fact, every newcomer to Abdullah Hall felt a similar sense of initial transportation to 'another world' where they had to learn to be with different others and in the process it humanized Abdullah's Aligs to appreciate the beauty of friends in 'ordinary female friendships'.[61]

As an educational institution, AMU is unlike any other university that I know of in India. The institution aimed beyond producing 'successful' professionals. In Sir Syed's philosophy the domains of ontology and epistemology were inseparably interlinked. The development of the Alig identity in everyday activities in the residential halls of AMU (such as Abdullah Hall) is a testimony to the knowledge of human dignity. This was encapsulated in the ethos of a lived *adab* or everyday ethics that emphasized the ideals of social cohesion, tolerance, moderation and accommodation for living peacefully and in close proximity to different Others. The actual practice of this in the day-to-day life of Abdullah Hall started with small lessons, at times painful for the juniors, for appreciating 'seniority', which is an AMU ethos. Seniority was earned by the number of years one is associated with the Hall. Thus an early lesson that all the residents learnt was to show respect to the workers, particularly the elderly menial workers who had served for several years in the hall. All male workers based on their age were addressed as either *baba* or *bhai* (father/brother), and women are addressed as *apa* or *baji* (sister). This did not mean that social and economic classes were overcome, but in the space of Abdullah Hall it was temporarily suppressed for practical purposes of creating an Alig community. Every elder had to be greeted with the salutation of *adāb*.[62] Being a nonreligious form of greeting (like good morning) the exchange of *adāb* allowed for overcoming religious divides and for acknowledging the other person irrespective of his or her cultural and religious background. Based on my experiences, I would argue that this living *adab* provided us with an actual illustration of the value of the other to build human relationships based on respect.

Friendship was not simply a discourse; it was a lived and actualized reality in Abdullah Hall. Routine played an important role in fostering this exchange. Within the Hall the workers had designated tasks and the students respected the boundaries, sometimes grudgingly. They had to because it was an AMU 'tradition'. The dining hall, in particular, symbolized this arrangement. Meals were cooked in a common kitchen, served at fixed times, and everyone ate together in the common dining hall. Even the food portions were equally measured and served on white china bowls and plates. Meals were generally simple vegetarian fares, meat was rarely served. Sir Syed's ethics that food should be simple and nutritious, and eaten in small quantity were carefully adhered to in Abdullah Hall. The kitchen workers and students both knew and maintained the boundaries of this arrangement. The regular meals were rather stripped down to a bare minimum for maintaining a nutritious diet; the richer girls often received care packages from home. However, this food, too, could not be consumed alone; it had to be shared in the communal living arrangement with roommates; with three, four, or five girls; based on number of roommates one had in the room. All meals were a shared activity, and mealtime provided the students with an opportunity to develop social skills of interaction. The strict maintenance of mealtimes meant that the kitchen staff was relieved of their duties on schedule, which made their workday manageable and humane. Workers were not viewed as servants, a normal tendency in Indian social class attitude, but were accepted as facilitators that made everyone better because of it.

The girls shared their mealtime as a way of catching up, but they also took it a step further to discuss schoolwork and help one another with their academic and extra-curricular pursuits. While academics continued to be a competitive endeavour, the general spirit of working with others to help their learning process and enable their success was also a collaborative and collective effort. This, one must acknowledge, was quite an exceptional happening at Aligarh in the context of the Indian education system that encourages cut-throat competition among students to motivate them to be successful. At Abdullah Hall, on the contrary, girls tutored one another in almost all aspects of learning – religious and secular. There was no economic exchange connected to this activity, but the generous spirit of give-and-take brought the girls together to know and appreciate one another better. Friendships that were strengthened during the collective study halls, particularly during exams, had a lasting effect of building exceptional trust.

Building the Abdullah Hall collective as a shared endeavour based on understanding between the resident students and the hall workers extended to small everyday matters. The use of water provides an important example of this spirit of accommodation. In the hot climate of Uttar Pradesh in northern India, water is a precious item; and in the hall the use of water was carefully regulated. Drinking water in particular was specially monitored and provided by a water carrier each morning. An old *baba* filled a *ghara* (jug) for each resident once a day. The *ghara*, a traditional cooler, kept the water cold and drinkable throughout the day. Everyone had their personal jug of water. Today in South Asia water has become one of the scarcest resources, and the competition to procure water for household use leads to violent confrontations between communities. Neighbours are 'at war' with one another in the struggle to have access to drinkable water. In a small but significant way, Abdullah Hall's water management system made it equally available to all, while it also taught the girls to respect the workers who provided them with the much-needed daily item of use.

Likewise, academic and extra-curricular activities were seamlessly woven within the daily routine. Respect for time and place was carefully maintained in every activity within the hall. Every activity was part of a routine. This enabled the people involved in servicing the hall to maintain its proper functioning. In the Women's College of Abdullah Hall, classes began at 8 a.m. and went until noon. At 1 p.m. after the lunch break classes resumed and finished at 4 p.m. This was followed by sports. The negotiations in the arena of games fostered collective team spirit, but because it was non-competitive, it never led to bitter rivalry between the opposing teams. Yet, everyone was involved. This unique aspect of sports as a space of enjoyment and not fierce competition was unusual because it expressed the seriousness for training without the need to prove prowess in the game. At 6.30 p.m. dinner was served in the Hall, and the flurry of daytime activities ended. Respect for this schedule in communal living meant adjusting and accommodating, at every instance. It also meant developing a keen awareness of the others' needs so that one did not infringe into their time and space. The understanding that developed in this intimate space produced positive human association rather than impose a rigid discipline. After the communal dinner, the roll call hour provided opportunity to interact with those one had overlooked earlier in the day. Weekly entertainment in the form of the Wednesday night indulgence of watching TV for one hour became another space for negotiating common consensus. In the 1980s, the programme called *Chitrahaar* (Bollywood movies song and dance) was very popular, and all the girls agreed by consensus to use the one hour of television time to watch this programme in their hostel common room.

During university celebration days such as the annual commemoration of Sir Syed and Papa Mian, or during the annual college convocation, the emphasis was once again on group activities. Occasionally, visitors from the boys' halls were allowed inside Abdullah Hall and inter-varsity competitions provided the space to engage and compete with one another, an established AMU tradition.[63] These activities and events reinforced the shared responsibility of upholding an Alig culture expressed in the conduct of AMU's boys and girls.

Another important feature of Abdullah Hall, as was the case in the boys' halls, was the tradition of 'Introduction' of incoming students. The process of Introduction is a kind of ragging/hazing that continued for many weeks before the 'Fresher's Party'. And although it was much dreaded by the new comers these exchanges during Introduction facilitated the process of getting to know the 'seniors', and one was inducted to the community of friends. After the Fresher's Party the seniors become sisters/friends to the new comers, and the community within Abdullah Hall thrived.

A 'timeless' tradition of Abdullah Hall is 'visiting' on Friday afternoon and Sunday that provided the girls, particularly those who came from traditional Muslim families, the opportunity to develop confidence in negotiating identity in the public sphere.[64] The simple activity of going outside the hall for an ice cream, a cup of tea, or a movie created a spirit of excitement to enjoy the company of others. It also created opportunities for socializing beyond the hall. It made small pleasures like preparing for this social activity significant, and the sense of gratitude to be able to share happy moments enabled the cultivation of a spirit of generosity that enabled Alig girls to wish others the same sense of happiness. The annual *numaish* (fair) was another occasion when the girls were allowed outside the hall, and it caused much excitement for preparing for the event. These seem like small matters of sociability in today's world, but for the Abdullah Hall girls it opened a new world of possibilities, and their *adab* was tested on these occasions. Earning the respect of outsiders was a critical lesson repeated by the wardens before each outing beyond the hall. Abdullah Hall girls were expected to live up to the expectation of being transmitters of excellent behaviour that was seen as symbolically dignifying the Muslim society.

At an external level, the humdrum of routine life within Abdullah Hall does not evoke a great understanding of how it contributed to peace in which friendship was the driving force. Precisely, it was the everydayness of the routine and the interactions fostered and nurtured in this daily rhythm of life that was naturalized and which produced extraordinary outcomes of forming a moral community that was inspirational. The shared experience of being the architects of this community meant that the Abdullah Hall girls were able to focus on benefitting one another for positive human development, and it reinforced the capacity of living with trust and in peace.

Curiously, the strictly codified and clockwork discipline of Abdullah Hall did not include religious training. Although AMU was founded as, and still remains, a Muslim 'minority' institution, the ethos of communal living easily accommodated the variety. This was a deliberate policy for fostering positive human relationships between the girls of different religious backgrounds. There was no censuring of religion, though. If one was inclined to practice a religion, she had the freedom to do so in the privacy of her room. No one was denied admission to the hall based on her religious or ethnic background. The majority of the residents of Abdullah Hall were Sunni Muslims, but Shi'a, Hindu and Christian students and staff also lived in the hall compound. Abdullah Hall functioned as a religion-neutral space. No one judged the other for good or bad beliefs. On certain occasions, the Sunni girls organized *milads*. *Milad* literally means 'birth'. *Milad-un nabi*, the celebration of the Prophet Muhammad's birthday, was organized by the girls and all activities were planned, managed and executed by them. Christmas was also celebrated. Likewise, the ceremony of *matam*, or mourning, a Shi'a ritual during *Muharram*, was observed by the girls. As well, the Hindu festivals of Diwali and Holi were celebrated in the hall with a special dinner. Religion was not a divisive space but an inclusive one to know one another, and it served as a cultural orientation for the variety that constituted the Abdullah family.

Furthermore, the spirit of religious inclusion and neutrality was extended to education. The classes held in the morning hours before lunch were based on disciplines, but the classes after lunch until 4 p.m. in the afternoon focussed on cultural studies. AMU's curriculum that was followed in the Women's College of Abdullah Hall provided the option of studying Sunni or Shi'i theology based on a student's personal religious background, and non-Muslim students did a course on 'Indian Civilization'. Together all students had to do a 'general education' class, as well as study Urdu and a foreign language, if a teacher was available.[65] Students were thus exposed and encouraged during their formative years of young adulthood to accept the variety of religious communities that constitute the Indian nation and respect the differences between them.

One may mistake this practice of coexistence and mutual respect that was the ethos at Abdullah Hall and AMU as an expression of Indian secularism. Secularism's impact on Indian society is questionable, in my opinion. Rather I argue that the religion neutral ethos of Abdullah Hall was based on a more refined and committed purpose of reaffirming an ethical outlook of living in a multi-religious, polycultural world and of creating a theoretical, and practical framework of coexistence. Central to this concept of ethics was sociability, though not of the kind we are celebrating today – technological marvels that enable connection and communication through Facebook, Twitter, My Space and so on from a distance. The sociability within Abdullah Hall, as I have described, was a face-to-face exchange. This meant investment in time, efforts and emotions; and unlike digital friendships, it was not instantaneous. There was no gregarious buzz of friendship. We were all part of one family. Although each one of us had the power to befriend whosoever we chose, no one had the power to overlook the unit or the family of friends because every member within this unit was a potential long-lasting friend. Friendship therefore developed without a network of consumers. Friendship was never defined or conceptualized; and because it remained unannounced, it improved the individual and the collective. As Naved Masood recalls based on a conversation with Mumtaz Jahan, Papa Mian's daughter and a lifelong worker of Abdullah Hall, the dictum of interaction was *aqal-e halal*.[66] This meant reasoned thought for doing good that would benefit the family of Abdullah Hall as a whole.

Obviously a women's space, Abdullah Hall functioned on a gender-egalitarian ethos. I am using this term conceptually drawing upon S'adiyya Shaikh's reading of Sufi spaces as providing a 'comprehensive framework for an egalitarian politics of gender'.[67] Within Abdullah Hall different kinds of relationships between people were evident that did not totally eliminate gender location, but the diminished significance of gender identity in framing hierarchy was evident in everyday practice. Subverting the traditional outlook of gender codification, menial workers who were mostly men, were visibly respected by the girls as well as the staff and administrators of the Provost office. The Provost set the example, and everyone had to emulate this conduct. The workers were never referred to by their first names (considered demeaning in the Indian tradition) and the formal 'you' was always used to address the *bhais* and *babas*. The poorest two male vendors who sold small quantities of home-cooked food and odds and ends inside the Abdullah Hall compound when I was a student there were especially respected as 'senior' members of the hall. The nature and dignity of men and women as understood and accepted within Abdullah Hall was radically different from what operated outside. Gender difference was not a threat or a ground for rivalry, fear or discrimination. In the extremely gender conscious world of today, Abdullah Hall's lived practice presents us with an example that explicitly engaged social hierarchy and economic class, but it also provided a reconceptualization of human equality in ways that were both spiritually and socially relevant.

Abdullah Hall's ethos emphasized care and empathy as the foundation for human interaction, which, one may say, feminized the world of a Muslim society in its true spirit. There is a general tendency to read Sir Syed's project of education in a residential environment as a masculinising endeavour that injected a culture of being virile and powerful, a way of regaining the lost pride of Muslim men. Some even claim that this revived manliness of Muslim identity became the launching site leading to the demand and creation of Pakistan. I would argue on the contrary that the culture of care and compassion for the other that was emphasized and continuously reinforced in AMU's lived culture undermined the masculinist ways of being that prize aggressive performance and macho social norms as marks of success. This was truly represented in Abdullah Hall; and as a female space, a marginal location within AMU, it emblematized Sir Syed's vision of education improving the human person and human qualities. Abdullah Hall's *adab* directed one to alternatives where positive values of sharing, obedience, respect, care and compassion were prioritized. It provided the rationale for cultivating a society that valued inclusiveness and peace as a way of living. Women were the agents of this peaceful ethos and the embodied concept of friendship for peace reflected in the day-to-day routine of Abdullah Hall and women's lives was amply demonstrated in the lived environment within and beyond the space of the hall.

Conclusion

The narrative ethnography of Abdullah Hall that I presented in this chapter interrogates the meaning of education and provides new interpretations of accommodating differences arising from proximity. It also raises questions and offers an alternative evaluation of Muslim identity in a specific context. Accepting that living with the other had a positive influence for the Abdullah Hall girls assertively challenges the fear of difference, class-biased formulations, and gender discrimination that is a repeated and misinformed story about Muslim women. The inclusiveness at Abdullah Hall provided possibilities for the residents to rethink the purpose of learning and offered for them an organic and ontologically grounded critique of power dividing people. Fostering friendship through education facilitated a space for peace in the lived world.

Much has changed in Abdullah Hall since the 1980s though. Some of the changes were generated by internal pressure of accommodating the growing number of new students and increasing the capacity of housing within the hall. New hostels and buildings encroached the open and green spaces. Abdullah Hall no longer looks like the place it was once. The bigger problem, however, is not about the spatial changes, but the rising trend of negative politics within AMU and the mixing of religion with education. The lack of a vision for combating these problems has had adverse effects on the student body at large. In the 1990s the rise of Hindu fundamentalism in India led by the BJP and the crisis they created with the *Babri Masjid-Ram Janambhumi* issue and the post-Godhra anti-Muslim violence in 2002 effected the psyche of Aligarh students. Religious riots spread from the city to the university campus. At the heart of this crisis then and now at AMU is the age-old question what is the Indian Muslim identity? Can Muslims truly be accepted as Indian? The problem of acceptance and integration of Muslims within India, of course, cannot be resolved by the Aligs. However, reviving the vision of Sir Syed – that the *Mussalman-e Hind* (Muslims of India) – can play a positive role in the development of community and country is particularly important. It is the only relevant approach for Aligs and the mission of positive contribution under the AMU banner that can be actualized without coercion because Aligs believe in it.

Returning to the specific case of Abdullah Hall's ethical code provides us with a model of social and human interactions, combining classroom academic work with actual performance of those lessons in real life for acknowledging human dignity as a way of cultivating peace. The capacity of personal progress alongside accepting and supporting the well-being of others is a critical lesson that genuinely marries academic knowledge with a vision of the larger project of human development. If this culture of *adab* or civility and friendship can be reinterpreted to fit the needs of communities, a progressive and peaceful way of negotiating identity in the multi-religious landscape of India is possible. It can provide guidance for developing a moral and just society for Muslims and others even beyond India. Paying attention to women's lives and their active participation in the process are crucial for successful outcome. Abdullah Hall and Alig women symbolize the possibility of actualizing such an endeavour of peace.

Notes

1. Ahmed Ali, *Twilight in Delhi* (London: Hogarth Press, 1940). The period known as the reign of the 'Company Bahadur' stretched over 100 years, from the fall of Bengal after the Battle of Plassey in 1757 to the Revolt of 1857. After the Battle of Plassey in 1757 and the acquisition of the Bengal *Diwani* (treasury) in 1765, the East India Company officials became directly involved in managing and administering their newly acquired Indian territories with the help of a large army manned by Indian sepoys, while they continued to pursue and expand their economic and commercial ventures. As well, in this period the British slowly and steadily started to make inroads in the courts of the local rajas with the aim to shift political power to their control. Gradually, the Company Bahadur became the de facto ruler of India that caused alarm and resentment among the local populous leading to the Revolt of 1857. The Indians, however, failed to regain political power. In consequence, Bahadur Shah Zafar II, the last Mughal emperor was dethroned by the British, and Queen Victoria of England became the monarch of India. India became a colony of the British. The British colonial rule in India, beginning from the early period of the East Indian Company until 1947, when India regained its freedom, is generally referred to as the Raj.

2. Malik Bennabi, *On the Origins of Human Society*, transl. and annotated by Mohamed Tahir El-Mesawi (London: The Open Press, 1968).

3. During the tenure of Dr Zakir Hussain as Vice Chancellor of the university, in the post-independence period, the segregation of students in the residential halls based on their religious background was abolished. Hindu and Muslim students lived together from then on.

4. Ashis Nandy, 'Telling the story of communal conflicts in South Asia: Interim report on a personal search for demystifying myths', *Racial and Ethnic Study*, 25/1 (2002), pp. 1–19.

5. Sana Haroon, 'Reformism and orthodox practice in early nineteenth-century Muslim North India: Sayyid Ahmed Shaheed reconsidered', *Journal of Royal Asiatic Society*, Series 3, 21/2 (2011), pp. 177–98.

6. Archival documentation on the Barelvi followers is available in the Peshawar archives, in particular, reports and sermons of one of his ardent followers, Maulvi Fazal Ellahi who sincerely believed in the mission of Sayyid Ahmed Barelvi as *Amirul Momineen*.

7. For example, see W. W. Hunter, *Indian Mussalmans: Are They Bound in Conscience to Revolt against the Queen?* (Calcutta: Government Printing Press, 1871).

8. Aziz Ahmad, 'Syed Ahmad Khan, Jamalaldin Afghani and Muslim India', *Studia Islamica* 13 (1960), p. 66; Mushirul Hasan, 'Pan Islamism versus Indian nationalism: A reappraisal', *Economic and Political Weekly* 21/24 (14 June 1986), pp. 1074–9; Irfan Habib, 'The envisioning of a nation: A defence of the idea of India', *Social Scientist* 27/9–10 (Sept/Oct, 1999), pp. 18–29; Irfan Habib,

'Viability of Islamic science: Some insights from the 19th century', *Economic and Political Weekly* 39/23 (5–11 June 2004), pp. 2351–5.

9. Abdulla Ahmed, 'Syed Jamaluddin Afghani's ideas blaze the trail', *Pakistan Horizon*, 34/2 (Second Quarter 1981), pp. 35–43.

10. Gyan Pandey, 'Can a Muslim be an Indian?' *Comparative Studies in Society and History* 41/4 (October 1999), pp. 608–29.

11. Habib, 'The envisioning of a nation'.

12. Pankaj Mishra, however, presents Jamaladin Aghani as a Muslim intellectual who liberated the Muslim mind and provided them with the intellectual ideas to chart a new course for themselves. Leaders like, Kamal Atatürk in Turkey, Gamel Naser in Egypt and the even the religious leader, Ayatollah Khomeni, he argues, were inspired by Afghani's political writings calling for the liberation of the Muslim mind; *From the Ruins of Empire: The Intellectuals Who Remade Asia* (New York: Farrar, Straus and Giroux, 2012).

13. Carl Ernst, 'Muslim studies of Hinduism? A reconsideration of Arabic and Persian translations from Indian languages', *Iranian Studies* 36/2 (2003), pp. 173–95; Franz Rosenthal, 'The stranger in Medieval Islam', *Arabica* 44/1 (1997), pp. 35–75; Amir Khusrau, the well-known poet, scholar, administrator and Sufi of the thirteenth century, produced an extensive body of literature on the relationship with the other. He took pride that he was an 'Indian Turk' and that 'Hind' was his home. The composite language of Hind combining Hindawi (Hindi dialects), Persian, Sanskrit and Turkish became his language of poetic expression that is sung in the Indian subcontinent even today.

14. Christian Troll, *Sayyid Ahmad Khan: An Interpretation of Muslim Theology* (New Delhi: Vikas Publications, 1978); David Lelyveld, *Aligarh's First Generation: Muslim Solidarity in British India* (Princeton: Princeton University Press, 1977). Jamalaldin Afghani was one of the trenchant critics of Syed Ahmad Khan. For an interesting parallel reading of these two men, see Aziz Ahmad, 'Syed Ahmad Khan, Jamalaldin Afghani and Muslim India'.

15. Habib, 'Viability of Islamic science', p. 2352.

16. Lelyveld, *Aligarh's First Generation*.

17. It is surprising that several decades later, AMU was transformed into an 'arsenal of Muslim India', as some claimed that Muhammad Ali Jinnah announced at AMU in 1945. At least, in Pakistan this is a repeated story; and many Indian Muslim friends who did not study at AMU claim that was the goal of the university – to make Muslim identity in India strong and separate – led to the creation of Pakistan. Somehow AMU in this imagination is the bedrock of the communal Muslim spirit. Some take pride in this outcome; others lament at the loss and partition of India. The shift from the original vision of empowerment of Indian Muslims through education to the process that made the educated Indian Muslim men the so-called frontline advocates for founding Pakistan needs careful study as to how and why this happened. Is this a reliable narrative for understanding the Muslim quest for belonging in South Asia?

18. David Lelyveld, 'The colonial context of Muslim separatism: From Sayyid Ahmad Barelvi to Sayyid Ahmad Khan', in Asim Roy and Mushirul Hasan (eds), *Living Together Separately: Cultural India in History and Politics* (New Delhi: Oxford University Press, 2005), p. 414.

19. I have personal experience of this crossing of boundaries and a sense of immediate mutual friendship with Aligs in Bangladesh and Pakistan during my research trips to these countries. It is due to the friendship shown by my Alig family in Bangladesh and Pakistan that I, although from India, could undertake research on my book project on the 1971 war of Bangladesh.

20. Bradley Bryan, 'Approaching the other: Aristotle on friendship's possibility', *Political Theory* 37/6 (2009), p. 768. I am using the term 'other-self' in the Aristotelian sense 'of the second self' as those who reflect the virtue of the other as discussed by Bradley Bryan. The great Sufi master Jalaluddin Rumi also makes the same point in his use of the mirror as metaphor of ourselves. We reflect the image of the other in ourselves, he reminds us, in many of his poems and discourses in the *Mathnawi* and *Fi-hi Ma-fi*.

21. Francis Robinson, 'Nineteenth-century Indian Islam: Review of David Lelyveld's *Aligarh's First Generation: Muslim Solidarity in British India* and Christian W. Troll's *Sayyid Ahmad Khan: A Reinterpretation of Muslim Theology*', *Modern Asian Studies* 14/4 (1980), p. 685.

22. Jacques Derrida, 'The politics of friendship', *The Journal of Philosophy*, 85/11 (1988), pp. 632–44.

23. Aristotle, *Nicomachean Ethics* (NE), transl. Terence Irwin, 2nd edn (Indianapolis: Hackett Publishing, 1999).

24. Derrida, 'The politics of friendship', p. 642.

25. Lelyveld, 'The colonial context', p. 414; Kwame Anthony Appiah, *Cosmopolitanism: Ethics in a World of Strangers* (New York: W.W. Norton & Company, 2006).

26. Aristotle, *Nicomachean Ethics*.

27. Leo Tolstoy, *War and Peace*, transl. Louise Maude and Almer Maude (New York: W. W. Norton, 2006 [1966]).

28. Aurelius Augustine, *Confessions of St Augustine*, transl. Edward N. Pusey (New York: Random House, 1999).

29. Daniel Hruschka, *Friendship: Development, Ecology and Evolution of a Relationship* (Berkeley: University of California Press, 2010).

30. Ahmad Achrati, 'Deconstruction, ethics and Islam', *Arabica*, 53/4 (2006), pp. 472–510.

31. Derrida, 'The politics of friendship'.

32. Felix Berenskoetter, 'Friends, there are no friends? An intimate reframing of the international', *Millennium – Journal of International Studies* 35/3 (2007), pp. 647–76.

33. Ahmed Achrati reading Abu Al Fath Uthman Ibn Ginni (1001 CE) on the subject of hospitality in Islam, against the grain of Derrida's deconstructivism, suggests a close relation between language and philosophy. He argues that

speaking about something is associated with a view of the spoken, voicing the spoken and its response in listening, to hear, which is a responsibility and an ethical position. This ethical position when applied to friendship makes it clear that it does not exist in itself but requires a process of actualization. Achrati very eloquently reminds us 'man is an ontological inter-mediate, inter-ness, capable of both equity and inequity, authenticity and inauthenticity. Man is also ontologically a natural (in-the-world), and naturally (*'an fitratin*) inclined towards justice and hospitality.' Friendship is part of the process of the advancement of man to his full status as a human being. See Achrati, 'Deconstruction, ethics and Islam'.

34. Berenskoetter, 'Friends, there are no friends?'.

35. The cornerstone of Islamic ethics according to Achrati 'is that of the voice and of listening, of the cry of Isma'il and the prayer of which were heard at a certain well. The question for Islam is one of hospitality and the hospitable reception of Hagar and Isma'il among the Arabs, the event that changed an act of abandonment into abandoning to Allah. The question of reception is also a question of receptivity to the divine truth, the Qur'an, the voice of *wahy* that resonated through Muhammad in Arabia', 'Deconstruction, ethics and Islam', pp. 502–3.

36. Jalaluddin Rumi often reminds us for the need to be silent to hear and respond to the intellect, the heart, which is the location of knowledge that makes men and women human beings. See Omaima Abou-Bakr, 'Abrogation of the mind in the poetry of Jalal al-Din Rumi', *Alif: Journal of Comparative Poetics* 14 (1994), pp. 37–63.

37. Derrida 'The politics of friendship'; Paul J. M. van Tongeren, 'Politics, friendship and solitude in Nietzsche (confronting Derrida's reading of Nietzsche in 'Politics of friendship')', *South African Journal of Philosophy* 19/3 (2000), pp. 1–24.

38. Francis Robinson, *Separatism among Indian Muslims: The Politics of the United Provinces' Muslims, 1860–1923* (London: Cambridge University Press, 1974).

39. Edward Said, *Orientalism* (New York: Vintage Books, 1978).

40. Samuel Huntington, *The Clash of Civilization and the Remaking of the World Order* (New York: Simon and Schuster, 1997).

41. Emmanuel Levinas, *Totality and Infinity: An Essay on Exteriority*, transl. Alphonso Lingis (Pittsburgh: Duquesne University Press, 1969); Emmanuel Levinas. *Otherwise Than Being: Or Beyond Essence*, transl. Alphonso Lingis (Pittsburg: Duquesne University Press, 1974).

42. Fatima Keshavarz, "Much have I roamed through the world': In search of Sadi's self-image', *International Journal of Middle East Studies* 26/3 (1994), pp. 465–75; Abou-Bakr, 'Abrogation of the mind'.

43. Franklin Lewis, *Rumi: Past and Present, East and West* (Boston: OneWorld, 2000); Abou-Bakr, 'Abrogation of the mind'; Rosenthal, 'The stranger in Medieval Islam'; Achrati, 'Deconstruction, ethics and Islam'; Stanley Milgram, 'The familiar stranger: An aspect of urban anonymity', in S. Milgram, J. Sabini

and M. Silver (eds), *The Individual in a Social World* (Reading: Addison-Wesley, 1977).

44. Mikhail Mikhailovich Bakhtin, *The Dialogic Imagination: Four Essays*, Michael Holquist (ed), transl. Caryl Emerson and Michael Holquist (Austin: University of Texas Press, 1981).

45. Achrati, 'Deconstruction, ethics and Islam', p. 495.

46. Maulana Rumi sums this up in a beautiful poem extending a hand of friendship: 'Come, come, whoever you are, wonderer, worshipper, lover of leaving. It doesn't matter. Ours is not a caravan of despair. Come, even if you have broken your vow a thousand times. Come, yet again, come, come.' This verse is inscribed on the walls of his *khanqah* (hospice) that today serves as a museum in Konya, Turkey.

47. Maurice Blanchot, *L'Amitie'* (Paris: Gallimard, 1997 (1971)), pp. 328–9.

48. Dobrota Pucherova, 'Re-Imagining the other: The politics of friendship in three twenty-first century South African novels', *Journal of Southern African Studies* 35/4 (2009), p. 943.

49. Qias Mujeeb, 'Abdullah Hall,' *Aligarhnama* (23 February 2008). Available at http://aligarhnama.blogspot.com/2008/02/Abdullah Hall-hall.html (accessed 27 October 2012).

50. Martin Heidegger, *Sein und Zeit, (Being and Time)*, transl. Joan Stambaugh (Albany: State University of New York Press, 1996), pp. 54, 191, 193.

51. Worldwide there are AMU associations that bring together Aligs in multiple organizational activities and support groups. Every year, on 17 October, Sir Syed Day is observed by Aligs in their local chapters.

52. Generally, scholarship on Muslim women focusses on their oppressed private lives, piety and reform efforts guided by the elite. The literature on *purdah* and life behind it is the dominating theme in this genre. Azra Ali Engineer and Zoya Hasan have made some attempts to redeem this problem and highlight the organizational efforts for modernization led by ordinary Muslim women with a definite understanding of feminism. See Azra Asghar Ali, *The Emergence of Feminism among Indian Muslim Women, 1920–1947* (New York: Oxford University Press, 2000); Zoya Hasan and Ritu Menon (eds), *The Diversity of Women's Lives in India* (New Brunswick: Rutgers University Press, 2005).

53. Gail Minault, *Secluded Scholars: Women's Education and Muslim Social Reform in Colonial India* (New Delhi: Oxford University Press, 1999).

54. Lelyveld, *Aligarh's First Generation*.

55. Troll, *Sayyid Ahmad Khan*; Hafeez Malik, *Sir Sayyid Ahmad Khan and Muslim Modernization in India and Pakistan* (New York: Columbia University Press, 1980).

56. Shadaf Bano, 'Rashid Jahan's writings, resistance and challenging boundaries: Angaare and onwards', *Indian Journal of Gender Studies* 19/1 (2012), pp. 57–71.

57. Ismat Chughtai, 'Lihaf' [The Quilt], in Ismat Chughtai (ed), *The Quilt and Other Stories*, transl. Tahira Naqvi and Syeda S. Hameed (Delhi: Kali For Women, 1990 [1942]).

58. For further reading on the history of creative writing in Urdu see Shaista Ikramullah, *A Critical Survey of the Development of the Urdu Novel and Short Story* (London: Longmans, Green and Co., 1945).

59. See Amber Abbas's dissertation *Narratives of Belonging: Aligarh Muslim University and the Partitioning of South Asia* for an ethnography of the AMU boys experiences and their memories of friends, PhD dissertation (Austin: University of Texas: 2012).

60. Berenskoetter, 'Friends, there are no friends?'; Sibyl A. Schwarzenbach, 'On civic friendship', *Ethics* 107/1 (October 1996), pp. 97–128.

61. Leila J. Rupp, 'Sexuality and politics in the early twentieth century: The case of the international women's movement', *Feminist Studies* 23/3 (Autumn 1997), p. 578.

62. Adab and Adāb are different. The former signifies civility and the latter is a form of greeting.

63. Lelyveld, *Aligarh's First Generation.*

64. The tradition of 'visiting' was initially very restrictive because the reputation of girls, a very sensitive topic in Muslim community, was at stake. In the 1980s when I was an undergraduate student at Abdullah Hall, we were given permission to visit with approved family and friends.

65. I studied Russian language at Aligarh.

66. Naved Masood, 'Mumtaz Apa – reminiscences', *Aligarh Movement* (2010). Available at http:aligarhmovement.com/aligarians/Mumtaz_Jahan_Haider (accessed 27 October 2012).

67. Sa'diyya Shaikh, 'In search of 'al-insān': Sufism, Islamic law, and gender', *Journal of the American Academy of Religion* 77/4 (December 2009), p. 782.

CHAPTER 11

THE LIVING MONUMENTS OF MOURNING: STRUGGLES FOR MEMORY AND PEACE IN POST-REVOLUTIONARY IRAN

Shahla Talebi

The Flower Garden of Martyrs

'What was your relationship to him?' I ask the woman on the grave.[1] 'He was my cousin', she tells me. 'You must have been very close to him that after all these years you still keep coming here', I suggest. As if, in response to a possible judgment in my tone, she explains:

My parents are buried in a different section here [*Beheshtzahra* Cemetery]; I come for them anyway. So I may as well pay a visit to his grave as his sister visits those of my parents. It is much easier to travel this long distance having company.

I wonder if she is trying to distance herself from the State and its utilization of 'state martyrs', which had led to a strong resentment among many Iranians by the time of my research in Iran between 2002 and 2005.

'His children don't have time to come here', she adds interrupting my thoughts. 'What about his wife?' I ask, to which she goes on to answer in length:

> His wife is remarried. She no longer visits the cemetery and his three children are now accomplished professionals. His oldest son is a well-known surgeon in Shiraz; the younger son and his only daughter are lawyers and reside in Tehran. They have no time to come to the cemetery. Her sister is the only remaining family member who comes on a regular basis. Both of his parents died soon after he was martyred.

'The sister?' I ask, with my eyes looking around for her. 'Yes, she is gone to fetch water', she responds.

Just then I see the sister coming towards us, carrying a jar of water. The cousin continues, now in a louder voice, apparently to include the sister in our conversation:

> You know how busy people are nowadays! Life has become so much harder and everything so different. Martyrs' kids enter the best universities, get the best education because they're martyrs' children. But they are often too busy to remember their fathers.

Already on the grave, the sister greets me and Freshteh, a friend who accompanies me with her camera. Squatting on the grave, the sister begins pouring the water from the jar onto the plants and the flowers at the head of the grave. Freshteh's camera and I watch as she washes the gravestone with the palm of her hand and her fingertips, so amiably and softly, as though caressing her brother's injured face.

*****

I open this chapter on a gravesite in an attempt to highlight those modes of remembering and mourning the dead that are intertwined with, and allow for, a different conceptualization of life and death; peace and violence; and self and community. The views and practices of many of the families with whom I worked during my field research was informed by the Islamic Shi'i discourses on life, death and martyrdom as well as the sociopolitical milieu of the time and space in which these discourses were redefined and constantly renegotiated and revived. *Shahadat* or martyrdom is the apex where the blurred boundaries between life and death are particularly highlighted. In this conceptualization, as the lives of these grieving families and their relationship with their 'martyred' loved ones illuminate, neither life nor death are necessarily seen as the opposite of one another; nor is peace envisioned in a binary oppositional relationship with war. The self and the community are not separable from one another either. Peace is imagined not as absence of war or violence but as a state of being-becoming and an act of the mind, at once cognisant of the ever-presence of violence yet constantly aspiring and working to recreate a serene world in the midst, and in spite of, and in constant resistance to violence. This state of mind and mode of action recognizes the never-ending and necessary struggle one needs to undertake to remain present to the violence of history, language and the everyday. It is an urge, a desire and an assumed responsibility to stand as a witness to injustices of one's time and community while striving to regenerate and sustain a state of peace.

This chapter hinges upon the premise that remembering those lives cut short by violence is not merely about the dead, a compelling realization to which I arrived especially while working with the families of State and dissident martyrs in Iran.[2] Neither, as I also learned from these families, are their visits to the graves of their loved ones a mere act of mourning in the conventional sense of the term, to simply put the dead to rest and move on with 'life as we know it'.[3] While the experiences of these two groups of families differ in drastic ways, considering the fact that 'state martyrs' have been venerated by the state while 'dissident martyrs' are forced into silence, marginalized and stigmatized, I have chosen to explore the convergences in their remembrance and mourning attitudes and practices. Remembrance and mourning are here envisaged in connection with and embedded in a deep desire for justice. This chapter strives to illustrate how through remembering and mourning some of the grieving families, in Elizabeth Povinelli's words, seek '[m]aximally embodied social relations', and express a desire for 'thick life'.[4] Rather than bracketing the dead in an absolutely unreachable space so that the living can evade facing their mortality,[5] this alternative conception foregrounds interconnected genealogies and geographies of life and death, one that brings the living and the dead into new forms of sociality.[6] Through sharing their grief with one another, a gift, the gift of their friendship, and other forms of gift exchanges, they recognize the other and themselves in the other and hence engender the possibility of a peaceful existence. Mourning as such is itself a gift – to the living *and* to the dead. It confirms the survival of the living while keeping the dead in the bonds of sociality. It allows for life and gifting relationship to continue between the dead and the living. Many of these families refer to the Islamic discourse that does not assume impermeable boundaries between life and death and between the realm of the living and the dead. The gift exchange does not only occur in this perspective among the living but between the dead and the living, through visitations, guidance and other means. As the living often remind the dead of the principles of their religion, the dead too visit the living in their dreams and may offer guidance or even protection to the living. Life keeps going on in these new forms of sociality.

Remembering the dead is thus construed here, on the one hand, as a way of struggling against two commonplace amnesias – the existential amnesia concerning our mortality and the historical amnesia that remembers only selectively at the cost of forgetting others. I suggest that both struggles are paramount not merely for living an ethically just and humane life but for generating a spirit of peace. Acknowledging and recognizing the grief of the individuals and the community and allowing the space of remembrance and mourning for their unjust losses are necessary steps both to working through trauma and to creating a sense of serenity for the individual and the community. On the other hand, through opening up the space between the living and dead, by way of their gifting sociality, these families create a different kind of recognition. This recognition, as Paul Ricoeur suggests, 'in a different context' is not about a struggle for 'the affective, judicial and social recognition', which he argues has the risk of begetting 'unhappy consciousness' and 'a sense of incurable victimization' (2005:218).[7]

Through gifting these families rather seek out an, 'albeit symbolic, experience of mutual recognition' (Ricoeur 2005:226). This recognition is not sought between themselves and the enemy but between the dead and the living, and as the recognition of the structural and contingent condition of human existence. This carries a power that in turn has profound political force and implications. Such an attitude and mode of action leads to a 'state of peace' in their minds and in the communities they create. Yet they never give up on the struggle to remain witnesses to the injustices that pollute even the air they breathe. This alternative mode of remembering and mourning not only the dead but the living creates new genealogies and temporalities. In regard to mourning the living I think the statement by Adorno and Horkheimer is fitting in that they suggest: 'Hatred of the dead is made of envy no less than of a feeling of guilt' (1997:215).[8] While their notion of life and death are based on their reading of Freud and his idea of death wish, I deploy their view to consider not only the fact that in the people we lose we also lose part of ourselves, hence the mourning for the other is also about the loss of ourselves. Mourning could also be about the living whose life may have been rendered so impossible that death seems to be a liberating possibility; thus possible envy for the dead who seems freed from the often-degrading realities of life.

This manner of mourning and remembrance ventures to create links between the past and the present with eyes already on the future. Through such embodied remembrance, the dead and the living remain in a socially embedded relationship with one another. Remembrance allows them to reconnect to life, to others and to their own multiple selves, to those of the past and those yet to emerge. As this chapter attempts to show, the women I met on the gravesites and later in their daily spaces of life and work play a seminal role in propagating and preserving these life-bearing, peace-generating and community-sustaining connections. They give life to new geographies of friendship and bonds of kinships through their active work of remembering, mourning and surviving – for without mourning there would be no survival; only a survivor can really remember and mourn. They continue mourning and sharing their grief as a gift and the mutually recognize their own losses, survival and mortality as well as those of others, while bearing witness to the dead and the injustices of their time and place; and of other times and places.

By emphasising these modes of sociality and their power to create new relationships between the living and the dead, I hope to highlight a different perception of justice and peace – one in which remembering injustices is not about revenge or forgiveness. This perception rather shifts away from dichotomising approaches and instead thinks along the line of Paul Stoller's 'sensuous scholarship', and its 'local wavelength of theory'. This means seeking out not only 'local epistemologies' but their constructions 'by way of the "lower" senses, by way of the body' in order to learn about 'the order of experience and the nature of epistemologies in the contemporary world'.[9] Such an approach also underscores the potential of pain and grief in creating empathies and organic bonds rather than leading, as is often assumed, only to misery and depressive mode and to mournful communities in the conventional sense of mourning. In the particular case of my project, conversing with the local wavelengths introduces a different notion of mourning deeply rooted in a particular reading of Iranian Shi'i discourses of *shahadat*; as an act of witnessing injustice and as a gift of presence.

To remember in this manner is to connect to pain on a different register, simultaneously keen to its singularity and corporality. It is to expose those attempts that revive some memories only to ignore others or force them into erasure from collective memory and to deprive them from becoming historical events. In post-revolutionary Iran such attempts have tended to refuse both groups of surviving families the singularity of their grief while stripping their dead from thick sociality with the living. To remember and mourn the dead, as practiced by many of these families, however, is to reckon not merely with the reality of their death, but with the imminence of their own deaths. It means to never let the dead fall into absolute oblivion, for the connections between the living and the dead to be severed, for the cosmos to shrink.

Against these dangerous possibilities, as this ethnographic account shows, many of the families who lost loved one(s) during the violent events of the Iran—Iraq war or the political suppression of the 1980s have struggled to sustain a dynamic relationship between the dead and the living, one that has led to the formation of new forms of sociality, subjectivity and citizenry in post-revolutionary Iran. These modalities are hinged upon a specific symbolic exchange between life and death, and mourning as a form of *shahadat* or witnessing.

Shahadat in this sense is itself a figure of the gift − a symbolic exchange between the living and the dead that enables a new form of life to emerge.[10] These women's continuous mourning and hence connection to their dead is not, I argue, a failure to 'liberate' themselves from the 'lost object' − a collapse into a pathologically prolonged mourning as a simplified reading of Freud's notion of melancholia may have us believe.[11] Anchored in a radically different sense of the boundaries of life and death, and relationship to pain and mourning, this ceaseless 'attachment' to the dead undermines the conventional notion of 'economy of mourning', and its measured emotional investment in the 'lost object'.[12]

These women's relationship to the dead does not atomize or individualize mourning.[13] Pain for them is not an entirely private and incommensurate phenomenon. As Freud and other later psycho-analysts working from the tradition of 'mourning and melancholia' such as N. Abraham and M. Torokor, scholars like Michel Foucault, Talal Asad and Elaine Scarry show pain is at once a social and a personal reality, a semiotic practice.[14] In the words of Sheikh Sa'adi, the Persian poet of the twelfth and thirteenth centuries:

> Human beings are members of a whole
> In creation of one essence and soul.
> If one member is afflicted with pain,
> Other members uneasy will remain.
> If you've no sympathy for human pain,
> The name of human you cannot retain![15]

The women of whom I speak here embrace pain as a reality, which, instead of seeking to 'overcome' or resolve, they weave into new bonds of friendship. In recognition of each other's pain, they discover multiple sites of humanity – that of their own and of the other – through sharing, generosity, kindness, defiance and refusal to forget and, in short, through living, grieving and surviving. The inclusion of the dead into a web of bonds and new kinship relations puts the living in an ontological relation with the limits of life, where life is both lost and regenerated, at once highlighting culture and its limits. As C. Nadia Seremetakis suggests, anthropologists, including Michelle Rosaldo, George Lakoff, Lila Abu-Lughod, Catherine Lutz and Geoffrey White have written of the 'expression of emotions as embodied, conceptual, moral and ideational construct that place the self in a dynamic relation to social structure'.[16] Women's expressions of pain, Seremetakis suggests, are instruments of cultural power and truth claiming.[17]

Rather than allowing their grief to foreclose the world and the language on them, these women embrace a much thicker and larger world and its symbolic exchange. They recognize that one's pain is never entirely one's own.[18] They simultaneously defy attempts to preclude the violent roots of their sufferings, while accepting loss and pain as the condition of humanity. Their ever-presence to injustice and their acceptance of pain generates the desire for peace in the world and serenity in the mind. As a mother of an executed dissident told me, these women live their lives as a testimony to injustices to which their loved ones were subjected. Yet, they never wish such grief even for their killers, for killers too have mothers, and the pain of their loss would be too unbearable for their mothers. In her essay in this collection, Arzoo Osanloo also writes of the same spirit of forbearance and forgiveness that compels some of the mothers and sisters whose children and siblings have been killed to refuse to seek the death penalty for their killers. They too, do not tolerate seeing the pain of loss even for the mothers of their children's killers. This attitude introduces a departure, at least discursively, and a mode of imagination from that which reinforces the vicious cycle of violence. This does not mean that families of dissidents are not interested in seeking out other forms of accountability from the State. Nor does this mean that the families of state martyrs, and nearly all Iranians, do not feel the injustices of the global politics that imposed eight years of bloody war on Iran, cost millions of lives, so much destruction, and particularly of the role of the United States which encouraged and stood behind Iraq all those years. I have heard this from so many of these families that knowing the reality of the unfair global system they are not going to spend too much energy on seeking out judicial restitution. What these families, particularly the women, seem to rather focus on is creating and sustaining their communities. Mother Zahra, a state martyr's mother, explains this in the following words:

> We will keep our children alive by remembering them and by living a good life that is true to them. These powerful countries try to destroy us, to break our spirit. We will remain powerful by being connected to one another. Friendship helps us to endure the pain of so much injustice we have endured. But it is not only that. It also keeps us strong. It keeps us serene. It brings peace to our hearts. It helps us not to harm ourselves. Harming the self is a big sin for we are not our own. We are God's *amanat* (Sacred Trust). See this mother who set herself on fire after losing all her three sons, she lost heart for she could not see other's pain and find her connection with them. But you know what is most important is to know that God is always in our heart. The loneliest are those who forget that God is always present. Their heart becomes so darkened that they do not see God in it. That is when they lose peace and feel really lonely. They can then turn against themselves or others. This is very dangerous. We need to remain connected in pain with each other and with God.

Life, Death, the Gift of Peace

This state of peace in mourning is also rooted in a belief in life as an *amanat*, or divine entrustment, from God, a common view among many Shi'i Iranians. With life as an *amanat*, self-sacrificing deaths cannot be simply delineated as offerings, for how does one give as a gift that which one does not own? If life is not one's own, one's parents', or the State's, how can they claim to be the givers or receivers of these gifts, sacrifices or their beneficiaries? How does one offer to God that which is already His? This implies that one has no right to end one's life without a claim to being called by God. In fact, many of the families of those martyred in the Iran–Iraq War suggest that their children knew, either through a dream, a vision or a premonition of their imminent martyrdom and of God's call for them.

With the notion of life as an *amanat*, which God may reclaim at any given moment, death and martyrdom take different meanings. If life is an *amanat*, then death is truly 'a precious gift to the believer' or 'an atonement for every Muslim', as Al-Ghazali cites the Prophet's saying.[19] To end one's life before one's time means one's failure as an *amanatdar* (trust keeper). The common saying of many Iranians about the loss of their loved ones, '*khoda amanatesho pas gereft*' (God reclaimed his trust), or the Qur'anic verse that Muslims recite upon someone's death or misfortune, '*Ena llah va ena elaiyeh rajeoon*' (Surely we belong to God and to God we shall return), are allusions to these beliefs of life and death.[20] Mrs. Mahshour, the mother of a leftist executed dissident, exemplifies the serenity resulting from this belief:

> The night before hearing the news [of her son's execution], I dreamed of a white rooster I had raised and nurtured. God was asking me to set it free, to let it fly away. To no avail, I pleaded to keep it. Finally I raised it high and let it fly in the sky. When I woke up I knew that my son was gone. So when the news came, I already knew. I was calm. I assured my children that he was now with God.[21]

In Mrs. Mahshur's view, mothers have greater affinity with and understanding of the concept of *amanat* for they nurture, carry within and give birth to the children that they then have to let go. Mothers, she argues, offer their children love, protection and guidance, but have to trust that, on their own, they would be safe and make right choices. This, she explained, is how God too trusts and guides us not to harm ourselves for we are God's *amanat* on earth. She explains:

We, mothers, have to give our gift [their children] to others. When we send them to school, we have to trust that they would be treated well; when they marry, they become that of others. But the worst is when the state sends them to war. We bring them to life, but our children are never really ours. We raise them as God's gift, God's *amanat*, but we have to trust His *amanat* with others. We are doubly worried; we worry that we may not have raised them right and worry that others may harm them. All along we know that any moment God may call them.

For this mother the possibility and the responsibility of not having done right with one's *amanat* may have profound implication for the defected *amanat* can become harmful to other lives, which are also *amanats* from God.

She goes on to explain:

Although the biggest fear of a mother is for her children to die before her for this is a mother's worst grief, at least I know my child was raised to become a fine man. God called him young for he loved him; because he was such a fine man. So my grief is less devastating than those who killed him, for it is them, those killers, who would be lost forever. My son, he will be with God. He is a *shahid*. He will be with us forever. He will live on forever.

For this mother serenity is as present as is the grief and cognisance of the injustice of her son's killers. Yet there is a different kind of visibility of the death that may overshadow life and become disruptive of normative socialization. The Revolution of 1979, the eight years of bloody war with Iraq, the internal conflicts, and the harsh political suppression of 1980s rendered death too visible in the Iranian landscape. The overwhelming visibility of death in a

Central African City of Kinshasa compels Filip De Boeck to ponder the dwelling of death in its slums and cemeteries. He writes:

> But what happens if the very nature of the imaginary as flexible but organized field of social practice has become disorganized and has lost, at least to some extent, its localizing force and its capacity to create continuity, to produce sociality? The imaginary is the dimension of the invisible, but what if the invisible becomes visible, and the dead replace and become more alive than the living?[22]

In Kinshasa, De Boeck sees the birth of a new form of sociality created by the youth, a new symbolic exchange on the debris of the old and in the rejection of all legacies. In *Beheshtzahra* Cemetery a different kind of socialization is engendered, though not so much through the rejection of all legacies but in drawing on the discourses of *shahadat* and in mourning and remembering, and in bearing witness. This is a perspective of *Shahadat* in the spirit of witnessing and mourning, it is mourning as a way of witnessing and witnessing by way of remembering and mourning, as performative gifting. As with the tradition of mourning for the martyrdom of Hussein, the third Shi'i *Imam*, and his companions in Karbala, (680 CE) in Ali Shariati's[23] rendition, here too mourning becomes an act of witnessing, a gift that is given in a way of negating the self and as a way of reminding and striving for an ethical life.

This notion of *shahadat*, in Shariati's reading, insinuates living present to the time and community, to memory and to injustice. For Shariati, *shahadat* does not mean 'to be killed', but rather it 'implies that something which has been covered and is about to leave the realm of memory, and gradually forgotten by people' is brought back to light. By resisting amnesia, one becomes a *shahid*. In this reading of *shahadat*, not only an individual but 'the Islamic community established by the Qur'an has the status and responsibility of a shahid'. In their continuous work of mourning, which is also an act of remembrance, the Iranian mourning women seemed to live the idea that 'every Muslim should make a shahid community for others, just as the Apostle is an 'uswah (pattern) – [or an exemplar] – on the basis of which we make ourselves'.[24]

In the remainder of this chapter, I speak of this relational kind of mourning and of the productive role of women and their gendered gift, keen to the relations of power and the subjects' attachment to their obligations to others, and to particular forms of domination in the society.[25] Women's gendered gift of mourning reinforces and disrupts the dominant discourses and practices while radically differing from the nacropolitics exemplified in the hyper-memorialization of state martyrs and the deprivation of executed dissidents from the sociality of their death.

Life of the Cemeteries

In one of my many visits to *Beheshtzahra*, on this particular Friday, following a few hours of wandering on the graves and talking with martyrs' families, a friend, Freshteh, and I take a coffee break and sit on a bench in the Flower Garden of Martyrs, the section allocated for the graves of state martyrs. Surrounding us are tall trees, a pleasant scent of colourful flowers, fresh green grass, blue running streams, ponds and fountains. From nearby the children's laughter can be heard. Holding hands, young couples pass us by, leaving behind the smell of their perfumes and bits and pieces of their conversations. The ambiance resembles that of the parks in the northern parts of Tehran where the air is less polluted compared to the densely populated poor neighbourhoods of the southern part of the city. Under the shade of the trees, nearly intoxicated by the smell of flowers and dozing off under the caressing fingers of the breeze, if one could ignore the graves, perhaps death and destruction, the craziness of life in the city too could be forgotten.

Strolling around we come across groups of families in different sections of the Flower Garden of Martyrs who are sitting on blankets spread on the grass along the graves, chatting, eating and drinking. The inviting aroma of tea emanates from the teapots on their samovars. The smell of their food reminds me of the atmosphere of a typical outing in Iran. In the playground, children scream as swings take them to the heart of the blue sky; here and there we see men resting their head on their partners' laps; one may hear the lovers' whispers as they walk around, sit on the benches or relax on the grass. These common scenes of a picnic leads one to wonder if people have in fact become oblivious to the reality of death or that they have forsaken all those perished lives buried in this cemetery. However, soon one learns that the dead have not been forgotten but included in this sociality.

One cannot forget the dead, not merely, because the moment one walks into any of the sections one comes face to face with the graves and the mourners, on and around them. Frequently one encounters elderly mothers with tearful eyes who carry tins of water to the graves or notices visitors who cry for their loved ones more than 20 years after their death. Even if one ignored all this and confused the ambiance of the cemetery with that of a normal picnic, the lives of the dead individuals signified by brief words or poems on their gravestones would prevent the forgetting. Nor would the laughter of the dead caught and framed in their photos allow forgetting. Perhaps in the *Flower Garden of Martyrs* one might have become oblivious to the presence of the dead if their entire life had not been compressed in those tiny home-boxes, indexing their absence from their 'real' homes. Forgetting would have been perhaps possible had it not been for the bizarre objects within these crude metallic houses. However, not only none of these may be ignored or forgotten, one could not lose sight of the writings on the abundant boards in the cemetery that constantly remind visitors of their indebtedness to martyrs. All those monuments of martyrdom and war, these objects of memory,[26] and the stories of the mourning mothers demarcate this cemetery as the site of death, as the ultimate *destination* of war and violence, and a place where new life and new friendship bloom beyond and over, these devastating losses.

With graves in sight, all the similarities between a picnic and this cemetery fade away. It is not merely the sight of death that reminds one of violence and war. Death and the dead are present even when one is invited to share *ãsh reshteh* (Persian noodle soup) and *hendevãneh* (watermelon) with a group of mothers of martyrs on the graves of their beloved sons. As you listen to the stories of their lives and deaths and the new life these mothers have labouriously bore in their absence, your mouth takes a mixture of bitterness of grief and the sweet they offer you along with tea. The sweetness of their friendships emerging out of their grief remains with you, as a testament to the role these women play in sustaining life and community against the destructive force of war and violence.

New Life on the Ruins

Beheshtzahra teaches one a great deal about death and violence, but more importantly, it teaches about the multifarious ways these women cope with their traumatic consequences and the creation of life in their aftermath. It demonstrates the novel ways people build their future over and out of the ruins. An example of these new relationships and communities built on the sites of death is illustrated in the story of the four mothers of state martyrs who welcomed Fereshteh and me into their company. As we greeted them while walking by, they invited us to join them and offered us *āsh reshteh*, tea and *hendevāneh*. They made room for us to sit with them around a tablecloth beside the graves of their martyred sons. With no question, they shared their stories, laughter, grievances and food with us:

> 'We come here every week', one of the women said while another explained.
> 'We have been coming here since our sons were martyred.'
> Still the third woman added.
> 'If you come on Thursdays, you'll find us here. We are often here for the entire day; sometimes we cook here, but other times, like today, we bring our food and heat it here. We bring fruits, sweets and other stuff, and eat, drink and chat, usually till late in the evening.'

As they poured us tea, I informally inquired about their stories, which they generously shared along with their food, fruits, sweets and tea. They commented about one another's lives, interfered with and completed each other's stories and filled in the gaps born of forgetfulness, or even difficulty in articulation. This interconnected relationship between their own stories and emotions, and those of the others, as well as the detailed knowledge of each other's lives, testified to their deeply intimate friendship.

'Did you know each other before the War?' I asked them.

'No! We met here, on the graves of our sons. We live so far away from one another and have such different lives. See, for example, she lives in Karadj, (a town about 12 miles west of Tehran) while I come from Hasan Ābād' (a poor neighbourhood at the outskirts of Tehran),' one of the mothers responded.

Her worn out black chador, coarse hands and deeply wrinkled face revealed her working-class background. The woman in a long *mānto* and *maghneh* (a particular kind of head cover), pointing to a third woman in a flowery black chador, added:

The two of us live in Tehran, but the four of us do a lot together. We go to Jamkarān or take trips to holy Mashhad, or Qom.

[The woman from Karadj interjected.]

We consult one another about our problems, marriages and ...

Throughout the conversation, they kept interrupting and completing each other, so much so that in the end, I was no longer able to tell exactly which one said what; but from all this I conjured that their friendship was a by product of their martyred sons' new houses neighbouring one another and that their friendship had gone far beyond the neighbourhood.

In this geography of friendship, the dead are as actively involved as are the living, who in the inclusion of the dead in their midst give rise to new 'communities of pain and healing' of which Taussig and Comaroff[27] have written. As in the cities of the living wherein war has created new neighbours, neighbourhoods and friendships, the cities of the dead have also engendered new neighbourhoods and friendships, built on shared grief, sometimes by crossing the boundaries of class and social position. Friendship among women is also the site of peace, as Yasmin Saikia shows in this collection. These women's friendship has the power to engender peace, Saikia argues, not necessarily due to their conscious attempt but as in response to their feeling the need for being connected with, cared by, and caring for, the others. Like the mourning mothers in the Iranian cemeteries of whom I herein write, women's friendship, as Saikia suggests, bear new human relationships and new forms of life.

Yet, *Beheshtzahra* offers more than a single impression could capture – even a single person would have different impressions in various visits or even in a single trip to the cemetery if one visits some of its different sections. As with entering a large city, one's experience would greatly depend on one's point of entry and initial encounters; the impression of the ambiance of an upper-class neighbourhood, for instance, would remarkably differ from that of shanty houses. Here as well, various visits or even different entry points, or a more expanded journey in one visit might be impregnated with significantly divergent, and often surprising, outcomes. For, there are far more histories buried in *Beheshtzahra* than what lay in the well-maintained *Flower Garden of Martyrs*.

Beheshtzahra also contains the stories and bodies of many who have died of suicides, heart attacks and strokes that occurred in direct, or indirect relation to the violent history of war and political suppression in Iran. Grief can also generate more deaths, illustrated, for instance, in the story of the parents whose three sons were killed in the Iran–Iraq War. Shortly after the death of the third son, the father died of a stroke. Struck by intense grief, the mother then set herself on fire. While stories like this often remain outside of the pages of the official history, as dead they are buried in accordance with the religious and social norms and often receive regular funerary rituals and mourning processions.

The dead of the leftist dissident martyrs, however, are neither allowed into the mainstream cemeteries nor do their stories even enter into the pages of the official history. They live on as secretive, underground stories, unwritten and marginal, while their bodies are thrown into the unmarked, sometimes even mass, graves. Pushed to the margins of mainstream social structure in these remote and marginalized gravesites, 'Bauman's (1977) notion of performance spaces as disruptive and disjunctive and as an alternative social structure within or at the margins of the social structure',[28] finds an example in the way, in sharing their grief and friendship, the families of 'dissident martyrs' create their own alternative performative space.

There are also sections within the mainstream cemeteries that are kept at the margin and are allocated for the dissident martyrs. Wandering in the cemetery Freshteh and I came across one of these nearly hidden sites, section 33. This is the site where the contrast between the dominant topography of the territorializing discourse of the state − manifested in the *Flower Garden of Martyrs* − and the peripheral landscape of dissident martyrs becomes vividly visible. This quasi-burial ground is the site of an 'oppositional consciousness',[29] a site of struggle for humanity of the dead and the living. The banning of any funerary ritual, or any tombstone, urges the grieving families to seek, in De Certeaue's terms, nomadic tactics of creating spaces rather than mapping places.[30] They walk, both metaphorically and literally, in the venues of spatial narratives and on the unmarked graves at the margins of the cemetery.

Transition: Images of the Words and Words of Images

After a long ride on the subway and then the bus to the cemetery on that early Friday, Freshteh and I get off the bus on a distinct site, which would overshadow our experience of that day. The bus passes through the perfectly paved, wide boulevards along which in the blue-painted brooks the water shines under the sun's rays. I recall Marziyeh's remarks about the *'ābad'* (developed) status of this cemetery and its contrast with the gloomy condition of life in the city. As a political prisoner who spent five years of her life in prison under the Shah's regime and a widow who lost her husband to execution under the Islamic Republic, Marziyeh has grown intimate with pain and death. Her large extended family experienced so many losses in the War and the political suppression, both under the Shah and the Islamic Republic, that in her own words, 'for years since 1980, nobody in my family could stop wearing black, for before the mourning period ended for one loved one, another was executed'. In 2004, as a single mother of two college age children, she related to me how this constant state of mourning impacted her children:

> For several years my children did not see me in anything but black. I had gotten so used to it that I had totally lost sight of it till one day my three-years-old son's teacher told me that the only colour he used in painting was black.

The bus passes by the writings on the boards, murals and photos of state officials and famous state martyrs on the walls. Contemplating how huge the cemetery has grown, I recall the words of Ferdous, a former political prisoner who is also an executed dissident's widow and a single mother of two: 'These days the cemeteries are not exclusively for the dead. Where else could the poor afford to take their children for an outing but these well-maintained cemeteries?' My own frequent visits would in fact confirm the multipurpose quality of this cemetery as a site to pay heed to the dead, perform pilgrimage,[31] picnic, socialize, make friends, fall in love and initiate marriages.

The Name of the Nameless

Off the bus, Fereshteh and I look around. On one side of the road, the tall trees invite our gaze, but the very instant we turn to the other side, only a couple of feet across one of the 'regular' sections, we are faced by a tastelessly built brick and mud wall circumscribing a barren graveyard. Too short to conceal what lay behind, the wall segregates this plot from the rest of the cemetery. Against its purpose, which is to separate this graveyard from the rest, the wall urges one to wonder what kind of life and death it is to isolate or conceal.

The drastic contrast between this dry dirt site and the beautiful trees and well-maintained condition of most other sections, especially the *Flower Garden of Martyrs*, epitomizes the realities of the marginalization of the dissident martyrs vis-à-vis the hyper-memorialization of the state martyrs. It feels as though the tall trees on the other side are to evoke the envy of the dwarfish and dry bushes in this section. Yet the absence of flowers, trees and water arrest one's attention.

Now on the plot, Freshteh and I search for the names of the dead amidst the smashed gravestones, trying to identify them by reading the fragments of writings on the scattered broken pieces of tombstones. Once in a while we recognize a name and excavate our memories of those 're-presented' by these broken tombstones, shattered names and fragmented identities.[32] Most of those lying here have no traces by which one could identify them – nothing to prove their deaths and hence their once-lived lives. In the absence of a grave, signifier, symbolic manifestations, or any demarcating object or evidence, their death is rendered absolute. Their once-existence may become obscure.

'Where has my entire life work gone? I have lost them all, the fruits of my life?' These were the only words Mrs. Sadeghi uttered when she heard the news of the execution of all her three children in the massacre of political prisoners in Iran in the summer of 1988. In their stead, in one day, she received three small bags – each supposedly containing one of her children's belonging. Mechanically she followed her husband home, but the moment they entered their entrance hall, she seemed to have gone paralysed. Sitting at the doorway, she opened the bags, pulling pieces in and out. Nobody could separate her from the bags, nor would she move from the doorway. Neither eating, nor drinking, she just remained there.

It was as if her entire life work of motherhood was condensed in these three bags. As if by looking through them she was somehow trying to find something of her children that could be salvaged or something that remained of them. As if she could find no place for herself at home without her children, sitting at the doorway seemed to signal her readiness to go-die. The loss of all her children, unmarried with no offspring and no graves, seemed to mean not merely the loss of life but of community.[33] Experiencing the loss of all her children, all 'fruits of her life', she seemed to have lost herself and hence all her connections to the community, and the world around her. She had fallen into oblivion. The struggle for the mourning mothers not to allow their lives, and the lives of their dead loved ones to fall into such oblivion was hence existential, paramount not merely to their own existence but the sustaining of the community. For many dissidents' families the ban of mourning, not receiving the body of their executed loved ones for proper funerary rituals of ablution and burial, and the absence of real burial sites make the possibility of generating a community of mourners incredibly challenging.

Historian Vicente Rafael writes of the 'hopelessly out of place' quality of the dead in regard to the 'numerous photographs of Filipinos killed in a battle' during the Filipino–American War of 1899–1902.[34] In Rafael's view, this 'hopelessly out of place quality' of the corpses of the Filipinos killed in the battle is due to their being transformed, in Roland Barthes' words, into the 'living images of the dead'. In the barren graveyard of the Iranian dissidents, the entire landscape has an out of place quality, compelling one to echo Rafael's question: what sort of sociality could exist that did not have a place for the dead?'[35] If in the case of the Filipino dead, the living images of the corpses 'resist the closure of mourning', and create a sociality in which the dead lives on by eluding mourning and memorialization, the families of the dissident martyrs in Iran do not even seek to put their dead to rest.[36] They rather struggle to reclaim their social existence both as the living and the dead.

In this sense, these families mourn not merely the death of their loved ones but the unjust erasure of their death and the inhumane banning of public mourning. Through their unceasing mourning, which is also a way of witnessing, they strive to transform their traumatic experiences, in psychoanalytical terms of Nicholas Rand, through 'introjection' and their inter-subjective relation in this collective mode of mourning.[37] Against all the obstacles, like younger Javel in the story 'At Sea' that Rand re-narrates, they refuse to mutely mourn; instead they create 'the opportunity to adjust to [their] loss through a public display of grief'.[38] They attempt, in Rand's words, 'to find and renew [themselves] [...] be able to remember the past, recall what was taken from [them], understand and grieve over what [they] have lost to trauma.'[39]

In *Khavaran*, a segregated cemetery for the leftist dissidents, the mourning mothers tried very hard to locate their dead, because the regime kept bulldozing the graveyards. As if reading an ancient map in search of treasure, they searched the cemetery step-by-step, by taking, for instance, 'three steps to the right from the south-east corner, then five steps to the north, and finally two steps to the left'. The more the Regime dislocated the graves by erasing their signs, the more the families turned into walkers, who, in De Certeau's metaphor, navigated their own itineraries. Navigating the graveyard, this is how a woman helped Fereshteh and I find the grave of a former inmate. This urge to locate the grave, to know where the dead is, Jacques Derrida would tell us is paramount for the work of mourning. In his words:

> Nothing could be worse, for the work of mourning, than confusion or doubt: *one has to know* who is buried where – and it is *necessary* (to know – to make certain) that in what remains of him, *he remains there*. Let him stay there and move no more![40]

In Derrida's view, in knowing 'what remains there' we want to know that the dead remains there. This may be conjured as a way of fixing a place for the dead to prevent it from 'invading' the space of the living. However, the mourning women I worked with sought for the dead to still have a place among the living, to inhabit a space in our memory and our sociality. This mode of mourning, I believe, brings serenity to them rooted in their interconnected yet singular pain.

In the early 1980s, Mrs. Rouhi was one of those mothers who searched for any trace of her lost daughter in the endless alleys and streets in the east of Tehran. She told me how months after her disappearance, she still woke up from her recurring nightmares in which she would hear her daughter's whispers imploring her to look for her body. 'I walked in my waking hours, day after day, week after week, month after month, from one valley to another, but neither in my dreams nor in my waking hours I could find any trace to locate her body.' Nobody seemed to know what had happened to her after her arrest in 1981. She had obviously not even given her name to the interrogators. Had she died under torture? Was she executed? The uncertainty made her loss so much more excruciating, especially for her mother. She did not know how to mourn her.

This space of *barzakh*, between places, between life and death, or neither life nor death, renders Mrs. Rouhi's suffering so unimaginably incommensurate. Her daughter is long dead but has no space among the dead. Mrs. Rouhi hears her whisper but cannot find her; nor can she visit her grave where she can communicate with or cry for her, and see others communicating with and crying for their loved ones, with whom she may feel a sense of kinship based on pain and loss, with whom she can work towards sustaining a peaceful and dynamic sociality with the dead. While ceaselessly haunting her, her daughter does not have a place from which she can relate to the living or the dead. She has no place to remain, either here or there.

The refusal of the State to deliver the body or allow proper funerary and burial rituals and graves, and its ban on public mourning posed great obstacles for the families of dissident martyrs. Even when the family was given a location for the grave, the constant bulldozing of the graveyard agonized the mourners.[41] Locating the dead is precarious, especially when the same grave has been given to more than one family.

Despite the revered status of state martyrs, among them too some dead remain 'gomnam' (unidentified), for either the body was not found or was too severely damaged to be identified. (In the 1980s running a DNA test was not that common, particularly because too many bodies returned from the front.) Aside from hygienic concerns, the dead had to be buried as soon as possible in accordance to the Islamic dictate. For these families too, the work of mourning proved hazardous.[42]

In the liminal space between life and death, social relations and communication become suspended. For both groups of mourning families, locating the lost one is of great significance for without it they seem to find it impossible to relate to an utter void; nor do they accept the exclusion of the dead from their cosmos. The dead belongs, as most of these families as Muslims believe, to a larger cosmos, residing in a neighbouring country, to which we will all travel in due time. However, the space between life and death, neither life nor death, renders sociality complicated if not impossible.[43]

The concern of these surviving families is not, therefore, about forcing the dead or the ghost to 'stay in its place', but to allow the dead a place of existence, to let the dead remain in conversation with the living and to remain social. To know that the dead *remain there* is to know they are present as witnesses, *shahids*.[44] Visiting the grave is hence as much about the living as it is about the dead. The freshness of the flowers on the grave speaks for the living, who still remember the dead. In an eerie sense, one comes to realize that one's recognition of death is mainly reliant on the signs that index life; as though it is the material objects of this world that imply the dead being dead, and 'being' in the other world.

Simultaneously, though, these material objects, these indicators of one's death, perhaps more crucially allude to one's once-upon-a time existence. Without a body, burial or a chance for public mourning, not only the death is rendered traceless but the very existence of the dead is undermined or utterly denied. Without visitors, mourners, graves, tombstones, flowers and/or heirs, nothing remains of the dead to verify that she or he ever lived. In this absolute departure, life itself is disclaimed. Refusing this sheer disappearance, this seemingly never appearance, the families, especially of dissident martyrs, diligently continue to visit the graves and work on creating new webs of relations.[45]

Against this total disavowal of life, they continue to hold on to the photos, letters and/or any other objects of their dead; some, like Shirin, a wife of an executed dissident, even carry a portable tombstone to the cemetery and take it back home. She put this portable tombstone, on which the name of her executed husband and his birth and death dates were carved, in the living room of a house in which she lived with her second husband, and her children when I visited her in 2003. In the apprehensive words of an elderly mother whom I met on the graveyard of her dissident martyred son: 'who will come to his grave when I die?' She dreaded not her own death but the double loss of her son in her death. This was the agony of her son's death and its non-recognition, fear of his forsaken life, of an utter unimaginable void in the place of a son she had raised and watched to grow!

In these forgotten departures, there are also the forsaken ever-arrivals: the death whose precondition – life – is not remembered. Death, in and of itself, is never as absolute or as other as we claim, not as long as the living keep the dead alive in the material objects, in retelling of stories, in their own living, in carrying them in their own body and even in the form of a ghost. Death is absolute only when the dead are dead to the living, when they are cut from the social bonds. It is not only the living whose survival depends on outliving the dead, but living allows for the dead to live on by surviving and carrying them within, by continuing to remain in relation with them and by never forsaking them. The families of State and dissident martyrs hence continue mourning not to liberate themselves from the dead but to bring them to their midst against the imposed hyper-visibility or invisibility to which their respective lost loved ones have been subjected. Resisting the mere 'perishing' of their dead, they strive to claim, in Derrida's term, their 'cultural death'.[46]

Of Mourning and Peace

The complaints about the youth not paying heed to the dead, as the one in the opening story, are mainly derived from the anxiety that the dead may die, to their children. The dead die all over again in the death of the mother or family members, in being forgotten by the youths, or in being erased from history. Faced with an impossible abyss, mourners implore the attention of the youth, fight for their dead to enter the pages of history and for a counter-narrative while all along working to sustain a peaceful community. Of this desire for peace, which is so much more than a momentary absence of violence, Mrs. Rohani, a mother of two executed dissident sons and a daughter-in-law, speaks to me on one early Friday morning in the summer of 2004 as we ride on a bus from one cemetery, where we have just visited the graves of one of her sons and the wife of the other, to another cemetery to visit her other son. 'My daughter-in-law's last wish was to be buried along her husband but the regime not only denied her wish by burying her along my other son but made my life harder for now every Friday I have to travel the long distance between the two cemeteries', she tells me. In the same breath, however, she goes on to speak of peace:

> As a woman and a mother, I cannot but desire peace for I cannot imagine any mother to live the grief of outliving her children. Nowadays, so many mothers like me have lost their flesh and blood to war, revolution, to torture, to execution. We, mothers, we like to create not destroy. You know, we have been created, already with a gift. Our womb is God's gift to us. Our womb is the most precious place for it is in our womb that God's creation becomes complete. It is in our womb that we carry and nurture God's *amanat* (trust) on earth. But God's gift to us does not end here. We breastfeed our children; this too is a gift so we can nourish God's gift and *amanat*, his gift and our gift, our children.

[She goes on to say:]

> But you know of course that with gift comes responsibility. You have to protect God's *amanat*. You cannot harm it. A mother's task is not merely to bring children to this world but to nurture them, to love them, to protect them, to teach them how to love themselves and others as God's *amanat*. This is why I say motherhood is like prophethood. See if the Prophets are the messengers of God on earth. If they are His *'amanatdar'* in whom He trusts with His divine message, divine words, with mothers God trusts with his creation. It is through mothers that human beings come to this world to whom then God sends His guidance. So you see it is not only the condition of our womb and our home that we have to keep safe for our children. It is also the larger world that we should make a safer and more peaceful place for everyone.

I interrupt Mrs. Rohani. 'But this is a huge responsibility on women you seem to suggest. No?' She nods, affirmatively and goes on to assert:

> Of course being a woman is a huge responsibility. But our gift is also huge. We have been trusted to assist God with his creation. You think this is not a huge gift? That is why our grief is even deeper when our children act violently; when they create such a violent world, when instead of love, they disseminate hatred. It is like turning God's message of peace, Islam, to message of hate and war, as these state heads have. Seeing the prison guards act so violently and rudely toward the grieving and mourning mothers made my heart bleed. It made me cringe inside. Every time they disrespected me or other families while visiting our children or when they heartlessly told us of our children's execution, I told them that they could be my son and that their mother would not be happy to see them cursing and disrespecting someone's mother or killing a mother's child. I mourned not only the loss of my children, but the loss of these children who have been lost to God. It is our responsibility and gift to nurture and love all children in a way that brings serenity and love to their heart. We have to overwhelm their heart with love, put them under the spell of love, so they become incapable of harming one another.

'But how?' I ask. She explains:

> As mothers, we are capable of loving other's children as if our own for all children are God's *amanat* and we have to be ready to let go of them when necessary. That is why even in pregnancy, filled with joy, we already begin mourning for we know that what is growing inside us, in our womb, will soon depart from us and go on a separate way. Mourning and motherhood are inseparable.

Journal, 31 July 2014

I have come to see the sisters of the three executed Rashidi brothers. The family is very well known among dissidents. The mother, a highly respected and active 'mother of martyr', as she was usually referred to by other families, has passed away about five months ago. Her death has brought great sadness and anxiety to the 'community of the executed dissidents', and generated concerns about their relationship to their 'martyrs', and to one another. As I ring the bell and right before Zohreh, one of the sisters, opens the door, my eye catches the funeral announcement on the door, still not removed five months after the mother's death.

The content of the announcement instantly introduces me to a peculiar reality: the expression of sadness in this poetic prose is less about the loss of the mother to her living children than to her martyred sons. It conveys the concern that 'she would no longer be around to commemorate our loved ones', and that 'this burden is now on our {the sisters'}, shoulders'. The main goal of mother's life, the announcement seems to imply, was to live so her sons would live on in, and be remembered by, her. Her death thus engenders anxiety about her sons' utter deaths.

Whose Monument?

Mrs. Rashidi,[47] a mother of three executed sons, three 'Rashids' (tall standing men), as their sister, Zohreh, refers to them, was an embodiment, a manifestation and an exemplary motherly figure whose whole existence rotated around her sons' lives and preservation of their memories as the dead. Since the arrest of her sons during the Shah's regime, Mother Rashidi had played a crucial role in organizing and participating in activities against imprisonment, torture and execution of dissidents. Her efforts in establishing a community of the families of political prisoners had proven vital and effective. Her presence appeared imperative to all the gatherings, be it in the graveyards, at anniversaries held at home, or in coming together in front of the jail to protest maltreatment of their children in jail.

She was an example of those mothers, to whom I refer to as 'loyal mourners', those for whom mourning becomes a defining aspect of their subjectivity. These mothers stand, as if a monument, to the memory of their dead sons or daughters. Their life turns into an object of memory, for remembering the life and death of their dead. For the Rashidi family, that monument is now gone; in its stead remains a hollow space and a void to be filled by other monuments built as though on its ruin. The anxiety is immense, the burden unbearable. Those who are to take on the role of the new monument wonder if they will effectively represent the great task the mother had so efficiently carried on. What would their failure mean? What if they die too? Who would take over their place? What enables one to inherit the position of a mourner–witness? What of the time of no replacement?

As I sit there and listen to Zohreh's stories and concerns and to her sister's worries about Zohreh's chain smoking and ill health, suddenly a shiver runs down my spine. The realization collapses on me – like an avalanche – a revelation from which no escape seems possible. Am I not here, at Zohreh's, privy to all the stories so that I could take on the role of a substitute, another monument? Am I – the anthropologist – capable of carrying this burden?

Zohreh smokes incessantly as she narrates the stories of the lives, the struggles and the deaths. Tears wash her face, while the smoke of her cigarettes and her frequent coughs punctuate my senses, my sight and my hearing. As she relates details of the predicaments of the surviving families facing, constant surveillance, arrests and beatings simply for mourning and commemorating their dead, I scrutinize the room like an archaeologist who searches for artifacts to trace and make sense of the past.

The living room is illustrative of the presence of the dead in the lives of the living. The walls are covered by the photos of three handsome young men, with dried roses decorating the frames. There are also photos of the father and the mother. The mother's smile is frozen, along with her eyes, which stare at her sons' photos. The handicrafts made in prison by the sons, and their letters sent from there, are also hanging on the walls, as are the embroideries, paintings, poems and other related objects offered by others in the memories of the three 'martyred comrades'. The cemetery has come home. The home has turned into a cemetery, and a museum. On one of the walls, a poem by Shamloo commemorates those who 'face the thunder, enlighten the house and die'.[48]

Where is the line between life and death? We are born to our life as well as our death, socially, culturally, politically and linguistically. We cope with our lives and deaths by resisting the kind of life and death that erases us from our sociocultural and historical existence, that throws us outside sociality, outside language, that forces us to die an unimaginable, impossible and inhumane 'natural death'. Against this im-possibility mother Rohāni, another mother who has lost two sons and a daughter-in law to the State execution, insists on her son's right to die, be buried and mourned like any other human being, as *yek ensān-e-ejtema'e* ('a social being'). Asserting their humanity, these mourning families strive to reclaim a social and historical death for their loved ones. In light of this, standing on that barren site in *Beheshtzahra* Cemetery, Freshteh and I attempt to decipher the significance of the material objects carried to and left on these graves by the living as indicators of the humanity of the dead, the evidence of their once-lived lives, their struggles, their dreams, their unfulfilled desires, and their unjust and violent deaths.

Here, in this vital matrix of life and death, every piece of a tombstone appears as a valuable treasure. Walking around and reading the fragments of carved words on the pieces of shattered tombstones, we search for traces and for signs. Freshteh films, carefully, meticulously, as if trying to preserve the decaying indicators of these deaths and lives. I try to put the letters together: here a word '*āghāz*' (beginning-birth) with the date of birth, there a '*parvāz*' (flight-departure) and the date of death, having survived the cruelty of destruction. The rest we have to imagine, outlive and survive so the dead can survive.

We watch a mother carry a jar of water to the grave of her son, a metaphoric gesture of her mourning as a way of giving life, a way of boosting life and sustaining communities, by weaving the dead into the social fabric of society, by living as a *shahid*. Through their exemplary generosity, through giving voice to their grief and through communicating and connecting with others in grief, many of the families of state and dissident martyrs create new geographies of friendship and bonds of kinship, and a radically different conceptualization of peace. While the State insists on the selective memorialization of state martyrs, which is in fact often at the cost of the singularity of their memory and of the grief of their families, the reality of the lives of these families and the performative sociality created on their singular yet shared pain have a different lesson to teach us about peace. They teach us that peace is not achieved by a selective revitalization of some memories, and the forced erasure of others, always a false calm before the storm, always already anticipating its opposite. It is rather a process, a state of mind, and a mode of action projected in the kind of mourning, remembrance and witnessing that include not only one's own dead, but those of others. It is mourning—witnessing the inhumanity of the other. It seeks a space beyond the boundaries of the self and the other based on the idea that somehow even with language there is something more to flesh and pain than political and legislative corporality connote.[49] This peace is inviting and binding, in grief and joy, those who work to create, rather than destroy communities.

Notes

1. These are excerpts of conversations I had with 'martyrs" families during my ethnographic field research. This particular one took place in *Beheshtzahra* Cemetery in Tehran in May 2004.

2. I refer to those killed in the Iran–Iraq War, or internal conflicts and whose death was death the State officially recognized as martyrdom as 'state martyrs' or 'official Martyrs'. The dissidents who were killed by the State were, however, stigmatized and forced into silence, though still often considered as martyrs by their families or their affiliated organizations. Following their families' sentiment, I call this group of dead 'dissident martyrs'. See Shahla Talebi, 'From the light of the eyes to the eyes of the power: State and dissident martyrs in post-revolutionary Iran', *Visual Anthropology* 25/1–2 (2012), pp. 120–147.

3. This is an allusion to the title of a book which shows how a routine everyday life of a family is turned upside down with the birth of their son with Downs Syndrome. The book illustrates how sustaining a sense of normalcy of the everyday entails a systematic violence to the child and the family and the only

way out seems to embrace the abnormal and to create a different sense of normalcy and a different relation to the everyday. Michael Bérubé, *Life as We Know it: A Father, a Family, and an Exceptional Child* (New York: Vintage Books, 1998).

4. Elizabeth A. Povinelli, *The Empire of Love: Toward a Theory of Intimacy, Genealogy, and Carnality* (Durham: Duke University Press, 2006), p. 45.

5. In his piece, 'Storyteller', Walter Benjamin writes:

> today people live in rooms that have never been touched by death, dry dwellers of eternity, and when their end approaches they are stowed away in sanatoria or hospitals by their heirs. It is, however, characteristic that not only a man's knowledge or wisdom, but above all his real life – and this is the stuff that stories are made of – first assumes transmissible form at the moment of his death. Just as a sequence of images is set in motion inside a man as his life comes to an end – unfolding the views of himself under which he has encountered himself without being aware of it – suddenly in his expressions and looks the unforgettable emerges and imparts to everything that concerned him that authority which even the poorest wretch in dying possesses for the living around him. This authority is at the very source of the story.

See Walter Benjamin, *Illuminations: Essays and Reflections*, Hannah Arendt (ed), transl. Harry Zohn (New York: Schocken, 1969), pp. 83–110.

6. Here one may think with Samuel Weber and what he says about translation and history, which is also relevant in this translation between life and death, the exchanges between the living and the dead, in Weber's words:

> What survives, survives in a modified form. Can it thereby be said to 'outlive itself?' What might it mean to outlive oneself? In no case does it mean to be simply immortal. Rather it is a form in which the uniquely modern relation of life and death defines its own ambiguous, ambivalent character (68).

See Samuel Weber, *Benjamin's – Abilities* (Cambridge: Harvard University Press, 2008).

7. Paul Ricoeur, *The Course of Recognition*, transl. by David Pellauer (Cambridge: Harvard University Press, 2005).

8. See Theodor W. Adorno and Max Horheimer, *Dialectic of Enlightenment* (London: Verso, 1997).

9. Paul Stoller, *Sensuous Scholarship* (Philadelphia: University of Pennsylvania Press, 1997), p. 1.

10. See Veena Das, *Life and Words: Violence and the Descent into the Ordinary* (Berkeley: University of California Press, 2007); See also Veena Das, 'Wittgenstein and anthropology', *Annual Review of Anthropology* 27 (October 1998), pp. 171–95.

11. Sigmund Freud, 'Mourning and melancholia', *The Standard Edition of the Complete Psychological Works of Sigmund Freud*, Vol. XIV (London: Vintage,

1914/2001), pp. 237–58; also see his 'On the History of the Psycho-Analytic Movement', *The Standard Edition of the Complete Psychological Works of Sigmund Freud*, pp. 3–68.

12. For a reading of the complexity and yet limitation of Freud's notions of mourning and melancholia see Shahla Talebi, 'Who is behind the name? A story of violence, loss, and melancholic survival in post-revolutionary Iran', *Journal of Middle East Women's Studies* 7/1 (Winter 2011), pp. 39–69; see also Tammy Clewell's 'Mourning beyond melancholia: Freud's psychoanalysis of loss', *Journal of the American Psychoanalytic Association* 52/1 (2004), pp. 43–67. Available at www.apsa.org/portals/1/docs/japa/521/clewell.pdf (accessed 15 July 2013).

13. In the context of South Africa and TRC, reading Ruth Wilson Gilmore's discussion of women who testified, Allen Feldman suggests that they did not take the stand, 'as atomized traumatized victims, but as representatives and embodied signifiers for the disappeared and the dead'. He argues that 'the entire call and response performance existed in an emotionally powerful relation to absence – to the silenced and the dead who would never testify. The presence of these women, and the shadows they brought into the hearing room, evoked the historical depth and recesses of their witness that could not be captured in literal speech. Refusing to ground their language in individualized knots of the traumatic, these women invoked a dialogic of presencing the unreachable, of giving 'impossible witness'. Allen Feldman, 'Memory, theatres, and the trauma-aesthetic', *Biography* 27/1 (2004), p. 176.

14. See, for instance, Nicolas Abraham, Maria Torok and Nicholas Rand, 'A poetics of psychoanalysis: 'The lost object: Me', *SubStance* 13/2, Issue 43 (1984), pp. 3–18; Michel Foucault, *Discipline & Punish: The Birth of the Prison*, 2nd edn., transl. Alan Sheridan (New York: Vintage, 1995); Talal Asad has taken issue with Elaine Scarry's view on the incommunicability of pain, and pain as a private matter; see Asad's *Formations of the Secular: Christianity, Islam, Modernity* (Stanford: Stanford University Press, 2003), pp. 80–1; Elaine Scarry, *The Body In Pain: The Making and Unmaking of the World* (Oxford: Oxford University Press, 1987); Nadia C Seremetakis, *The Last Word: Woman, Death, and Divination in Inner Mani* (Chicago: University of Chicago Press, 1991).

15. M. Aryanpoor's translation.

16. See Michelle Rosaldo 'Toward an anthropology of self and feeling', in R. A. Shweder and R. A. LeVine (eds), *Culture Theory: Essays on Mind, Self, and Emotion* (Cambridge: Cambridge University Press, 1984), pp. 137–7; see also Catherine Lutz and Geoffrey M. White, 'The anthropology of emotions', *Annual Review of Anthropology* 15 (October 1986), pp. 405–36; Lila Abu-Lughod and Catherine Lutz (eds), *Language and the Politics of Emotions* (Cambridge: Cambridge University Press, 1990).

17. Seremetakis, *The Last Word*.

18. This reminds me of the indigenous people of Belyuen, 'a small community in the Northern Territory of Australia and its hinterlands' (Povinelli, *The Empire of*

Love, p. 2). As Povinelli suggests, the sore of her body is not only hers. She writes how her journey to figure out whose sore it is 'may lead [her] into the mud of Maliya or simply to the kinship of husbands and wives. In any case, here at Belyuen, my flesh is always already stretched across multiple possible material anchors'. See Povinelli, *The Empire of Love*, p. 46.

19. Al-Ghazāli, *The Remembrance of Death and Afterlife*, transl. Tim J. Winter (Cambridge: Islamic Texts Society, 1989).

20. The verse is 'Inna lillah wa inna ilaihe raji'un' in Sura *Al-Baqara*, Verse 156. The verse reads as: '*When a misfortune overtakes them, they say: "Surely we belong to Allah and to Him we shall return"'*.

21. Mrs. Mahshour, from our conversation in April 2004.

22. Filip De Boeck, 'Mourning and the imagination of political time in contemporary central Africa', *African Studies Review* 48/2 (2005), p. 14.

23. Ali Shariati was a scholar of Islam and a sociologist whose reading of *Shi'ism* and *shahadat* was extremely influential in paving the way for an Islamic revolution in Iran.

24. See Ali Shariati, 'Jihad and Shahadat', *Iran Chamber Society*. Available at http://www.iranchamber.com/personalities/ashariati/works/jihad_shahadat.php (accessed 10 June 2012).

25. Marilyn Strathern, *The Gender of the Gift: Problems with Women and Problems with Society in Melanesia* (Berkeley: University of California Press, 1990).

26. A reference to Susan Slyomovics, *The Object of Memory: Arab and Jew Narrate the Palestinian Village* (Philadelphia: University of Pennsylvania Press, 1998).

27. See Michael Taussig *Shamanism, Colonialism, and the Wild Man: A Study in Terror and Healing* (Chicago: University of Chicago Press, 1991); Jean Comaroff, *Body of Power, Spirit of Resistance: The Culture and History of a South African People* (Chicago: University of Chicago Press, 1985).

28. Seremetakis, *The Last Word*, pp. 4–5.

29. The term used by Jane J. Mansbridge and Aldon Morris in an edited book of the same title: Jane J. Mansbridge and Aldon Morris (eds), *Oppositional Consciousness: The Subjective Roots of Social Protest* (Chicago: University of Chicago Press, 2001).

30. Michel De Certeau, *The Practice Of Everyday Life* (Berkeley: University of California Press, 1988).

31. In my visit to the Museum of War in Shalamcheh, a small war-ridden town in the south of Iran which was destroyed by Iraqis, I was struck by the sign at the entrance that welcomes the visitors for their *ziyarat* (pilgrimage) and addressed them as *zayerin* (pilgrims) as well as a sign at the exit, which wishes that God would accept their *ziyarat*.

32. For a history of attacks on graves see Mehrdad Amanat's 'Set in stone: Homeless corpses and desecrated graves in modern Iran', *International Journal of Middle East Studies* 44 (2012), pp. 257–83.

33. Those killed in the massacre of the summer of 1988 were thrown into mass graves.

34. Vicente Rafael, *White Love and Other Events in Filipino History* (Durham: Duke University Press, 2000), p. 87.

35. Ibid., p. 91.

36. Ibid., pp. 91–2.

37. Nicholas Abraham and Maria Torok, *The Shell and the Kernel: Renewals of Psychoanalysis*, Nicholas T. Rand (ed), Vol. 1 (Chicago: University of Chicago Press, 1994); Abraham and Torok's concept of intro-jection, according to Rand, 'appears to be a synthetic enlargement of abreaction, binding, working out, working-through, and the work of mourning': Rand, 'Introduction', in *The Shell and the Kernel*, p. 7.

38. Ibid., p. 10.

39. Ibid., p. 11.

40. Jacques Derrida, *Specters of Marx: The State of the Debt, the Work of Mourning & the New International* (London: Routledge, 1994), p. 9.

41. In fact now *Khavaran* Cemetery (the remote Cemetery allocated for the dead of the Bahai and leftist dissidents) has been closed and the families are no longer allowed to enter and visit the graves (many of them mass-graves) of their dead loved ones killed by the State.

42. There were many stories of the 'tragic' return of those believed to be dead. I have written of one of these stories. A family, who was living right across from our house, received the news of the death of their son who was in the early stages of the Iran–Iraq War. Not that long after his pregnant wife gave birth to his child, the family had her married to her brother-in-law, the family's younger son. With a child from the first son, and pregnant with the second, one night the family opened to door to their first son who was obviously wrongly thought dead and now returned, only to learn that his wife and child were no longer his. 'Tragedies' like this one made seeing the body essential to the peace of mind of the families. See Shahla Talebi, 'Mourning for the loss of mourning', *Connect* 3 (2001), pp. 107–14.

43. My book, *Ghosts of Revolution*, deals with this suspended state of *barzakh*, in madness and in dying while still physically alive, and of the complexity of relating to this State. See Shahla Talebi, *Ghosts of Revolution: Rekindled Memories of Imprisonment in Iran* (Stanford: Stanford University Press, 2011).

44. Derrida, *Specters of Marx*, p. 90.

45. Since *Khavaran* has been closed on these families, the private spaces of their homes have become the site of their collective mourning/witnessing. Cybermedia has also been essential though with a different characteristic. Many of the mourning mothers have made videos of their stories about their dead loved ones and how the State has treated them, and their families, and posted on Youtube, or even Facebook. While this has changed the intimate way they related to one another and to their dead, it has also allowed for the expansion of the community of mourners and a sense of witnessing on a global scale. The ethnographic study of this transformation is begging a new project.

46. Jacques Derrida, *Aporias* (Standford: Stanford University Press, 1993), p. 43. This statement might appear to somewhat simplify the complicated concept of dying. For, 'dying is neither entirely natural (biological) nor cultural. And the question of limits articulated here is also the question of border between cultures, languages, countries, nations and religions as well as that of the limit between a universal (although non-natural) structure and a differential (non-natural but cultural structure'. Derrida, *Aporias*, p. 42.

47. Even my choice of name for her I later noticed was somehow a reference to her sons.

48. From my field notes, 31 July 2004; For the official translation of the poem, see Ahmad Shamloo, 'Funeral oration', Available at http://shamlu.com/trama.htm (accessed 13 July 2013).

49. An allusion to Elizabeth Povinelli's discussion of carnal and corporal body in Povinelli, *The Empire of Love*, pp. 7–8.

CHAPTER 12

MERHAMETLI PEACE IS WOMAN'S PEACE: RELIGIOUS AND CULTURAL PRACTICES OF COMPASSION AND NEIGHBOURLINESS IN BOSNIA AND HERZEGOVINA

Zilka Spahić-Šiljak

For the last 19 years, I have worked with women's organizations[1] engaged in peace-building in Bosnia and Herzegovina (BiH) and the Balkans. I explored their agency and their dedication to rebuilding and healing broken inter-ethnic relationships. Their work focusses on providing the secure legacy of a peaceful society for future generations. Despite deep ethno–national and ethno–religious divisions within BiH after 1990, women were determined to rebuild peace by working towards inter-faith and inter-ethnic cooperation.[2] Their major message is that the three BiH constituencies – Bosniaks–Muslims, Serbs–Orthodox Christians and Croats–Catholics – must learn to live together; their cultural and ethnic hybridities and the shared past experience of peaceful coexistence can serve as a guide for their future and for the future of conflict resolution in other multi-ethnic societies.

For four years I worked as a peace worker with a dozen Muslim women. I interviewed nine women, in particular, as often as once every two months over the course of these years.[3] I was able to look deeply into issues that were of intimate importance to them. This ethnographic work is particularly focussed on the experience of these nine women who were from three Muslim villages of BiH near Mostar, Sanski Most and Bijeljina.[4] As a part of the 'Social Inclusion of Women Returnees' project, I met these women during regular visits to their villages over the span of four years.[5] Together, we discussed the social inclusion of women in their local communities as well as the institutional, social and political obstacles they faced in their struggles to obtain basic social and economic security. Thus, the primary goal was not to speak about peace-building and reconciliation. However, these themes appeared to be important especially in villages at the borders, which are neglected both by State and local authorities. These are the self-same authorities who promised a better life, employment and social benefits if they received support for ethno–national political goals of ethnic division and separation from those who belong to other ethnic groups. Yet, these promises remain unfulfilled.

Due to sensitive and sometimes dangerous political implications that these initiatives could have had in the ethnically divided political and social realms of BiH, all of the interviewed women wanted to remain anonymous. They explained that their peace-building activities were driven by *merhamet* (compassion, mercy) and *komšiluk* (neighbourliness). These signify good will, good deeds and faith in human goodness, but are often judged to be the naïve, foolish and irrational endeavours of sensitive women 'who always find a way to forget and forgive'.[6]

In this chapter I discuss women's agency in peace-building and how the nine women I interviewed were motivated by *merhamet* and *komšiluk*. These are social and cultural norms and concepts that pre-date the 1992–5 war and the socialist period. *Merhamet* stems from the Arabic word *rahmat*, which is translated as 'mercy', and it is the most important of God's 99 names.[7] Moreover, this word is feminine in gender, implying that God comprises both the feminine and the masculine. *Komšiluk* is from the Turkish *komşu*, a word that translates as neighbour and implies a prescribed set of social relations between neighbours. However, it is also a richly loaded term in the Balkans. For example, *komšiluk* might mean regular coffee visits, the celebration of major life events together, or the extension of unsolicited aid. The women I worked with re-enacted these concepts as useful channels for peace-building and reconciliation, despite ethno–nationalist rhetoric and a patriarchal culture that undermine the *merhamet* approach to peace-building: as a purely female, naïve, foolish and, therefore, less valuable sociopolitical activity.

Gendered Peace Initiatives on the Ethno–National Borders

Rebuilding peaceful social relationships in politically divided and economically impoverished BiH society was a difficult enterprise. Women in BiH, as in many other post-conflict countries, became the most prominent actors in peace-building initiatives during and after the war. As many feminist scholars emphasize, peace-building is always gendered.[8] Feminist scholars also emphasize that women are not inherently peaceful, and they can be as warmongering as men. Nevertheless, forms of masculinity and femininity embedded in different societies define psychosocial features and roles of women and men. Elizabeth Porter explains this idea more fully:

> However, because women are universally the nurturers in relationships, families and communities, they play crucial roles in peace building, often in a very informal and unofficial way. These roles often emerge out of the experience of oppression, knowing what it is like to be excluded and seeking the society that is really inclusive.[9]

What drew my attention during the four years I worked with women in rural areas on the entity borders was how returnee Muslim women cope with war trauma, expulsion from their homes and family losses and how they conceived of rebuilding inter-ethnic relations among Muslim, Orthodox Christian and Catholic women. I was surprised at the courage and readiness of some women, who became more religious during or after the war, to re-establish communication with their pre-war neighbours. The driving force in re-establishing peace was the sociocultural and religious concept of *merhamet*, which is part of their Islamic and cultural legacy. *Merhamet* was channelled through the concept of *komšiluk* that was nurtured by all ethnic and religious groups, primarily in rural areas but also in urban settlements where people lived in private houses and created small neighbourhoods.[10]

At the same time I heard judgmental comments from both men and women that '*Merhametli* peace is woman's peace.' It means that peace out of *merhamet* is a woman's way of building peace, because women are more emotional and sensitive, and they better understand and connect with those who experience suffering and pain. In general, this is valued and recognized as a positive characteristic of a 'woman's nature' and expected of gender roles in patriarchal societies like BiH. However, if it is extended beyond the expected roles, such as in the post-war political context of BiH, acting out of *merhamet* becomes a naïve and foolish activity of women or of those who imitate 'woman's nature'. Once somebody moves outside the ethno–national authority, it is understood as crossing gender and ethnic borders – ethnic boundaries assigned to each ethno–national group and imposed gender boundaries for women and men in the context of the ethno–national and patriarchal society of BiH.[11] Male ethno–national leaders control the BiH political realm, particularly in the field of inter-ethnic relations. This includes activities such as peace-building and reconciliation at the higher level of decisionmaking – and these male leaders do not have an interest in bringing people together and rebuilding a multi-ethnic society. Why would they? This would lead directly to their loss of power. Therefore, ethno–national leaders rely on the Constitution of BiH, which recognizes ethno–national divisions and the rights of members of three ethnic constituencies and *not* the rights of citizens first. It legitimizes their politics of ethnic division, separation and isolation into ethnically homogenized communities.

Merhamet can have both positive and negative connotations and political implications. When it is practiced within the 'permissible' boundaries of gender roles and ethnic relations, it is viewed with approval by both the authorities and the public at large. However, when *merhamet* is used as a way to cross inter-ethnic borders – for example, when a Muslim woman visits her Christian neighbours across the border, or when women use it to step outside their permitted gender roles and take on leadership in their communities – it becomes a transgressive act for the ethno–patriarchal order.

Examining the etymology of *merhamet* to better understand its ambiguous interpretation for peace-building, I found the linguistic root in the Arabic *rahma* (mercy, compassion, love). In the Bosnian cultural context, *merhamat* is known as a universal humanistic value derived from Islam, marking the lives of BiH Muslims who have lived for generations alongside religious 'others'.[12] A *merhametli* person shows mercy, compassion and unconditional openness, and puts another's needs first.

The Arabic word *rahma*, however, also refers to the womb or uterus. In Sufi literature,[13] the concept of the feminine is coupled with mercy and the capacity to embrace and love as God does.[14] The creative force of life in a woman's womb draw women close to the primordial condition of human existence, which is signified by the submission of created souls to God as Lord. (Q7:172). Submission to God is thereby the primary and defining human act. Sachiko Muratta says that a true *muslim* 'accept[s] freely and joyfully that one is a 'woman' that one cannot be fully human without actualizing the light of femininity'.[15] To reach the state of full, primordial submission to God (*islam*), one needs to therefore move beyond the normative gender binaries of femininity – as weak, corporeal or sensitive – and masculinity – as the strong, rational, protector, maintainer and leader – to incorporate the best of both female and male. This gender unification also allows unification within our communities and with God.

If *merhamet* is understood as the positive qualities of women and men, then *merhametli* peace-building should be valued and recognized as beneficial for the entire community, but especially the vulnerable: women and returnee families living in rural places on the borders. While ethno–national and religious elites live in the comfortable majority in urban centres where they need not understand the everyday challenges on the borders, they nevertheless impose boundaries, in particular on women, judging when their acts of *merhamet* are acceptable or transgressive.

Women in BiH villages on the ethno–national borders face double marginalization. One marginalization is related to their lives at the edge of two politically divided entities within BiH (the Federation of BiH and the Serb-dominated Republic of Srpska). The other stems from when they act 'outside the social and cultural borders' of their assigned gender roles. For instance, they can be mothers, helpers, supporters and even national heroines; but, if they dare to show compassion outside ethno–national borders, they are overstepping their bounds. Acting out of *merhamet* to rebuild interethnic relationships can be seen as a sign of disorientation and even betrayal of the national identity by some Bosniac Muslims. For these Muslims, the important prerequisites for peace-building and reconciliation, namely the prosecution of war criminals, have not been fulfilled. However, for women on the ethno–national borders who are committed to peace-building, waiting for retribution (although important) is not a practical way to survive and rebuild lives in their divided society.

When I met with returnee women in three villages, they came to me with stories about peace-building and reconciliation. They told me what they do, individually and in informal groups, to re-establish communication with their neighbours and, more importantly, how they wrestle with their war memories and the betrayal of their neighbours. They shared with me the difficulties of their attempt to resolve the riddle of peaceful multiculturalism in Bosnia, and to provide a secure place for themselves and their children. These formal and informal peace-building initiatives in the border villages mark an important step in the restoration of peaceful life in small communities where minorities feel more socially excluded, than majority ethnic groups.

Remembering *Komšiluk*

Women who lived on the entity border within BiH are in particular caught in the middle of two social imperatives. On the one hand, they must show loyalty to their ethnic group and to the suffering that their community underwent during the war. On the other hand, there is also the impetus to rebuild and re-establish lines of communication with their pre-war neighbours and friends. Men also had to show loyalty to the nation but they were not controlled as women whose bodies were perceived as a 'territory of a nation' and 'national pride' or 'shame' depending whether men were able to protect that 'territory' or it was conquered by other nations.[16] However, as Svetlana Slapšak explains, it is the marginalized position of women that made them more inclined to peace and building networks of support.[17] This 'no man's land' of opposing imperatives is fraught with tension and danger for those women who attempt to navigate it. I heard dozens of stories over the four years that showed the importance of *merhamet* in Muslim cultural and religious life, and how life on the borders between different ethnic and religious groups in BiH caused Muslim women to develop dialogue and peace-building initiatives.

The concepts of *merhamet* and *komšiluk* are deeply rooted in the religious teachings of Islam and Bosnian culture. Today, these concepts are suppressed under the surface of ethno–national identities and the attempt to homogenize the three ethnic groups. However, in some areas where more refugees and displaced persons returned to their previous homes, and in particular in the border villages, there are attempts to re-enact and heal ethno–national and neighbourly relationships. These women recall the socialist era, which was a time of belief in brotherhood and unity when they lived peacefully. Several researchers show how people in BiH lived together and how they appreciated *komšiluk* as the best channel of interaction and collaboration with people in the same neighbourhood.[18] This research also clarifies how ethno–nationalist rhetoric turned these people against each other and devastated their peaceful relations to the extent that people still fear the homes and neighbours they once fled.

Jasmina from a village around Mostar tells us about life among her pre-war Catholic Croat neighbours:

We lived in two houses, but we were like one family. We shared everything and I did not mind when I brought my children to school to take my neighbour's children too, or when I made a good lunch I shared it with them, or if we had bad or good news we shared it first with our neighbours [...]. They were also friendly and supportive and helped us when we sought help.[19]

Her friends Alma and Azra had similar experiences about nurturing these neighbourly relationships across ethnic and nationalist lines, and they genuinely believed that they could live together in mutual respect and friendship. They learned to respect differences. For example, they told me about how their Catholic neighbours did not offer food with pork in it to their children out of respect for the prohibition against pork. Azra reflected on this relationship as something valuable, noting that mutual respect among neighbours in her area was a unique experience in her life. When she lived in Italy after the war, for example, she did not find that her neighbours had any real respect for her eating restrictions. Her Italian hosts did not know and did not want to know. For her it meant eating cheese, pasta and tomatoes for months. (However, she added that was still much better than being in BiH during the war without any decent food.) So, these women were aware of the fact that sometimes it was not easy for their Catholic neighbours to remember every time, to exclude pork from the meals. Yet, it was how they showed their commitment to Komšiluk (neighbourliness) with Muslims.

Alma added that her Catholic neighbours sometimes paid more attention to the food restrictions and other customs than Muslims did! She explained that Muslims in some regions were lax in observing dietary restrictions (like not eating pork or not drinking alcohol) before the war, but were more observant afterwards. For Alam and similar less-observant Muslims, the war was a time of religious awakening and a 'coming to yourself', as she says: 'to become aware that we are coming from Allah and will be back to Him in the Hereafter, so all our deeds should be measured and estimated through the lenses of our belonging to God'.[20] She said that she was laughed at by some of her neighbours because of her desire to re-establish her faith by attending some courses and workshops at various NGO's and faith-based organizations. According to Alma, for a woman or man over 40 to go to school again and learn something new was considered shameful in the community. However, she did not listen to these negative voices. She was eager to learn more, and she was courageous enough to exercise her agency in the pursuit of self-education.

Muslim women in the northeastern part of Bosnia around Bijeljina (Mirzeta, Enisa and Nadija) also confirmed great neighbourhood relations that sometimes went beyond regular neighbourliness. For example, many in these villages observed the old Slavic custom of assigning a Godmother (*kuma*) and Godfather (*kum*) to married couples and newborns. Mirzeta reported that they did not differentiate between Muslims and non-Muslims in terms of having *kumstvo* ties (godfather and godmother relations) for their families. They entrusted their non-kinship relations in marriage and in the celebration of newborn children to their Muslims and non-Muslim friends alike. Enisa added that Muslims in that part of BiH produced and drank alcohol alongside non-Muslims, and that they were not attached so much to religion and the mosque, except for some rituals. Therefore, they did not feel any impediments to establishing close and friendly interactions with non-Muslims, and they felt free to share very intimate ties of family and friendship.

Nadija's experience is similar, and she reported that her family was so secularized and distant from Islamic customs that in her house eating pork and drinking alcohol was not questioned at all. Her family's best friends were Serb neighbours, and her first child's *kum* was a Serb who helped her family and many other Muslims to escape death in 1992 when soldiers from Serbia entered the Bijeljina region and killed hundreds of Muslims. She said that when the war started:

> I became aware that it did not matter if I drink alcohol or eat pork and do not follow any of the religious obligations like praying and fasting, they (Serbs) will put me in my ethnic box just because I have a Muslim name and formally belong to that ethnic and religious group. I even did not know so much about

my Muslim identity at that time, but they made me to become aware of it.[21]

Women from villages around Sanski Most (Sena, Kana and Latifa) have not had such close relationships, but they developed good relationships with their neighbours and would borrow machines and equipment for agriculture. They would invite them to work together and even to borrow money if they were in need. Sena, who was a refugee in Slovenia during the war said that she had two friends from the Serb–Orthodox Christian village. She could not conceive that one day they would be separated by ethno–national borders in BiH and that her neighbours would leave the region without speaking a word to her.

Her neighbour Kana, who used to be a teacher in the primary school, says that she perceived all children as equal and did not notice any disrespect by Serb–Orthodox Christian families before the war. Therefore, she was surprised when she heard that some families were involved in terrible crimes and that some of them were prosecuted for war crimes. One of her students in the village's primary school told her that he had to go to the war. He explained to her that he could not avoid killing Muslims, but he drank in excess to be able to 'survive it'. Today he suffers from depression and insomnia. His family had good relations with Kana's family when he was a student, and he felt he could come to his teacher and tell his story. Kana commented at the time that he knew how *Merhametli* (full of compassion) she was as a teacher and family friend. He probably counted on these qualities when he later decided to reconnect and ask for forgiveness. She told him, however, that she could not forgive him for something he did against other people and urged him to ask forgiveness from the families of his victims.

Another neighbour, Latifa, who had a grocery shop on the border between two villages (Bosniac – Muslim and Serb – Orthodox Christian) described her neighbourhood relations as family relations. On two occasions she was short of cash, so she knocked on the door of her Serb – Orthodox Christian neighbours and borrowed money for a few months. She added:

Once even my mother and father and brothers did not know that I was short with money. I could turn to my neighbours for help and continue my grocery shop business. They respected my situation and never mentioned that to my family or somebody in the village. You know your friends in difficult situations.[22]

All nine women with whom I communicated regularly over that four-year period glorified the *Komšiluk* relationships and the close friendships they had with their non-Muslim neighbours. At the same time all of them expressed their disappointments with the war, the ethno-national divisions and the expulsion from their homes. However, after the return to their villages these women understood that if they wanted to rebuild life on the border with their Serb neighbours, they would need to communicate with one another; although, they limited this call for communication to those who did not commit war crimes. These women expressed incredible courage when they decided to reopen dialogue with their neighbours who now live on the other side of the (ethno-national) border.

Breaking Isolation and Marginalization

All of the women who I interviewed are aware of the social and political divisions in BiH, and they do not want to forget or invalidate their experiences during the war. However, as one of the women explained:

We do not want to spend our lives in isolation, enslaved by hatred. We also learned that in some other areas Serb/Orthodox and Croat/Catholics were displaced and experienced losses and pain, and *as mothers we know that pain and suffering does not have nation or religion* (emphasis mine).[23]

This kind of 'maternal thinking' – understanding the suffering and pain mothers feel for their children and families – is helpful in connecting women from opposite sides of ethnic borders.[24] The pain and care of motherhood are common ground for them, and at the same time the ethics of care make them more sensitive and receptive to the stories and experiences of their neighbours.

Women were encouraged through various educational programmes to understand that other people also suffered, and that they needed to open their hearts to hear experiences from the other side of the ethno–national border. Rediscovering the concept of *merhamet* that was always part of the BiH religious and cultural mosaic was important for these women, because as pious believers, or women with revived BiH cultural identity, they wanted to show how their lives were enlightened by their faith. They were committed to using their faith and the positive legacy of BiH culture channelled through *Komšiluk* and other forms of socializing in order to rebuild relations with their neighbours.

Sena's story is a good illustration of this commitment to rebuilding community through traditional cultural and Islamic religious ideas. She felt betrayed by two friends who left BiH and did not inform her about the coming attacks on her village, but she found peace in Islam. She learned from the Qur'an that forgiveness is the better part of faith, that Muslims should strive for forgiveness as a way of life, and that it is a superior moral trait (42:43). After attending some workshops on trauma healing she understood the disappointment and anger she felt against her two friends. She realized that the anger imprisoned her and that she was not able to move on in her life because she was holding onto these intensely negative emotions.

With the support of a psychosocial therapist (who happened to be an observant Muslim woman) she was able to discuss her trauma from a religious perspective. She began the healing process in earnest when she decided to forgive her friends, but not to forget what happened to her people in that region. She emphasized the idea of forgiving without forgetting, because often women who work for reconciliation in the region are accused of being 'traitors' to their ethnic or national identities; it is assumed that they have forgotten the pain their community has gone through.

Despite the negative atmosphere in the village, Sena went to visit her pre-war neighbours with the former schoolteacher Kana. They brought coffee and sugar, which are the standard *poklon* (guest gifts) in their communities. She felt relieved when she told them that she was ready to rebuild their neighbourly relations. Her former friends were happy to see her again, because they also were isolated and lonely. They too suffered loss and sorrow in the war. Exchanging these stories of loss brought both perspectives to the surface; it allowed the women to empathize with each other and to help them overcome the overwhelming pain of silence and isolation.

However, as Sena emphasizes, 'it was easier to visit my pre-war friends than to come back to my village and be exposed to judgments and offences by my Muslim neighbours, who felt that two of us betrayed the village or the Bosniac ethnic group'.[25] Unfortunately, judgments came from men and women. Sena's brother-in-law commented that 'she does not even respect her husband, who was injured during the war and if he was a "real" husband he would discipline her'.[26] Her husband is a very patient man who loves Sena deeply, and he merely advised her not to go against the village. However, when he saw that she was healing psychologically he supported her and stood behind her decision to continue in her peace-building efforts. Sena, Kana and Latifa established a small coalition in the village to pursue peace-building activities despite negative popular opinion. They believed that people needed time to process their traumas and anger, and to come to a reconciliation first with themselves and then with their larger community.

Alma from Mostar experienced a spiritual awakening during the war and became a fully observant Muslim in every way except that she does not wear the *hijab* (head cover). She discussed the issue of the *hijab* with Muslims scholars and with her friends who do wear the *hijab*. She came to a very interesting interpretation of this issue. She reasoned that because the purpose of the *hijab* in the Qur'an is to promote the safety of women, and if wearing the *hijab* in her village threatened her safety,[27] she could be a good Muslim woman by observing the heart rather than the letter of the law. Her reasoning was very similar to that of other Muslim women in the region who are attempting to integrate their new religious ideas with their ethnic and feminist identities.[28] Although Alma accepted the observation of

Islam on a daily basis, she found a way to adjust the expression of her religious identity to the context in which she lives, to be protected and also to have better chances for communication with her non-Muslim neighbours.

She decided to stay with her children in BiH even though her husband died soon after the war and the rest of her family emigrated to other countries, to Europe and the United States. After her return from Germany to BiH she rebuilt her house and was able to provide for her children from the land she owned, but she felt that she also needed to rebuild her connections with her pre-war neighbours. Alma recalls a lecture at the mosque in Mostar during one of the big feasts when she heard a story about Jalal al-Din Rumi and his interpretation of faith in God. She learned that there were as many paths to God as people on earth and that God will decide in the Hereafter who was on the right path. Meanwhile, people need to 'compete in good deeds' (Q5:44–48). For her it meant that there is plenty of room in the world for everybody and for every expression of faith, and as a Muslim she should respect this multiplicity. It motivated her to start reading the *Mathnawi* by Jalal al-Din Rumi. She deeply enjoyed the book and was drawn to its teaching of tolerance and mutual respect. It helped her to open her heart to God through opening her heart to other people. Alma describes herself as a *Merhametli* person. She says, however, that *merhamatli* means something different to her now than it did before the war. Now that she is armed with a different quality in comparison to the pre-war *merhamet*, with the new knowledge and a new understanding of Islam, she has become an informed and responsible believer:

> For the first time I have not done something just because I was told to do that or because it was the rule or commandment that need to be followed or because it followed some inherited traditions in my religion. When I came in contact with Rumi's work I knew deeply in my heart and my mind that the right path is the path of love and *merhamet*.[29]

However, her neighbours did not welcome her ideas and her new approach in understanding social relations, because it ignored all

borders and barriers imposed as a consequence of the war and ethno—
national politics. She finally found support in Azra, her sister-in-law,
who was an observant believer and who had lost her husband during
the war. As an older respected woman in the village, Azra was in a
better position than Alma to bring about meaningful change.
Jasmina, her cousin, also joined them; and these three women
reopened communications with their pre-war neighbours. Jasmina
says that it was terrifying for her for the first time to visit the Catholic
village, because she did not know how they would react and if they
would accept their visit. The first visit was not easy because of the
tensions of the spoken and unspoken parts of their gathering.
However, the grandmother of her pre-war Catholic friend finally said,
'thank you for coming after all, and since you did the first step we
should respect it based on our faith and our customs'.[30] She then asked
her daughter and daughter-in-law to pay a visit back to her and to
accept the hand of reconciliation. She started crying, and Alma reports
that all of them cried for losses they had experienced and had been
unable to prevent during the war. The following visits were more
relaxed, and they shared stories of suffering and understanding, related
to the war from each perspective. Most importantly, they as women,
found a common ground to renew their relations. Men on both sides
either disapproved of these initiatives or remained silent, but as Alma
explains, 'it is Azra's status in this village as a pious Muslim woman
before and after the war that gave us the credibility to proceed with
these activities without so much judgment, at least not publicly'.[31]

The stories of Mirzeta, Enisa and Nadija from Bijeljina are
different. Their rediscovery of *merhamet* was not so much motivated
by religion as by the Muslim cultural tradition through which they
channelled *komšiluk*. As refugees in the cities of Tuzla and Zagreb,
they spent a few years in refugee camps with older Muslim women
whose stories about neighbourly relationships in the pre-war days
were compelling and forced Mirzeta, Enisa and Nadija to rethink
their relationships with their own pre-war neighbours.

Since they were so close to their Serb neighbours and were tied
with *kumstvo* before the war, displacement and family losses brought
deeper anger, and wounds that festered and did not heal.

They believed in their close ties to their neighbours and felt that they were betrayed. They lost everything they believed in, and they did not know how to start building their lives again. When they were invited for the first time to join some women's groups that gathered Muslim and Serb women they were reluctant and did not respond. After a while they recalled in memory the narratives they heard from the grandmothers in exile. These narratives taught them that the neighbour is as important as family and that one owes respect to neighbours because they have their own *hak* (Arabic: *haqq*, Engl: right, truth, reality). Again if we look into the genesis of this word and the ethics behind these relations, we inevitably end in Islamic tradition and its teachings about neighbourliness and the *huquq* (rights) of neighbours. These women did not find refuge in religion or attend any educational programmes that involved their religious perspectives as the women from Mostar or Sanski Most did. Yet, they found their local traditions to be an important framework for rebuilding their lives with their neighbours. Today, they find *merhamet* as a relevant framework of human relations, but it needs to be grounded in a deep awareness of one's ethnic and religious identity. Mirzeta is convinced that the giving hand is always better than the receiving hand, which she recalls from her religious education during childhood. Once the Muslim village was in a better socioeconomic position, she thought that they should help their Serb neighbours who lived in poor conditions after their expulsion from Croatia. However, Enisa says:

> It is perhaps easier to communicate with those who have had similar experiences and status like we Muslims have. Our new neighbours are also refugees and lost their homes and family members. The real challenge is to renew relations with our pre-war friends who mostly were not involved in the war activities, but did not say anything against crimes and ethno–national divisions.[32]

Further, many of the Muslim women I worked with are the primary breadwinners, and they face judgment by other women who criticize them for being *Merhametli* towards their Serb neighbours and accuse these peaceworkers of forgetting what the Serbs have done to Muslims. These three women from Bijeljina region feel strong pressure to stay faithful to their community but also to build good relations with their neighbours, especially with those who had a destiny similar to theirs. Mirzeta says that they will not have the same neighbourhood relations as they did before that war, but at least they will make life easier for their children. These children – a new generation of Serbs and Croats – grow up mere streets apart from one another, divided by ethnicity but united by geography. Their mothers work to build a safe community within which divisions of faith and ethnicity are mediated through the concepts of *merhamet* and *Komšiluk*.

Conclusion

In this ethnographic work, I have examined how women in the border villages of Bosnia and Herzegovina utilize the culturally mediated concepts of *merhamet* and *komšiluk* to rebuild their communities across boundaries of faith and ethnicity. These women inhabit a treacherous no man's land, caught between hardening boundaries of identity and the need to re-establish communal harmony. Their peace-building efforts are at once derided as 'women's peace' but also viewed as deeply subversive when they entail stepping out of assigned gender roles by attempting to bridge ethnic divisions. This grassroots peace-building, informed by a renewed sense of themselves as *Muslim* women, provides a model for how religion can be an effective tool for rebuilding war torn communities from the bottom up. These women have found in Islam – denigrated by the West as divisive and oppressive to women – a tool for self-empowerment. Their courageous work illustrates for us the immense power of faith as a means to bring about communal reconciliation.

Notes

1. I worked with the following women's and human rights NGOs: Forma F Mostar, Žena BiH Mostar, Li-Woman Livno, Association Grahovo, B. Grahovo,

Krajiška suza Sanski Most, Glas žene Bihać, Lara Bijeljina, Forum žena Bratunac.

2. The last war in BiH from 1992–5 divided people on three main constituent groups (Bosniacs–Muslims 40 per cent, Serbs–Orthodox Christians 30 per cent, Croats–Catholics 17 per cent and Others–Minorities 13 per cent). This ethno–national division was legalized by the Dayton Peace Accord and the Constitution in 1995, strengthening tripartite democratic ethno-polis.

3. I use different names for the nine women I interviewed: Alma, Azra and Jasmina from Mostar region, Mirzeta, Enisa and Nadija and from Bijeljina Region, and Sena, Kana and Latifa from Sanski Most Region.

4. After the war BiH was divided into two entities: Republic of Srpska and the Federation of BiH with ethnically homogenized parts of the country. Mostar city is located in the southern part of BiH with Croats–Catholics as the majority population. Sanski Most is in the western part of BiH with the Bosniaks–Muslims population and Bijeljina city in the northeastern part of BiH is home to the Serbs–Orthodox Christian population.

5. The 'Social Inclusion of Women Returnees' project was implemented by The TPO Foundation Sarajevo (*www.tpo.ba*) in the period from 2008–11. It helped women to get better insight into their rights and taught them how to achieve those rights in practice, but it also included peace-building trainings that helped some of them to find the way to peace.

6. Latifa, interview conducted on September 2008.

7. *Merhamet* is a Bosnian local expression for universal values of mercy, good, openness, hospitality and respect. It derives from the Arabic word *rahma*, which means mercy, love and openness. Bosnian Muslims used *merhamet* to describe their personal sentiments. They say: 'we are *merhametli* people'. They use this expression towards other people and especially towards those in need. The phrase has different meanings depending on the context and the concrete situation. If somebody is good, nice, attentive and shows compassion and understanding, he or she may get the label, *merhametli* person. Or, if somebody forgives and tries to reconcile people in conflict, he or she is also named as a *merhametli* person. If somebody is taking the needs of others before his or her own needs, he or she will be recognized as *merhametli* person. If somebody tries to give a hand and to help even if he or she is not asked to do it, she or he will be named as *merhametli* person. If she or he gives charity, and is engaged in philanthropic activities, she or he is *merhametli* person. Finally women are mostly called *merhametli* because of their love and mercy to children and family, but sometimes if the husband is a difficult and robust person, and his wife succeeds in calming him down, she will be described as *merhametli* person because her mercy, compassion and love are so strong that they melt his robust character.

8. Cynthia Enloe, *The Morning After: Sexual Politics at the End of the Cold War* (Berkeley: University of California Press, 1993); Zillah Eisenstein, *Hatreds: Racialised and Sexualised Conflicts in the 21st Century* (New York: Routledge,

1996); Jean Bethke Elshtain and Sheila Tobias (eds), *Women, Militarism and War: Essays in History, Politics and Social Theory* (Savage: Rowman & Littlefield, 1990); Julie Mertus (ed), *The Suitcase: Refugee Voices from Bosnia and Croatia* (Berkeley: University of California Press, 1999); Elizabeth Porter, *Peacebuilding Women in International Perspective* (New York: Routledge, 2007); Donna Pankhurst (ed), *Gendered Peace: Women's Struggles for Post-War Justice and Reconciliation* (New York: Routledge, 2009).

9. Porter, *Peacebuilding Women*, pp. 1–4.

10. Tone Bringa, *Being Muslim the Bosnian Way: Identity and Community in a Central Bosnian Village* (Princeton: Princeton University Press, 1995).

11. Zilka Spahić-Šiljak, *Women, Religion and Politics: The Impact of Religious Interpretations of Judaism, Christianity, and Islam on the Status of Women in Public Life and Politics* (Sarajevo: IMIC, Center for Interdisciplinary Postgraduate Studies & TPO Foundation, Sarajevo, 2010); Asim Mujkić, *We, The Citizens of Ethnopolis* (Sarajevu: Centar za ljudska prava Univerziteta, 2008).

12. Meša Selimović, *Pisci, mišljenja, razgovori* (Authors, Thoughts, Conversations) (Beograd: Brogradski izdavačko-grafički zavod, 1983).

13. God's mercy is of the highest quality, and it prevails over all other qualities, therefore, the Muslim Sufi poet Mevlana Jalaluddin Rumi (1207–73) once wrote: 'Woman is the radiance of God; she is not your beloved. She is the creator – you could say that she is not created', *The Mathnawi of Jalalu'ddin Rumi*, transl. Reynold A. Nicholson (Cambridge: Gibb Memorial Trust, 2002), pp. i–2437.

14. Sachiko Muratta, *The Tao of Islam: A Sourcebook on Gender Relationships in Islamic Thought* (New York: State University of New York Press, 1992), pp. 143–48.

15. Sachiko Muratta, 'Women of light in Sufism', *The Muhyiddin Ibn 'Arabi Society*. Available at http://www.ibnarabisociety.org/articles/womenoflight.html (accessed 22 October 2012).

16. Vesna Kesić, 'Gender and ethnic identities in transition: The former Yugoslavia-Croatia', in Rada Ivekovic and Julie Mostov (eds), *From Gender to Nation*, (Ravena: Longo Editore, 2001), p. 65; Zilka Spahić-Šiljak, 'Images of women in Bosnia and Herzegovina, and neighboring countries, 1992–1995', in Faegheh Shirazi (ed), *Muslim Women in War and Crisis: From Reality to Representation* (Austin: University of Texas Press, 2010).

17. Svetlana Slapšak, 'The use of women and the role of women in the Yugoslav War' in Skjelsbaek Inger and Smith Dan (eds), *Gender, Peace and Conflict* (London: Sage Publications, 2001), p. 181.

18. Slavenka Drakulić, *How We Survived Communism and Even Laughed* (New York: Harper Perennial, 1993), pp.183; Tone Bringa, *Being Muslim the Bosnian Way*, pp. 66; Xavier Bougarel, 'Bosnia and Herzegovina – state and communitarianism', in David Dycker and Ivan Vejvoda (eds), *Yugoslavia and After* (London: Longman, 1996), pp. 67–115; Paula M. Pickering, *Peacebuilding in the Balkans: The View from the Ground Floor*, (Ithaca and London: Cornell University Press, 2007), pp. 1–38.

19. Jasmina, Personal interview (November 2010).
20. Alma, Personal interview (November 2010).
21. Nadija, Personal interview (May 2011).
22. Latifa, Personal interview (June 2011).
23. Kana, Personal interview (September 2009).
24. Sara Ruddick, 'The Rationality of Care' in Jean Elshtain and Sheila Tobias (eds), *Women, Militarism and War: Essays in Politics, History and Social Theory* (Savage, Md.: Rowman and Littlefield, 1990).
25. Sena, Personal interview (September, 2009).
26. Ibid. (July 2010).
27. Only a small percentage of Muslim women in BiH today wear *hijab*; however, before the war in many villages women wore traditional scarfs that mostly covered half of the head. It was common for Muslim and non-Muslim women alike. After 1990 some women started wearing *hijab* out of piety, or simply because they thought it was the right way to show their religious identity. The new image of Muslim women, especially in urban areas with the non-Muslim majority population was not received well. Thus *hijabi* women who live on the ethnic border in BiH face many challenges when they appear with *hijab* as a visible marker of their religious identity. There were assaults on women and provocations by Croat or Serb ethno–nationalists, and many women gave up *hijab* to be safe when comuting in non-majority Muslim areas in BiH.
28. Zilka Spahić-Šiljak, *Contesting Female, Feminist and Muslim Identities. Post-Socialist Contexts of Bosnia and Herzegovina and Kosovo*, (Sarajevo: Center for Interdisciplinary Postgraduate Studies of the University of Sarajevo, 2012).
29. Alma, Personal interview (October 2010).
30. Jasmina, Personal interview (November 2010).
31. Alma, Personal interview (June 2009).
32. Enisa, Personal interview (May 2009).

CONCLUSION

GENDER, PEACE AND WAR

Sally L. Kitch

Are peace and war gendered? Are men inevitably war makers and women inevitably peacemakers? These questions have long inflected debates about particular wars, about the relationship of warfare to human nature, about war's purpose in human social systems, about gender roles and their implications in various societies and even about evolutionary biology, which supports genetic explanations for most human behaviour, including war- and peacemaking. *Women and Peace in the Islamic World: Gender, Agency and Influence* offers a new test case for exploring such questions in the context of contemporary and historical Muslim societies.

In my analysis of the book's arguments, I will use that theme as a lens through which to view its contributions. I will consider what the essays taken together say or imply about gender's associations with peace and war. I will explore the authors' explanations for women's historical association with peacemaking and, especially, their understanding of gender, war and peace in the context of Islamic precepts and values in an array of Muslim-dominated societies. I will ask whether the book suggests that women in general have a biological/genetic or a cultural propensity for peace and explore to what extent any such propensity, especially among Muslim women, is related to maternal roles or experiences. In addition, I will discuss a few issues related to the gender of war and peacemaking that the book's essays do not directly address.

War: Nature or Nurture?

In their consideration of the gendered nature of war, contributors to this volume strongly suggest that biology (genes, hormones and DNA) is not the primary reason that men are the world's principal war-makers. miriam cooke and others argue that war is gendered because misogyny promotes war (Husin, Chapter 5) and because war is fostered by 'structural violence', especially against women. Such misogyny shapes thought, values and popular culture in many Muslim societies and inheres in rigid patriarchy, and some religious fundamentalisms. In other words, the authors suggest, social systems that keep war a priority option (war systems) and 'gender systems' (values and beliefs related to gender roles and identities) that devalue and subordinate women are intertwined.[1] cooke quotes Tawakkul Karman as she demonstrates how that interconnection works: 'When women are treated unjustly and are deprived of their natural right all social deficiencies and cultural illnesses will be unfolded [including war], and in the end the whole community, men and women, will suffer.'

Such arguments implicitly contradict sociobiological claims that men are genetically programmed for war because they are genetically programmed to fight off competitors for access to women, who are essential for spreading their genes to the next generation. Instead the book's claims reinforce conclusions that feminist research in other contexts have also reached. That is, if even the most allegedly biologically-based acts, such as sexual and reproductive behaviour, are shaped by sociocultural expectations and values, as recent studies make clear, then it must also be the case that acculturation shapes conventional gender associations with war and peace.[2] Indeed, it is possible that war systems have evolved, in part, in order to reduce anxiety-producing gender ambiguity by providing an arena for clearly defining gender distinctions. It is not by chance, according to Joshua Goldstein, that the most warlike society he has studied, the Sambia, is also 'the most sexist'.[3]

Many authors in this volume also implicitly support the idea that violence is deeply implicated in 'the construction and reproduction of hegemonic masculinity' in many societies.[4] That is, social 'constructions of masculinity motivate soldiers to fight' across a variety of cultures and belief systems. (Indeed, it is probable that increased male hormone levels result from, rather than cause, aggressive feelings and actions in men).[5] Rather than genes or hormones, 'norms of masculinity contribute to men's exclusive status as warriors', often to the extent of making war a test of manhood.[6] Societies typically define manhood in ways that overcome men's reluctance to fight (promises of rewards in heaven or of earthly sexual conquest) and define womanhood in ways that support a war mentality – by, for example, asserting that men will be judged effeminate for refusing to fight and associating peace with women.[7]

Of particular interest to this volume, gender norms can be quite diverse outside the arena of war. Within that arena, however, they are surprisingly stable and consistent over time and across geopolitical boundaries. That is the case, despite the fact that 'none of the gender differences arising from biology is sufficient to explain gendered war roles'.[8]

Peacemaking: Biological or Cultural Determinism?

The gender of peace discussed in *Women and Peace in the Islamic World* is more direct and complex. Indeed, it is this discussion of peace and gender that makes the cultural specificity of the book's essays so important. Many writers, such as cooke, do not consider peacemaking a universal female characteristic, let alone a genetically determined one, in any society. However, as in the case of war, peace is gendered for sociocultural reasons. The book's contributors suggest that women's support of peace reflects, in part, its positive relationship to social justice for all, and to environments in which women are valued.[9] In addition, these authors contend, women's affinity for peacemaking is shaped by their socially mandated identities and, especially, their roles as mothers.

This perspective has a special meaning for the Muslim women represented in *Women and Peace in the Islamic World*. Many of them see motherhood, with its inherent dread of losing children, as inspiration for feeling compassion toward enemies and, therefore, for engaging in 'a process, a state of mind and a mode of action' that recognizes 'the in-humanity of the other' and empathizes with the 'other's' fears and losses (Talebi, Chapter 11). 'As *mothers we know that pain and suffering does not have nation or religion*' (Šiljak, Chapter 12). As mothers, many Muslim women also interpret Islam's holy texts from a particular perspective.

Zilka Šiljak chapter on women's peacemaking methods in the border villages of Bosnia and Herzegovina (BiH) offers an example. These women regard the pain and care of motherhood as common ground, and the 'ethic of care makes them more sensitive and receptive to the stories and experiences of their neighbours', whom many of their husbands have regarded as absolute enemies since the 1990s wars. For their efforts, women's peacemaking gestures are both recognized and derided as 'women's peace', and disparaged by many BiH men, precisely because women's bridge-building undermines the beneficial power inequities among men that ethnic divisions promote.

For the women of BiH and many others discussed in this book, mothers' greater compassion reflects 'the Islamic nature of forbearance', which allows former combatants to 'move away from a discourse of rights towards one of humanity' (Osanloo, Chapter 8). In BiH women utilize 'the culturally mediated [Islamic] concepts of *merhamet* [compassion] and *komšiluk* [neighbourliness] to rebuild their communities across boundaries of faith and ethnicity' that have been hardened by war (Šiljak, Chapter 12). One of Arzoo Osanloo's Iranian interviewees also explains that mercy is what God prefers and that, '"being merciful will bring about peace." This peace is not just a peace that aims to bring about reconciliation between parties but "peace in the heart of the individual".' This is true despite the Qur'an's explicit permission to retaliate for deaths, since 'throughout the Qur'an, believers are [simultaneously] compelled to forgive others for transgressions, even the ultimate one, the killing of a loved one'.

Through their understanding of womanhood shaped by their experiences as mothers, the women Osanloo interviewed prioritize forbearance and compassion over retaliation, although both are permissible in Islam: 'If we talk about how the mother of the victim lost a child, and if she pursues retaliation, there will be another mother that loses a child, it seems to address the humanity of the other' (Osanloo, Chapter 8). Sufi literature goes even further to connect the feminine identity 'with mercy and the capacity to embrace and love as God does'.[10]

As important as it is, however, motherly compassion is not the only source of Muslim women's situationally inspired everyday peacemaking, according to several of the book's contributors. For example, Osanloo quotes Janet Afary, who considers how the tradition of women's activism in their own behalf in the Muslim world, going back to the early twentieth century, has inspired their current peace activism. Husin also regards Acehnese women's history as inspiration for their contemporary activism for peace (Chapter 5). However, Husin further attributes women's affinity for peace to their closer connection to the State and their longer experience in navigating administrative and legal systems, presumably because of their greater poverty and dependence on and restriction by State entities. Perhaps women have learned how systems of all kinds ensnare individual will and undermine good intentions. Therefore, they may understand better than the men caught up in them how war systems work. Azza Karam notes that 'women form the majority of those working in faith-based services', where they 'seek to reclaim their religious heritage and reinterpret the understandings of religion such that the faith becomes central to practice ... a Religious feminism is not merely a concept, but a reality borne of the struggles of women of faith for their rights – with their faith as a constructive part of that struggle' (Chapter 9).

Yasmin Saikia attributes Muslim women's peacemaking procliv-ities to the instruction in care and empathy (at least some of them receive) through their close friendships with other women. Saikia discusses Abdullah Hall, a women's residential facility at Aligarh Muslim University in India, where girls receive training in forming empathic and respectful friendships. She argues that such training creates a template for being 'at peace with self and others'

(Chapter 10). 'Abdullah's ethos emphasized care and empathy as the foundation for human interaction, which, one may say, feminized the world of a Muslim society [and] undermined the masculinist ways of being that prize aggressive performance and macho social norms as marks of success' (Chapter 10).

Souad Ali's essay argues that such gendered experiences do not necessarily result in women's peacemaking acts, but even that lapse reinforces the importance of enculturation in making women into peacemakers. Ali explains, for example, that combatant political parties in Sudan have manipulated mothers well-versed in the Qu'ran to disregard 'their knowledge of the principle of peace in Islam' and have kept them from using that knowledge, 'to help their society move from conflict and war to reconciliation and peace' (Chapter 6).

Significant Contribution and Unanswered Questions

Women's understanding of their own identities as Muslims and as mothers in terms of Qur'anic messages about compassion, mercy and forbearance, even in the face of extreme offences, is a powerful message of this book. It resonates with the work of several Western feminists, such as Sara Ruddick, Carol Gilligan and Jean Bethke Elshtain, who have also noted the emotional and social learning – the 'ethic of care', 'maternal thinking' and capacities for *ascesis* (restraint) and forgiveness – that motherhood induces in women.[11] Such theorists also understand motherly compassion as situationally constructed, rather than biologically mandated, although their views have been critiqued as biological determinism. *Women and Peace in the Islamic World* charts a slightly different path, however, by grounding the values of compassion and concern for others not only in motherhood but also in the same holy texts that are so often used to justify male dominance, vengeance and even violence against women, all of which arguably contribute to war systems. That Muslim women's Islamic rationale for compassionate peacemaking crosses the many geopolitical locations discussed in this book suggests that it has become an important model for Muslim women's activism toward peace around the world.

In addition, the book's presentation of Muslim women's uniformly calm and rational approach to the troubling questions of violence and retribution across many regions situates their everyday peacemaking well beyond the realm of genetic programming. Instead, their peacemaking overtures occur in a deliberate, reasoned arena in which female wisdom supersedes male-associated emotional heat (a neat reversal of traditional expectations). The essays further support a democratization of Islamic religious interpretation, as female believers claim the right to make their own theological judgments. Indeed, many contemporary Islamic feminists now argue that 'the female is an autonomous moral being with a direct relationship with God as her only Guardian' (Ali, Chapter 6).

Despite these important accomplishments, the book's juxtaposition of women, peacemaking and religion raises some issues that the volume only partially addresses. One of them is whether the association between women, everyday peacemaking and religion can or will actually promote peace. As Goldstein points out, the association of women with peace and peacemaking may simply reinforce social preconceptions about 'the feminine' as a value system and about women as exponents of those values. Of particular relevance to *Women and Peace in the Islamic World*, 'even women peace activists can reinforce masculine war roles'.[12] Attaching the values of peacemaking to motherhood could further diminish their impact, especially in situations where nurturing is considered contrary to masculine values and imperatives. As Šiljak essay demonstrates, a 'woman's peace' in a misogynistic world can be discounted as out of touch with allegedly higher (male-identified) values and, especially, with the power issues that drive many armed conflicts in the first place.

Put another way, a female-associated rationale for peace does not necessarily counteract or replace complementary and competing male-associated values and imperatives, such as honour, valour, bravery and aggression (depending on the particular sociopolitical system). Moreover, if women are the main proponents of the Qur'an's tenets of compassion and forbearance, then men seeking to distance themselves from 'the feminine' may embrace even more firmly the alternative scenario of revenge and retaliation as their appropriate masculine domain.

That potential unintended consequence raises doubts about possibilities for increasing social justice for women through their dedication to peacemaking. A few writers in *Women and Peace in the Islamic World*, including Osanloo, do link Muslim women's support for peace with their activism on their own behalf throughout history. However, other contributors seem less optimistic. Indeed, they suggest that war, especially in the regions they discuss, is frequently *about* women's rights, either directly or indirectly. For example, S. Ayse Kadayifci-Orellana explains that many Muslims are resentful towards the West 'particularly in relation to [the] empowerment and rights of women'. Those issues are likely to be 'associated with the colonization experience and thus rejected strongly', sometimes to the point of violent resistance or attack (Chapter 7). Indeed, Karam points out that women's empowerment is a 'symbolic terrain' that lies at the heart of the 'contention between diverse protagonists', whether from foreign lands or within a particular society (Chapter 9). In Afghanistan, for example, struggles for power have for centuries entailed contests over women's proper roles, dress and demeanour – sometimes as a pretext for other issues.[13]

In short, arguments over women's rights and empowerment can and do incite wars, meaning that the war systems in many Muslim nations are inextricably intertwined with resistance to women's increased status, rights or public roles. By the same token, establishing peace might always already suggest empowering women, which could further decrease its appeal to many men. Promoting social justice for women as an element of long-lasting peace is further hampered by the lack of basic terms for the discussion, since *feminism* and *gender*, for example, have no equivalents in many regional languages.

Another related issue the book raises but does not directly address arises from a paradox that underlies many of the essays. That is, the same cultural tenets of sex distinction and segregation that make motherhood so important in the lives of Muslim women and encourage them to value compassion and forbearance also reinforce the war mentality women must fight against. Equally paradoxical, the strongly sex-segregated societies that mandate women's motherhood/peace mentality may actively discourage men from assuming the nurturing roles that engender compassion and promote peace through the recognition of combatants' shared humanity. Sex-segregated societies may also mandate different educational experiences for males and females, so that the kind of friendship training Saikia received at Abudullah Hall, though available to Aligarh Muslim University boys, may be unavailable to most Muslim males. Such separate and unequal educational experiences may even be considered necessary to maintain the strict sex distinction and segregation that characterize many Muslim societies. Saikia's chapter suggests that increased access to such training for Muslim boys as well as girls would help to combat gender distinctions with regard to war and peace.

These ironies reinforce peace theorist Johan Galtung's argument that segregated social structures almost inevitably support war systems. Galtung identifies rigid sex distinction and patriarchy as prime examples of the dualistic worldview underlying cultures of violence. He calls that worldview the 'Dualism-Manichenism-Armaggeddon' syndrome, in which black vs. white, or good vs. evil thinking is considered not only inevitable, but also righteous. Patriarchy exemplifies that worldview because its vertical hierarchy and male vs. female thinking virtually require force in order to maintain and legitimize men's domination of women.[14]

Moving the Mountain

What *would* validate Muslim women's compassionate Islamic construction of peacemaking as a legitimate political standpoint? Many intersecting challenges must be overcome to produce that result. The first is transforming the private experience of women peacemakers, as well as the religious support for that role, into more public sources of guidance for family and community action, especially in response to external aggression and insult. *Women and Peace in the Islamic World* obliquely suggests that simply revealing the depth and extent of Muslim women's peacemaking rationales and activities in everyday life could be a step in that direction. Indeed, demonstrating the scope of women's peacemaking roles is a critical contribution of this book. However, it may also be important to look to other models for transforming women's private peacemaking values and activities into public action, such as the United Nations' Resolution 1325, which requires member states to make women central in conflict prevention, peacemaking and social reconstruction.

The second challenge is connecting women's Islamic peacemaking rationales with a broader interpretation of Islam that also speaks to male imperatives. Key to meeting that challenge is establishing that *male* and *female* are constructed by practice and custom, and not by natural laws. They are, therefore, subject to revision. They also command equal respect, even in an Islamic context. This book supports that conclusion by representing varied degrees of sex distinction and segregation in Muslim societies, thereby undermining the concept of a universal or eternal Islamic gender system.

The third challenge is linking women's engagement in everyday peacemaking with wider campaigns for social justice in Muslim (and other) societies, which is necessary for establishing long-lasting peace systems. That means assessing and ameliorating the ways in which sex segregation and misogyny support the war systems that link masculinity to violence and retribution.

This volume implies some ways those challenges might be met. Richard Martin's and Chad Haines's chapters provide useful examples. Haines recognizes Muslim women's perspectives on peace as fundamental to Islam and not an aberration. He wants Islam to be included in international dialogues about peace as a way to counter 'received wisdom [about] nationalist hubris' and assumptions that Islam is 'violently singular'. He asks the world to 'recognise the extent to which [ideas about peace] do flourish amongst Muslims and are part of the debate about what it means to be Muslim in the world today' (Chapter 2).

Martin offers an historical model to help Muslims themselves recognize peace as an Islamic tenet. He chronicles the history of dialogue 'among Muslim disputants on issues that "mattered"' in the Middle Ages, where spokespersons for various positions on Shari'a law and Islamic theology 'engage[d] each other according to behavioural norms that were grounded in Islamic understandings and cultural customs' (Chapter 3). Although these councils probably paid scant attention to gender issues, Martin believes that their dedication to finding common threads among various and conflicting theological and legal interpretations of Islam could be a model for contemporary discussions about gender, war and peace in light of the varied and sometimes conflicting beliefs and practices related to gender norms within and among Muslim societies.

Martin hopes that the deliberative model of these now abandoned councils will be resurrected via Habermas's concept of *communicative rationality*, which favours increased communication 'across factional and theological boundaries within a broad cultural and political ethos', such as Islam. Communicative rationality could also enable various religious and secular groups, both within and beyond Islam, to find and share common goals on the way to synthesis, peaceful coexistence or at least agreeing to disagree (Chapter 3).

Martin agrees with Haines that 'Islamic feminism is an active contributor to the redynamisation of Islamic theology across societies, namely through asserting the significance of gender as an important category of thought' (Chapter 3). Although many barriers remain to making Islamic feminists equal partners in discussions of war and peace, rights and social justice, both authors hope that the theologically-based compassionate elements of 'women's peace' will be recognized as a common thread in Islamic thought, worthy of inclusion in regional and global politics of war and peace. Such an elevation of 'women's wisdom' into sanctioned public peacemaking deliberations could simultaneously challenge hierarchical sex segregation, and promote social justice, and women's increased status as important components of peace.

Elora Chowdhury's chapter in this volume offers another model for shifting women's peacemaking agency from the interpersonal to the public political realm. She argues that women's peacemaking analyses should be crucial to understanding 'the interface of globalization, national development and rising militant Islamic politics' (Chapter 4). Writing about Bangladesh, Chowdhury urges the international NGO community to recognize the insights of indigenous women's activism in developing a 'more nuanced intersectional analysis of gender, ethnicity, militarism, nationalism and class in thinking about violence' (Chapter 4). That same advice could be given to international governments and to intra-national forces. In short, Chowdhury's essay offers a template for recognizing Muslim women's interpersonal peacemaking gestures, rationales and perspectives, formed within 'localised analysis, debate, contestation, understanding and struggle', as a critical challenge to typically male-dominated political analysis of war, aggression and honour (Chapter 4). Again, acknowledging women's understanding of the big issues related to war and peace is in itself a gesture towards increased status and social justice for women.

Chowdhury's essay makes another significant point that could also help transform women's private, interpersonal peacemaking into a political force in Muslim societies. In her critique of NGO behaviour and attitudes, Chowdhury insists that feminism and fundamentalism should both be seen as 'part of modernity instead of . . . [as] opposing discourses'. Maintaining the dichotomy obscures the dual identities of many women as both Muslim and feminist (Chapter 4). I would say that it also relegates Islam to an archaic rather than a living religious and political force. In contrast, recognizing that women's rights and social justice exist in the same political and historical register as Islamic theology and law allows them to be seen as interacting with rather than countermanding one another. That recognition helps to promote dialogue rather than conflict between them.

Transforming Gender Distinction: Biology and Feminism

Scientific study teaches that sex and gender are culturally constructed, as are the differences in desires, values and capacities that some societies consider innate to the two sexes, but that genes and brain structures cannot really explain. Indeed, a deep understanding of biological facts includes recognizing the contextual way – both chemically and socially – that human genes express themselves.[15] Biological research also cautions that there are more overlaps in gendered physiology and behaviours than there are differences. In fact, despite outward appearances, 'men and women are extremely similar genetically'.[16] Biologically reductionist conclusions ignore 'the entire historical course of cultural development of human society', which makes it nearly impossible to differentiate between sociocultural and genetic causes of human behaviour.[17] For many, these revelations from the sciences argue for creating full social, political and economic equality between men and women. They fuel a variety of *liberal* or *equality* feminist perspectives around the world, and they complicate some *difference*, or *cultural* feminisms, which consider many gender differences innate.

Women and Peace in the Islamic World occupies a nuanced position between those poles by tempering the wish for equality, even sameness, between the sexes with the recognition of significant gender differences. The argument underlying many of the book's essays is basically this: even though neither nature nor Islam decrees that gender distinctions are absolute, and even though Muslim societies should promote social justice for all, and equitable status for women, certain valuable gender distinctions can arise from men's and women's different experiences and social locations. Thus, even as some Muslim women seek greater freedom to determine their own social roles, they may also embrace and promote certain aspects of their gendered experiences and social situations, including their valuation of peace. Societies' commitment to social justice demands that women's perspectives, derived from their social positions and roles, play a larger part in determining their societies' values and policies.

Such a view resonates with many Western feminists who recognize that social location can determine worldview without at the same time conceding that such worldviews are biologically determined, or morally, or religiously mandated. In some cases, men and women and members of various other groups or classes will share worldviews; in other cases, people of different racial, ethnic, gender, or class groups (which are themselves socially-constructed) will hold different worldviews. True social justice must entail mechanisms for recognizing, evaluating and incorporating the contributions of such worldviews into a society's political and social structures. Excluding them *ad hominem* (because of who holds those views rather than what they say) produces social tyranny.

The gender standpoint advanced in this book emerges from many Muslim women's roles and experiences – including but not limited to motherhood – that lead them to value peace and prioritize Islam's support for compassion, mercy and forbearance towards enemies. As mothers they understand viscerally the horrific price paid for the war systems that others (especially men, embrace as authentically Islamic.) The co-existence of these apparently competing interpretations of Islam identifies the religion as a dynamic and complex living system with a history of debate and deliberation (not just war) over differing religious interpretations. To replace the fiats of fundamentalism with the precepts of dialogue helps to elevate women's perspectives from interpersonal to public realms and inserts 'gender' and 'feminist' into the panoply of modifiers that characterize multiple versions of Islam around the world.

Women and Peace in the Islamic World is right to pay attention to gendered issues of peace. The book adds important voices to those of women around the globe who bring their situational knowledge to this important topic. It shows why women's perspectives should be relevant to the politics of peace and war in Muslim societies, and beyond without dismissing or attributing those perspectives to genetic programming. The book further invites readers to consider not only how women's social locations (and not their genes) shape their views but also how men's social locations (and not their genes) determine their beliefs, political perspectives, and support for war systems. In addition, the book's suggestion that Islam is not and should not be a religion or a social system for one sex or the other, also resonates with other social and religious contexts. The future the book anticipates depends on a deep understanding of principles and values, and on dialogue and debates that do not make gender differences automatic grounds for either dominance or irrelevance.

Notes

1. Catia C. Confortini, 'Galtung, violence and gender: The case for a peace studies/feminism alliance', *Peace & Change* 31/3 (2006), p. 343.
2. Joshua Goldstein, *War and Gender: How Gender Shapes the War System and Vice Versa* (Cambridge: Cambridge University Press, 2003), p. 181.

3. Ibid., 20.

4. Confortini, 'Galtung, violence, and gender', p. 336.

5. Betty Rosoff, 'Genes, hormones and war', in Anne E. Hunter and Catherine M. Flamenbaum (eds), *On Peace, War, and Gender: A Challenge to Genetic Explanations* (New York: The Feminist Press at CUNY, 1993), pp. 43–4; Goldstein, *War and Gender*, also reports that testosterone levels do not cause corresponding levels of aggressive behaviour and that aggressive behaviour might increase testosterone levels rather than the other way around (pp. 148–54).

6. Confortini's 'Galtung, violence and gender', offers an alternative possibility for interpreting sexist imagery in military training. She explains that certain imagery might actually serve homoerotic functions that contribute to the bonding of male groups (p. 344).

7. Rosoff, 'Genes, hormones and war', p. 47; Goldstein, *War and Gender*, p. 9.

8. Goldstein, *War and Gender*, p. 182).

9. This perception reinforces the view of peace theorist Johan Galtung who regards peace as both negative in its cessation of violence and positive in its association with social justice. Galtung does not fully explore the role of gender in the social construction of both violence and peace, however. See Confortini, 'Galtung, violence and gender', pp. 335–6.

10. Sachiko Muratta, *The Tao of Islam: A Sourcebook on Gender Relationships in Islamic Thought* (New York: State University of New York Press, 1992), pp. 143–48, as quoted in Šiljak Chapter 12, this volume.

11. Carol Gilligan, *In a Different Voice: Psychological Theory and Women's Development* (Cambridge: Harvard University Press,1993); Sara Ruddick, *Maternal Thinking: Toward a Politics of Peace* (Boston: Beacon Press,1995); Jean Bethke Elshtain, 'Reflections on war and political discourse: Realism, just war, and feminism in a nuclear age', *Political Theory* 13/1 (February 1985), pp. 39–57.

12. Goldstein, *War and Gender*, p. 5.

13. See Sally Kitch, *Contested Terrain: Reflections with Afghan Women Leaders* (Urbana-Champaign: University of Illinois Press, 2014).

14. Confortini, 'Galtung, violence and gender', pp. 339–40.

15. Rosoff, 'Genes, hormones and war', p. 41; Joshua Goldstein corroborates this analysis by explaining that sex hormones translate social contexts and events rather than determine them, Goldstein, *War and Gender*, p. 156.

16. Goldstein, *War and Gender*, p. 143

17. Doris Grieser Marquit and Erwin Marquit, 'Gender differentiation, genetic determinism, and the struggle for peace', in Anne E. Hunter and Catherine M. Flamenbaum (eds), *On Peace, War, and Gender: A Challenge to Genetic Explanations*, (New York: The Feminist Press at CUNY, 1993), p. 156.

EPILOGUE:
DIALOGUING PEACE

Daisy Khan and Cemalnur Sargut

Perspectives of Two Muslim Peacemakers

The concept of peace needs more than theory and policymaking. We believe it needs to be seen as everyday practice, illuminated by lived examples. The challenges to peace can be understood when we engage with ground realities that make-up our everyday concerns. Exploring these questions can be difficult and potentially murky because they require keen sensitivity to interpretation and context. We have decided to end this book with a discussion between two peacemakers, Cemalnur Sargut, a Sufi sheikha of the Rifai'i Order and President of TURKAD, Istanbul, and Daisy Khan, Founder President of The Women's Islamic Initiative for Spirituality and Education (WISE), New York. The two of them engaged in a public conversation at the Center for the Study of Religion and Conflict at Arizona State University on the subject of peace and Muslim women's role in leading peace initiatives on 12 March 2011. Yasmin Saikia moderated the discussion.

In the discussion, the two women focussed on the work of peace beyond the confines of national boundaries and local communities.

They approached peace as a holistic project involving public participation in their efforts. This conversation became an interactive site involving the speakers and audience in a common dialogue. In closing, we offer a few excerpts from this conversation for our readers to engage with and appreciate the struggle for achieving peace as an ongoing process.

Cemalnur Sargut: I was born into a Sufi family where things were not just explained, they were lived. The Prophet of Islam, Muhammad (peace be upon him) when he was asked, what is *Deen* (religion), he replied that 'religion is *akhlaq* or good manners'. I believe if we accept this simple lesson and engage others in good *Akhlaq* then the wars would all end.

Professionally, I was a chemical engineer, but when I was given permission by my teacher to give *sohbet*, discourses, I slowly emerged as a human being. I owe this to Mevlana Rumi. My teacher used to tell me there are three different types of eyeglasses. The first one sees only the near. These glasses are the kind that generally the politicians wear because they are programmed to see one as two. The other pair is the pair that sees only the far, like I have. Those people wearing these glasses fly unaware of the realities of this world. However, from Rumi, I learned that *Sufism* means wearing both types of glasses together at the same time. In other words, when looking at this world, we have to always think whether God is pleased with us. This consciousness will lead us to service. We believe that *Sufism* will actually bring peace to everyone across the world.

The enemy of a human being is conceit. There is no other enemy. If we become people with *akhlaq*, we will have a positive impact in the world. Becoming a human being is what counts. It starts with developing the capacity to be good, having good manners. For me, to speak this message and reach to a wide variety of audience is not too difficult. I can reach people in Turkey and abroad because the television does the work for me. Sometimes it is challenging when people call me a *kafir* or disbeliever because they think their Islam is the only correct version. Then it makes me sad, but I continue with my work.

Sufis are generally wrongly considered to be people preferring to be isolated and always calling for Allah. I would like to tell you a story about this. There was this person who climbed up a mountain and thought he attained divine favours by reciting 'Allah! Allah!' To test his powers, he put some milk in a container and turned it upside down. When he saw that the milk did not pour out of the vessel he became sure that he had attained special powers. He wanted to show this ability to others. He went to the city and met his brother who was a cobbler. He showed off to his brother, 'Look, what I can do. I am special'. His brother said, 'Masha Allah [by the grace of Allah] you have become special. It is well done. Why don't you come and help me? Why don't you repair the shoes of that lady?' The lady had very beautiful long legs. All of a sudden the milk that the man was holding started to pour out. The brother remarked, 'Well, you naughty boy, come and live your life here in this world and attain your powers. It is very easy to become special up in the mountains'. We're trying to do this in our work here in our communities and societies, in this world. It is a challenge, but we do our work. We work all the time. We do this to please Allah.

Daisy Khan: I was raised in a home where the patriarch of the family was my grandfather, a highly educated man, but also an Islamic scholar. I learned the concept of justice from him, because he was a very just man. I was also fortunate to have a maternal grandmother who was a Sufi sheikha. As a child, I remember sitting in her room where she had young men and women, everybody sitting around her, learning from her.

I came to America to pursue an education in architectural design. Like many other immigrants I lost my faith, found my faith, went through this whole journey of identity. It was *Sufism* that brought me back to my faith. Unknowingly I walked into a mosque, which was a Sufi mosque. They welcomed me. Also, in that very mosque, I met the man I was later going to marry. In some ways now that I look back on it, I think it was my insurance policy because I married a man of God to make sure that I would always stay on the right path.

And then 9/11 happened, and my husband was in the spotlight. I had worked in the Towers for four years. It was our neighbourhood that was attacked, and everybody wanted to know who Muslims were. I had no choice but to teach myself. In this process I discovered about women and Islam from a new perspective. The important thing for me to do was to learn from the experience of other women and how they overcame their obstacles. I got engaged with the feminist movement that helped me to learn the importance of public participation. This led me to create WISE in 2006.

WISE is a network of Muslim women. Its efforts are to help Muslim women to create informed strategies for change. The idea is to transform self and society. Towards this goal, we created four channels for change. Number one: we have to tell our own story. If we don't define ourselves, they will define us. I created a website called wisemuslimwomen.org. The second thing is change through collaboration. We work with women around the world from different faiths to learn from their struggles. We come together in an annual conference. At the conference we conduct instant polls. The instant polling gives us a sense what Muslim women around the world are thinking, what are their priorities. In the last poll we asked Muslim women what is the biggest barrier for women's advancement; 90 per cent of the women told us the biggest problem is Qur'anic interpretation. It is not the lack of education or resources, but the interpretations that powerful bodies make about women's rights that create impediments for women. For example, preventing women from driving, or going outside their home on their own in Saudi Arabia.

We learned that change through interpretation is critical. For this we created a Muslim women *shura* or council, because no one person can interpret the text that will be acceptable to all. The council consists of 22 women from around the globe. We are reinterpreting the Qur'an with a holistic approach, including a spiritual side, as well as keeping in mind issues of jurisprudence and views of society. We are looking at different issues, including female genital mutilation, violent extremism, Jihad against violence, adoption and many more issues of direct relevance to Muslim communities worldwide.

Recently, we launched a campaign against violence. Our effort is to show the link between domestic violence and public violence in the community because there actually are linkages between the two. Women have realized that they have to step into this arena and address this difficult issue within Muslim communities. We are teaching ourselves to step down from the mountain to really take back our religion because it is being hijacked by too many others. This is no easy task, but our work continues.

Cemalnur: The life of the Prophet Muhammad offers a wonderful story. There was a person in the Prophet's neighbourhood who threw garbage at him every time he would walk down the alley. He would duck to avoid the garbage. It became a routine, but one day there was no one throwing garbage at him. He asked about the whereabouts of the person and found out that she was sick. So he said, 'I'll go visit her'. Everybody discouraged him. But he visited her. The woman was so moved by this act; that the person she used to throw entrails and garbage at was actually coming to meet her, that she said, 'I accept your message'. Our struggle, first and foremost, is with our *nafs* (ego). If you do that, we will move to a better place, a more peaceful and happy place. Others around us, too, will be happy. We have to start with ourselves and seek peace in our communities first. That is our work as women and Muslims.

CONTRIBUTORS

Souad T. Ali is Chair of the Council for Arabic and Islamic Studies and Associate Professor of Arabic Literature, Middle Eastern and Islamic Studies in the School of International Letters and Cultures at Arizona State University. She is the author of *A Religion, Not a State: Ali 'Abd al-Raziq's Islamic Justification of Political Secularism* (2009), co-editor of *The Road to Two Sudans* (forthcoming), and numerous articles. Her current projects include *Kuwaiti Women in Leadership Positions: Social Change* (2015); modern perspectives on women and gender in Islam, and a translation of Ali 'Abd al-Raziq's *Al-Islam wa Usul al-Hukm*.

Elora Halim Chowdhury is Associate Professor in the Department of Women's and Gender Studies at the University of Massachusetts-Boston. Her research and teaching interests include transnational feminisms, gender and development, violence and human rights advocacy in South Asia. She is the author of *Transnationalism Reversed: Women Organizing against Gendered Violence in Bangladesh* (2011), which was awarded the Gloria E. Anzaldua book prize by the National Women's Studies Association in 2012. Her current scholarship focusses on dissident cross-border feminist alliances, friendships and solidarity projects.

miriam cooke is the Braxton Craven Distinguished Professor of Modern Arab Cultural Studies and Director of the Middle East Studies Center at Duke University. Her research interests include war and gender, Islamic feminism, dissidence under authoritarian rule and construction of identity in new nations. Currently, she is working on the role of women's art and literature in the 2011 Arab revolutions. Her major publications include: *Women and the War Story* (1996); *Women Claim Islam* (2000); *Dissident Syria: Making Oppositional Arts Official* (2007); *Nazira Zeineddine: Biography of a Pioneer of Islamic Feminism* (2010); and *Tribal Modern: Branding New Nations in the Arab Gulf* (2014).

Chad Haines is Assistant Professor of Religious Studies at Arizona State University. He received his PhD in Cultural Anthropology from the University of Wisconsin-Madison. His publications include *Nation, Territory and Globalization in Pakistan: Traversing the Margins* (2012) and he is currently working on a new manuscript titled *Being Muslim, Being Global: Everyday Ethics, Urban Sociality, and Traces of Islamic Modernity in Dubai, Islamabad and Cairo*. His research engages the complex ways post-coloniality and globalization reshape the Muslim world, focussing on everyday lives of Muslims and the performance of ethics, and sociality in the urban sphere.

Asna Husin teaches Philosophy of Education and Islamic Civilization at the Ar-Raniry State Islamic University, Banda Aceh, Indonesia, and is the Founder-Director of the Peace Education Program (PPD). She received two Fulbright Scholarships to Harvard University for her MA in Middle Eastern Studies, and Columbia University for her PhD in Religious Studies. Through PPD she works closely with major Ulama organizations and educational institutions in Aceh to promote Islamic education and gender equity. She has served on Aceh's Provincial Commission on Education and the Acehnese Council for the Preservation of Culture and advised Aceh's Governor on education and social issues.

S. Ayse Kadayifci-Orellana is Visiting Assistant Professor in Georgetown University's Program in Conflict Resolution and directs the Conflict Resolution Field Program. She is the author of *Standing on an Isthmus: Islamic Narratives of War and Peace in the Palestinian Territories* (2007) and co-editor of the volume *Anthology on Islam and Peace and Conflict Resolution in Islam: Precept and Practice* (2001).

Azza Karam serves as a Senior Advisor on Culture and Social Development at the United Nations Population Fund and coordinates a UN system-wide task force on engaging with faith-based actors around issues of development, democratization and human rights. Her books include: *Islamisms, Women, and the State* (1997); *A Woman's Place: Religious Women as Public Actors* (2004), *Women in Parliament: Beyond Numbers* (2005), *Transnational Political Islam: Religion, Ideology and Power* (2004) and *Religion, Development and the United Nations* (2012). She is a recipient of a Distinguished Alumni Award from the American University in Cairo.

Sally L. Kitch is Director of the Institute for Humanities Research and Regents' Professor of Women's and Gender Studies at Arizona State University. She specializes in feminist theory and epistemology, gender and racial ideology and gender representation. Her book, *The Specter of Sex: Gendered Foundations of Racial Formation in the U.S.* (2009), was a top-two finalist for the John Hope Franklin Prize of the American Studies Association. Her current book, *Contested Terrain: Reflections with Afghan Women Leaders,* explores Afghan women leaders' resistance to the gender ideologies and practices that tradition, as well as invasion and war, enshrine in their society.

Richard C. Martin is Professor Emeritus of Islam and the History of Religions at Emory University. He is author or editor of many books and articles on Islamic religion including: *Approaches to Islam in Religious Studies* (1985); *Defenders of Reason in Islam: Mu'tazilism and Rational Theology from Medieval School to Modern Symbol* (1997) and *Rethinking Islamic Studies: From Orientalism to Cosmopolitanism* (2010). Currently he is the editor of MESA's *Review of Middle East Studies* and editor-in-chief of the forthcoming second edition of the *Encyclopaedia of Islam and the Muslim World.*

Arzoo Osanloo is Associate Professor at the University of Washington's Law, Societies and Justice Program. She holds a JD from American University, Washington College of Law and a PhD in Cultural Anthropology from Stanford University. Her book, *The Politics of Women's Rights in Iran* (2009), analyses the politicization of 'rights talk' and women's subjectivities in Iran. Her new project examines the Islamic mandate of forgiveness, compassion and mercy in Iran's criminal sanctioning system. Her research and teaching focus on the intersection of law and culture, including human rights, refugee rights and identity, and women's rights in Muslim societies.

Yasmin Saikia is the Hardt-Nickachos Chair in Peace Studies and Professor of History at Arizona State University. She is the author of three books and numerous articles and book chapters. Her recent book *Women, War and the Making of Bangladesh: Remembering 1971* (2011) won the Oral History Association best book prize, 2013. She is currently undertaking two research projects – children learning peace and violence in South Asia and utopia in South Asian Muslim thought and politics.

Zilka Spahić-Šiljak is Research Associate and Visiting Scholar at the Women's Studies in Religion Program at Harvard University. Her research focusses on gender, religion, feminism, human rights, politics, education and peace-building. Her major publications include: *Sjaj Ljudskosti – životne priče mirotvorki u Bosni i Hercegovini* (Shining Humanity – Life Stories of Women Peacemakers in Bosnia and Herzegovina (2013)); 'Contesting Female, Feminist and Muslim Identities – Post-socialist Contexts of Bosnia and Herzegovina and Kosovo' (2012); 'Women, Religion and Politics' (2010); 'Women Believers and Citizens' (2009) and *Three Monotheistic Voices: Introduction to Judaism, Christianity and Islam* (for public school use) (2009).

Shahla Talebi is Associate Professor of Religious Studies at Arizona State University. She received her BA from the University of California, Berkeley, and her MA and PhD from Columbia University in social cultural anthropology. Her research explores the experiences of revolution, martyrdom and self-sacrifice, and mourning and memorialization, with philosophical and ethnographic reflections on modernity, submission and subjectivity, and on Islam in its multiple expressions and dimensions and the specificity of its Shi'a history, imaginations, symbols, metaphors, and embodied practices. She is the author of the award winning book, *Ghosts of Revolution: Rekindled Memories of Imprisonment in Iran* (2011).

BIBLIOGRAPHY

Abaza, Mona, *Changing Consumer Cultures of Modern Egypt: Cairo's Urban Reshaping* (Leiden: Brill, 2006).

Abbas, Amber, *Narratives of Belonging: Aligarh Muslim University and the Partitioning of South Asia*, PhD Dissertation (Austin: University of Texas, 2012).

Abdullahi, Abdurrahman M., 'Women and constitutional debate in Somalia: Legal reforms during reconciliation conference (2000–2003)'. Available at http://www.scribd.com/doc/15421298/Women-and-Constitutional-Debate-in-Somalia (accessed 15 July 2013).

Abou-Bakr, Omaima, 'Abrogation of the mind in the poetry of Jalal al-Din Rumi', *Alif: Journal of Comparative Poetics* 14 (1994), pp. 37–63.

Abou El Fadl, Khaled, *Speaking in God's Name: Islamic Law, Authority, and Women* (Oxford: OneWorld, 2001).

———— 'The place of tolerance in Islam', in Joshua Cohen and Ian Lague (eds), *The Place of Tolerance in Islam* (Boston: Beacon Press, 2002), pp. 13–14.

———— *The Great Theft: Wrestling Islam from the Extremists* (New York: HarperCollins, 2005).

Abou El Fadl, Khaled, Joshua Cohen and Deborah Chasman (eds), *Islam and the Challenge of Democracy* (Princeton: Princeton University Press, 2004).

Abraham, Nicholas and Maria Torok, *The Shell and the Kernel: Renewals of Psychoanalysis,* in Nicholas T. Rand (ed), Vol. 1 (Chicago: University of Chicago Press, 1994).

Abraham, Nicolas, Maria Torok and Nicholas Rand, 'A poetics of psychoanalysis: The lost object: Me', *SubStance* 13/2, Issue 43 (1984), pp. 3–18.

Abu-Lughod, Lila, 'Do Muslim women really need saving? Anthropological reflections on cultural relativism and its others', *American Anthropologist* 104/3 (2002), pp. 783–90.

———— 'The social life of "Muslim women's rights": A plea for ethnography, not polemic, with cases from Egypt and Palestine', *Journal of Middle East Women's Studies* 6/1 (2010), pp. 1–45.

———— *Do Muslim Women Need Saving?* (Cambridge: Harvard University Press, 2013).

Abu-Lughod, Lila and Catherine Lutz (eds), *Language and the Politics of Emotions* (Cambridge: Cambridge University Press, 1990).

Abu-Nimer, Mohammed and S. Ayse Kadayifci-Orellana, 'Muslim peacebuilding actors in the Balkans, Horn of Africa and the Great Lakes Regions', *Salam Institute for Peace and Justice* (23 May 2005). Available at http://salaminstitute. org/MuslimPeacebuildingActorsReport.pdf (accessed 15 July 2013).

Achrati, Ahmed, 'Deconstruction, ethics and Islam', *Arabica*, 53/4 (October 2006), pp. 472–510.

Adorno, Theodor W., and Max Horkheimer, *Dialectic of Enlightenment* (London: Verso, 1997).

Afary, Janet, *The Iranian Constitutional Revolution, 1906–11* (New York: Columbia University Press, 1996).

Afghan Institute for Learning. *Creating Hope International* (CHI). Available at http://www.afghaninstituteoflearning.org/learning-centers.html (accessed 15 July 2013).

Afsaruddin, Asma, *The First Muslims: History and Memory* (Oxford: OneWorld, 2008).

Afshar, Haleh, *Women In The Middle East: Perceptions, Realities, And Struggles For Liberation* (New York: Palgrave, 1993).

Ahmed, Abdulla. 'Syed Jamaluddin Afghani's ideas blaze the trail', *Pakistan Horizon*, 34/2 (Second Quarter 1981), pp. 35–43.

Ahmad, Aziz, 'Syed Ahmad Khan, Jamalaldin Afghani and Muslim India', *Studia Islamica* 13 (1960), pp. 55–78.

Ahmed, Fauzia E., 'Hidden opportunities: Islam, masculinity and poverty alleviation', *International Feminist Journal of Politics* 10/4 (2008), pp. 542–562.

Ahmed, Leila, *Women and Gender in Islam: Historical Roots of a Modern Debate* (New Haven: Yale University Press, 1992).

Ahmed, Sadaf, *Transforming Faith: The Story of Al-Huda and Islamic Revivalism among Urban Pakistani Women* (New York: Syracuse University Press, 2009).

Alexander, M. Jaequi, *Pedagogies of Crossing: Meditations on Feminism, Sexual Politics, Memory, and the Sacred* (Durham: Duke University Press, 2005).

Al-Ghazāli, Abu Hamid, *The Remembrance of Death and Afterlife*, transl. Tim J. Winter (Cambridge: Islamic Texts Society, 1989).

Ali, Ahmed, *Twilight in Delhi* (London: Hogarth Press, 1940).

Ali, Ayaan Hirsi, *The Caged Virgin: An Emancipation Proclamation for Women and Islam* (New York: Free Press, 2008).

Ali, Azra Asghar, *The Emergence of Feminism among Indian Muslim Women (1920–1947)* (New York: Oxford University Press, 2000).

Ali, Kecia, *Sexual Ethics and Islam: Feminist Reflections on Qur'an, Hadith, and Jurisprudence* (Oxford: OneWorld, 2006).

Ali, Souad T., 'Religious practices: Preaching and women preachers (Sudan)', *Encyclopedia of Women and Islamic Cultures*, Vol. 5, (Leiden: Brill, 2007).

——— 'Women in Islam and civil society: An overview of the disparity between religion and culture', in Sibel Halimi (ed), *A Lecture on Gender Issues* (Prishtina: Kosovar Centre for Gender Studies, 2009).

Altorki, Soraya and Camillia El-Solh (eds), *Arab Women in the Field: Studying Your Own Society* (Syracuse: Syracuse University Press, 1988).

Amanat, Mehrdad, 'Set in stone: Homeless corpses and desecrated graves in modern Iran', *International Journal of Middle East Studies* 44 (2012), pp. 257–83.

Amnesty International Public Statement, 'Indigenous land dispute turns deadly in Bangladesh', (20 April 2011). Available at http://www.amnesty.org/en/library/asset/ASA13/003/2011/en/0e39431c-934e-4fb8-8c23-efa1e42a3cf5/as a130032011en.html (accessed 13 July 2013).

Anderson, Benedict, *Imagined Communities: Reflections on the Origin and Spread of Nationalism* (London: Verso, 1991).

Andrews, Helena, 'Muslim women don't see themselves as oppressed, survey finds', *New York Times* (8 June 2006). Available at http://www.nytimes.com/2006/06/08/world/middleeast/08women.html (accessed 19 June 2012).

Anidjar, Gil, 'Secularism', *Critical Inquiry* 33/1 (2006), pp. 52–77.

An-Na'im, Abdullahi Ahmed, *Islam and Global Justice* (Pennsylvania: University of Pennsylvania Press, 2011).

Appiah, Kwame Anthony, *Cosmopolitanism: Ethics in a World of Strangers* (New York: W.W. Norton & Company, 2006).

Arendt, Hannah, *The Origins of Totalitarianism* (New York: Harcourt, 1973).

Aristotle, *Nicomachean Ethics*, transl. Terence Irwin, 2nd edn. (Indianapolis: Hackett Publishing, 1999).

Arkoun, Muhammad, *Rethinking Islam: Common Questions, Uncommon Answers* (Boulder: Westview Press, 1994).

Asad, Talal, *Formations of the Secular: Christianity, Islam, Modernity* (Stanford: Stanford University Press, 2003).

Atiya, Nayra, *Khul-Khaal: Five Egyptian Women Tell Their Stories* (Syracuse: Syracuse University Press, 1982).

Augustine, Aurelius, *Confessions of St Augustine*, transl. Edward B. Pusey (New York: Random House, 1999).

Baderin, Mashood A., *International Human Rights and Islamic Law* (Oxford: Oxford University Press, 2003).

Badran, Margot, *Feminists, Islam and Nation: Gender and the Making of Modern Egypt* (Princeton: Princeton University Press, 1996).

——— 'Feminism and the Qur'an', in *The Encyclopedia of the Qur'an*, Vol. 2 (Leiden: Brill, 2002), pp. 199–203.

——— *Feminism in Islam: Secular and Religious Convergences* (Oxford: OneWorld, 2009).

——— 'From Islamic feminism to a Muslim holistic feminism', *Institute of Development Studies Bulletin* 42/1 (2011), pp. 78–87.

Bakhtin, Mikhail Mikhailovich, *The Dialogic Imagination: Four Essays*, transl. Caryl Emerson and Michael Holquist (Austin: University of Texas Press, 1981).

Ballington, Jullie and Azza Karam (eds), *Women in Parliaments: Beyond Numbers*, 2nd edn (Stockholm: International IDEA, 2005).

Bano, Shadaf, 'Rashid Jahan's writings, resistance and challenging boundaries: Angaare and onwards', *Indian Journal of Gender Studies* 19/1 (2012), pp. 57–71.

Barazangi, Nimat Hafez, *Women's Identity and the Qur'an: A New Reading* (Gainesville: University Press of Florida, 2004).

Barlas, Asma, *Believing Women in Islam: Unreading Patriarchal Interpretations of the Qur'an* (Austin: University of Texas Press, 2002).

Bauman, Richard, *Verbal Art as Performance* (Prospect Heights: Waveland Press, 1977).

Benjamin, Walter, *Illuminations: Essays and Reflections*, Hannah Arendt (ed), transl. Harry Zohn (New York: Schocken, 1969).

Bennabi, Malik, *On the Origins of Human Society*, transl. and annotated by Mohamed Tahir El-Mesawi (London: The Open Press, 1968).

────── *Islam in History and Society* (Islamabad: Islamic Research Institute, International Islamic University, 1988).

Berenskoetter, Felix, 'Friends, there are no friends? An intimate reframing of the international', *Millennium - Journal of International Studies* 35/3 (2007), pp. 647–676.

Bergeron, Suzanne, *Fragments of Development: Nation, Gender, and the Space of Modernity* (Ann Arbor: The University of Michigan Press, 2006).

Berkley Center, 'Interview series: Women, religion, and peace', Berkley Center for Religion, Peace and World Affairs (February 2012). Available at http://repository. berkleycenter.georgetown.edu/1202WomenReligionPeaceInterviewSeries_webversion.pdf (accessed 15 July 2013).

Bérubé, Michael, *Life as We Know It: A Father, a Family, and an Exceptional Child* (New York: Vintage Books, 1998).

Bilgrami, Akeel, 'The importance of democracy', in Joshua Cohen and Ian Lague (eds), *The Place of Tolerance in Islam* (Boston: Beacon Press, 2002), pp. 55–60.

────── 'The clash within civilizations', *Daedalus* 132/3 (2003), pp. 88–93.

Blanchot, Maurice, *L'Amitié* (Paris: Gallimard, 1971).

────── *Friendship {L'Amitie'}*, transl. Elizabeth Rottenberg (California: Stanford University Press, 1997).

De Boeck, Filip, 'Mourning and the imagination of political time in contemporary central Africa', *African Studies Review* 48/2 (2005), pp. 11–32.

Bose, Sugata and Ayesha Jalal, *Modern South Asia: History, Culture, Political Economy* (London: Routledge, 1998).

Bougarel, Xavier, 'Bosnia and Herzegovina – state and communitarianism', in David Dycker and Ivan Vejvoda (eds), *Yugoslavia and After* (London: Longman, 1996), pp. 67–115.

Bowen, John R., *Muslims through Discourse: Religion and Ritual in Gayo Society* (Princeton: Princeton University Press, 1993).

Boyd, E.B., 'Women to women: In Afghanistan, Zoe Bedell '07 led female marines in a new role', *Princeton Alumni Weekly* (1 June 2011). Available at http://paw.p rinceton.edu/issues/2011/06/01/pages/5436/index.xml?page=2& (accessed 2 May 2012).

Bringa, Tone, *Being Muslim the Bosnian Way: Identity and Community in a Central Bosnian Village* (Princeton: Princeton University Press, 1995).

Bryan, Bradley, 'Approaching the other: Aristotle on friendship's possibility', *Political Theory* 37/6 (2009), pp. 754–779.

Bulliet, Richard W., *The Patricians of Nishapur: A Study of Medieval Islamic Social History* (Cambridge, Mass: Harvard University Press, 1972).

Burgat, Francois, *Islamic Movement in North Africa*, transl. Austin Dowell (Austin: University of Texas, 1993).

Butler, Judith, *Gender Trouble: Feminism and the Subversion of Identity* (London: Routledge, 1990).

Cady, Linell Elizabeth, *Religion, Theology, and American Public Life* (Albany: State University Press of New York, 1993).

De Certeau, Michel, *The Practice of the Everyday Life*, transl. Steven Rendell (Berkeley: University of California Press, 1984).

Chatterjee, Moyukh, 'Reflecting on 30 years of subaltern studies: Conversations with Profs. Gyanendra Pandey and Partha Chatterjee', *Cultural Anthropology Online* (1 December 2011). Available at http://www.culanth.org/curated_collections/6-subaltern-studies/discussions/14-reflecting-on-30-years-of-subaltern-studies-conversations-with-profs-gyanendra-pandey-and-partha-chatterjee (accessed 5 June 2012).

Chittick, William, 'The theological roots of peace and war according to Islam', *The Islamic Quarterly* 34/3 (1990), pp. 145–63.

Chittick, William and Sachiko Murata, *The Vision of Islam* (New York: Paragon Books, 1994).

Chowdhury, Najma, 'The politics of implementing women's rights in Bangladesh', in J.H. Bayes and N. Tohidi (eds), *Globalisation, Gender, and Religion: The Politics of Women's Rights in Catholic and Muslim Contexts* (New York: Palgrave, 2001), pp. 203–30.

Chugtai, Ismat, 'Lihaf' (The Quilt), in Ismat Chughtai (ed), *The Quilt and Other Stories*, transls. Tahira Naqvi and Syeda S. Hameed (Delhi: Kali For Women, 1990 [1942]).

Clewell, Tammy, 'Mourning beyond melancholia: Freud's psychoanalysis of loss', *Journal of the American Psychoanalytic Association* 52/1 (2004), pp. 43–67. Available at www.apsa.org/portals/1/docs/japa/521/clewell.pdf (accessed 15 July 2013).

Coleman, Isobel, *Paradise Beneath Her Feet: How Women are Transforming the Middle East* (New York: Random House, 2010).

Comaroff, Jean, *Body of Power, Spirit of Resistance: The Culture and History of a South African People* (Chicago: University of Chicago Press, 1985).

Confortini, Catia C. 'Galtung, violence, and gender: The case for a peace studies/feminism alliance', *Peace & Change* 31/3 (2006), pp. 333–67.

Cook, Michael, *Commanding Right and Forbidding Evil in Islamic Thought* (New York: Cambridge University Press, 2010).

cooke, miriam, *War's Other Voices: Women on the Lebanese Civil War* (London: Cambridge University Press, 1987).

―――― *Women and the War Story* (Berkeley: California University Press, 1996).

Corbin, Henri, *Traites Des Compagnons – Chevaliers: Recueil de sept 'Fotowwat-Nameh'* (Teheran: IFRI, 1973).

Cushman, Thomas, 'A conversation with Veena Das on religion and violence, suffering and language', *Hedgehog Review* 6/1 (2004). Available at http://virginia.edu/iasc/hedgehog.html (accessed 10 June 2012).

Dabashi, Hamid, *The Arab Spring: The End of Postcolonialism* (London: Zed Books, 2012).

―――― *Being a Muslim in the World* (New York: Palgrave Macmillan, 2013).

Daiffalla, M.A. Wad, *Kitāb al-Tabaqātfī Khusūs al-Awliā al-Salihīnwa al-'Ulamāwa al-Shu'arāfī al-Sudan* [The Book of Stratifications of Holy People, Scholars, and Poets in Sudan] 3rd edn. (Khartoum: The University of Khartoum Press, 1985).

Danforth, John, *Faith and Politics: How the 'Moral Values' Debate Divides America and How to Move Forward Together* (New York: The Penguin Group, 2006).

Das, Veena, 'Wittgenstein and anthropology', *Annual Review of Anthropology* 27 (October 1998), pp. 171–95.

——— 'The apocalyptic interlude: Revealing death in Kinshasa', *African Studies Review* 48/2 (2005), pp. 11–31.

——— *Life and Words: Violence and Descent into the Ordinary* (Berkeley: University of California Press, 2007).

Derrida, Jacques, 'The politics of friendship', *The Journal of Philosophy* 85/11 (1988), pp. 632–44.

——— *Aporias* (Stanford: Stanford University Press, 1993).

——— *Specters of Marx: The State of the Debt, the Work of Mourning and the New International* (London: Routledge, 1994).

Drakulić, Slavenka, *How We Survived Communism and Even Laughed* (New York: Harper Perennial, 1993).

Duara, Prasenjit, *Rescuing History from the Nation: Questioning Narratives of Modern China* (Chicago: University of Chicago Press, 1995).

Eaton, Richard, *Islamic History as Global History* (Washington: American Historical Association, 1990).

——— *The Rise of Islam and the Bengal Frontier, 1204–1760* (Berkeley: University of California Press, 1993).

Ebadi, Shirin, *Iran Awakening: One Woman's Journey to Reclaim her Life and Country* (New York: Random House, 2006).

Eck, Diana L, *A New Religious America: How a 'Christian Country' has become the World's Most Religiously Diverse Nation* (San Francisco: Harper Collins, 2001).

Eisenstein, Zillah, *Hatreds: Racialised and Sexualised Conflicts in the 21st Century* (New York: Routledge, 1996).

Elshtain, Jean Bethke, 'Reflections on war and political discourse: Realism, just war, and feminism in a nuclear age', *Political Theory* 13/1 (February 1985), pp. 39–57.

Elshtain, Jean Bethke and Sheila Tobias (eds), *Women, Militarism and War: Essays in History, Politics and Social Theory* (Savage: Rowman & Littlefield, 1990).

Enloe, Cynthia, *The Morning After: Sexual Politics at the End of the Cold War* (Berkeley: University of California Press, 1993).

Ernst, Carl, 'Muslim studies of Hinduism? A reconsideration of Arabic and Persian translations from Indian languages', *Iranian Studies* 36/2 (2003), pp. 173–95.

Esack, Farid, 'The contemporary democracy and the human rights project for Muslim societies', in Abdul Aziz Said, Mohammed Abu-Nimer and Meena Sharify-Funk (eds), *Contemporary Islam: Dynamic not Static* (London: Routledge, 2006), pp. 117–28.

Expatica, 'German interior minister says Islam must accept female equality', *Expatica.com, German News Archive* (13 May 2008). Available at http://www.exp atica.com/de/news/local_news/German-interior-minister-says-Islam-must-accept-female-equality-.html (accessed 28 June 2012).

Feinman, Ilene Rose, *Citizenship Rites: Feminist Soldiers and Feminist Antimilitarists* (New York: New York University Press, 2000).

Feldman, Allen, 'Memory theatres, virtual witnessing, and the trauma-aesthetic', *Biography* 27/1 (2004), pp. 163–202.

Ferguson, Niall, *Civilization: The West and the Rest* (London: Penguin, 2011).

Fernea, Elizabeth and Basima Bezirgan (eds), *Middle Eastern Muslim Women Speak* (Austin: University of Texas Press, 1977).

Foucault, Michel, *Discipline & Punish: The Birth of the Prison*, 2nd edn., transl. Alan Sheridan (New York: Vintage, 1995).

Fraser, Nancy, 'Rethinking the public sphere: A contribution to the critique of actually existing democracy', *Social Text* 25/26 (1990), pp. 56–80.

Freire, Paulo, *Pedagogy of the Oppressed* (New York: Continuum Press, 2000 [1968]).

Freud, Sigmund, 'On the history of the Psycho-Analytic Movement: Papers on metapsychology and other works', *The Standard Edition of the Complete Psychological Works of Sigmund Freud*, Vol. XIV (1914–16) (London: Vintage, 2001), pp. 3–68.

———— 'Mourning and melancholia', *The Standard Edition of the Complete Psychological Works of Sigmund Freud*, Vol. XIV (1914–16) (London: Vintage, 2001), pp. 230–38.

Friedman, Elisabeth, 'The effects of "transnationalism reversed" in Venezuela: Assessing the impact of UN global conferences on the women's movement', *International Feminist Journal of Politics* 1/3 (autumn 1999), pp. 357–81.

Galtung, Johan, 'Editorial' *Journal of Peace Research* 1/1(1964), pp. 1–4.

———— *Theories of Peace: A Synthetic Approach to Peace Thinking* (Oslo: International Peace Research Institute, 1967).

———— 'Violence, peace, and peace research', *Journal of Peace Research*, 6/3 (1969), pp. 167–91.

———— 'Keynote address at the global conference "Women and the 21st Century - Feminist Alternatives"', Cairo, Egypt (16–18 December 2010).

Ghannam, Farah, *Remaking the Modern: Space, Relocation, and Identity in a Global Cairo* (Berkeley: University of California Press, 2002).

Gholami, Hussein, 'Restorative traditions in violent conflicts in Iran', in Hans-Jorg Albrecht, Jan-Michael Simon, Hassan Rezaei, Holger-Christoph Rohne and Ernesto Kiza (eds), *Conflicts and Conflict Resolution in Middle Eastern Societies: Between Tradition and Modernity* (Berlin: Duncker & Humblot, 2006), pp. 457–70.

Gilligan, Carol, *In a Different Voice: Psychological Theory and Women's Development* (Cambridge: Harvard University Press, 1993).

Goldstein, Joshua S., *War and Gender: How Gender Shapes the War System and Vice Versa* (Cambridge: Cambridge University Press, 2003).

Göle, Nilüfer, *The Forbidden Modern: Civilization and Veiling* (Ann Arbor: University of Michigan Press, 1996).

Goodman, Aaron, 'Thailand: Women for peace-offering solace to victims of conflict', *PBS Frontline World* (9 August 2007). Available at http://www.pbs.org/frontl ineworld/rough/2007/08/thailand_women.html (accessed 12 May 2008).

Griffith, Sidney H., *The Church in the Shadow of the Mosque: Christians and Muslims in the World of Islam* (Princeton: Princeton University Press, 2007).

Griswold, Charles L., *Forgiveness: A Philosophical Exploration* (New York: Cambridge University Press, 2007).

Guhathakurta, Meghna, 'Women negotiating change: The structure and transformation of gendered violence in Bangladesh', *Cultural Dynamics* 16/2–3 (2004), pp. 193–211.

Gupta, Akhil and James Ferguson, 'Discipline and practice: "The field" as site, method, and location in anthropology', in Akhil Gupta and James Ferguson (eds), *Anthropological Locations: Boundaries and Grounds of a Field Science* (Berkeley: University of California Press, 1997), pp. 1–46.

Habermas, Jürgen, 'Modernity versus postmodernity', transl. Seyla Benhabib, *New German Critique* 22 (1981), pp. 3–14

Habib, Irfan, 'The envisioning of a nation: A defence of the idea of India', *Social Scientist* 27/9–10 (Sept/Oct 1999), pp. 18–29.

——— 'Viability of Islamic science: Some insights from 19th century', *Economic and Political Weekly* 39/23 (5–11 June 2004), pp. 2351–55.

Haines, Chad, 'Cracks in the facade: Landscapes of hope and desire in Dubai', in Ananya Roy and Aihwa Ong (eds), *Worlding Cities: Asian Experiments and the Art of Being Global* (London: Blackwell, 2011), pp. 160–81.

——— *Nation, Territory, and Globalization in Pakistan: Traversing the Margins* (London: Routledge, 2012).

Al Hakim, Suad, 'Islam and peace', transl. Tara Aziz and Karim Crow (paper presented at the symposium Islam and Peace in the 21st Century, February 1998).

Halliday, Fred, *Islam and the Myth of Confrontation: Religion and Politics in the Middle East* (London: I.B.Tauris, 1995).

Hällzon, Patrick, 'The Gülen movement: Gender and practice', *Gülen Conference in Washington* (15 November 2008). Available at http://fgulen.com/en/gulen-movement/conference-papers/gulen-conference-in-washington/26438-the-gul en-movement-gender-and-practice (accessed 13 July 2013).

Hambly, Gavin R.G., *Women in the Medieval Islamic World: Power, Patronage and Piety* (New York: Palgrave MacMillan, 1999).

Hammoudi, Abdellah, *A Season in Mecca: Narrative of a Pilgrimage* (Cambridge: Polity Press, 2006).

Har-El, Shai, 'From peace process to actual peace', *World Policy Blog* (3 April 2012). Available at http://www.worldpolicy.org/blog/2012/04/03/peace-process-actu al-peace (accessed 18 April 18 2012).

Haroon, Sana, 'Reformism and orthodox practice in early nineteenth-century Muslim North India: Sayyid Ahmed Shaheed reconsidered', *Journal of Royal Asiatic Society*, Series 3, 21/2 (2011), pp. 177–98.

Hasan, Mushirul. 'Pan-Islamism versus Indian nationalism: A reappraisal', *Economic and Political Weekly* 21/24 (14 June 1986), pp. 1074–79.

Hasan, Zoya and Ritu Menon, *The Diversity of Women's Lives in India* (New Brunswick: Rutgers University Press, 2005).

Hashemi, Nader, *Islam, Secularism, and Liberal Democracy: Toward a Democratic Theory for Muslim Societies* (New York: Oxford University Press, 2012). Available at http://www.irsprc.org (accessed 8 August 2012).

Hassan, Riffat, 'The role of women as agents of change and development in Pakistan', *Human Rights Quarterly* 3/3 (August 1981), pp. 68–75.

Heidegger, Martin, *Sein und Zeit (Being and Time)*, transl. Joan Stambaugh (Albany: State University of New York, 1996).

Heschel, Suzannah (ed), *On Being A Jewish Feminist* (New York: Knopf Doubleday, 1987).

Hruschka, Daniel, *Friendship: Development, Ecology and Evolution of a Relationship* (Berkeley: University of California Press, 2010).

Huda, Qamar-ul (ed), *Crescent and Dove: Peace and Conflict Resolution in Islam* (Washington, DC: US Institute of Peace Press, 2010).

Hunter, Shireen (ed), *The Politics of Islamic Revivalism: Diversity and Unity* (Bloomington: Indiana University Press, 1988).

Hunter, W.W., *Indian Mussalmans: Are They Bound in Conscience to Revolt against the Queen?* (Calcutta: Government Printing Press, 1871).

Huntington, Samuel P., 'The clash of civilizations', *Foreign Affairs* 72/3 (summer 1993), pp. 22–49.

——— *The Clash of Civilization and the Remaking of the World Order* (New York: Simon and Schuster, 1997).

Husin, Asna, 'Summary of the conference: "Islam, Women and Peace Building"', Center for the Study of Religion and Conflict, Arizona State University, Tempe, Arizona (10–12 March 2011). Available at http://nonviolenceinternational.net/wp-content/uploads/2011/03/Islam-Women-Peacebuilding-Asna-Husin.pdf (accessed 15 July 2013).

Hussain, Shafqat, 'Of tea and snow leopards', *Counterpunch* (8 April 2011). Available at http://www.counterpunch.org/hussain04282011.html (accessed 3 May 2011).

Ikramullah, Shaista, *A Critical Survey of the Development of the Urdu Novel and Short Story* (London: Longmans, Green and Co., 1945).

International Committee of the Red Cross (ICRC), 'Convention on the Rights of the Child, 20 November 1989', *International Committee of the Red Cross*. Available at http://www.icrc.org/ihl.nsf/NORM/301345982738E9FBC1256402003FCA24?OpenDocument (accessed 11 May 2011).

International Crisis Group, 'Southern Thailand: Insurgency, not jihad', *Asia Report* no. 98 (18 May 2005).

Jabri, Vivienne, *War and Transformation of Global Politics* (New York: Palgrave Macmillan, 2007).

Jamal, Amina, 'Transnational feminism as critical practice: A reading of feminist discourses in Pakistan', *Meridians* 5/2 (2005), pp. 57–82.

Jawad, Haifaa, *The Rights of Women in Islam: An Authentic Approach* (London: MacMillan, 1998).

Johansen, Robert C., 'Radical Islam and nonviolence: A case study of religious empowerment and constraint among Pashtuns', *Journal of Peace Research* 34/1 (1997), pp. 53–71.

Kabeer, Naila, 'Between affiliation and autonomy: Navigating pathways of women's empowerment and gender justice in rural Bangladesh', *Development and Change* 42/2 (2011), pp. 499–528.

Kadayifci-Orellana, S. Ayse, *Standing on an Isthmus: Islamic Narratives on Peace and War in Palestinian Territories* (Lanham: Lexington Books, 2007).

——— 'Exodus in the Qur'an: Mercy, compassion, and forgiveness', in *Freedom Journeys: The Tale of Exodus and Wilderness across Millennia* (Woodstock: Jewish Lights Publishing, 2011), pp. 210–16.

——— 'Interfaith dialogue', in Natana J. DeLong-Bas (ed), *The Oxford Encyclopedia of Islam and Women* (Oxford: Oxford University Press, 2013), pp. 474–79.

———— 'Islam and peacebuilding', in Natana J. DeLong-Bas (ed), *The Oxford Encyclopedia of Islam and Women* (Oxford: Oxford University Press, 2013), pp. 507–13.

———— 'Self-Orientalization and Occidentalization in the Muslim world', (unpublished paper, North Western MESA Conference, 2013).

———— 'Muslim women's peacebuilding initiatives', in Katherine Marshall and Susan Hayward (eds), *Women, Religion and Peace: Exploring the Invisible* (Washington: USIP Press, forthcoming).

Kadayifci-Orellana, S. Ayse and Meena Sharify-Funk, 'Muslim women peacemakers as agents of change', in Qamar-ul Huda (ed), *Crescent and Dove: Peace and Conflict Resolution in Islam* (Washington: USIP Press Books, 2010), pp. 17–204.

Kamali, Mohammad Hashim, *Maqasid al Shariah Made Simple* (Herndon, VA: IIIT Books, 2008).

Kandiyoti, Deniz, *Women, Islam and the State* (Philadelphia: Temple University Press, 1991).

Kaplan, Caren, *Questions of Travel: Postmodern Discourses of Displacement* (Durham, NC: Duke University Press, 1996).

Karam, Azza (ed), *A Woman's Place: Religious Women as Public Actors* (New York: World Conference of Religions for Peace, 1998).

———— *Women, Islamisms and the State: Contemporary Feminisms in Egypt* (London: Macmillan, 1998).

———— (ed), *Women in Parliaments: Beyond Numbers* (Stockholm: International IDEA, 1998).

———— (ed), *Transnational Political Islam: Religion, Ideology and Power* (London: Pluto Press, 2004).

Karim, Lamia, 'Democratising Bangladesh: State, NGOs, and militant Islam', *Cultural Dynamics* 16/2–3 (2004), pp. 291–318.

Karman, Tawakkul, 'Nobel lecture' (10 December 2011). Available at http://www.nobelprize.org/nobel_prizes/peace/laureates/2011/karman-lecture_en.html (accessed 13 April 2012).

Kāshif-Badri, Haja, *Al-Haraka al-Nisā'iyyafī Al-Sudan* [The Women's Movement in Sudan] (Khartoum: University of Khartoum Press, 1984).

Kazantzakis, Nikos, *Saint Francis*, transl. Peter A. Bien (New York: Simon and Schuster, 1962).

Kelly, Liz, 'Inside outsiders: Mainstreaming violence against women into human rights discourse and practice', *International Feminist Journal of Politics* 7/4 (2005), pp. 471–95.

Keshavarz, Fatima, '"Much have I roamed through the world": In search of Sadi's self-image', *International Journal of Middle East Studies* 26/3 (1994), pp. 465–75.

Kesić, Vesna, 'Gender and ethnic identities in transition: The former Yugoslavia-Croatia', in Rada Ivekovic and Julie Mostov (eds), *From Gender to Nation* (Ravena: Longo Editore, 2001), pp. 63–80.

Khadduri, Majid, *Islamic Law of Nations: Shaybani's Siyar* (Baltimore: John Hopkins Press, 1966).

Khan, Khan Abdul Ghaffar, *Thrown to the Wolves: Abdul Ghaffar* (Calcutta: Eastlight Book House, 1966).

———— *My Life and Struggle: Autobiography of Badshah Khan* as narrated to K.B. Narang (Delhi: Hind Pocket, 1969).

Khan, Zafar Alam, 'There are different paths to the Kaabah: Cemalnur Sargut', *The Pioneer* (25 November 2011). Available at http://www.sufinews.org/paths-to-the-kaabah/ (accessed 15 July 2013).

Kibria, Nazli, 'Muslim encounters in the global economy: Identity developments of labor migrants from Bangladesh to the Middle East', *Ethnicities* 8/4 (2008), pp. 539–556.

Kitch, Sally, *Contested Terrain: Reflections with Afghan Women Leaders* (Urbana-Champaign: University of Illinois Press, 2014).

Lazreg, Marnia, 'Feminism and difference: The perils of writing as a woman on women in Algeria', *Feminist Studies* 14/1 (Spring 1988), pp. 81–107.

Lelyveld, David, *Aligarh's First Generation: Muslim Solidarity in British India* (Princeton: Princeton University Press, 1977).

———— 'The colonial context of Muslim separatism: From Sayyid Ahmad Barelvi to Sayyid Ahmad Khan', in Asim Roy and Mushirul Hasan (eds), *Living Together Separately: Cultural India in History and Politics* (New Delhi: Oxford University Press, 2005), pp. 404–14.

Levinas, Emmanuel, *Totality and Infinity: An Essay on Exteriority*, transl. Alphonso Lingis (Pittsburgh: Duquesne University Press, 1969).

———— *Otherwise than Being: Or Beyond Essence*, transl. Alphonso Lingis (Pittsburgh: Duquesne University Press, 1974).

———— *Ethics and Infinity: Conversations with Philippe Nemo*, transl. Richard A. Cohen (Pittsburgh: Duquesne University Press, 1985).

Lewis, Franklin, *Rumi: Past and Present, East and West* (Boston: OneWorld, 2000).

Lewisohn, Leonard, 'Ali ibn Abi Talib's ethics of mercy in the mirror of the Persian Sufi tradition', in M. Ali Lakhani (ed), *The Sacred Foundations of Justice in Islam: The Teachings of 'Ali ibn Abi Talib* (Bloomington: World Wisdom Inc., 2006), pp. 109–46.

Little, David, *Peacemakers in Action: Profiles of Religion in Conflict Resolution* (New York: Cambridge University Press, 2006).

Lorde, Audrey, *Sister Outsider: Speeches and Essays* (Berkeley: Crossing Press, 1984).

Lutz, Catherine and Geoffrey M. White, 'The anthropology of emotions', *Annual Review of Anthropology* 15 (October 1986), pp. 405–36.

Macdonald, Sharon, Pat Holden and Shirley Ardener (eds), *Images of Women in Peace and War: Cross-Cultural and Historical Perspectives* (Madison: University of Wisconsin Press, 1988).

Mack, Beverly B., and Jean Boyd, *One Woman's Jihad: Nana Aama'u Scholar and Scribe* (Bloomington: Indiana University Press, 2000).

Mahameed, Ibtisam, 'Ibtisam Mahameed: Complete interview', (25 February 2009). Available at http://www.youtube.com/watch?v=L93qTw8_v0s (accessed 15 July 2013).

Mahmood, Saba, 'Feminist theory, agency and the liberatory subject', in F. Nouraie-Simone (ed), *On Shifting Ground* (New York: Feminist Press, 2005), pp. 111–152.

———— *The Politics of Piety: The Islamic Revival and the Feminist Subject* (Princeton: Princeton University Press, 2005).

Mahmoudi, Firouz, 'The informal justice system in Iranian law', in Hans-Jorg Albrecht, Jan-Michael Simon, Hassan Rezaei, Holger-Christoph Rohne, Ernesto

Kiza (eds), *Conflicts and Conflict Resolution in Middle Eastern Societies: Between Tradition and Modernity* (Berlin: Duncker & Humblot, 2006), pp. 411–28.

Malik, Hafeez, *Sir Sayyid Ahmad Khan and Muslim Modernization in India and Pakistan* (New York: Columbia University Press, 1980).

Mamdani, Mahmood, *Good Muslim, Bad Muslim: America, the Cold War, and the Roots of Terror* (Lahore, Vanguard Books, 2005).

Manji, Irshad, *The Trouble With Islam Today* (New York: St. Martin's Press, 2004).

Mansbridge, Jane J and Aldon Morris (eds), *Oppositional Consciousness: The Subjective Roots of Social Protest* (Chicago: University of Chicago Press, 2001).

Marafi, Safa, *The Neoliberal Dream of Segregation: Rethinking Gated Communities in Greater Cairo (a case study of Al-Rehab City gated community)*, MA thesis (Cairo: American University in Cairo, 2011).

Marsden, George M, *Understanding Fundamentalism and Evangelicalism* (Grand Rapids, MI: William B. Eerdemans Publishing, 1991).

Marshall, Katherine and Susan Hayward, *Women, Religion, and Peace: Exploring an Invisible Force* (Berkley Center for Religion, Peace, and World Affairs and the United States Institute for Peace, 2010).

Martin, Richard C., 'Public aspects of theology in Medieval Islam: The role of kalam in conflict definition and resolution', *Journal for Islamic Studies* 13 (1993), pp. 101–20.

Martin, Richard C. and Abas Barzegar (eds), *Islamism: Contested Perspectives in Political Islam* (Palo Alto: Stanford University Press, 2010).

Martin, Richard C., Mark R. Woodward, and Dwi S. Atmaja (eds), *Defenders of Reason in Islam: Mu'talizism from Medieval School to Modern Symbol* (Oxford: OneWorld Publications, 1997).

Marty, Martin E., *When Faiths Collide* (Oxford: Blackwell Publishing, 2005).

Masood, Naved, 'Mumtaz Apa – Reminiscences', (2010). Available at http:al igarhmovement.com/aligarians/Mumtaz_Jahan_Haider (accessed 27 October 2012).

McLuhan, Marshall and Quentin Fiore, *War and Peace in the Global Village* (New York: Bantam Books, 1968).

Mernissi, Fatema, *Beyond the Veil: Male-Female Dynamics in a Modern Muslim Society* (Cambridge: Schenkman Pub. Co., 1975).

——— 'Muslim women and fundamentalism', *Middle East Report* 18/153 (July/August, 1988), pp. 8–11.

——— *The Veil and the Male Elite: A Feminist Interpretation of Women's Rights in Islam*, transl. Mary Jo Lakeland (New York: Basic Books, 1991).

——— *Women and Islam: A Historical and Theological Inquiry*, transl. Mary Jo Lakeland (London: Basil Blackwell, 1991).

——— *Islam and Democracy: Fear of the Modern World*, transl. Mary Jo Lakeland (Reading, CA: Addison-Wesley, 1992).

——— *The Forgotten Queens of Islam*, transl. Mary Jo Lakeland (Minneapolis: University of Minnesota Press, 1993).

Merry, Sally, *Human Rights and Gender Violence: Translating International Law into Local Justice* (Chicago: University of Chicago Press, 2006).

Mertus, Julie, (ed), *The Suitcase: Refugee Voices from Bosnia and Croatia* (Berkeley: University of California Press, 1999).

El-Mesawi, Mohammed El-Tahir, 'Religion, society, and culture in Malek Bennabi's thought', in Ibrahim M. Abu-Rabi' (ed) *The Blackwell Companion to Contemporary Islamic Thought* (London: Blackwell Publishing, 2006), pp. 213–56.

Milgram, Stanley, 'The familiar stranger: An aspect of urban anonymity', in S. Milgram, J. Sabini and M. Silver (eds), *The Individual in a Social World* (Reading: Addison-Wesley, 1977), pp. 51–3.

Minault, Gail, *Secluded Scholars: Women's Education and Muslim Social Reform in Colonial India* (New Delhi: Oxford University Press, 1999).

Mindanao Commission on Women. Available at http://www.mindanaowomen.org/mcw/ (accessed 15 July 2013).

Minow, Martha, *Between Vengeance and Forgiveness* (Boston: Beacon Press, 1998).

Mir-Hosseini, Ziba, *Islam and Gender: The Religious Debate in Contemporary Iran* (Princeton: Princeton University Press, 1999).

———— 'Muslim women's quest for equality: Between Islamic law and feminism', *Critical Inquiry* 32 (summer 2006), pp. 629–45.

Moallem, Minoo, 'Transnationalism, feminism and fundamentalism', in C. Kaplan, N. Alarcon and M. Moallem (eds), *Between Woman and Nation: Nationalisms, Transnational Feminisms, and the State* (Durham: Duke University Press, 1999), pp. 320–48.

Mohanty, Chandra Talpade, *Feminism Without Borders: Decolonizing Theory, Practicing Solidarity* (Durham: Duke University Press, 2003).

Moosa, Ebrahim, 'The dilemmas of Islamic rights schemes', *Journal of Law and Religion* 15/1–2 (2000), pp. 189–215.

Morgan, Robin, 'Women of the Arab Spring', *Ms. Magazine* (spring 2011). Available at http://www.msmagazine.com/spring2011/womenofthearabspring.asp (accessed 15 July 2013).

Mubarak, Fatheena, 'Women's interfaith initiative in the UK: A survey', *The Inter Faith Network for the United Kingdom* (2006). Available at http://www.interfaith.org.uk/publications/all-publications/cat_view/6-all-publications (accessed 15 July 2013).

Mujeeb, Qias, 'Abdullah Hall', *Aligarhnama* (23 February 2008). Available at http://aligarhnama.blogspot.com/2008/02/abdullah-hall.html (accessed 27 October 2012).

Mujkić, Asim, *We, The Citizens of Ethnopolis* (Sarajevu: Centar za ljudska prava Univerziteta, 2008).

Murata, Sachiko, *The Tao of Islam: A Sourcebook on Gender Relationships in Islamic Thought* (New York: State University of New York Press, 1992).

———— 'Women of Light in Sufism', *The Muhyiddin Ibn 'Arabi Society*. Available at http://www.ibnarabisociety.org/articles/womenoflight.html (accessed on 22 October 2012).

Mushtaq, Faiza, 'Al-Huda and its critics: Religious education for Pakistani women', *ISIM Review: International Institute for the Study of Islam in the Modern World*. Vol. 22 (2008) pp. 30–1.

Nandy, Asish, 'Telling the story of communal conflicts in South Asia: Interim report on a personal search for demystifying myths', *Racial and Ethnic Study*, 25/1 (2002), pp. 1–19.

————*Time warps: Silent and Evasive Pasts in Indian Politics and Religions* (New Brunswick: Rutgers University Press, 2002).

Nasser, Sheikha Moza Bint, 'Q&A: Her Highness Sheikha Moza Bint Nasser', *Qultura* (December 2011). Available at http://www.qatar4unaoc.org/wp-content/uploads/2011/12/SHEIKHA+MOZAH + INTERVIEW.pdf (accessed 16 April 2012).

Nateri, Mohammad E. Shams, 'Formal and informal means of conflict resolution in murder cases in Iran', in Hans-Jorg Albrecht, Jan-Michael Simon, Hassan Rezaei, Holger-Christoph Rohne, Ernesto Kiza (eds), *Conflicts and Conflict Resolution in Middle Eastern Societies—Between Tradition and Modernity* (Berlin: Duncker & Humblot, 2006), pp. 401–09.

Nazneen, Sohela, Maheen Sultan and Naomi Hossain, 'National discourses on women's empowerment in Bangladesh: Enabling or constraining women's choices?' *Development* 53/2 (2010), pp. 239–46.

Neuburger, Luisa de Cataldo and Tiziana Valentini, *Women and Terrorism*, transl. Leo Michael Hughes (London: Macmillan, 1996).

Neumann, Iver, *Uses of the Other: The 'East' in European Identity Formation* (Manchester: Manchester University Press, 1999).

———— 'Nigerian Muslim and Catholic women's groups unite to promote peace', *IslamToday, Ahlul Bayt* News Agency (27 March 2012). Available at http://abna.ir (accessed 15 July 2013).

Nobel Women's Initiative, '"Real" democracy guarantees equal rights, security & peace' (13 May 2009). Available at http://nobelwomensinitiative.org/2009/05/real-democracy-guarantees-equal-rights-security-peace/ (accessed 13 April 2012).

Nomani, Asra, *Standing Alone in Mecca: An American Woman's Struggle for the Soul of Islam* (New York: HarperCollins, 2005).

Nur, Ibrahim, *Gender Sensitive Programme Design and Planning in Conflict-Affected Situations-Annex 5: Somali Case Study* (London: ACORD, 2002).

Oh, Irene, *Islam, Human Rights and Comparative Ethics* (Washington, DC: Georgetown University Press, 2007).

Osanloo, Arzoo, 'The measure of mercy: Islamic justice, sovereign power, and human rights in Iran', *Cultural Anthropology* 21/4 (2006), pp. 570–602.

———— *The Politics of Women's Rights in Iran* (Princeton: Princeton University Press, 2009).

Pandey, Gyanendra, 'Can a Muslim be an Indian?' *Comparative Studies in Society and History* 41/4 (October 1999), pp. 608–29.

Pankhurst, Donna (ed), *Gendered Peace: Women's Struggles for Post-War Justice and Reconciliation* (New York: Routledge, 2009).

Pathways of Women's Empowerment, 'Women and religion in Bangladesh and Pakistan: Pathways South Asia case study', *Pathways of Women's Empowerment* (2010). Available at http://www.pathwaysofempowerment.org/Bangladesh_Pakistan_religion.pdf (accessed 6 May 2011).

Perez, Michael Vicente, 'Muslim women in the push for peace', *Huffington Post* (27 August, 2011). Available at http://www.huffingtonpost.com/mobileweb/2011/08/27/muslim-women-in-the-push-_n_934469.html (accessed 8 July 2013).

Phiri, Isabel Apawo, Betty Govinden and Sarojini Nadar (eds), *Her-Stories: Hidden Histories of Women of Faith in Africa* (Pietermaritzburg, South Africa: Cluster Publications, 2002).

Pickering, Paula M., *Peacebuilding in the Balkans: The View from the Ground Floor* (Ithaca: Cornell University Press, 2007).

Pierson, Ruth Roach, "'Did your mother wear army boots?'" Feminist theory and women's relation to war, peace and revolution', in Sharon MacDonald, Pat Holden and Shirley Ardener (eds), *Images of Women in Peace and War: Cross-Cultural and Historical Perspectives* (Madison: University of Wisconsin Press, 1988), pp. 205–27.

Porter, Elizabeth, *Peacebuilding Women in International Perspective* (New York: Routledge, 2007).

Postel, Danny, 'Last words from Richard Rorty', *The Progressive* 71/8 (August 2007). Available at http://progressive.org/mag_postel0607 (accessed 8 July 2013).

Povinelli, Elizabeth A., *The Empire of Love: Toward a Theory of Intimacy, Genealogy, and Carnality* (Durham: Duke University Press, 2006).

Power, Carla, 'Muslim women demand an end to oppressive family laws', *Time* (17 February 2009). Available at http://www.time.com/time/world/article/0,8599,1879864,00.html (accessed 15 July 2013).

Press Secretary, White House Office of the, 'President Obama names medal of honor recipients', *The White House Office of the Press Secretary* (July 30, 2009). Available at http://www.whitehouse.gov/the_press_office/president-obama-names-medal-of-freedom-recipients/ (accessed 24 May 2009).

Pucherova, Dobrota, 'Re-imagining the other: the politics of friendship in three twenty-first century South African novels', *Journal of Southern African Studies* 35/4 (2009), pp. 929–43.

Qassim, Hamza, 'Umm Umara: The Prophet's shield at Uhud', *Nida'ul Islam* 22 (Feb/March, 1998).

Rafael, Vicente, *White Love and Other Events in Filipino History* (Durham: Duke University Press, 2000).

Rahman, Fazlur, *Major themes of the Qur'an* (Minneapolis: Bibliotheca Islamica, 1980).

——— *Islam and Modernity: Transformation of an Intellectual Tradition* (Chicago: University of Chicago Press, 1982).

Ray, Raka, *Fields of Protest: Women's Movements in India* (Minneapolis: University of Minnesota Press, 1999).

Reinbold, Jenna, 'Radical Islam and human rights values: A "religious-minded" critique of secular liberty, equality and brotherhood', *Journal of the American Academy of Religion* 78/2 (2010), pp. 449–76.

Reinhardt, Emma Dorothy, 'Kenyan women lead peace effort', *National Catholic Reporter Online* (26 April 2002). Available at http://natcath.org/NCR_Online/archives/042602/042602p.htm (accessed 5 July 2012).

Rhouni, Raja, *Secular and Islamic Feminist Critiques in the Work of Fatima Mernissi* (Leiden: Brill, 2010).

Riaz, Ali, *God Willing: The Politics of Islamism in Bangladesh* (Lanham: Rowman & Littlefield Publishers, Inc., 2004).

Ricoeur, Paul, *The Course of Recognition,* transl. David Pellauer (Cambridge: Harvard University Press, 2005).

Roald, Anne Sofie, 'Feminist reinterpretation of Islamic sources: Muslim feminist theology in the light of Christian tradition of feminist thought', in Karin Ask and Marit Tjomsland (eds), *Women and Islamization: Contemporary Dimensions of Discourse in Gender Relations* (Oxford and NewYork: Berg, 1998), pp. 17–44.

Robinson, Francis, *Separatism among Indian Muslims: The Politics of the United Provinces' Muslims (1860–1923)* (London: Cambridge University Press, 1974).

——— 'Nineteenth-century Indian Islam: Review of David Lelyveld's *Aligarh's First Generation: Muslim Solidarity in British India* and Christian W. Troll's *Sayyid Ahmad Khan: A Reinterpretation of Muslim Theology*', *Modern Asian Studies* 14/4 (1980), pp. 683–88.

Roff, William R., *Studies on Islam and Society in Southeast Asia* (Singapore: National University of Singapore Press, 2009).

Rogers, Paul, 'Introduction to the special issue of *Peace, Conflict & Development*', *Journal of Peace, Conflict & Development* 18 (December 2011), pp. 1–6.

Rosaldo, Michelle, 'Toward an anthropology of self and feeling', in R.A. Shweder and R.A. LeVine (eds), *Culture Theory: Essays on Mind, Self, and Emotion* (Cambridge: Cambridge University Press, 1984), pp. 137–57.

Rosenthal, Franz, 'The stranger in Medieval Islam', *Arabica* 44/1 (1997), pp. 35–75.

Rosoff, Betty, 'Genes, hormones and war', in Anne E. Hunter and Catherine M. Flamenbaum (eds), *On Peace, War, and Gender: A Challenge to Genetic Explanations* (New York: The Feminist Press at CUNY, 1993).

Roy, Olivier, *The Failure of Political Islam* (London: I.B.Tauris, 1994).

Ruddick, Sara, *Maternal Thinking: Towards a Politics of Peace* (Boston: Beacon Press, 1989).

——— 'The Rationality of Care', in Jean Elshtain and Sheila Tobias (eds), *Women, Militarism and War: Essays in Politics, History and Social Theory* (Savage: Rowman and Littlefield, 1990), pp. 229–54.

Rumi, Jalalu'ddin, *The Mathnawi of Jalalu'ddin Rumi*, transl. Reynold A. Nicholson (Cambridge: Gibb Memorial Trust, 2002).

Rupp, Leila J., 'Sexuality and politics in the early twentieth century: The case of the international women's movement', *Feminist Studies* 23/3 (autumn 1997), pp. 577–605.

El Saadawi, Nawal, *The Hidden Face of Eve: Women in the Arab World*, transl. and edited Sherif Hetata (London: Zed Press, 1980).

Sachedina, Abdulaziz, *The Islamic Roots of Democratic Pluralism* (New York: Oxford University Press, 2001).

Safi, Omid, *Memories of the Prophet: Why the Prophet Matters* (New York: HarperOne, 2009).

———, 'A Muslim spiritual perspective on Israel Palestine (with a dash of Obama)', *Tikkun* (12 June 2009). Available at http://www.tikkun.org/article.php/20090617013141275 (accessed July 8, 2013).

Said, Edward W., 'Opponents, audiences, constituencies, and communities', in W.T.J. Mitchell (ed), *The Politics of Interpretation* (Chicago: University of Chicago Press, 1983), pp. 7–32.

——— *Orientalism* (New York: Vintage Books, 1994 (1978)).

Saiyidain, K.G., *Islam: The Religion of Peace*, 2nd edn. (New Delhi: Har Anand Publications, 1994).

Salime, Zakia, *Between Feminism and Islam: Human Rights and Sharia Law In Morocco* (Minneapolis: University of Minnesota Press, 2011).

Salmi, Ralph H., Cesar Adib Majul and George K. Tanham, *Islam and Conflict Resolution: Theories and Practices* (Lanham: University Press of America, 1998).

Samuel, Terence, 'The peak of political power', *US News and World Report*, 23 December 2002.

Saudni, 'Tayyibah Taylor (Editor-in-Chief, Azizah Magazine)', *Muslim Heroes* (25 November 2010). http://muslimheroes.wordpress.com/page/23/ (accessed 15 July 2013).

Scarry, Elaine, *The Body in Pain: The Making and Unmaking of the World* (Oxford: Oxford University Press, 1987).

Schwarzenbach, Sibyl A., 'On civic friendship', *Ethics* 107/1 (October 1996), pp. 97–128.

Selimović, Meša, *Pisci, Mišljenja, Razgovori* (Authors, Thoughts, Conversations) (Beograd: Brogradski izdavačko-grafički zavod, 1983).

Seremetakis, Nadia C., *The Last Word: Women, Death, and Divination in Inner Mani* (Chicago: University of Chicago Press, 1991).

Shah-Kazemi, Reza, 'A sacred conception of justice: Imam 'Ali's letter to Malik al-Ashtar', in M. Ali Lakhani (ed), *The Sacred Foundations of Justice in Islam: The Teachings of 'Ali ibn Abi Talib* (Bloomington: World Wisdom Inc., 2006), pp. 61–108.

————— *My Mercy Encompasses All: The Koran's Teachings on Compassion, Peace and Love* (Berkeley: Counterpoint Press, 2007).

Shaikh, Sa'diyya, 'In search of '*al-insān*': Sufism, Islamic law, and gender', *Journal of the American Academy of Religion* 77/4 (December 2009), pp. 781–82.

Shamlu, Ahmad, 'Funeral oration', *Ahmad Shamlu*. Available at http://shamlu.com/trama.htm (accessed 13 July 2013).

Shariati, Ali, 'Jihad and shahadat', *Iran Chamber Society*. Available at http://www.iranchamber.com/personalities/ashariati/works/jihad_shahadat.php (accessed 10 June 2012).

Sharify-Funk, Meena, 'Peace and the feminine in Islam', in Abdul Aziz Said, Nathan C. Funk, and Ayse S. Kadayifci (eds), *Peace and Conflict Resolution in Islam: Precept and Practice* (Lanham: University Press of America, 2001), pp. 277–98.

Shehabuddin, Elora, 'Contesting the illicit: Gender and the politics of *fatwas* in Bangladesh', *Signs: Journal of Women in Culture and Society* 24/4 (1999), pp. 1011–44.

————— *Reshaping the Holy: Democracy, Development, and Muslim Women in Bangladesh* (New York: Columbia University Press, 2008).

Shehadeh, Lamia, *The Idea of Women in Fundamentalist Islam* (Gainesville: University of Florida Press, 2008).

Shura Council, the Global Muslim Women's, 'Violent extremism: A violation of Islam', *American Society for Muslim Advancement*. Available at http://www.wisemuslimwomen.org/pdfs/shura_council_violent_extremism_digest.pdf (accessed 15 July 2013).

Siddiqi, Dina M., 'Taslima Nasreen and others: The contest over gender in Bangladesh', in H. L. Bodman and N. Tohidi (eds), *Women in Muslim Societies: Diversity Within Unity* (Boulder: Lynne Rienner Publishers, 1998), pp. 205–27.

————— 'In the name of Islam? Gender, politics, and women's rights in Bangladesh', *Harvard Asia Quarterly* 10/1 (winter 2006), pp. 4–14.

Sidiqi, Fatima, 'Morocco's veiled feminists', *Project Syndicate* (2006). Available at http://www.project-syndicate.org/commentary/morocco-s-veiled-feminists (accessed 1 June 2011).

Slapšak, Svetlana, 'The use of women and the role of women in the Yugoslav War', in Inger Skjelsbaek and Dan Smith (eds), *Gender, Peace and Conflict* (London: Sage Publications, 2001), pp. 161–83.

Slyomovics, Susan, *The Object of Memory: Arab and Jew Narrate the Palestinian Village* (Philadelphia: University of Pennsylvania Press, 1998).

Soroush, Abdolkarim, *Reason, Freedom, and Democracy in Islam*, transl. and edited Mohammad Sadri and Ahmad Sadri (New York: Oxford University Press, 2002).

Spahić-Šiljak, Zilka, 'Images of women in Bosnia and Herzegovina and neighboring countries, 1992–1995', in Faegheh Shirazi (ed), *Muslim Women in War and Crisis: From Reality to Representation* (Austin: University of Texas Press, 2010), pp. 213–24.

——— *Women, Religion and Politics: The Impact of Religious Interpretations of Judaism, Christianity, and Islam on the Status of Women in Public Life and Politics* (Sarajevo: IMIC, Center for Interdisciplinary Postgraduate Studies & TPO Foundation, 2010).

——— *Contesting Female, Feminist and Muslim Identities: Post-Socialist Contexts of Bosnia and Herzegovina and Kosovo* (Sarajevo: Center for Interdisciplinary Postgraduate Studies of the University of Sarajevo, 2012).

Steele, David, 'An introductory overview to faith-based peacebuilding', in Mark M. Rogers, Tom Bamat, and Julie Ideh (eds), *Pursuing Just Peace: An Overview and Case Studies for Faith-Based Peacebuilders* (Baltimore: Catholic Relief Services, 2008), p. 5–42.

Stewart, Kathleen, *A Space on the Side of the Road: Cultural Poetics in an 'Other' America* (Princeton: Princeton University Press, 1996).

Stoller, Paul, *Sensuous Scholarship* (Philadelphia: University of Pennsylvania Press, 1997).

Stowasser, Barbara, *Women in the Qur'an, Traditions, and Interpretation* (New York: Oxford University Press, 1994).

Strathern, Marilyn, *The Gender of the Gift: Problems with Women and Problems with Society in Melanesia* (Berkeley: University of California Press, 1990).

Taha, Mahmoud M., *The Second Message of Islam*, transl. Abdullahi Ahmed An-Na'im (Syracuse: Syracuse University Press, 1987).

Talebi, Shahla, 'Mourning for the loss of mourning', *Connect* 3 (2001), pp. 107–14.

——— *Ghosts of Revolution: Rekindled Memories of Imprisonment in Iran* (Stanford: Stanford University Press, 2011).

——— 'Who is behind the name? A story of violence, loss, and melancholic survival in post-revolutionary Iran', *Journal of Middle East Women's Studies* 7/1 (winter 2011), pp. 39–69.

——— 'From the light of the eyes to the eyes of the power: State and dissident martyrs in post-revolutionary Iran', *Visual Anthropology* 25/1–2 (2012), pp. 12–147.

Taussig, Michael, *Shamanism, Colonialism, and the Wild Man: A Study in Terror and Healing* (Chicago: University of Chicago Press, 1991).

Timmons, Debra, 'The sixth clan – women organize for peace in Somalia: A review of published literature', *University for Peace* (2004), pp. 1–30. Available at http://www.africa-upeace.org/Uploads/Publications/de99de80–057e-47c3–995d-318423d93a72/de99de80–057e-47c3–995d-318423d93a72.pdf (accessed 15 July 2013).

Tolstoy, Leo, *War and Peace*, transl. Louise Maude and Almer Maude (New York: W. W. Norton, 1966).

van Tongeren, Paul J.M., 'Politics, friendship and solitude in Nietzsche (confronting Derrida's reading of Nietzsche in 'Politics of friendship')', *South African Journal of Philosophy* 19/3 (2000), pp. 1–24.

Tröger, Karl-Wolfgang, 'Peace and Islam: In theory and practice', *Islam and Christian Muslim Relations* 1/1 (1990), pp. 12–24.

Tutu, Desmond, *No Future without Forgiveness* (New York: Doubleday, 2000).

USAID, 'Alternative Nobel Prize goes to Kenyan peacemaker', *USAID East Africa* (2 December 2007). Available at http://eastafrica.usaid.gov/en/Article.1117.aspx (accessed 24 November 2009).

Victor, Barbara, *Army of Roses: Inside the World of Palestinian Women Suicide Bombers* (Emmaus, PA: Rodale Inc., 2003).

Wadud, Amina, *Qur'an and Woman: Rereading the Sacred Text from a Woman's Perspective* (Oxford: Oxford University Press, 1999).

———— 'Muslim women as citizens?' in Nissim Rejwan (ed), *The Many Faces of Islam: Perspectives on a Resurgent Civilization* (Gainesville: University Press of Florida, 2000) pp. 206–09.

———— *Inside the Gender Jihad: Women's Reform in Islam* (Oxford: OneWorld, 2006).

Walther, Wiebke, *Women in Islam: From Medieval to Modern Times* (Princeton: Markus Weiner Publishers, 1995).

Warner, Michael, *The Trouble with Normal: Sex, Politics, and the Ethics of Queer Life* (Cambridge: Harvard University Press, 1999).

Weber, Samuel, *Benjamin's -abilities* (Cambridge: Harvard University Press, 2008).

Weeden, Curt, *How Women can Beat Terrorism: How Women in the U.S., Europe and Other Developed Nations can Empower Women in Poor Countries – and Move the World Towards a More Peaceful Tomorrow* (Mount Pleasant: Quadrafoil Press, 2003).

Williams, Jody, 'Conclusions', *Conference Report: Women Redefining Peace in the Middle East and Beyond, Nobel Women's Initiative* (2007). Available at http://nobel womensinitiative.org/2009/02/nobel-womens-initiative-conference-reports/ (accessed 2 July 2013).

Winichakul, Thongchai, *Siam Mapped: A History of the Geo-Body of a Nation* (Honolulu: University of Hawaii Press, 1994).

Women's Initiative in Islamic Spirituality and Equality, *Jihad against Violence: Muslim Women's Struggle for Peace', WISE* (July 2009). Available at http://www. wisemuslimwomen.org/images/uploads/Jihad_against_Violence_Digest(color). pdf (accessed 15 July 2013).

Wolf, Eric, *Europe and the People without History* (Berkeley: University of California Press, 1982).

Zentgraaff, H.C., *Aceh*, transl. Aboe Bakar (Jakarta: Buena, 1983).

Al-Zuhayli, Wahbah, *Al-Tafsir al-Munir fi al-Aqidah wa al-Shari'a wa al-Manhaj* [A Clear Exegesis about the Doctrine, Law, and the Path], Vol. 22 (Beirut: Dar al-Fikr, 1411/1991).

INDEX

men-women partnerships, 136–38, 139
National Democratic Party, 161
NGOs in, 157, 158–59, 167n.77
religious court gender project, 158–59
Tsunami (2004), 153, 158, 161–62
women's peacemaking networks
 Adiwarni Husin and, 150–51
 Consultative Assembly of
  Acehnese Women, 151–52, 154–55, 156–57, 166n.50
 Nonviolence International, 166n.50
 Peace Education Program, 157–58, 167n.77
Aceh Freedom Movement (*Gerakan Aceh Merdeka*, GAM), 149–50, 151, 153, 155, 156, 158
Achrati, Ahmed, 283, 284–85, 286, 305n.33, 306n.35
adab, 19, 292–94, 297–98, 301, 302, 308n.62
Adl, 199
Adorno, Theodor W., 313
Afary, Janet, 369
Afghani, Jamalaldin, 204n.14, 278, 304n.12
Afghan Institute for Learning (AIL), 195–96
Afghanistan
 Revolutionary Association of the Women of Afghanistan, 32
 Taliban control of, 184, 195–96
 US foreign policy, 53, 55–56
afu, 200
agency
 of Acehnese women, 136–38, 139
 deploying forgiveness, 228, 229–32
 in the everyday, 3
 friendship and, 284–85, 286, 307n.46
 ihsan and, 9
 of individuals in peacemaking, 1

of Muslim women not recognized by Western liberals, 53
 Sabr and, 201
 through piety, 12–13
 See also peacemaking
Ahmed, Fauzia, 128
Ahmed, Sadaf, 12–13
Ali, Ayaan Hirsi
 The Caged Virgin, 14
Ali, Kecia, 82–83, 84
Ali, Souad T., 18, 169–88, 385
Aligarh Muslim University (AMU)
 curriculum, 299, 302
 friendship ethos, 276–77, 281–82, 303n.3
 gender egalitarianism and, 300–301
 goals of, 276, 293–94, 304n.17
 guiding values, 19
 history of, 276, 279–80
 Hussain, Zakir and, 303n.3
 as lived culture, 290
 Mussalman-e Hind, 280, 281, 304n.17
 religious training at, 298
 reunions, 207n.51
 students selected for, 279, 280, 281
 Women's College, 281
 See also Abdullah Hall (Aligarh Muslim University, AMU)
'Ali ibn Abi Talib, 234–36, 244n.24
 Nahj al-Balaghah, 234, 235
Alliance of Civilizations Project (AOC), 30–31
al-Mirghani family, 173
Al-Nahda, 271n.11
Altorki, Soraya
 Arab Women in the Field, 12
amanat, 19, 317–20, 334
Anidjar, Gil, 132n.8
An-Naim, Abdullahi Ahmed, 8
Ansar al-Sunna, 176–77, 188n.26
Anwar, Zainah, 194
Arab Spring
 characteristics of results, 267–69